Fourth Edition

Teaching Physical Education In Elementary Schools

Illustrated

MARYHELEN VANNIER, Ed. D.

Professor and Director, Women's Division
Department of Health and Physical Education,
Southern Methodist University

MILDRED FOSTER, B.S.

Dallas Public School System,
Dallas, Texas

W. B. SAUNDERS COMPANY
Philadelphia   London   Toronto

W. B. Saunders Company: West Washington Square
Philadelphia, Pa. 19105

12 Dyott Street
London, WC1a   1DB

1835 Yonge Street
Toronto 7, Ontario

Teaching Physical Education in Elementary Schools   SBN 0-7216-8977-9

Print No.:   9   8   7   6   5

"I keep six honest serving men;
(They taught me all I knew)
Their names are What and Where and When
And How and Why and Who."

RUDYARD KIPLING

PREFACE TO THE FOURTH EDITION

This book is first a presentation of physical education —what it is and what its place should be in our rapidly changing world and educational system. Second, it is a source book of physical education activities for children in grades one through six. Third, it contains methods for teaching children through these activities, as well as directing the numerous sports, rhythms, dances, games, and activities that have been included.

It has been written for three groups: (1) the specialized physical educator, (2) the classroom teacher, and (3) the college student who is professionally preparing to become an elementary teacher.

This fourth edition contains many significant changes. Briefly stated, these include: (1) the addition of a new chapter on Movement Exploration; (2) the enlargement of all previous chapters to include many new materials and suggested teaching methods in each one, especially in creative activities, class management, ways of teaching physical activities to mentally retarded, blind, deaf, and other exceptional children, ways of conducting a more productive program when hampered by limited facilities and large classes, outdoor education and school camping experiences, methods of teaching physical activities by closed circuit television, and competencies to be reached at each grade level; (3) the inclusion of many new activities in all areas of the program, especially in the noon hour, recess, and after-school program, rhythmic activities, and basic movement skills; and (4) the addition of many new illustrations, including photographs.

The enlarged list of the latest and best books in

physical education following each chapter and the list of recommended films will serve as a means of supplementing the materials included in the text, for both the elementary teacher on the job and the college instructor using this book in professional preparation classes.

It is imperative that every teacher make *each* and *all* physical education class periods more meaningful and purposeful, linking more securely what is learned today with that mastered yesterday. Likewise, the elementary physical education must become more skillfully planned to contain a wider variety of progressively more difficult and challenging educational experiences that will help all children to grow up successfully. The aim of education, through its curriculum, should be to develop all youth physically, socially, mentally, and morally to their highest potential so that they *do* become well-rounded, happy, intelligent, socially-sensitive, and productive democratic citizens, as youth as well as adults. To this great endeavor each teacher on every educational level, regardless of her area of specialization, has much to contribute. May this book help each one to discover significant ways for doing so through the teaching of physical education most successfully in the elementary school.

MARYHELEN VANNIER

MILDRED FOSTER

Dallas, Texas

ACKNOWLEDGMENTS

The authors are indebted to many persons who have made this book possible. Especial gratitude and appreciation are due our families and professional colleagues for submitting photographs for illustrations and helpful suggestions for improving the contents of this fourth edition.

We are thankful to numerous students in our classes, both on the elementary and college level, who have helped us learn and play the games and other activities presented in this book, as well as collect new materials.

We are especially grateful to Dr. Delia Hussey of the Detroit Public Schools and to Dr. Joan Tillotson, Director of the Title III, ESEA Project for the Elementary School of Plattsburgh, New York, for their helpful suggestions regarding the new chapter on Movement Exploration. We are also grateful to all persons who submitted photographs for inclusion in this new edition, including our two professional colleagues mentioned above as well as Dr. Robert Lamp of Stanford University, Norman Barnes of the Nissen Corporation, G. Lindkirst of the Lind Climber Company, Asher Etkes of the Playground Corporation of America, and Elizabeth Glidden, Specialist in Elementary Physical Education for the Los Angeles City Schools. Mrs. Dorothy Good deserves our special vote of thanks for typing the manuscript.

CONTENTS

PART ONE. THE WHY

Chapter 1

THE PLACE OF PHYSICAL EDUCATION IN SCHOOLS 3

What Is Physical Education? 3
The Aim of Physical Education 5
The General Objectives of the Elementary School 7
The Goals of Physical Education 7
The Value of Play and Recreation 13
When Is One Educated? 16
When Is One Physically Educated? 16
Suggested Readings 18

PART TWO. THE WHO

Chapter 2

THE TEACHER 21

Who Should Teach Physical Education in the Primary
Grades? 21
Teacher Preparation 22
The Role of the Supervisor 22
Qualities Necessary for the Physical Education Teacher.. 24
Desirable Principles and Philosophy 24
Professional Growth 26
Suggested Readings 30

Chapter 3

THE CHILD 32

ix

Significant Facts About Today's Children   34
Basic Needs of All Children   37
Conflicts That Arise from Unfilled Needs   40
Recognition   41
Discipline Techniques   42
Characteristics of Children   43
Atypical and Exceptional Children   51
Enlisting the Cooperation of Others   52
The Use of Behavior Records   52
Suggested Readings   52

PART THREE. THE WHERE

Chapter 4

THE GYMNASIUM, PLAYGROUND, POOL, AND CLASSROOM   57

The Gymnasium   57
The Pool   59
The Classroom   60
Increased Use of Facilities   61
Legal Liability   62
The Playground   64
Supplies and Equipment Needed   69
Accident Safeguards   71
Suggested Readings   74
Sources of Equipment and Supplies   75

PART FOUR. THE HOW

Chapter 5

HOW CHILDREN LEARN   79

Learning Theories   81
Kinds of Learning   86
Learning Principles   86
Suggested Readings   87

Chapter 6

THE TECHNIQUES OF SUCCESSFUL TEACHING   89

Teaching Methods 89
Teaching Motor Skills 92
Class Management 94
Class Organization 99
Team Teaching 105
Teaching by Closed Circuit Television 105
Suggested Readings 106

Chapter 7

THE PROGRAM 107

The Total Program 107
Planning the Program 108
Competencies To Be Developed 118
The Need for Progression in the Program 121
The Teaching Unit 121
The Daily Lesson Plan 121
Courses of Study 124
Suggested Readings 124
Suggested Physical Education Curriculum Guides ... 125

Chapter 8

PHYSICAL DEVELOPMENT AND YOUTH FITNESS 126

What Is Physical Fitness? 128
Essentials for an Effective Program 128
Screening Tests for Fitness 130
Postural Fitness 132
Posture Exercises 133
Correlation with Health and Safety Programs 135
Suggested Readings 136

Chapter 9

SIMPLE AND CREATIVE GAMES 138

Fundamental Play and Simple Games 138
Constructed Creative Games 148
Pitching Games 149
Skills and Rules Related to Team and Individual Sports .. 150
Target Skills 153
Other Suggestions 156
Suggested Readings 157

Chapter 10

RELAYS 159

    Organization of Teams 159
    True Relay 159
    Modified Relays 160
    Relay Formations 160
    Types of Relays 161
    Suggested Readings 172

Chapter 11

BASIC SKILLS AND LEAD-UP GAMES TO TEAM SPORTS .. 174

    Suggested Games Listed According to Degree of Difficulty 174
    Class Organization 178
    Fundamental Skills Related to Team Games 179
    Suggested Readings 193

Chapter 12

RHYTHMS AND DANCE 194

    Rhythms 194
    Fundamental Movements 199
    Singing Games 201
    Safety and Other Singing Games 205
    Square Dance 206
    Mixers 213
    International Dances 214
    Social Dancing 225
    Dancing Terminology 229
    Suggested Readings 231
    Record References 232
    Visual Aids, Words, and Music 233
    Suggested Records for Creative Movement Experiences .. 233

Chapter 13

MOVEMENT EXPLORATION 234

    The Teacher's Role 234
    Teaching Techniques 236
    Suggested Equipment 237

Suggested Activities 238
Creative Play 240
Games Created by Children 246
Progressive Presentation 247
Suggested Readings 254
Suggested Films 255

Chapter 14

GRADED STUNTS, SELF-TESTING ACTIVITIES, TUM-
BLING, AND TRAMPOLINING........................... 256

Uniforms 257
Equipment 258
Safety Precautions 258
Class Organization and Presentation 259
Suggested Lesson Plan 260
Graded Stunts 260
Couple Stunts 261
Graded Self-testing Activities 261
Description of Stunts 262
Couple Stunts—Primary 273
Couple and Group Stunts—Upper Elementary 275
Tumbling Stunts Listed as to Difficulty and Grade Level 277
Description of Tumbling Activities 277
Pyramid Building 280
Poses for Pyramids 285
Rebound Tumbling (Trampolining) 286
Suggested Readings 290
Instructional Aids 290

Chapter 15

ELEMENTARY GYMNASTICS 291

Warm-up Exercises 291
Apparatus Used in Gymnastics 294
Suggested Readings 306

Chapter 16

TRACK AND FIELD 308

Suggested Indoor Activities 308
Suggested and Official Outdoor Events 309

Needed Facilities and Equipment 309
Suggested Readings 312

Chapter 17

AQUATICS 313

Class Organization 313
Preliminary Skills 316
Methods of Staying Afloat with Minimum Effort 318
Strokes 319
Aquatic Fun Time 322
Testing Procedures 324
Suggested Readings 326

Chapter 18

CLASSROOM AND QUIET GAMES 327

General Techniques 327
Criteria for Choosing Activities 328
Safety Precautions 328
Equipment 328
Game Leadership 329
Active Circle Games 330
Quiet Circle Games 334
Table and Card Games 337
Stunts and Games of Skill 337
Active Relays 339
Quiet Guessing Games 341
Games from Other Lands 342
Suggested Readings 346

Chapter 19

CAMPING AND OUTING ACTIVITIES 347

Types of Experiences 348
The Outdoor Learning Laboratory 349
The Program 350
Suggested Readings 372

Chapter 20

ADAPTED PROGRAMS FOR ATYPICAL CHILDREN 373

Number of Handicapped Children 373
Classifications 374
Needs of Exceptional Children 374
The Adapted Program 375
Program Objectives 376
Teacher Qualifications 376
Sample Letter Sent to the Family Physician 377
Parent Cooperation 378
Class Work 378
Teaching Methods 380
Administrative Details 380
Specific Cases 381
Suggested Readings 393
Organizations from Which Helpful Information Can Be
Obtained 394

Chapter 21

RECESS AND NOON-HOUR ACTIVITIES 395

Administrative Details 396
Safety Precautions 398
Activities 398
Suggested Readings 408

Chapter 22

INTRAMURAL AND AFTER-SCHOOL ACTIVITIES 409

Class Competition and Tournaments 409
Types of Competition Suitable for Children 412
Suggested Competitive Activities in Upper Elementary
Children 412
Organization of Programs 414
Classification of Players 414
Club Organization 416
The Seasonal Program 416
Special Events 417
Suggested Readings 424

Chapter 23

EVALUATING THE RESULTS 425

The Purpose of Evaluation 426

Evaluation of Health Status and Physical Growth 427
Evaluation of Social Growth and Pupil Behavior 428
Evaluation of Motor Skills and Physical Fitness 430
Evaluation of Pupil Knowledge and Attitudes 431
Evaluation by the Pupils 433
Teacher Evaluation 435
Evaluation by the Physical Education Supervisor 436
Evaluation with the Principal 438
Evaluation of the School Program 438
Grading and Reporting to Parents 440
Suggested Readings 440

APPENDICES 443

Recommended Films on Elementary Physical Education .. 443
Recommended Film Strips 444
Film Sources 444
Film Guides 445

INDEX 447

Part I

THE WHY

A child's world is fresh and new and beautiful, full of wonder and excitement. It is our misfortune that for most of us that clear-eyed vision, that true instinct for what is beautiful and awe-inspiring, is dimmed and even lost before we reach adulthood. If I had influence with the good fairy who is supposed to preside over the christening of all children I should ask that her gift to each child in the world be a sense of wonder so indestructible that it would last throughout life, as an unfailing antidote against the boredom and disenchantments of later years, the sterile preoccupation with things that are artificial, the alienation from the sources of our strength.

—Rachel Carson

Chapter 1

The Place of Physical Education in Schools

WHAT IS PHYSICAL EDUCATION?

Physical education is as old as man. The very existence of our primitive ancestors depended upon their ability to secure food, to erect crude shelters in caves, forests, or on mountain slopes, to battle successfully with changing weather elements, and to refresh their bodies through sleep, rest, and play. To know how to use their bodies meant life; failure to utilize this knowledge brought death.

In ancient Greece and Rome physical training held an important place in the educational program for boys and girls. Since then physical education has swung back and forth from favor to disregard in the eyes of the educator, churchman, and citizen. Bowed down by the narrowed vision of the man of the Middle Ages, who was concerned largely with his soul and saving it, the physical self was held to be an evil thing of the devil. Modern man thinks differently; his vision has widened, his knowledge increased. He now sees the folly of trying to separate the mind from the body, knowing that the mind is of the body and vice versa—that it is impossible to educate or use either singly. Thus, the parent, the school teacher, and the college professor speak of developing the "whole child" and likewise, then, the "whole man."

Physical education today is regarded as a vital part of general education. However, there are those both in and outside of schools who confuse big-time athletic contests for a few players with physical education for all, 1-2-3 bend type of mass exercise learned in order to pass a physical fitness test with a wide range of games and sports, or muscular boxers and drill teams for girls with a full program of sports and games, rhythmic activities, and recreational pursuits for all people of all ages.

Just as primitive man had to learn to use his body wisely or perish, so must modern man, for biologically they are almost identical. Just as our ancestors needed vigorous activity to keep themselves fully functioning, so do we today. The difference lies only in degree. There are those among

3

us who claim that all too rapidly Americans are becoming a race of on-
looking softies rather than doers. Others claim that we let our bodies
rust out rather than wear out. Some declare that as a race of people we
need to get off our seat and onto our feet, doing meaningful, vigorous
physical activities. Man, primitive or modern, is an animal and as such
his basic physical needs are the same. His emotional, social, and mental
needs are greatly intensified. Failure to satisfy properly his physical
needs, or the balance wheels, often throws him out of gear. Wise men
among us declare that in this push-button age of "cocktails and catas-
trophe" modern man is already obsolete. Some even claim that organic
degenerate disease will destroy man provided that his own created
weapons of destruction do not beat the diseases to it.

Just as youth may learn more outside of schools than they do in
them, and just as they often learn more from their peers than from their
teachers, so do they gain through life experiences a type of physical education. Learning to play successfully a game of hide and seek with policemen is a type of physical education; learning to use harmful narcotics is
another. For in spite of adults, youth will learn. *Because* of adults what
children learn can be socially good as well as good for them. Physical
activity programs must be directed if desired results are to accrue. If we
would develop strong, courageous, loyal citizens, conscious of their role
in society, we, as adults, must help children to do better the things they
will do anyway, and teach them to do those things we can and they might
do. Above all, we must enlist their enthusiasm and desires to preserve
and pursue further that which man throughout history has found to be
good. Educators have long claimed that the purpose of education is to
enable people of all ages to judge and to transfer our cultural heritage,
as well as to live successfully and happily while *in* it. Education, which is
a carefully planned developmental program, helps people to discover, use,
judge, and improve upon those things that our ancestors found to be
good as well as workable in solving the many problems of living.

Physical educators, as well as classroom teachers who teach physical
activities to children, have a great as well as a grave responsibility. Educationally speaking, they are in a choice spot, for they have the opportunity to guide children, to direct and observe their play, and to teach
them the enduring lessons of life through an informal approach. Psychologists tell us that children are their real selves when they play. Educators
claim that all people, regardless of age, learn more, faster, and remember
longer when they are doing something they enjoy, when they become
absorbed in the adventure of learning. Joseph Lee, an early leader of
recreation in America, held that play for children is creating or the gaining of life, whereas play for adults is recreation or the renewal of life.
Educators declare that if adults want to know what a child is really like
they should *observe* his play, but if they are truly concerned about what
a child may become they should *direct* his play.

Physical education in schools is directed, purposeful activity centered around the total body, its development, movement, care, and use. As such it stresses the development of skills—physical, social, and mental. A good program in this field should enable one to become a highly-functioning individual who is full of zest for life, capable, and desirous to serve well both himself and society. Such a person would posses a number of physical skills and have a desire to build and maintain total fitness throughout life. Regardless of age, he would know *how* and would *want* to use these refined movements while working, recreating, and living with others.

The majority of states in the nation have mandatory laws decreeing that physical education be included in the public school curriculum, whereas some few have permissive laws for its inclusion. Likewise, most states have state directors of physical education, health education, and safety. Each state has established by law minimum minutes for daily class instruction. Although the amount of time designated for daily instruction periods varies, a majority of the states require a recess period for supervised play *plus* a minimum instruction period of thirty minutes daily from grade 1 through 12. All schools and communities must provide better-planned and broader programs of physical activity for *all* children on a day-to-day, year-round basis.

Much has to be done on a national and local level to improve both the *status* and *content* of this program in the school curriculum. Laws alone will not do this, just as laws set up to punish criminals will not prevent crime. People can and will get around laws as long as they do not really believe in their value. Thus, in some states the recess period is counted as physical education. Some administrators even record the noon lunch period or the walking to and from school as physical education. Professional leaders who realize the value of directed physical education instruction must sell the purpose and value of a well-planned and directed physical education program to their colleagues, their administrators, and to the general public. Only then will state laws regarding education in general and its component parts be enforced and improved upon. Youth has the legal and the moral right to receive the best general and physical education possible.

THE AIM OF PHYSICAL EDUCATION

Physical education provides opportunities for the individual and the group to learn from skilled teachers activities that are invigorating, developmental, educational, and will lead to positive physical, social, mental, and emotional growth. This aim, in short, is to develop each individual to his highest potential as a democratic citizen.

This connotes that the resultant growth and development of children through directed physical activities should affect the total child. Social, mental, and emotional growth are closely related. The teacher of physical education must understand these interrelationships and accordingly conduct a well planned and progressive physical education program toward their development. Small classes are essential if this worthy aim is to be fulfilled and opportunities should be provided for after school intramural participation.

Such a directive also means that: (1) both the specialized and classroom teacher be professionally prepared in methods of teaching youth *through* and *in* physical activities; (2) the physical education class be no larger in size than those in English, history, or any other subject; (3) all youth be guided toward mastering skills that will help them grow in organic vigor, knowledge, appreciations, and ability to contribute to their own development as well as to group endeavors.

Because all life is mostly group life, it is vastly important for youth to learn early how to find peer status and gain adult approval legitimately as well as how to contribute and receive benefits from being with and working with others. A child adept in sports and games, in playing on a team, squad, or in a small group, will reach this goal earlier and with more ease than one lacking such skills. A good teacher somewhere along the academic ladder has helped such a youth to learn from and through a wide variety of experiences lessons vital to his existence.

Figure 1.　The major learnings of children come from and through movement. (Courtesy of AAHPER.)

THE GENERAL OBJECTIVES OF THE
ELEMENTARY SCHOOL

The broad objectives of physical education are those of education in general. Schools should assume the responsibility to see to it that every child, regardless of sex, economic status, geographic location, or race has equality of opportunity to receive the best balanced and meaningful education possible. Such an education should:

1. Equip him to enter an occupation suited to his abilities and offering reasonable opportunity for personal growth and social usefulness.
2. Prepare him to assume the full responsibility of American citizenship.
3. Give him a fair chance to exercise his right for happiness.
4. Stimulate intellectual curiosity, engender satisfaction in intellectual achievement, and cultivate the ability to think rationally.
5. Help him to develop an appreciation of ethical values which should undergird all life in a democratic society.[1]

Obviously these worthy objectives can best be achieved when the school, home, church, and other institutions in the community work closely together for their accomplishment.

THE GOALS OF PHYSICAL EDUCATION

Literally, to educate means "to lead forth." The aim of the elementary school curriculum should be to teach each child in each new rising generation to understand, believe in, and value democracy as a way of life, as well as to inspire each pupil to strive for personal distinction in order that he may contribute toward the advancement of a more highly cultured, productive, happier, and meaningful life for himself and all people. Consequently, the elementary school in terms of individual and societal needs should:

1. Help each child to grow in emotional security.
2. Provide experiences in democratic living that help each child to gain status or a feeling of belonging in his group and in his community.
3. Provide daily situations in which each child can enjoy feelings of success or achievement in terms of his own potentialities or of group goals.
4. Provide the facilities and relationships which foster the physical security and health of each child.
5. Provide for the purposeful and functional acquisition by the child of the tools and basic skills contributing to effective living in today's world.
6. Provide experiences rich in opportunities for the development of aesthetic and moral values.
7. Provide rich contacts with the accumulated cultural heritage in the solving of present problems and in the pursuit of leisure.

---

[1] Educational Policies Commission: *Education for All American Youth.* Washington, D. C., National Education Association, 1944, p. 21.

8. Provide experiences demonstrating how science and democracy promote constructive change through problem-solving and group deliberation.
9. Provide experiences that help children understand the problems of world cooperation and encourage them to work creatively for universal peace.[2]

The unique contribution of physical education is in the area of effective, efficient, and purposeful movement. This is of great importance to all educators who realize the impact of the scientific truth that "the basic tool for performance of any task in life is the human body."[3] The specific developmental goals of physical education are in the areas of (1) physical fitness, (2) increased skill range and accuracy, (3) knowledge, (4) attitudes and appreciation, and (5) better use of leisure time.

Physical Fitness

Because it is impossible to separate the mind and body of man, in the true sense of the word there is no such isolated thing as "physical" fitness. Actually, the mutually interdependent and inseparable components of total fitness are mental, emotional, social, and spiritual, as well as physical. Fitness, then, is a total phenomenon. Taking part in vigorous activities contributes to organic development and general well-being. To build intelligent and socially sensitive youth we must work toward that goal. The muscles of the body grow in strength, size, and tonus through exercise.

The vital organs of the body are likewise favorably affected by exercise. Through activity, the rate and force of heart beat is increased; breathing becomes deeper and more rapid; heat production and body waste are stepped up; improved appetite and sleep, and accelerated energy build-up and energy breakdown result. In children, physical activity serves as a stimulus to growth.

Physical fitness is the result of planned activity and regularity of exercise, sleep and rest, eating, engaging in play or recreation, keeping in a state of emotional well-being, and regularity of waste elimination habits. Abundant, buoyant health gives one the drive to work, to play, and to live with zest. Children need approximately four hours of rugged, big-muscle activity daily through outdoor play in order to develop, to be, and to stay healthy. On the Kraus-Weber Body Flexibility Test, and other more recent tests, American children placed alarmingly low in comparison with European youth. The widespread publicity given to this and other fitness test results has succeeded in arousing the people of the United States to the need for better physical education programs for *all* children in *all* schools.

[2] Rucker, W. Ray: *Curriculum Development in the Elementary School.* New York, Harper & Brothers, 1960, p. 41.

[3] Broer, Marion: *Efficiency in Human Movement.* Philadelphia, W. B. Saunders Company, 1960, p. 3.

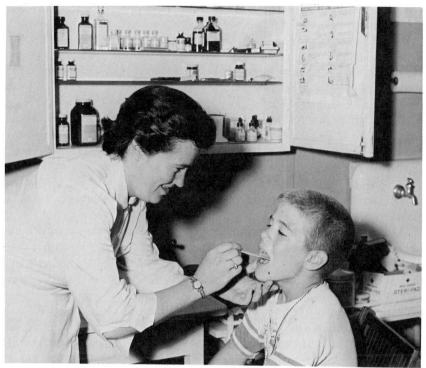

Figure 2. All elementary school children should have a periodic physical examination and their program in physical education should be built upon the physical needs of each individual child in that program. (Courtesy of AAHPER.)

Increased Skill Range and Accuracy

Skills result when the whole body learns to coordinate properly. Children increase their ability to master certain skills as they grow older. This is known as maturation: one will best learn to play baseball, tennis, or other sports when he is ready to learn them, or has a desire to do so. Seven year old George may not want to learn to play badminton, but because of urging by a doting aunt, will try and fail. He throws down the racket is disgust and walks away. George at fifteen, however, may be a skilled player and rabid badminton fan. There are many sport skills a child of six cannot do, but the same child may be a masterful player at eleven. Skilled teachers can detect this maturation period, and when the student is ready to learn, skill improvement can be accomplished. They must know what these individual maturation levels are, how they can be seen, and at what age they are most likely to appear.

Skill coordinations are learned mostly through trial-error plus imitation. Jane learns to roller skate by trying to copy the movements of her older brother. She tries until she masters the skill, or, if she fails, will keep on practicing either alone or before a small group until she is an old hand at it—but will drive herself to skate, in spite of repeated falls and skinned knees, only as long as she is determined to learn. The will to do is a dynamic driving force. It can be both instilled in others and guided; it is the basis for learning *how* to do things. Mistakes are a vital part of all learning, for there can be no end result without initial attempts. Children are eager to learn and to do.

Because youngsters learn sport skills largely by imitating others and practicing what they have seen, the most productive teachers of physical education know how to perform a number of skills well. They know how to throw and catch balls of all sizes, how to aim and hit targets, how to coordinate arm and leg movements, how to do the polka and other dance steps, as well as numerous other kinds of physical activities. But most of all, such teachers know how to teach a wide variety of physical skills to others.

If, however, the teacher is unskilled and unable to demonstrate how to do a movement correctly, she may be able to describe it in such a clear, concise way that the best student in the class can do it well enough from her description for the others to copy. Not all teachers who can perform a beautiful tennis shot can teach others to do likewise. Chances for successfully getting others to want to learn to play tennis well may be greater, however, if the player-teacher is highly skilled, is admired and respected by the learner, and knows how to help others learn joyfully.

It is important for the teacher to know that practice makes perfect *only* if the correct way to perform a skill is being repeated. It is harder to unlearn faulty movement habits than to learn new ones. Susan tends to learn to swim faster if she is taught from the beginning by someone who knows how to teach than if she learns to do a few dog paddles on her own and in some magic way learns to stay above water. Charles will learn to make more baskets if he works with someone who is a whizz at basket shooting than if he takes a ball and practices unguided in his own back yard.

The role of the teacher in skill teaching is that of (1) recognizing learning readiness, (2) motivating the learner, (3) demonstrating the correct way to do the movements, and (4) helping the child teach himself how to master them. Speed, strength, timing, and increased movement range can be developed through practice under skilled directions of the teacher who can help the learner correct his mistakes.

Knowledge

Increasing the ability to make correct judgments, to do things well, and to know about other people as well as one's self is another goal of physical education. Children must learn early in life the meaning of signals and symbols, and how to react to them. They must learn how to move with ease and safety in the environment of the home, school, playground, and community. This social knowledge becomes increasingly important as the child goes from his primary home group to the larger secondary group of the school and the community. Furthermore, children must learn to find security, love, recognition, and belonging in each of the many environments or groups they join hourly, daily, and weekly, throughout life. And as they move from group to group they learn the rules of the groups, of the game of life. They get to know about the other fellow. Through movement or play Johnny learns also about himself, whether his classmates consider him a "swell hitter" or an "easy out." He also soon knows what his teammates are like, if they are good or poor sports, if they will cheat in order to win or if they will play fairly. Likewise, Johnny learns through activity that if he steps over this line he is out, or if he shoves and pushes other players he will be penalized. Johnny learns much about grownups, too, through games. He soon masters techniques for getting along with them with the least effort. He also discovers the right time to swing the bat to connect it with the ball or where to aim to hit the bull's eye. He learns how to modify games for his immediate purpose, how to play baseball in the narrow confines of the back alley or the city street. He learns to use, find, and substitute equipment in his environment when he wants to play a game learned at school; thus the shinny stick replaces the hockey club or the broom handle is used as the baseball bat. Through experiences of movement, through games, and through activity Johnny learns about life itself. Children must have much vigorous activity in order to grow, learn, and develop.

Can we as adults teach the child to know, appreciate, and want the beautiful and best throughout his own life? Can we teach him the real value of material wealth against the wealth of living a successful, abundant life which may make him and society better, wiser, healthier, and happier?

Attitudes and Appreciation

People continue to do throughout life things they most enjoy. Children will play baseball or prisoner's base on playgrounds, vacant lots, and in narrow city streets as long as they gain deep satisfaction from the game. This joy of playing, of participation, increases as they gain in ability. Children and adults alike choose to do the things they can do best in their leisure time. If we would build in youth a feeling of success at playing games, if we would have them like their physical education classes, we must teach this activity in such a way that coming to class is an adventure![4]

Through games, rhythms, and other types of body movements children learn to appreciate more than the activity itself; they become cog-

---

[4] Jones, Violet: *Hooray, P.E. Today!* New York, Pagent Press, 1959.

nizant of the rights and privileges of others. They may regard the adult teacher highly or they may distrust and disrespect her, for appreciation or lack of it collects and dams up within the child in whatever he is doing.

Through instruction in physical education, selfish "I" drives, so markedly strong in many young children, can gradually be rechanneled to reach the deeper "We" drives. As children grow both in age and experiences of learning to share with others, to give and take, they become more mature in their social relationships. Possessing and using a "We" feeling is one sign of maturity. It must be learned if one is to live a full, happy, adjusted, and useful life.

Attitudes control, shape, and color everything the individual does in life. How the child *feels* about what he is learning is as important as what he is learning. Motives (often hidden as well as apparent in children) that can spur on or checkrein a child's desire to learn are:

Wants and needs	Knowledge of progress
Individual behavior traits	Purposes
Attitudes toward self and	Emotions
what is being learned	Rewards
Interests	Punishment
Habits and skills	Group recognition

Because all children learn *experimentally* with their *whole* bodies, it is the role of the teacher not only to provide meaningful and progressively difficult learning activities but also to help each pupil shape constructive attitudes toward himself, life, the rights of others, his parents and family, teachers and other adults, as well as help him gain a real respect for the value of learning and education. Because no two persons are born exactly alike, but each differs in his natural endowments, the skilled teacher will be ever alert to "teachable moments" that abound in all learning situations which will help the child shape desirable behavior. She must also develop in each pupil attitudes that are favorable toward physical education. Those who race children through a strenuous activity period en masse, or sour them on physical activity because of rigid physical fitness performance standards and testing procedures, fail to realize that such negative experiences also produce negative attitudes toward physical activity. Children who "have had it" in physical education classes become the adults of the future who "don't want it."

Better Use of Leisure Time

Today's children have inherited a rich legacy of leisure. Every American now has more leisure than any citizen in any age has ever had, yet this is only the dawn of a fast-breaking glorious new day of work-free time. However, many Americans of all ages remain trapped in their own-created quagmire of mediocrity, existing in their own mechanical push-button environment wherein they "grab" at this or that fleeting pleasure, and "dash" here, there, and yet nowhere.

Misused leisure is dangerous and extremely costly. Bored, unhappy, thrill-seeking children and adults get into serious trouble, for it is during free time that both crime and accident rate shoot up to dizzying heights. Positive leisure, on the other hand, when used to its fullest, will (1) re-create the mind, body and spirit through activities that have meaning and value, and (2) bring forth renewed physical and/or emotional and mental creative effort. Factors that determine what one does in his leisure time are: geographical location, cultural conditioning which has already labeled activities as positive or negative, sex, age, amount and depth of education, opportunities, economic and social status, religion, personal desires and drives, race, and ability. Those wishing to guide youth toward positive, beneficial use of free time need to know much about what *moves youth toward choices,* and much, much more about the *feelings, wants,* and *desires* of each individual child. They must also do a much better job of teaching children many kinds of physical skills and games to play when they are out of school as well as in it.

THE VALUE OF PLAY AND RECREATION

Play is one of the great physical needs of man, along with food, rest, elimination, and sex. It is leisure-time activity voluntarily selected and done that brings satisfaction and recreation to the individual. Life abounds with the rhythm of work-play, energy breakdown—energy build-up, sorrow-joy, health-sickness. "All work and no play makes Jack a dull boy," but it can also make Jack a sick boy, indeed. People need to get away from the drabness, dullness, and monotony of their lives whether they are six, sixteen, or sixty. They need a change to do activities that are challenging, adventurous, and fun!

What is work for one person may be play for another. The manual laborer who lays brick upon brick eight hours a day for five days is working. Winston Churchill, on the other hand, when prime minister of England, was known to lay bricks for fun; it was one of his many hobbies. It has been said that the main difference between work and play is the degree of pleasure that comes from either. What is hard work for one brings much joy to another. What one does during his hours of free time may be recreative provided that it brings deep satisfaction and release from tension, is done voluntarily without pay, and gives one a change from his usual routine. Children need to be taught to play as much as they need to be taught to work, for play and work are inseparable. We work so that we can play, but we play so that we can work more productively, whether we are young or old.

There are three types of play: (1) motor (hitting a tennis ball, swimming, riding a bicycle), (2) sensory (watching a sunset, listening to a symphony or jazz, or tasting a cake one had made), and (3) intellectual (going to lectures, the movies, reading a comic book or Shakespeare).

Through recreative activity the child and the adult are revitalized, refreshed, and recreated. Since many children sit most of their time in school and are directed in their many activities by an adult, they must become more active and self-directed in their play during their free time.

To Children

Children are dynamic, exploratory creatures. The vast portion of their early learning comes from and through movement. One is amazed at the number of things a one year old child can do. His greatest life learning period is between the years 1 to 6, and the more a child hears and sees the more he wants to hear and see. By the time a child is three years old he has pretty much learned how he *should* and *will* deal with the world. If he is normal, throughout life he will continue to add skill upon skill until a peak is reached. Children find deep satisfaction in the big muscle movements of running, skipping, hopping, and jumping. Joy comes in pretending, in moving to sounds, in playing tag and "it," and in chasing and being chased.

Some adults have erroneously believed that children, because they naturally seem to enjoy movement, pretense, and rhythms, do not need to learn how to play. These people have claimed that it is as silly to try to teach children how to play as ducks how to swim. We now realize that these oldsters knew as little about ducks as they did about children. Although play is universal, each child in each culture (whether he is an Eskimo, Pygmy, or a freckle-faced American boy or girl) must be and is taught by adults the games of the clan, tribe, and city block, plus those most favored ones of his own sex, race, and religion. A boy is taught games thought best for boys. Little girls are given dolls and baby carriages. Sociologists and anthropologists call this cultural and social conditioning through play. Both tradition and education influence the child through the adult. Games such as "Run, Sheepie, Run," "Fox and Geese," and "Red Rover," are passed on down to children. They are eager to learn them, for children crave to be like grownups, to do the things adults would like them to do, to play games favored by adults. Often the cry is "teach us a game you played when you were little."

Children up until the age of three largely take part in narcissistic play or playing alone. This is followed by parallel play in which they can play for a short time with one or two other children. They refuse to share their playthings, and will scream bloody murder when the girl next door grabs their toys and runs away. As they grow older they become more social in their play interest and will voluntarily play with two or three or four others. They also become more socially conscious, more willing to share. Just how many games they will play, with how many other children they want to and can play successfully depends upon their age, how well they were taught to play, when they were taught, and by whom. The first grader who has learned to play well with others in a small group and can follow simple directions has learned much, indeed.

Children from rural areas need directed play just as much as do city children in spite of the fact that they have wide fields in which to roam and trees to climb. Indeed, among rural children this need to learn how to play with others is often intensified.

To Older Youth

Because of differences in strength, play interests, and physical capacity, boys and girls are usually separated at the fourth grade for instruction in physical education. Boys tend to like rugged games in which they can show their strength, while girls tend to favor rhythmical activities and team games. As each sex grows older, activities are favored in which they can meet members of the opposite sex. During the adolescent period, which has been called often the time of temporary disorganization, youth is awkward, ill-at-ease, moody, and rebellious. He is more apt to bridge the gap successfully between childhood and adulthood if he can play several sports with more than average skill, and if he has mastered some social graces fairly well or at least well enough not to be completely miserable at a social gathering. Above all, it is vastly important that somewhere between the ages of ten to fifteen skill patterns laid down in previous years be refined, reinforced, and relearned. Unless youth can dance, play tennis, swim, ride horseback or do other sport skills well, their chances for learning to do so at the age of twenty, thirty, forty or later are very small. As one grows older he is more fearful of losing face among his peers. It is only the unusual adult who learns how to swim or play golf or other sports unless basic movement patterns similar to those found in these activities were learned during early life.

To the Adult

As one grows older he tends to become physically, emotionally, and mentally sluggish. Too often he is a victim of heartburn, headaches, or ulcers. One reason why heart disease is the chief cause of death among American people is that people burn themselves out too early; they become frustrated and unhappy, not from physical fatigue, but from overworking their emotions and their minds. Some medical authorities claim that modern man works all day and worries all night. Many American adults tend to be pleasure-mad without finding real or peace-abiding pleasure in many of the things they do or seek. They rarely spend their leisure time leisurely or recreatively. Recreation alone will not cure our national present-day problems or the personal problems of each citizen.

It can help, however, especially if one knows how to choose physical and recreational activities best suited for his age, and finds meaning, joy, release from tension, and renewed purpose from doing them.

Whether or not one develops a state of physical, emotional, and mental fitness depends, among other things, upon practicing good health habits regularly. Routinized daily health habits of early childhood become habitual and tend to carry over to later life. A healthy, happy childhood is the foundation upon which a healthy, happy adulthood rests.

WHEN IS ONE EDUCATED?

One is never completely educated, for opportunities for more learning are everywhere at all times. When the desire for learning is gone, one is in a rut. The only difference between a rut and a grave is depth. Education involves learning, which in its last analysis means changed behavior. If a person's behavior does not change, or if his actions are not altered because of the amount of education he has received, he has not learned. Time and energy have been wasted. Increasingly one is being considered educated because of what he *does,* rather than what he knows. Education should and must make a difference.

One is educated when he:

1. Can communicate with others and has something of real value to communicate; when he has command of fundamental communicative arts.
2. Can face, adjust to, and solve his own personal problems, or knows how to go about solving them and is working toward a solution, and is actively engaged in helping to solve the bigger problems of society.
3. Knows how to live abundantly, and knows the things he can do in order to use his total body best when he is a child, youth, adult, and aged citizen.
4. Can make a living doing the things that bring satisfaction to him; that are creative to him.
5. Can accept sorrow; when he can find happiness, and lives a balanced life.
6. Can live and act rationally by using his education in his daily life.
7. Can face courageously the many everchanging complexities of his life, time, environment, and work by utilizing what he knows and believes in as a human being.

WHEN IS ONE PHYSICALLY EDUCATED?

One is never completely physically educated, for each year of life brings new adjustments that must be made, new techniques that must be mastered. Physical education, like education in general, is continuous. It can be measured or evaluated by what one does, how one lives, and how one utilizes himself. Those who have taken courses in this subject in schools should act differently from those who have not had this opportunity.

As the twig is bent, so grows the tree. The kind of education the child receives determines the kind of adult he will be. What type of product do we want to turn out from our schools and colleges? What kind of boys· and girls do we want to put our stamp of approval on or pass in our classes as physical education teachers and professional educators?

An individual in our culture is physically educated when he:

1. Knows about his body and how to use it wisely, whether he is six, sixteen, or sixty, and possesses organic health and vigor.
2. Knows how to play one or more individual sports with above average ability and gains satisfaction for having participated.
3. Knows how to play one or more team sports with above average ability and gains satisfaction from participating.
4. Knows how to move his body gracefully to rhythm and knows how to do one or more social, folk, or square dances.
5. Knows how to save himself from drowning and has adequate skill in first aid, in safety and survival techniques, and in the avoidance of injury related to activity.
6. Knows how to use his body without undue fatigue.
7. Can move at different speeds with ease, can change directions, and can judge distances.
8. Can throw balls of various sizes with a fair degree of accuracy.
9. Can hit, strike, kick, and catch moving objects with a fair degree of accuracy.
10. Can hit stationary and moving targets with a fair degree of accuracy.
11. Can fit into several groups and contribute to each one.
12. Is happy and has a zest for living.
13. Does a wide variety of activities in his leisure time regardless of age and is recreated by doing them.
14. Has periodic medical and dental check-ups and has defects corrected.
15. Has positive, beneficial, and regulated daily health habits.
16. Knows the role physical activity plays in relationship to weight control, prevention of fatigue, stress, aging, degenerative diseases, poor mental health, and psychosomatic disorders.
17. Has a deep regard for the meaning and value of life, his own and that of others.

This list may be incomplete but it will serve as a guide for youth and adults, pupils and educators. Teachers of physical education, like all other educators in the public school and on the college campus, need to determine for themselves *what* they are trying to do through their teaching, and *how* they are going to bring about learning or changed behavior among their students. Each pupil must understand *what* physical education is, *why* it is important to him, *how* to have and maintain total fitness, and how to *be* and *keep* in good condition.

Someone once compared teaching to taking a trip. First you must choose the place you want to go, next you must discover how you are to get there in the most economical way in time, money, and energy, and then to gain the real satisfaction from your planning and your dreams, you must go. The skilled physical educator helps students *go* forward to better things in life.

Whether or not civilization will endure during our age of ever-increasing wars at more frequent intervals depends upon the greatest race the world has ever known, or seen—the race between education and world destruction. Education of the present type will neither cure nor save the world. For if education will win the race it must find new and better methods of changing selfish "I" drives to "We" drives in people and in nations. It must devise new ways to change immaturity into maturity. It must help a sick society full of feelings of fear, frustration, and futility become a healthy one full of courage and strong moral convictions. It must help each person to help himself to find and live an abundant life. This is a challenge that education and every teacher, regardless of his or her field of specialization, must accept, believe in, and work for with united and dedicated effort.

SUGGESTED READINGS

American Association for Health, Physical Education, and Recreation: *This Is Elementary Physical Education* (A policy statement). Washington, D.C., 1967.

Anderson, Marian; Elliot, Margaret; and La Berge, Jeanne: *Play with a Purpose*. New York, Harper & Row, 1967.

Dauer, Victor: *Fitness for Elementary School Children Through Physical Education,* 2nd Ed. Minneapolis, Burgess Publishing Company, 1965.

Erikson, Eric: *Childhood and Society,* Rev. Ed. New York, W. W. Norton & Company Inc., 1964.

Fraiberg, Selma: *The Magic Years.* New York, Charles Scribner's Sons, 1959.

Halsey, Elizabeth, and Porter, Lorena: *Physical Education for Children: A Developmental Program,* Rev. Ed. New York, Holt, Rinehart and Winston, 1961.

Kirchner, Glenn: *Physical Education for Elementary School Children.* Dubuque, Iowa, Wm. C. Brown Company, 1966.

Mead, Margaret, and Heyman, Ken: *Family.* New York, The Macmillan Company, 1965.

Miller, Arthur, and Whitcomb, Virginia: *Physical Education in the Elementary School Curriculum.* Englewood Cliffs, N.J., Prentice-Hall, Inc., 1963.

Part II

THE WHO

CHILDREN LEARN WHAT THEY LIVE

If a child lives with criticism,
*   He learns to condemn.*
If a child lives with hostility,
*   He learns to fight.*
If a child lives with ridicule,
*   He learns to be shy.*
If a child lives with shame,
*   He learns to feel guilty.*
If a child lives with tolerance,
*   He learns to be patient.*
If a child lives with encouragement,
*   He learns confidence.*
If a child lives with praise,
*   He learns to appreciate.*
If a child lives with fairness,
*   He learns justice.*
If a child lives with security,
*   He learns to have faith.*
If a child lives with approval,
*   He learns to like himself.*
If a child lives with acceptance and friendship,
*   He learns to find love in the world.*

—DOROTHY LAW NOLTE

Chapter 2

The Teacher

The teacher of physical education on the elementary level may be the regular classroom teacher or the specialized physical educator. Often in smaller schools it is the teacher, who in a self-contained classroom assumes the responsibility of teaching all subjects offered in the curriculum. In the larger city system, however, it is the trained physical educator who is in charge of the program. It is also customary in larger public schools to separate the sexes from the fourth grade level on through high school for instructional purposes, and for the girls to be taught by a woman and the boys by a man. However, the sexes should not be completely separated at and following the fourth grade level. There are many coeducational activities that should be included in the program. Just how often coeducational classes should meet and what activities are included in the program depend upon desired objectives to be realized.

WHO SHOULD TEACH PHYSICAL EDUCATION IN THE PRIMARY GRADES?

There are arguments pro and con to this question. Some educators believe that it is better for the children in the primary grades to have their physical education classes and playground periods supervised by their own classroom teacher. Those who believe in this school of thought claim that since play is so significant it is important for the teacher, who will be with the children for the longest period of time, to see how they play so that she can best guide them into desirable physical and social growth patterns. Other educators hold that only those persons certified to teach physical education activities should do so. Those who cling to this line of thought believe that children learn faster when they are taught correctly from the beginning by a professionally prepared physical educator.[1]

---

[1]AAHPER. *Professional Preparation in Health, Physical Education and Recreation Education.* N.E.A., Washington, D.C., 1962, pp. 58–70.

In smaller schools the classroom teacher usually is the only one available to give instruction in all subjects offered in each grade. This includes basic skill in the broad fields of language arts, physical education, art, and music. In schools organized under the self-contained classroom plan the teacher must be a jack-of-all-trades. Too often she is master of none, or of fewer than she might be, had she fewer responsibilities.

It is imperative that the person selected to teach physical education be the best one available. The teacher above all should be the one most skilled in methods of teaching children through physical activities as well the one who teaches them a wide variety of physical activities. Such a person may well be the classroom teacher, especially in the first three grades.

TEACHER PREPARATION

Physical educators must be certified to teach by the state in which the training was received. Although states vary considerably in specific requirements, the majority require over 20 hours of specialized professional preparation for a major in this field. Broad educational areas center around theory and practical courses in activities, organization and administration, principles and methods of teaching physical education. Ten to twelve hours in the biological sciences including anatomy, kinesiology, physiology, and hygiene are usually required. Supervised practice teaching is required in most states for certification. Gradually teacher certification standards are being raised throughout the country on both the elementary and secondary levels. This is a hopeful trend, for better selected and prepared teachers should produce better educational results.

THE ROLE OF THE SUPERVISOR

It is increasingly becoming the practice in many American schools for the classroom teacher, who may be unprepared to teach physical education, to be under the supervision of an experienced physical education specialist. This form of guided in-service training can be of invaluable assistance. Together the expert and novice in this specialized field should plan, carry out, and evaluate a physical education program for which each particular grade teacher has responsibility. All such teachers in the entire elementary school should have regularly scheduled group conferences with the supervisor to establish goals to be accom-

Figure 3. Nonverbal communication from the teacher to her pupils is often more important than what is actually said to them. (Courtesy of Dr. Robert Lamp, Stanford University.)

plished, program content for each grade, and testing procedures to be used. In this way each grade teacher can see the relationship and contribution her program has with that of all other teachers in the school.

The role of the supervisor should be that of guiding the teachers, and he or she will be most successful if democratic methods of leadership are used. Guidance in its broadest sense means helping others to help themselves. Democratic leadership rests upon the principle that a real leader makes more leaders. As the expert consultant, the supervisor should help all teachers grow in their understanding of the importance of skills in teaching children through physical activities. The supervisor should visit each classroom teacher periodically to observe the effectiveness of both her teaching and program—their strengths and weaknesses —and, acting in the role of a co-worker, should aid the teacher to improve in those areas in which assistance is needed. The regular classroom teacher should be visited under her poorest and best teaching situations. Above all, no special program should be prepared to impress the supervisor. A friendly atmosphere should prevail throughout the supervisor's visit. In modern education "snoopervision"—as supervision was once called and practiced—is as outdated as teacher-dominated classes and dictatorial school administrators.

QUALITIES NECESSARY FOR THE PHYSICAL EDUCATION TEACHER

The qualities most desired in a physical educator are the same as those desired in any other teacher. All good teachers in any field must have technical skills, personality, integrity, and good health. They must have a genuine and sincere feeling for people, in contrast to a feeling for things. They must know how to use desirable methods of democratic leadership, realizing that a good leader is also a follower at times, and that a real leader aids others to develop good leadership traits. A teacher is like a good parent—both want to help children to help themselves to grow into strong, healthy, useful individuals and group members.

Teaching requires much stamina. One has to be physically fit to withstand the wear and tear of being with children over a long period of time. Too often weary teachers project their own feelings of fatigue, disappointment, anger, and pent-up emotions upon children. This is a fairly safe choice of victim, for children are less apt to fight back than adult colleagues. Teachers, like their youngsters, need to be able to get away from it all through recreative play. Increasingly, they must do themselves what they want others to do. Emerson's phrase, "What you *are* sounds so loudly in my ears that I cannot hear a word you are saying," is well worth remembering! If one wants to teach physical education, she must be well educated herself, as well as have a deep desire to help others become educated in this field.

DESIRABLE PRINCIPLES AND PHILOSOPHY

Principles, or basic beliefs regarding what is known in all fields of knowledge, should guide all teachers; these are the foundations upon which one's philosophy of teaching, of education, and of life are built.

Teachers continually search for short cuts in their work, practical ways in which to solve their problems. Such solutions come best out of each individual's experiences. They cannot be passed on very successfully from one person to another. Bernard Shaw believed that if you teach a man anything he will never learn. Materials in this book can be valuable to the readers only when tried and improved upon, modified, or reshaped to fit into their own unique situation, and when they are added to things learned from their own experiences. Suggested teaching methods, materials, and books will be, however, most valuable to readers when they have been rooted in educationally sound principles. Both basic beliefs and objectives require continual modification as we push further back to explore into regions previously marked "unknown." One's philosophy must keep pace with the result of man's eternal quest to *know,* to find out *why,* and to *grow.*

Principles of Teaching

Teaching is both an art and a science. To some, it is a struggle, a bore, a job in which one does too much work for too little pay. To others teaching is a joy, an adventure, a challenge. To still others it is a leadership service to be rendered to the development of mankind.

Each teacher's philosophy—whatever it is—governs, colors, spurs on or retards her results in working with others. The best and most fruitful results can come only from the skilled teachers who enjoy working with others. Such teachers improve constantly in their methods and continue to grow professionally.

Principles basic to education are:

1. People are educable.
2. Every experience from which people learn involves their whole being.
3. Education goes on wherever there is life. It can be good or bad depending upon the teacher in the learning environment.

Figure 4. All teachers should know that skill mastery is one of the great desires of youth. This boy is working hard on his own to develop muscular and sensory coordination at the school playground during after-school hours because he has been motivated to do so. (Courtesy of Youth Services Section, Los Angeles City Schools.)

Principles basic to teaching are:

1. Everyone can learn something.
2. Learning means changed behavior.
3. The learner masters materials more readily if he shares in the planning, doing, and evaluation of what he is to learn.
4. Teaching is largely motivating people to *want* to do things.
5. The learner, in reality, teaches himself. The role of the teacher is to help him find short cuts toward mastery and satisfaction in accomplishment.
6. Good teaching is guiding people to help themselves.
7. Teaching can be a conducted tour shared by the teacher and learner through a thrilling world of experience.
8. The most fruitful results accrue in a warm, kindly, friendly atmosphere, in which the learner feels secure.
9. Good teaching is progressive. Skills, knowledge, and appreciation are built upon each other.
10. Good teaching develops initiative, self-reliance, confidence, and independence.

Each teacher should discover her own methods based upon these and other educational principles. It is this leader who is the key to successful accomplishments in physical education, more so than adequate or elaborate facilities and equipment, small classes or sufficient time given to the program. Often the best instructors in the field have the poorest equipment with which to work and the most crowded room space. Creative master teachers are few. Resourcefulness, coupled with enthusiasm, can sometimes produce better results than superior technical knowledge and training.

Integration

Physical education offers many opportunities for integration with other subjects, such as:

1. Arithmetic—counting, scoring, and laying out courts.
2. Art—making costumes, posters, scenery, charts, and creating dances.
3. Language arts—speaking distinctly in games, dramatizing stories, choral speaking, reading and writing game rules, and keeping squad records.
4. Music—working with rhythms of all types; making and playing various kinds of instruments.
5. Social studies—folk dances, playing period games, developing understanding and appreciation of other persons and groups, developing group consciousness, leadership-"followership" activities.
6. Science and health—building desirable health habits and attitudes, developing physical fitness, good body mechanics, planning one's daily schedule for rest, work, and play.
7. Practical arts—making and repairing game equipment; laying out play areas.

PROFESSIONAL GROWTH

Preliminary professional education is but one aspect of effective teaching. Each professional leader is obligated to do her best and contribute to the growth and improvement of her own chosen specialized field. There are many challenges that a teacher faces but perhaps none is more important than the ever-deepening desire every real educator has to improve herself and her teaching ability. There are two chief ways to grow professionally: (1) through in-service training programs, and (2) engaging in further professional pursuits.

In-Service Education

In-service education is an on-the-job self-improvement program. Educators must learn how to teach and can do so by capitalizing upon their own trial and error attempts. The old folk sayings "live and learn" and "experience is the best teacher" are only true if one is wise enough to profit from experience. For some, the longer one stays in the profession, the greater the temptation becomes to teach in the same old way and stay in the same old well-worn groove. Fortunately, most teachers have high professional goals and are keenly interested in improving their effectiveness as educators.

The physical education supervisor working with classroom teachers can do much to improve elementary physical education programs through careful supervision and well planned follow-up conferences, as well as by conducting teacher-education workshops. One of the finest means of in-service education can be found in the development of a graded course of study by a group of teachers aided by the physical education specialist.

STAFF MEETINGS

Democratically led staff meetings with fellow teachers can be a splendid way to grow in understanding and appreciation of the unique and valuable contribution each makes to the school program. Such meetings should be well planned, and real problems that affect all who attend the school should be studied carefully. The old saying "two heads are better than one" is not necessarily true, for this depends largely upon the kind of heads involved. Likewise, merely bringing a group of teachers together after a long school day to discuss cooked-up business is a waste of time and effort. In order that staff meetings be beneficial, each participant must feel that he or she has a real contribution to make for the benefit of the group as well as be aware that her time is being well spent in a pursuit that will help her become a better teacher, and a member of an important educational team. Short, frequent staff meetings wherein an agenda is followed are better than long ones. Everyone should contribute both to the making of the agenda and to the meeting itself.

CURRICULUM STUDY

Increasingly, schools are providing released time for teachers to work on curriculum improvement, and regard such work as part of their job, rather than compelling them to take part in such a project during after-school hours. All schools should periodically and continuously evaluate their objectives and programs, and be assisted in this task by a small group of experts. The total school program should be revised at frequent and needed intervals, but no special area needing revision should be allowed to remain as it is until the time comes for a major "house cleaning" or curriculum change.

SURVEYS

Although community surveys will not provide teachers with the needed answers to educational problems, it is imperative that educators know much more than they do about the locality in which they work. Those who engage in community surveys or capitalize upon the information gained by local community social agencies or a community council *will* know more about the area in which they work, and the kind of backgrounds and homes from which their pupils come. All teachers should conduct or take part in various surveys of their own school in order to gain valuable information that will enable them to become more productive and understanding youth leaders. The more any teacher knows about each student the better she can help each child develop to reach his potential as a human being capable of contributing to the society of which he is a vital part.

RESEARCH

Many teachers fail to realize that research and experimentation that they do on their own teaching situation, teaching effectiveness, and learning outcomes can be far more valuable and meaningful to them and lead to their own professional growth much more than reading about the research findings done by others. All great teachers are those who have found their own unique teaching methods and have dared to be different and creative.

WORKSHOPS

Teacher workshops are rich sources for self-improvement. These often provide opportunities to obtain new teaching methods and materials, as well as help instructors gain a renewed interest and enthusiasm for their work. Such workshops should be carefully planned by a steering committee that should select, from returned questionnaires sent to teachers, problem areas they want to learn more about. The services of physical education specialists and/or supervisors as resource persons will add much to the value of such an experience.

HOME STUDY

Correspondence extension courses are now available in most communities. Although there may be merit in securing materials via the correspondence course method, most teachers will profit more from attending an extension course and gaining inspiration, along with other things, from working with a well-known educational authority and exchanging ideas with other teachers from other schools. Even if only one teacher from each building in the system attends such a course, her fellow instructors can profit from her experience by reading suggested new materials, and by having her share with them the new ideas and concepts she has learned.

PROFESSIONAL ORGANIZATIONS

All teachers should be members of and contribute to their professional organizations. Likewise, each should read the official publications of these groups, as well as contribute articles to them either individually or as a committee. All should attend as many as possible of local, state, regional, and national meetings of their professional organizations.

Organizations that teachers of health and physical education can join with profit are: The American Association for Health, Physical Education, and Recreation; American School Health Association; and the National Education Association.

TRAVEL AND HOBBIES

Although aimless wandering is fun for a few days, travel for the purpose of gaining new or deeper understandings is far more rewarding. Increasingly, teachers are going abroad as exchange instructors, graduate students, or tourists. Those with keen interest in their work and specialized field will return home from any trip with newly gained enthusiasm and new materials for their work, and will pass these on to pupils. Teaching is a de-energizing business, as anyone knows who has been in it long. Those who are the most successful educators are those who have learned not to take school home with them, nor identify too closely with their pupils, realizing that each child must learn to live his own life; such persons have leisure hours through which they gain recreation and refreshment. Only faulty planners have no leisure for themselves. Those who declare "they haven't time" need to be gently reminded that everyone has the same amount of time—24 hours, no more and no less, every single day. What one does with it is a matter of value, for first things do come first for those who make them so. Experts tell us that in order to be healthy, all people, regardless of age, need to spend some time every day doing things that bring pleasure and joy. Those who have recreative leisure usually become the most productive workers. Experienced teachers are those who have profited from their experiences and have learned many short cuts in their work, so that they do have free time in which to enjoy life. Hobbies can add much to one's joy in life, for they lead to an ever-widening new world of interests and friends.

Further Professional Education

Most large school systems require that teachers take a refresher course in their field every three years. Increasingly, those with a bachelor's degree are going on for advanced work or to receive their master's degree. This usually takes one year or 30 hours of advanced work obtained in summer school or night courses. Some institutions require a written thesis; others require the student to take additional hours and write one or more long research papers.

Those who wish to advance themselves professionally, teach on the college level, or become national leaders in their field usually obtain further study beyond the master's degree. Supervisory and administrative positions increasingly are requiring broad professional experience and the doctor's degree. If candidates qualify for admission and pass preliminary examinations, they then work toward the Doctor of Philosophy or Doctor of Education degree. Both degrees are similar in admission standards, matriculation procedures, residence and other time requirements. The Ed. D. differs largely in that it tends to be more appropriate for those who wish to become education specialists. The Ph. D. is largely aimed at a more finely specialized subject area of knowledge. Graduate teaching fellowships, assistantships, scholarships, and loans are available for those qualified to receive them.

Every teacher, regardless of the educational level she works on, must be well selected, well prepared professionally, and a leader who continues to grow in productive skill as an educator. Through the united efforts of every such individual, a happier, healthier, safer, and better world can become a reality.

SUGGESTED READINGS

American Association for Health, Physical Education, and Recreation: *Professional Preparation in Health, Physical Education and Recreation* (A National Conference Report). Washington, D. C., 1962.

Association for Supervision and Curriculum Development, N.E.A.: *The Way Teaching Is.* Washington, D. C., 1966.

Bucher, Charles: *Foundations of Physical Education,* 4th Ed. St. Louis, C. V. Mosby Company, 1964.

Clarke, Harrison, and Haar, Franklin: *Health and Physical Education for the Elementary School Classroom Teacher.* Englewood Cliffs, N. J., Prentice-Hall, Inc., 1964.

Humphreys, Alice: *Heaven in My Hand.* Richmond, Va., The John Knox Press, 1950.

National Commission on Teacher Education and Professional Standards, N.E.A.: *The Real World of the Beginning Teacher.* Washington, D. C., 1966.

Peterson, Dorothy: *The Elementary School Teacher.* New York, Appleton-Century-Crofts, 1964.

Purchell, Carl: *Teach Me!* (A photographic essay on the joys of teaching and learning). Washington, D. C., National Educational Association, 1966.

Sanborn, Marion, and Hartman, Betty: *Issues in Physical Education.* Philadelphia, Lea & Febiger, 1964.

Sharp, Louise: *Why Teach?* New York, Henry Holt & Co., Inc., 1957.

Chapter 3

The Child

Each child reacts to others according to his own growth patterns. Although teachers have long claimed allegiance to this belief, too often many of them compare Johnny, age ten, with Jackie, age ten, or Mary, age six, with Alice, age five, or lump all children in one grade together as a group, comparing this year's batch with last.

If it is true that each child is an individual, then we must teach him individually and know his own unique growth pattern. Johnny, age five, may be an uncooperative bully, but his social growth by his tenth year, when compared to behavior patterns of the five previous years, may show remarkable progress.

Growth is influenced by many environmental and physical factors. Proper development can be retarded by sibling rivalry, constant criticisms and rebuffs, unbalanced by lack of praise for things done well or even tried, or feelings of guilt welling up within from being called "bad" or "naughty." Lack of love and security, the right amount of proper foods, and not enough sunshine and rugged outdoor play can hold a child back from developing along lines in his own unique growth channels. Increasingly, parents are wearing their children out by pushing them into too many activities. Boys and girls who are going to school have room in their already full lives to work and play for one or, at the very most, two additional activities a week. Foolish is the parent who has her child taking dancing, music, and figure skating lessons or other outside activities during the busy school year, for childhood is the time for few responsibilities and the high adventure of discovery.

Growth might be compared to a ladder, each rung representing a developmental stage. Each child must progress up three such ladders, one marked "physical growth," the second "social growth," and the third "mental growth." Every boy and girl must climb up to, and pass, each developmental rung in order, for there can be no skipping. The best adjusted youngsters are those whose progress up all three growth ladders is relatively even. Thus, adults will claim that a child reacts like most other ten year old children if that child is ten years in physical growth, socially advanced to levels of behavior characteristic of the average ten year old child, and can learn materials suitable for his mental age. Other youngsters may be five in chronological age and physical development, may be eight from the standpoint of mental age, but only comparable to the average three year old child in social development. It is imperative that all teachers study the special needs and growth patterns of each individual child. Although growth cannot be forced, it can be encouraged, for children, like plants, grow best in a warm, favorable environment. Both plants and children suffer from neglect and overnourishment. Skillful, wise handling can aid all growing things to find the best that life contains.

Teachers need to learn more about each pupil, his family and environmental background, rate of development, and where he is in his own developmental stage. Chronological age of a single year's space is of little help. Age groupings that include a two- or three-year span may be more accurate and meaningful. Although it is relatively easy for the teacher to distinguish between boys and girls, colored and white children, it is more difficult to see maturation levels. Thus, not all children in the first grade can and will learn to skip correctly even though a majority may do so. The child who has difficulty may not learn to skip until he reaches the third grade, but meanwhile he may learn to perform other skills better than anyone else in his class. It is imperative that the teacher discover with each child activities in which he can succeed and gain positive peer recognition. This will yield more fruitful results than if she concentrated on trying to bring all pupils up to an unobtainable average in a chosen activity. Each child needs to be helped to accomplish the best he can do according to his own ability. Teachers should study each one carefully to discover what his maturation levels are as well as his differences, for these provide the basis upon which a rich personality may be built. A sign of a well taught class is the number of varied personalities of the pupils who have been allowed to develop as each one is—unique and individual.

The age span during which most children attend the elementary school is a difficult one to study. In seeking greater independence children often become hostile toward adults, or listen more to their peers than to their parents. Motives for actions are often concealed. From their point of view, children are more removed from any other age groups than their own. Mere babies are children a year younger; adults are but one or two years beyond. Faced with the dichotomy of "acting like a man" and being treated as a baby, of being "too big to cry" and not being trusted out of sight, children are more confused than we adults realize we have made them. Although grownups, including the teacher, may count for little in the eyes and world of the child, adults must provide much more guidance and help him grow in his own sight and his own world. Greater knowledge is needed about *when* to help children in their stages of confusion and *when* to keep hands off. Teachers, if they are worthy of the name, push children gently away from them—they do not keep them clutched to their breasts. Man cannot fly if he is chained in an abyss—learning how to fly can only come from learning how to stay aloft, from having tried.

It has often been said that the difference between an adult and a child is the difference between *being* and *becoming*. This implies that one must grow into adulthood, and that children change into adults slowly and often painfully. Above all, the teacher should help all children develop their own strengths and uniqueness. Studies show that children placed in an environment wherein they are expected to learn will learn the most. Consequently, every teacher must have a high degree of expectancy in each pupil. How the teacher regards each learner and her own temperament is as important, if not more so, as her skill to teach children in the many areas of the school curriculum, for in the final analysis what any good teacher really teaches is a reflection of herself and her love for life, learning, and other human beings.

Research discloses that inconsistent teachers are more damaging to children—not strict, bossy ones. Today we desperately need in our schools teachers who are eager to learn and who love to learn about many things in our exciting, ever-changing world. Such teachers will bring joy and individual challenge back into the school curriculum!

SIGNIFICANT FACTS ABOUT TODAY'S CHILDREN

Although all children are basically alike, each is as unique and different as every grain of sand or every snowflake. In order to be a successful teacher of youth, the teacher must know as much as possible about each pupil, his rate of development, where he is in his own developmental stage, his family background and living environment conditions, as well as his own special needs, interests, desires, and problems. Likewise, the teacher must know: (1) the characteristics of all children according to their class in school and what to expect of them as a group, (2) what materials to teach each grade, and (3) what methods are best to use to educate each pupil and the entire class most effectively.

There are many changes in recent times that drastically affect children today.[1] Our population is shifting and growing drastically and seven out of every ten Americans now live in cities; our nation has grown by 28 million people since 1950. By 1980 there will be far more children and old people than the number of citizens now in our most productive age groups. School enrollment will zoom upward on all educational levels. The individual child, the older student, and often the brightest in the class, will be lost in the crowd. Although at the present time 36 per cent of our total population is composed of those below the age of 18, this percentage will increase rapidly in each new decade. All families are

---

[1] Materials condensed from the publication, *Children in a Changing World* (A Book of Charts), prepared by the Interdepartmental Committee on Children and Youth for the 1960 White House Conference on Children and Youth, Washington, D.C., 1960.

getting larger, for 58 per cent of our children today are members of a family composed of three or more offsprings. Our child population is being concentrated into fewer states, however, and seven states (New York, California, Texas, Illinois, Michigan, Ohio, and Pennsylvania) now have 44 per cent of the total number of children under the age of 18. Although mobility rates are highest among non-whites, our cities are not growing as fast as our suburbs, in spite of the fact that larger numbers of our people are moving from one main geographic area to another. Home ownership is at an all-time high. We have more mothers working outside of the home than ever before in our history, and our greatest increase of all working mothers (83 per cent) has been among those with children under six years of age. Even today, four of every ten mothers of school-age children are working. By 1970, according to predictions, 30 million will be employed. Among older youth, many more teenagers are now in school, yet approximately *one million youth drop out of school yearly*. This occurs far more in rural than urban areas. Family income is rising with family spending patterns showing higher living levels. People are working fewer hours and today have more leisure than any Americans have ever known, yet this is only the beginning of tomorrow's new age of leisure, which will only be golden when those of all ages have been educated to use this free time in positive, creative ways, in contrast to the violent, passive, and mediocre leisure time use found among most Americans of all ages today. Likewise, more people are church members and go to Sunday and Sabbath schools. More people are living longer, for the life expectancy for the female today is 70+, for the male, 68+. By the end of this century, it is estimated that the life expectancy will be 76.8 years for the female and 71.2 years for the male. In each decade for at least the next 40 years we will have more people who will (1) live longer, (2) have more leisure, (3) have a better health status, and (4) be in and stay in school longer on all educational levels. In turn, we will have more serious problems in our homes, industries, the medical field, and especially in our schools. Today's children are now living in a world of speed and luxury that their grandparents could not even imagine. Science will bring even greater and more rapid changes in the next few decades.

Living in this time of sudden change, today's youth are being pressured by their parents and other adults both at home and at school in our tension-filled society. Actually, most of the major problems that so drastically affect children today grow out of the fact that there are just so many of them. The increasing number of pupils attending schools too often results in larger classes and diminishing personal relationships. Children today, living in a permissive yet pressure-filled atmosphere of the school as well as the home, are often insecure, undisciplined, "bratty," and rude. Their sense of security is further weakened by the ever-growing bigness of the school, church, and community. Most rarely have time alone, and most are lost when faced with free time for leisure pursuits, for they do not know how to create their own fun rather than be passively entertained. Children belonging to non-white or other minority groups have never been so faced with such serious problems of insecurity and hatred.[2] Many of these youngsters face special physical, mental, and emotional problems, others have economic and educational ones related to the geographic area in which they struggle to exist or compete. In this time of rapid change, there are far more broken homes, yet the number of births is increasing. Today in America almost half of all mothers of illegitimate babies are below 20 years of age, and too many are under the age of 15 years (significant facts for those who endorse and conduct family life education in our schools). Juvenile delinquency, a social cancer, is spreading at an alarming rate in rural as well as urban areas.[3] Manpower shortages in public health and welfare departments are serious. A few families require a large amount of community service. City slums, an unsolved problem, continue to be a hotbed for the increase in disease (e.g., tuberculosis and venereal disease), infant death, robbery with the intent to kill, and homicide. The poorest housing from the standpoint of healthful and sanitary facilities is found in our rural areas and small towns.

On the educational scene, although all but three states have compulsory school attendance laws, under many of these laws children may be excused to work in agriculture. Three out of every five children of migratory workers are found to be in grades far below normal for their age. Children who drop out of school are most likely to become common laborers or service workers, for unemployment now is, and will continue to be, highest among young workers with the least amount of schooling. The demand for highly trained workers is increasing rapidly; persons with a college education have the widest and best choice of jobs.

Today in all public and private schools, classroom and teacher shortages are serious. A few children receive a better education than the majority, depending largely upon which state or city area the child was fortunate enough to be born in or now lives in. Although mortality rates are improving, those for non-whites are still high, and for Indian children the situation today is similar to that of the general population 25 years ago. Accidents and cancer are the most common causes of death among children. Far too many children, on all economic levels, have poor diets. Regardless of our many advances in education and science, the number of children with mental and serious emotional problems is increasing steadily.

It is only when each teacher realizes the seriousness of these startling facts and is determined to help each child who is affected by them gain the fullest kind of a more meaningful education that our country can maintain the moral, economic, and political leadership it now holds among the nations of the world. Just as little drops of water and tiny

---

[2] Anderson, Margaret: *Children of the South.* New York, Farrar, Straus & Giroux, 1966.

[3] Moore, Bernice: *Juvenile Delinquency: Research, Theory and Comment.* Washington, D.C., Association for Supervision and Curriculum Development, N.E.A., 1960.

grains of sand do, indeed, make a mighty ocean and a mighty land, the contribution *each* teacher in every school could make through the real education of *each* of his or her pupils, could contribute tremendously towards the maintenance of that leadership.

All teachers should capitalize upon each child's eager curiosity to find out all he can about himself and the exciting world in which he lives. Above all, adults must do their utmost to *give childhood back to children,* for they are being robbed of this precious, slow but wonderful growth period so basic to their development as a socially sensitized adult and a contributing world citizen.

BASIC NEEDS OF ALL CHILDREN

Needs basic to all children are: (1) physiological, (2) social, and (3) ego or self needs. If children are to grow in the friendly, warm, healthy environment of school, gymnasium, and playground, answers to these inward pressures must be met. If and when these needs are ignored, submerged, or thwarted the child becomes disturbed, rebellious, and delinquent. Although ideally the home, community and school should work together as a team to provide for these inward urges, there are some cases of alarming neglect from any or all of the three in many of our public schools. When home and/or community factors exert negative influence the school must assume greater responsibility. Teachers need be much more informed of the background of each pupil than they are; only then can behavior otherwise unexplainable become understandable.

Physiological Needs

Food, elimination, rest, exercise, and fresh air are the center of all human needs. Proper balance between rest and activity is of great importance to the health of the elementary school youngster. Children must have daily from four to six hours of big-muscle activity that involves running, jumping, and hopping. They need eight to ten hours of sleep nightly, plus one hour daily of quiet, restful activity. Many elementary schools provide cots or pallets for mid-morning and mid-afternoon naps. Little if any homework should be assigned so that the children are free to choose what they want to do in their leisure time after school. It is important that children use this time to explore, roam, wander, and play games with their peers in which there are no set rules or anyone giving them directions. Children who play well together away from watchful adults grow as individuals and as group members. It is the lonely isolated child suffering from deep fears of insecurity who often is frail and sickly.

Figure 5. Bumping and pulling activities such as this help to release tension and pent-up feelings. (Courtesy of AAHPER.)

Such "loners" are costly to society, for many end up in prisons or mental institutions as did Lee Harvey Oswald and the Boston Strangler.

Social Needs

These needs are especially strong among all people of all ages. We all need to (1) belong, (2) feel secure, (3) gain recognition, and (4) be loved. These inner pressures are often intensified among children.

Behavior patterns are laid down early in life. Personality problems among adults usually are traced back to early home or school conditions or incidents. Children, regardless of age, need to belong, to be a part of a group. Those who have few, if any, friends, who are always alone, or are the last ones chosen, who are crowd-fringers rather than joiners are greatly in need of a friend. The teacher can best help such a child belong by aiding him to develop extra skills and abilities. She can push the youngster gently forward in the eyes of other children. Care must be taken that the child does not cling to the teacher friend, but gradually is weaned away.

Children must feel secure in what they are doing if they are to do their best. Two circumstances contribute greatly to insecurity: (1) feelings of not being wanted, and (2) a disturbed home life. Instability resulting from either or both can literally wreck a boy or girl, or an adult.

Day-by-day relationship with adults can build feelings of security. Teachers must, like parents, be consistent in methods of dealing with youth. One can not laugh on one occasion at conduct that may bring punishment or disapproval two days later. Insecure adult teachers who vacillate between being a friendly advisor and a hostile enemy confuse children. They cause those who are already insecure to be more so. Non-verbal communication through voice tone and facial expressions and in other ways can do much to help children feel more secure both at school and in their homes.

Studies show that children favor teachers who are firm, strict but fair, who do not show favoritism, and who are friendly and really like them. They dislike most teachers who are bossy, who do not know what to do in a situation but try to bluff their way out of it, and who are care-less in their own appearance.

Children crave to be noticed, to be "first," and to be singled out. When this need is thwarted and they fail to gain such recognition legiti-mately, they will get it by negative methods. Deceitfulness, tattling, bragging, stealing, or other such measures may be resorted to in extreme cases. "I can run further than *you*" or "my Dad can lick *your* Dad" are expressions of this normal need. Recognition should be given to all not only by the adult but by the other children as well. This can be made in the form of simple phrases such as "Johnny, you are really getting that step now" or "Mary did the best in this group today," or "Alice learned how to do this faster than anyone yesterday." It can also be given by posting on bulletin boards names of those who won class honors and class events, or squad members who played most cooperatively for a two-week period. Children are not as interested in elaborate awards, such as cups or pins, as they are in receiving earned praise from adults and their peers. Although older youth crave the approval of adults, still more they crave recognition from their friends.

Children also need love—the kind that says "I trust you," "I know you can do it," "Let's figure out how we can do that better," the kind that is consistent. Boys and girls need the security of knowing that adults will be available for help if they need it. They need to feel that the adult cares about their welfare and their pressing problems. Adults need to remem-ber that love or friendship is not a weapon, a big stick, or a favor to be used, denied, or removed when "Johnny is bad." In our society today we need to love each other truly, using love in the religious sense and not as in the popular songs or radio advertisements. Love, the highest emotion of the human being, is too often expressed by our cheapest phrases. Thus, foreigners find it difficult to understand how we can *love* that flavor or *adore* that book.

The American school has neglected too long to answer these basic needs of pupils. Too frequently little balance between activity and rest has been maintained; often only superior children or the poorly coordi-nated are singled out for praise or ridicule; all too often the extreme pressing concern of the pupil for the approval of his classmates is overlooked; all too readily we like children only when they do what *we* want them to do, or perform according to our adult standards.

Children are *not* miniature adults. They are children who can and will grow into adults. As teachers we can help them or we can be their stumbling block. We can aid them by providing for their basic needs. We can retard them or even be their albatross when we teach games, sports, or facts, and not primarily teach children *through* these activities. Educators must realize the great importance of helping all children have as many kinds of successful learning experiences as possible.

Ego or Self Needs

The need to be loved, to feel wanted, and to have a sense of security, which is pressing among all children, should be met in the school as well as the home. Children must also develop a sense of pride in themselves, a type of self-respect without egotism. They will acquire this self-respect from others according to their achievements. Teachers are morally responsible to see that each pupil receives praise for what he has accomplished each class period.

Youth must be aided to accept and make necessary compromises with life. They must know how to accept limitations and how to work, play, and live effectively within these boundaries. Those who are physically handicapped need to learn early in life how to compensate for their handicap and how to work around it.

In order to have good mental and emotional health every child needs to feel and know that:

1. he is loved and matters very much to someone
2. his parents and other adults will always accept him, even though often they may not approve of the things he does
3. he belongs to a group or a family and that there is a place where he truly belongs
4. adults are there to help him when he faces strange, unknown, and frightening situations
5. he has a set of socially-approved moral standards to live by
6. he has grownups around him who show him by example how to behave and get along with others at school and elsewhere
7. he must learn self-control and although it is all right to feel jealous or angry, he cannot be allowed to hurt himself or others when he has these feelings

CONFLICTS THAT ARISE FROM UNFILLED NEEDS

Physical, egotistic or self, and social needs fuse together and become closely interwoven to cause behavior. If a child's needs are gratified, he is a happy, well-balanced individual; when they clash, become thwarted, or submerged, atypical behavior often results unless the child can be taught to sublimate or re-channel these drives into socially approved patterns.

Regression, introversion, segregation, rationalization, dissociation, and projection are escape mechanisms through which the child may avoid self-realization or insight.

Regression means returning or going back to childish behavior. First graders who do not get their way with their playmates often resort to foot-stamping, temper tantrums, or other antics characteristic of three year olds.

Introversion frequently results from deep fears of inadequacy from which the child may escape through excessive daydreams. Children unskilled in play techniques often wander off from the group and sit watching others have fun. Basically such children often want to join their peer group but are held back by fears of failure.

In all children there is the ever-present possibility for the flood waters of pent-up feelings to gush out when ideas and emotions clash. Unless they have mastered the fine art of self-control, mere trifles that exert pressure upon an emotional sore spot can send them flying off into a rage. They become upset, broken up, or dissociated at tiny incidents that previously left them untouched. They may not only "fly off the handle" but strike back at classmates verbally and otherwise. A pupil who is teased by his peers because he is afraid to be at bat in a baseball game may suddenly turn on them and lash out at these tormentors. The child may or may not be aware of his fear of batting but also of many other things as well. Because he wishes to hide his "horrible secret" from others he may suddenly charge at them like a wild animal. This action expresses a form of dissociation common among children.

At school the child who deeply distrusts or resents the adult teacher may be afraid to show these feelings. He feels safe, on the other hand, in releasing his pent-up frustrations upon his classmates. They, not the teacher, become the butt of his pugnaciousness. Prejudice, intolerance, excessive criticism, and cynicism are closely related to projection. One becomes adept in discovering those discrepancies others display that he knows are also his own, regardless of age.

Wise is the teacher who recognizes sudden antisocial behavior in pupils as an expression of a need for adventure. Allowing the child to get away with it is not the answer if the actions are repeated. However, the child has had the thrill of trying, and usually passes on into his next growth pattern stage. Here again the teacher's attitude toward the child is the most important. It is suggested that the other children find how they can help the offender solve the problem.

RECOGNITION

This wish is apparent in all age groups. Some gain it in socially approved ways; others find it through exceptional or antisocial behavior. In

Figure 6.   All children need to have opportunities provided for them that enable them to gain recognition from their peers in socially approved ways. (Courtesy of AAHPER.)

class some children will gain peer recognition early by being fair or by cheating in their play, physically adept or poorly coordinated, willing followers or rebellious leaders. This drive to display or improve skill mastery is intensified in some children. Pupils must receive recognition and praise legitimately from adults and their classmates. Every child can do some things better than anyone else, and should receive recognition for that ability provided it is socially approved.

DISCIPLINE TECHNIQUES

Many school discipline problems are really caused by the teacher or the teaching techniques. There are times when children deliberately disobey and should be punished. Techniques for doing so vary with each one. Some, who are more sensitive, will wilt before disapproving glances or general statements directed to the whole class, while others who are bolder and used to physical punishment understand only harsher treatment. Suggested ways for handling group disciplinary problems include:

1. *Isolate the child.*   This will be most detrimental to those who are already group isolates or scapegoats and is not suitable for them. It works best with status-secure individuals or group show-offs.
2. *Increased activity.*   Although this is often used with most students it is a waste of

energy and time, or serves largely as a means of increasing individual and group antagonism. Children as well as teachers often "gang up" against each other. The punished one is usually strong enough in popularity to gain a protective cluster of rebellious followers who will join in defying the adult leader.

3. *Send the child to the principal.* A technique that is wise only if the superior is wise, or if he is far more skilled in handling children than the teacher.

4. *Denial of activity.* This works only if the youngster is given opportunity to have rugged play and exercise later that same day. The boy who is kept indoors every recess play period for a whole week as punishment has a teacher ignorant of the basic physical activity needs of all growing children.

5. *Individual conferences.* Two offenders should be separated and spoken to singly, for together they gain needed support. *Having a high degree of expectancy in each child* pays off in numerous ways, especially when the teacher says, "I am disappointed in you," and the child senses that she really is.

CHARACTERISTICS OF CHILDREN

The Physical, Social-Emotional, and Mental Characteristics of Children in Grades 1-3 with Implications for Physical Education

PHYSICAL CHARACTERISTICS

Can use big muscles of the body best. Hand-eye-foot-eye coordination poor. Period of rapid growth. Imitative play patterns.
Lose baby fat if heavy; also lose weight if thin.
Acquire communicable diseases easily; fatigue easily.
Enjoy rugged big-muscle activities.
Motor skills are important for acceptance and leadership.
Acquire respiratory diseases easily.
Show more daring exploratory behavior.
Less attentive to cleanliness.
Postural difficulties become more noticeable by age of 8.
Lungs relatively small; heart rapidly increasing in size; pulse and respiration rates are increasing.
Show gradual increase in speed and accuracy; have better hand-eye coordination by the age of 8.
Average gain during this period is 5½ pounds and 2 inches in height.
Slow reaction time.
By age of 6 can throw medium-sized balls with full arm swing; can bounce and catch a ball, and kick a ball on the run.
Ready to learn to swim.
Girls better at stunts and tumbling than boys.
Boys show superiority to girls in throwing and batting.
Boys like combative games more than girls do.

SOCIAL-EMOTIONAL CHARACTERISTICS

Ego centered.
Sensitive.
Fearful of being left alone, of failure, and loss of adult approval.
Seek and give affection.
Cry easily; those most insecure bite nails and grab at themselves.
Have emotional outbursts.
Seek approval for more aggressive behavior.

Poor group spirit or learn loyalty better by age of 7.

"Acting out" by saying cruel, taunting things takes the place of physical aggressiveness.

"Play" being tough characters to gain confidence and power.

Own sex role more easily identified by 8 years.

MENTAL CHARACTERISTICS

Curious.

Creative.

Like definite directions.

Inattentive and talkative.

Take school seriously.

Imaginative.

Not a marked sense of humor.

Short attention span but have a good memory.

Girls develop reading and writing skill more easily than boys.

Boys grasp number concepts more easily than girls.

Have short-range mental goals.

IMPLICATIONS FOR PHYSICAL EDUCATION

Stress rhythmic activities and combinations of locomotor movements such as hops with runs.

Provide for many large-group games and a happy, secure, non-competitive social climate in grades 1 to 2.

Use a wide variety of exploratory movement skills with many kinds of equipment, such as climbing, jumping ropes, jumping from various heights, the balance beam, stilts, and so forth.

Use graduated-sized balls for throwing and catching skill development.

Stress big-muscle activities such as running, jumping, hopping and skipping in grades 1 and 2; begin some skill refinement in grade 3.

Introduce a variety of small-group games of 6 to 8 pupils, such as Crows and Cranes or Frog in the Sea.

Stress climbing, hanging, and balancing activities.

Develop arm strength in stunts and tumbling activities such as wheelbarrow races, kneeling-position half push-ups, and inchworm relays.

Use dual and combative stunts to develop strength, such as pull across the line, Indian leg and arm wrestle, and so forth.

Stress creative play; provide for free play periodically in grades 1 and 2.

Avoid highly competitive activities, for children during these formative years will often push themselves too far.

In the second and third grade stress chasing and fleeing games that require agility and change of direction.

Help each child "feel" through rhythmic movement the differences between up and down, quick and slow, soft and hard, heavy and light.

Provide opportunities for each child to experiment with ball skills such as throwing a ball against a wall and catching it and O'Leary; start modified basketball shooting in the third grade using a volleyball and lowered ring.

Discuss play situations, "cheating," taking turns, and behavior problems with the class; let each express what he feels, sees, or thinks.

Provide opportunities to keep hands and bodies busy in grades 1 and 2; change activities often.

Have children help to make rules regarding safety, use of equipment, and other rules they are expected to understand and obey.

Begin swimming instruction. Provide shorter periods for those not physically able to keep up with the group or those who chill easily.

Stress good posture and health habits, and desirable social behavior and development activities.

Provide many opportunities for each child to make suggestions by providing free-play choices and small-squad activities.

Stress joyful activities.

Proceed slowly with skill development.

Emphasize safety while at play and work, at home, and coming to and from school.

The Physical, Social-Emotional, and Mental Characteristics of Children in Grades 4-6 with Implications for Physical Education and Health Education

PHYSICAL CHARACTERISTICS

Developing rapidly with danger of damage to heart which is slowly increasing in size.

Rapid increase in strength, especially in boys.

Robust, active, noisy.

By 11, have better coordination and skills are becoming automatic.

For many the beginning of the ugly-duckling, pimply stage by the age of 11.

Have growth spurts, with early physical development for some.

Some girls begin menstruating, and pubic hair and breasts appear; have imaginary and far-removed romantic attachments; show developing interest in opposite sex and want to know about boys and men; show increasing concern for their complexion, appearance, and figure.

Boys have abundant energy and huge appetites; limited skill in sports; slowly developing skill in use of the small muscles of the body.

Steady increase in size, arms and hands growing longer and bigger.

Around age of 9, girls are taller and heavier than boys.

Small muscles becoming more developed; large muscles growing.

Most are long-legged, gaunt looking, and always hungry.

Most are in good physical condition, a few fatigue easily and should be watched for over-activity.

Poor posture becomes more apparent and should be corrected.

Eyes focus well near and far; nearsightedness develops in some.

Locomotion is steadier and children move with more grace and skill.

Sex differences becoming more pronounced.

Speedy recovery and increasing resistance to disease.

Average gain in weight—7 pounds; in height—2 inches.

Long bones and hips susceptible to injury.

"The golden age of skill development."

Boys and girls perform equally well in many activities.

SOCIAL-EMOTIONAL CHARACTERISTICS

Emotionally unstable.

Show less attachment to adults.

Have strong peer ties; in the gang stage.

Seek independence.

Often have personality complexes.

Enthusiasm often exceeds wisdom.

Becoming increasingly conscious of others.

Have an ideal man and woman and copy the actions of each.

Still look to family for security when in a tight spot.

Sensitive to criticism.

Inquisitive about human relationships.

Slowly developing interest in opposite sex, and in sex life.

Have independence and security conflicts.

Importance of peer acceptance paramount.
Like responsibility and to be considered trustworthy.
Period of increased worry.
Quick to detect insincerity.
Like self challenges.
Period of hero worship.
Increased need for independence and recognition.
Easily discouraged and excited.
Adult influence marked.
Sulking and resentment increases at home; anger develops quickly at parents rather than peers.
Loyalty and belonging a vital need.
Girls form close cliques; boys join adventurous and often destructive gangs.
Short-lived and widely varied interests.
Value good sportsmanship, loyalty, moral conduct, and strive to do the right thing.

MENTAL CHARACTERISTICS

Interested in the world and the community; want to improve both.
Restless; discouraged easily at learning attempts.
Show initiative; are creative and curious.
Idealistic and like to read about great people.
Enjoy learning new things; short interest span.
Concerned about adult approval of school work.
Concerned with justice.
Read and think a lot.
Preoccupied often with thoughts of sex.
By 11, most outgrow laughing at others; intellectual growth parallels developing sense of values and humor.
Boys like to fight, yell and tease; girls more sedate.
More comfortable with adults; like to talk seriously with favored ideal.
Developing strong feelings of right and wrong, and of loyalty.

IMPLICATIONS FOR PHYSICAL EDUCATION

Provide longer activity periods in which skill instruction gradually receives more stress.
Provide opportunities for groups and individuals to release emotions and tensions through more rugged physical activities and cheering for one's team.
Stress vigorous exercise; help pupils know how exercise assists growth; alternate strenuous activities with less active ones.
Stress good body mechanics, posture, and movement in daily life as well as in sports.
Gradually emphasize movement accuracy and good form; use a wide variety of throwing, catching, and hitting activities through lead-up games to softball, volleyball, and basketball.
Avoid highly competitive activities; stress good sportsmanship, player consideration, and team loyalty.
Provide many activities that involve rhythm and balancing, and teach social, folk, and square dance to co-ed classes.
Give as much individual attention and help to each pupil as possible in skill development tasks; develop good individual and group rapport.
Provide a variety of activities using apparatus for chinning, vaulting, balancing, and hand traveling.
Develop a longer, more active class program for every pupil.
Provide for the need for belonging through team and squad games and relays.
Keep competition at the children's level; provide intramural activities for all pupils.
Emphasize tumbling, swimming, and dance for girls; provide more activities for boys that will develop strength, speed, and endurance by using balls of various sizes.
Stress track and field events for both sexes.
Seize upon all "teachable moments" in class for health and safety instruction and shaping life values.

Not all children will fit into the growth characteristics listed above according to age. However, the majority of them will. The teacher should realize that a child of 5 to 7 is undergoing a most important transition. Because of his boundless energy, never-ending curiosity as a "doing" creature, adults must be on the lookout that he maintains a careful balance between active and passive play.

As children grow in age, skill, and ability to play with others, they should not engage in competition with children less advanced. The transition from early childhood to adolescence is one of remarkable progress. In schools, children should have increased opportunities for real responsibilities, as well as increased freedom to select, do for themselves, and evaluate their own progress. Growth, like education, is a long, tedious process.

The characteristics of a healthy child are: an abundance of vitality, bright clear eyes, lustrous hair, good muscle tone, clear skin, good teeth, a hearty appetite, and freedom from remedial defects. Such a child gains progressively in weight and height. A healthy child is happy: he radiates and sparkles. An unhealthy child tires rapidly, is irritable, seems and is dull.

Although today's children are one to two years more advanced than those of a generation ago, their interests are still wide ranging and their need for instructional help in learning how to use their total capabilities well in work and play is perhaps even more intense.

The Six Year Old

Six year olds are eager to learn! They are often overactive and tire easily. Although they are less cooperative than they were at five, they are beginning to learn how to use their whole bodies. Often they are boastful and eager to show others how well they can fight. Interest periods are relatively short but are gradually increasing in length. Acting things out, as well as all other such forms of spontaneous dramatizations, are favored pastimes.

Children of this age need increased opportunity to take part in big muscle activities of many kinds. Teachers can best work with them by giving them indirect supervision with minimum interference. Increased opportunities for making decisions might well be provided.

All need encouragement, ample praise, warmth, and much patience from adults. The importance of the kindergarten and first grade teacher in the life of a child is vast. Some psychiatrists believe that if a child does not like his first grade teacher or sense love, acceptance, and security in her presence, he is a potential school dropout. Since all children of this age need a wide variety of activities involving the use of the large muscles of the body, as well as much freedom to explore, adult supervision with a minimum of interference is best.

Figure 7. Elementary children find great satisfaction in learning how to work well in a small group. (Courtesy of *The Instructor*. Photograph by Edith Brockway.)

The Seven Year Old

The seven year old suddenly seems to become sensitive to the feelings and attitudes of adults. Fear of their disapproval causes him to be less anxious to try many things than to do a few well. Fairy stories, rhymes, myths, nature stories, and comic characters bring delight to him. Although he is becoming increasingly more capable of some abstract thinking, he learns best in concrete terms and through activity. Boastfulness and exaggerated cocksureness show that he often prefers the word fight to fighting.

Both teachers and parents should help the seven year old find the right combination between independence and dependence. Warm, encouraging, friendly relations between the child and the adult are imperative.

The Eight Year Old

Although the eight year old regresses to becoming dependent upon mother or teacher again, he also is gradually becoming more interested in others. Gang life becomes a part of his play pattern. Although he may appear to adults to be noisy, aggressive, and argumentative, he tends to favor adult-supervised activities. Collections of all kinds fill his pockets, his bedroom, or den. He may have more accidents than the seven year old because of his increased daringness.

Special needs of the eight year old include receiving much praise and encouragement from adults. Wise supervision from friendly grownups can help him belong to groups. Opportunities to develop control over small intricate muscles should be provided. Wood carving, making model airplanes, sewing, sketching, and other forms of arts and crafts can furnish channels for needed creative urges.

The Nine Year Old

By the age of nine most children have formed a reasonably strong sense of right and wrong although they may argue long and loud over fairness in games, or decisions of referees. Prolonged interest and carefully laid out plans become increasingly apparent. Stories of other lands and people and love for his country cause him to desire to become a good citizen, to do a good deed daily. Much time is spent with gang members discussing people and events in his own environment. Active rough and tumble play keeps the nine year old on the go.

Children of this age need to be given frank answers to their questions about sex. They need to belong to a gang they can be loyal to, and should have increased responsibilities in the home, school, and community. Training in the advanced skills, such as learning to kick a ball or hit a target in the correct way, should gradually be included in the physical education program for both sexes.

The Adolescent

Although there is a wide range of individual differences in maturity levels among this age group, certain generalizations can be made. The adolescent prefers his gang to his girl friend and will be often more loyal to this gang than to his own parents. Although there is a marked interest difference between the sexes, both tend to like best team games, pets, television shows, radio programs, and comic books. Teasing and other forms of antagonism between boy and girl groups is a favorite pastime. Although the majority of adolescents tend to be overcritical and rebellious, and have an "I know it all" attitude, some do not display these characteristics. Nailbiting, daydreaming, and often impudence show a regression to habits characteristic of younger children. Fear of ridicule, of being different, becomes a nightmare.

The adolescent needs to know about and understand emotional and physical changes happening within him. A sense of belonging to a peer

Figure 8. A healthy child is happy: he radiates and sparkles. (Courtesy of Dr. Joan Tillotson, Plattsburgh Public Schools, Plattsburgh, New York.)

group and increased opportunities for independence are paramount. Adult guidance that is friendly and unobtrusive enough not to threaten his need for freedom is necessary. Increased opportunities for the adolescent to earn and spend his own money, pick out his own clothes, and set his own daily routine should be provided. Membership in clubs that work toward a "worthy cause" should be encouraged.

Skill mastery is one of the great desires of youth. They long to surpass others in strength, speed, and accuracy. Strict physical training to gain team membership is willingly accepted and should be encouraged.

ATYPICAL AND EXCEPTIONAL CHILDREN

The majority of children attending public schools are normal. However, there is a small percentage who suffer from physical, emotional, and mental handicaps. These children require additional attention. Because all children should take physical education, no student should be excused from his class because of defects. The social values of play are greater than adults have formerly believed. A neurotic, psychotic, or disturbed child first shows evidence of emotional illness when he withdraws from the crowd and refuses to play. Yet psychiatrists tell us that, oddly enough, the first sign of recovery from emotional involvement among all ages is the sudden desire to be active, to play with others. Physically handicapped children can profit often even more than normal youth from the social aspects of physical activities. The crippled child needs to be accepted. His chances for being taken into groups will be increased through the play approach. Every child can and should be taught to master some type of physical activity. An individual program should be tailored to fit his physical case should he deviate from normal.

Signs and Symptoms of Social or Emotional Maladjustment

Most teachers have children in their classes who have behavior problems. Those needing special assistance and often professional help will show the following signs of maladjustment:[4]

Overtimidity; seclusiveness.
Overaggressiveness; constant rivalry and quarreling with others.
Excessive daydreaming; persistent inattentiveness not due to any discoverable physical cause.
Extreme sensitiveness to criticism expressed or implied; feelings hurt easily; cries easily.
Difficulty in reading or reciting not due to any discoverable physical cause.
Failure to advance in school at a normal rate in spite of good physical health and adequate intellectual capacity.
Extreme docility or anxiety to please.
Excessive boasting or showing off—anything to attract undue attention.
Resistance to authority; constant complaints of not being treated fairly, of being discriminated against, "picked on."
Poor sportsmanship; unwillingness to engage in group activities that might result in losing and so in loss of face; not playing fair, or cheating in group games.
Undue restlessness; habit tics, stammering, nail-biting, or lip-sucking not due to any discoverable physical cause.
Frequent accidents or near accidents.

---

[4] *What Teachers See.* Metropolitan Life Insurance Company, New York, N.Y.

ENLISTING THE COOPERATION OF OTHERS

Teachers sometimes need help in understanding each child more fully. Cooperation with the parents, teachers, and other pupils can often prove fruitful. Frank discussions should be held with parents, but these should be carefully planned by the teacher. Suggested techniques for successful parent-teacher conferences are:

1. Quickly establish the feeling that, like the parent, you want to help the child, that you are working together.
2. Find out as much about the child as you can without probing or prying.
3. Visit the parents in their home, if possible.

THE USE OF BEHAVIOR RECORDS

Children express their inner strengths and weaknesses through their behavior. The more the adult can hear and see a child in action, the more she can learn about each one. Likewise, the more *she* talks, the less she will learn about a child, for the more freely a youngster can communicate and identify with her, the greater the learning and character shaping result will be. Suggested questions to ask yourself when observing children at work and play include:

1. Are there children who maintain leadership after the activity or game has been continuing for 5 or 10 minutes?
2. Are there children who are noisy, but who are on the side lines rather than in the center of activity?
3. Are there children in your class who are remaining in group activity only as long as they can have their own way?
4. Which children are always on the fringe of activity?
5. Are there some children who are using teasing as a source of power?
6. Are some children so considerate of others that they have little time to attend to their own work?

All children reacting to the type of behavior described are problem ridden; many of them are pre-neurotic. If growth is a slow process, the teacher must know more about ways in which the child needs to develop, and must aid him to help himself. If the teacher would teach the child, she first must know the child's developmental level in as many areas as possible.

In appraising the developmental rate of each child, the teacher should make, keep, and carefully study cumulative behavior records of each pupil. Although this is time consuming, it leads to better pupil understanding and teaching.

SUGGESTED READINGS

Breckenridge, Marian, and Vincent, Lee: *Child Development: Physical and Psychological Growth Through Adolescence,* 5th Ed. Philadelphia, W. B. Saunders Company, 1966.

Brisbane, Holly, and Riker, Audrey: *The Developing Child.* Peoria, Illinois, Charles A. Bennett Co., Inc., 1965.

Buck, Pearl: *The Joy of Children.* New York, John Day Company, 1964.

Espenschade, Anna: *Physical Education in the Elementary Schools* (What research says to the teacher). Washington, D.C., National Education Association, 1963.

Jenkins, Gladys: *Helping Children Reach Their Potential.* Chicago, Scott, Foresman and Company, 1961.

Lear, Martha: *The Child Worshippers.* New York, Crown Publishers, 1963.

Loughmiller, Campbell: *Wilderness Road* (The story of the Salesmanship Camp for Emotionally Disturbed Boys). Austin, Texas, The Hogg Foundation, University of Texas Press, 1965.

Missildine, Hugh: *Your Inner Child of the Past.* New York, Simon and Schuster, 1963.

Wheatley, George: *Health Observation of the School Child.* New York, McGraw-Hill Book Co., 1965.

Part III

THE WHERE

Mankind has always felt the need of good leadership, for the history of the world shows that we have never had enough leaders in the right place at the right time. The elementary school is the rich soil in which children can develop those traits necessary for positive democratic leadership. The hope for our American future is in the education of our present children.

Chapter 4

The Gymnasium, Playground, Pool, and Classroom

Usually physical education classes are held in a gymnasium or outside on a play field. Most public schools are fortunate enough to have one or the other. Schools that use a playground for outdoor recreational activities and a gymnasium for physical education instruction usually have the best programs. The use of the classroom, auditorium, stage, or school corridor has been found to be inadequate and results in a make-shift program fitted into make-shift space. A well equipped gymnasium, adequate play-ground space, sufficient time for a minimum of 30 minutes daily class instruction plus another 30 minutes of scheduled supervised play or recess period provide an ideal teaching-learning environment.

THE GYMNASIUM

A well lighted, ventilated, clean gymnasium is of prime necessity in all modern schools. The gymnasium should not be known as a "play-room," but rather as the gymnasium—the place where children receive instruction not in play but in physical education.

In determining the size of the gymnasium, the immediate concern must be for:

1. Adequate teaching space, with a minimum area of approximately 41 by 66 feet for 66 children. For larger classes there should be an increase of 40 square feet for each pupil.
2. Official-size courts for pupil and adult use with a ceiling height of 22 feet under all beams, tresses, or hanging obstacles.
3. Good sunlight and ventilation. The ratio of window space to floor space should be 4:5 with windows preferably placed along the two long sides of the room rather than at the end; room temperature maintained at 60 to 65 degrees.
4. Clean walls on which there are two or more bulletin boards.
5. A clean, smooth-surfaced floor marked with permanent lines for playing areas, marked with colored chalk or removable tempera paint for playing areas.
6. The room should be free from all removable hazards; unremovable hazards, such as posts, radiators, pipes, and so forth, should be covered with mats.
7. Accessibility to drinking fountains, either outside in the corridor or recessed in the wall.

8. An acoustically treated ceiling.
9. Spectator seating.
10. Single doors that swing out away from the play area.

In many schools there is often only one gymnasium. Although for grades 1 to 4 this presents no problem because the two sexes have their class together, on the upper elementary level, if boys and girls in separate classes are scheduled to use the gymnasium, an alternate plan must be worked out and care taken that the girls get to use the gymnasium as much as the boys. When both sexes are using the gymnasium together, both teachers should conduct their own classes, for one teacher trying to control such a large group of pupils would accomplish little in the way of instruction. Several plans for alternate use of the gymnasium are to provide:

1. Co-recreational periods of social, folk and square dance; mixed volleyball and recreational games such as shuffleboard, and constructed games.
2. Health instruction two days a week in the classroom, alternating with physical education two days a week in the gymnasium, and devoting the fifth day to co-recreational activities.
3. Two days in the gymnasium, utilizing more vigorous types of activities, and three days in the classroom wherein the chairs are moved in and out of the corridor by the pupils. Activity possibilities in such a space are exercises to music, teaching good posture and body mechanics, rhythmic activities, and quiet recreational games.
4. Activities for the separate sexes, with the boys using one side of the gymnasium; the girls the other. Each class can use ½ of the floor or ½ of the period for skill drills and then alternate the use of the center of the floor for team play.
5. A well planned alternate program of mass activities or skill drills played by one sex, with the opposite sex doing stunts and tumbling on mats at each end of the floor, and dual stunts (such as the Indian leg wrestle) or pyramids on the sidelines.
6. Activities for girls in the gymnasium in the fall and early spring while boys play touch football, softball, or other sports outside. Provide co-recreational activities for the remainder of the year or use plans 4 or 5 above.

Locker, shower, toilet and lavatory facilities should adjoin the locker rooms and be accessible from the playgrounds. Pupil enrollment determines the number of lockers needed. Lockers may be the individual steel type, 12"x12"x36"; the narrow type, 7"x18"x36"; the basket type; or those built flush into the wall. Each student should have a standard combination lock; the teacher should file away two copies of master sheets of all combinations. Each locker room should have stationary long benches, mirrors at the end of each row of lockers, scales, and built-in hair dryers if the school has a swimming pool.

The shower room should adjoin the locker room; preferably, it should be a separate unit. Several cubicle showers and one gang shower are recommended for girls, and all gang showers for boys. There should be one shower head for every three girls and one for every four boys, all spaced at least 4 feet apart. Liquid soap, properly controlled water and room temperature, and good ventilation should be provided in both the shower and dressing room areas. A well-drained drying room is recommended and should be located between the locker and shower rooms to prevent a flow of moisture and tracking water into the dressing area.

A special towel service booth should be located near the drying room, or towels may be issued at the main equipment counter, or may be exchanged in baskets. Preferably, towels, swimming trunks and pool suits, as well as regulation gymnasium uniforms, should be furnished by the school and provided, newly laundered and sanitary, for each pupil at the beginning of each class.

Adequate well lighted, clean and sanitary, and ventilated rest rooms with adequate toilets, urinals, and wash basins should be provided. Liquid soap, hot and cold water, and towels should be furnished.

Pupils should be encouraged rather than required to take showers after class periods at the fourth grade level when they begin wearing special uniforms for class instruction. Required showers are not only hard to enforce but can lead to serious teacher criticism from some parents. Pupils should be sold on the idea that taking a shower is a privilege as well as a social obligation to fellow students in the next class to which they will go following physical education, rather than a requirement. The positive approach provides for positive action. Sufficient time should be allotted to include showers in the daily program. For some few, taking showers will be a big part of their physical education program.

THE POOL

Increasingly, schools are building swimming pools that have been planned for maximum use by both the school and the community throughout the entire year. Others, who recognize the great value of having each child learn to swim, are using local pools in the community. The swimming pool should have a southern exposure, be 75 feet long and at least 35 feet wide. Depths should vary from 2'6" at the shallow end to 4'6" at the outer limits of the shallow area, and the deeper area should taper from 9' to 12'. The shallow, instructional area should comprise two-thirds of the pool area. Troughs at the water level should be used for hand-gripping by beginners. The deck space around the pool should be composed of non-slippery tile and be large enough for land instruction. The walls and ceiling should be acoustically treated. Recessed ceiling lights and the use of natural light coming through side windows will reduce glare as well as provide a more comfortable area for teaching. An office adjacent to the pool should be used for keeping records and first-aid equipment. Water temperature should be kept about 80 degrees for elementary children. Shower, dressing, and toilet areas should be provided adjacent to the pool; these might also be used for physical education purposes, thus avoiding expensive duplication. All of the pool facilities should be designed for maximum use and supervisory control. Spectator space is also recommended.

Figure 9.   The classroom can be used by the classroom teacher for some kinds of physical education activities if no gymnasium is available. (Courtesy of *The Instructor*. Photograph by Edith Brockway.)

Because the swimming pool is a costly operation, it is essential that it be planned by expert architects and swimming specialists. Such a facility should also be used to its maximum, for swimming is one of our finest physical activities and has high carry-over value throughout life. At all times when the pool is being used by the school, it should be made available to people of all ages in the community for after-school instructional and recreational use throughout each week yearly.

THE CLASSROOM

The specific objectives the teacher may well have in mind when conducting physical education activities in the classroom are to:

1. Use all available space to the best advantage.
2. Set up rules of conduct with the pupils while playing so that people in other classes will not be disturbed.
3. Discover with the pupils hazards that should be avoided in the room.

The general objectives the teacher may well have when teaching active games and contests in the classroom are to:

1. Develop within the child the knowledge, skills, and appreciation favorable to his fullest and wisest use of free moments in the present and future.

2. Guide toward mastering social response in a variety of situations.
3. Familiarize the pupil with a wide variety of activities.
4. Develop understandings and abilities involved in the planning, selecting, and conducting of games.

Although the classroom is not suitable as a place in which to do physical activities, it can be used during bad weather, provided the children have their physical education classes outdoors whenever weather permits. All children need, among other things, plenty of vigorous big muscle activity, fresh air, and sunshine.

INCREASED USE OF FACILITIES

School programs and facilities should serve the needs of the total community—both children and adults. Because of the increased national concern for the well-being and education of people of all ages, communities throughout the nation are becoming aware that less than four per cent of public school buildings are being used as community centers. Because school buildings belong to the people, they should be opened to serve all the people day and night and especially during Saturday and the summer months. If the school widens its service to the community, it enriches the lives of everyone. In turn, the prestige of the school will rise, its influence will grow, and its support will be strengthened.

The school gymnasium, pool, and multi-purpose outdoor play areas

Figure 10. All community facilities should be utilized for educational and recreational purposes. (Courtesy of AAHPER.)

Figure 11.   The playground area should be attractive, clean, and safe. (Courtesy of the Playground Corporation of America, New York, New York.)

should be designed for program flexibility and year-round usage by people of all ages in the community.

LEGAL LIABILITY

Few school boards can be sued for negligent acts of omission or commission because of their common-law immunity. This theory states that because the "king can do no wrong" and the state represents him, the state cannot be sued. Consequently, because each school district is a division of government, the school board is immune to lawsuits. Because school districts conduct nonprofit governmental functions, they are also non-liable. In contrast, all organizations that carry on profit-making or proprietary functions can be held liable. Teachers, on the other hand, as well as activity directors in profit-making organizations can be sued for proven acts of negligence. Legally, negligence is (a) conducting an act that any reasonable person would have known to be too unreasonable and risky for others to do, and (b) failing to do an act necessary for the protection of others.

Physical educators can be held liable for proved negligence for the following reasons:

1. Pupil injuries where playground or gymnastic equipment is defective. (Physical educators should make and periodically report in *written form* to their administrators of known

Figure 12. Outdoor play equipment should be chosen carefully from the viewpoint of safety and valued use. (Courtesy of Public Schools of Lincoln, Nebraska.)

defective, dangerous equipment and hazardous areas. They should keep a carbon copy of this report.)

2. Injuries that occur to pupils who attempt to do exercises or activities beyond their skill, such as handstands, running-jump somersaults, and so forth. (Teachers should not permit students to attempt exercises or activities for which they have not developed the necessary skills or for which they have not been danger-warned.)

3. Injuries caused by the negligence of another pupil. The other pupil's misconduct must be foreseeable. (All teachers should know what to expect from each student in behavior as well as performance.)

4. Leaving assigned groups, even though temporarily to get a drink of water, go to the bathroom, or answer a phone call. (Physical educators who teach class by throwing in the ball and leaving or other such types of instruction by remote control are *asking for trouble*.)

Accidents sometimes happen in spite of precaution, safety education programs, adequate emergency measures, or routinized habits drilled into students of what to do in case of fire or an air raid. Periodic surveys should be made and carefully studied to determine the real effectiveness of the school safety program. Only when comparative figures show (1) a reduction in the number of school accidents, and (2) a lessened degree of the severity of individual injuries, can progress be claimed or the program said to be of value.

THE PLAYGROUND

Playground space should be planned so that there is opportunity for the greatest number to play safely at one time. At least five acres should be provided for elementary schools. A minimum of 100 square feet per pupil should be an absolute requirement. Separate areas should be set off for the primary grades for safety purposes, and this group should be assigned the space that is the furthest away from the oldest, most active group. Space should be planned for use by as many age groups as possible. For example, baseball diamonds may be used for kickball with the lower grades and for softball with the upper grades at different periods of the day. The area should also be enclosed by a metal fence.

Playground surfacing is usually of dust-treated dirt, hard cement, blacktop, grass turf, or sawdust combined with asphalt. Regardless of which type is used, the area should be a safe and healthful one for children's play. It should be well planned so that it can be adequately and easily supervised, fenced, well shrubbed and shaded. Primary children should be assigned permanent play areas near the shaded side of the building where they will be well protected from the vigorous activities of older children. Backstop fences for softball and enclosed swing and apparatus areas are highly recommended. Space should be provided for sandbox and creative play for the younger children. The entire playground area should be attractive, clean, and safe. It should look like and be a place for great adventures!

Figure 13. Playground space should be planned so that there is opportunity for the greatest number to play at one time. (Courtesy of the Playground Corporation of America, New York, New York.)

Outdoor play equipment should be chosen carefully from the viewpoint of safety and valued use. Jungle gyms and horizontal hanging bars should be provided which hang 36 inches from the ground for primary children and up to 54 inches for those in the upper elementary grades. Swings with canvas seats from 10 to 12 inches high, slides, monkey rings, parallel bars and merry-go-rounds are highly recommended. Some physical educators believe that, because seesaws do very little to develop physical fitness or coordination, they are unwise investments of public funds.

Other than the above-mentioned items, the following permanent playground facilities should be included:

Apparatus:

Wood or pipe climbing apparatus.
Horizontal ladders.
Low graded to high circular traveling ring.
Hemp or Manila climbing ropes suspended from poles, or securely fastened to the building or trees.
Heavy rope giant stride.
Swings, frame 12′ high in sets of six.
Slides, 8′ high, approximately 16′ long.
Balance beams of various heights from the ground.
Traveling rings.
Seesaws in sets of 3 to 4.
Tether ball poles.
Horseshoe stakes.

Bicycle racks.
Automobile tires, suspended on ropes.
Several outdoor bulletin boards.
Suspended Manila climbing ropes.
Vertical climbing poles.

Play Equipment for Younger Children:

Sandboxes and tools.
Wide and narrow horizontal planks and boards several inches off the ground for running and balancing.
Barrels, kegs, and hoops for rolling.
Inclined boards for running up and sliding down on.
Stairs built with varied step heights to climb up and over and jump from.
Wheelbarrows.
Small tables and work benches.
Large wooden boxes and cartons.
Telephone poles laid flat on the ground for climbing on and jumping from, and others holed securely in the ground for vertical climbing.
Numerous tires and wheels of varying sizes for rolling with hands or a crossed T-shaped board.
Pipe tunnels of reinforced concrete sewer pipe, arranged in units of three, set at different angles three feet apart.
A "Whatnot," or small platform of 9x6 feet, surrounded on three sides by a low wall and reached on the fourth open side by steps.
Tables and benches.
As many box hockey sets as feasible.

The school administrator, assisted by a committee of classroom teachers and the physical education teacher and/or supervisor, should give serious consideration to the following factors regarding playground facilities and their use: location, arrangement for the protection of all pupils but especially the youngest ones, regular safety inspection forms and procedures, fencing and marking hazardous zones, care of the ground underneath apparatus, instruction in its correct use, and necessary safety rules.

Courts and playing fields laid north and south should be designated as permanent play areas and marked with paint or whitewash. Dry slaked lime or tennis tape markers can be used on turf or dirt areas. Fixed posts are superior to moveable standards for paddle-type games. Iron nets are better and cheaper in the long run than oil-treated ones, substituted wire fencing, or ropes. Track and field facilities should be laid out according to the recommendations made at the National Facilities Conference sponsored by the Athletic Institute.[1]

Multiple purpose courts of cement or macadam should be laid and marked on all permanent play areas. A tennis court can also be used for paddle tennis, volleyball, badminton, shuffleboard, basket shooting, hopscotch, ice and roller skating. Electric outlets, if provided, will make it usable for dancing or showing films at night. Lighted courts and play

---

[1]Athletic Institute: *A Guide for Planning Facilities for Athletics, Recreation, and Physical and Health Education.* Revised Ed. Chicago, Illinois, 1957.

Figure 14.   Activities for the playground should add to the pleasure of the moment and enrich the recreational life of the child. (Courtesy of Elizabeth Glidden, Specialist in Elementary Physical Education, Los Angeles City Schools, Los Angeles, California.)

areas increase participation to such an extent that they are wonderfully inexpensive investments.[2]

Standard game areas that should be established are:

Outdoor badminton courts	Softball and baseball diamonds
Basketball courts	Speedball court
Croquet courts	Speed-a-way fields
Handball courts	Tennis courts
Shuffleboard courts	Touch football field
Soccer fields for both boys and girls, if possible	Volleyball court
	Paddle tennis courts
Lawn bowling courts	

Outdoor equipment, other than balls of varying size, includes:

Aerial darts	Individual and long jump rope sets
Badminton sets	Jumping standards and crossbar
Basketball or Goal Hi standards	Lawn bowling sets
Bat-O-Net sets	Marbles
Box hockey sets	Putting game sets
Croquet sets	Shuffleboard sets
Deck tennis rings	Tennis equipment
Horseshoe sets	Tether ball sets
Hurdles	

[2]Vannier, Maryhelen, and Fait, Hollis: *Teaching Physical Education in Secondary Schools,* 3rd Ed. Philadelphia, W. B. Saunders Company, 1968, pp. 123.

Activities for the playground should add to the pleasure of the moment and enrich the recreational life of the child so that he uses new activities in his leisure time away from school. By teaching obedience to rules and regulations, games help teach children to get along with others. Activities should be selected that are suitable to sex, playing space, clothing and weather, as well as age level.

Some suggestions to assure proper conduct on the playground are to:

1. Provide a varied program appealing to all.
2. Have a few concise rules and enforce them.
3. Make frequent tours of the playground with pupils, looking for hazards and having the children paint these hazards bright yellow.
4. Always maintain a spirit of fairness and justice.
5. Foster a spirit of self-government by giving children a share in the making of conduct rules on the playground, and have them help supervise and officiate at activities.
6. Use pupil-game rotation plans so that all get equal use of the best facilities and equipment.

For recess and supervised free-play periods pupils should be assigned to a specific play space. Those in the primary grades should be given a section near the building and have certain pieces of fixed equipment such as swings, slides, and a jungle gym for their exclusive use.

Children in the upper elementary grades should also have a section of the play field which is their own. Boys should not be allowed to monopolize the baseball diamond or soccer field but should rotate with the girls the privilege of using all marked areas. A weekly schedule of play space assignments should be worked out by a student committee and teacher. Coeducational games can be encouraged when at least one assigned weekly period is set aside for them.

HANDLING EQUIPMENT

All equipment, uniforms, and gear should be marked by stenciling the name or initials of the school on it. All items of one type should be numbered consecutively. There should be a definite set of rules and procedures for handing out and returning all equipment. A good plan is to have each squad leader do this. The teacher should make certain that all equipment is ready before each class enters the gymnasium or goes out to the playground. All bats, balls, squad cards, and other needed items should be easily accessible and as many items as possible placed together. Baseballs should be stored near bats, croquet mallets and wickets near balls.

A complete inventory of all items should be made at the beginning and end of each semester's work. Worn-out equipment may be sent to charitable institutions if the items are in good enough shape to be repaired and used.

SUPPLIES AND EQUIPMENT NEEDED

The materials listed below are minimum essentials needed to conduct an adequate program in elementary schools. The amount and variety to be purchased will be dependent upon class size. Rubber balls are cheaper than leather ones and may prove to be just as serviceable.

Supplies

Balls:
Basketball, official
Basketball, rubber
Football, official
Football, rubber
Indoor, 12"
Rubber, 5", 6", 8", 10"
Soccer, official
Soccer, rubber
Volley, official
Volley, rubber
Baseball gloves, balls, bats,
  protective equipment
Beanbags, 6x6, and targets
Broomsticks of various lengths
Chalk
Deck tennis rings
Five-pin bowling sets
Hoops
Hula hoop rings
Indian clubs
Jump-off boxes
Jump ropes, 3'8" sashcord
  Individual, 6', 7', 8'
  Long, 12', 15', 20', 25'
Phonograph needles
Phonograph records
Shuffleboard sets
Squad cards
Tape measure, 50'
Tempera paint

Equipment

Balance beams of varying height from the floor
Ball inflator
Bases
Bats
Bicycle racks
Blackboard, portable and permanent
Bulletin board
Cabinet, steel
Canvas bags in which to carry balls
Chinning bars
Equipment box
Flying and stationary rings
Game nets
Hurdles, 12", 15", 18", 20"
Jump and vault standards
Jungle gym
Junior jump standards
Landing nets
Lime and markers
Low parallel bars
Mats, 33"x60", 3'x5', 4'x6'
Microphone and speaker system
Net standards
Percussion instruments
Portable phonograph
Recreational games (checkers, horseshoes, etc.)
Slides
Stall bars, vertical and horizontal bars
Stop watch
Storage cabinets or lockers
Surplus parachutes
Swim fins, unsinkable boards, hair dryers
Swings
Table hockey
Targets
Teeter boards
Tin can walkers
Traveling rings, vaulting buck and horse, Swedish
  box, springboard, parallel bars, climbing stairs
Wooden stilts of varying heights
Whistles, timers

All equipment should be carefully selected, kept, and repaired. The pupils can aid in oiling balls, repairing nets, and sewing ball rips. Sporting goods companies can usually provide better equipment for money spent than local department stores.

Each teacher needs to have a yearly budget provided for the purchase of equipment, rather than being given a certain sum upon the sudden whim or urge of the school principal.

Figure 15. Physical education includes adventurous, joyful experiences. (Courtesy of the Playground Corporation of America, New York, New York.)

UNIFORMS DESIRED

Beginning in grade 4 it is desirable for both sexes to wear regulation uniforms for their class work in the gymnasium or on the playground. One-piece suits of dark material, white tennis shoes and socks are recommended for girls. Dark trunks, a white "T" shirt, high tennis shoes, and heavy socks are recommended for boys.

In order to secure the cooperation of the parents, letters may be sent to them explaining the costume requirement and places from which the clothing may be bought. They should also be informed that the clothing may be used for several years, and that provisions will be made to re-sell used garments. Upon request, parents from low income groups and mothers who sew should be sent patterns for making the uniforms.

Companies that sell regulation gymnasium uniforms usually provide superior garments at lower cost than can local stores. Recognized serviceable companies are advertised monthly in the *Journal of Health, Physical Education, Recreation.*

Regulation class uniforms aid in building desirable attitudes regarding the program; they also allow for freedom of movement, and build group unity and morale. Then, too, this is one way to encourage boys and girls to keep clean, because part of their bodies is seen by their classmates.

ACCIDENT SAFEGUARDS

Physical education includes activities wherein children can have adventurous, joyful experiences. Many of the games and sports can be dangerous if improperly supervised. Under proper guidance and good teaching a physical education class, however, need not be any more potentially dangerous than one in any other subject. One way of safeguarding against accidents is to be sure that pupils engage only in those activities for which they are prepared in coordination, strength, and skill.

Children are not as interested in safety or being careful as they are in taking chances, in being daring. Consequently, adults must help them see that they can have the most fun over a longer period of time if they can avoid handicaps that may result from injuries. Safety education is learning to take chances wisely.

Accidents, when they do happen, can often be the best teachable moments to instruct youngsters to be careful. A boy who sprained his ankle while running in the shower room may help impress upon his classmates the importance of obeying the no-running rule. However, it must be remembered that parents whose children are hurt at school often develop negative attitudes toward the school or the teacher in charge of the activity wherein the child was injured.

All teachers of physical education can safeguard against accidents by:

1. Checking all apparatus and equipment periodically and keeping both in good repair at all times.
2. Finding and marking all hazards with the pupils.
3. Directing all pupils and especially squad leaders in safety measures.
4. Using plans, materials, and programs that will reduce the possibility of accidents.
5. Insisting that all pupils wear suitable apparel for all activities.
6. Organizing and classifying pupils for class participation according to the results of physical examinations and motor ability tests.
7. Insisting that all rules for playing games be obeyed at all times.
8. Never leaving an assigned class or group.

Pupils have a right to enjoy all their physical education periods in clean, safe, and attractive surroundings. Although elementary children are not safety conscious, it would be educationally foolish and costly to remove all hazardous equipment, facilities, and activities from their physical education experiences, for they must learn early in life how to survive in an ever-increasingly danger-filled world. Teachers should stress *how* to play safely and wisely in order that one may play longer, and more skillfully. The following suggestions will prove helpful for increased protection for pupils during physical education and after-school activities:

The Gymnasium, Pool, and Locker Rooms:

1. Check to see that all equipment is in good condition. Discard and replace that which is not.
2. Avoid slippery floors.
3. Cover all exposed dangerous areas with protective pads or paint them bright yellow.
4. Have all doors swing out.
5. Fountains should be in safe recessed locations.
6. Post, and strictly enforce, all rules regarding the use of the pool, restrictions against running and horseplay in the showers, and use of the equipment when the instructor is not present.
7. Require all students to be properly dressed for athletics; require all to wear socks and tennis shoes.
8. Stay with all assigned classes for the entire time of duty. Strive for close supervision of the whole class. Stand where you can see and be seen by the majority or the entire group.

Playgrounds, Sports Fields, and Intramural Areas:

1. Allocate space so that all teams and individuals can participate without danger to themselves or others.
2. Check all equipment. Discard and replace that which is dangerous.
3. Discover hazards with each class group; encourage them to point these out to you. Paint all immovable hazards bright yellow.
4. Mark fields and play areas; play according to the official rules, for they have been made for the safety of the players.
5. Supervise all groups. Place yourself on the field where you can best do so. Do not leave the area until your assigned duties are over.
6. Help all assume responsibility for their own safety and that of others.

Competitive Athletics:

1. Lay out all playing areas from the standpoint of the best player and spectator safety protection.

2. Remove all hazardous obstructions.
3. Use only equipment approved and/or recommended by the governing association for secondary school competition in your locality.
4. Provide all players with properly fitting and safe protective clothing. Require them to keep it on while playing.
5. Receive medical approval for every participant.
6. Allow only those who have been properly trained and "warmed up" to play or enter games as substitutes.
7. Supervise all practices and competitive events: keep player safety uppermost in mind.
8. Supply proper first-aid treatment and needed medical care for all injured.
9. Insist upon adherence to training rules; avoid too frequent competition and long distance travel.
10. Make all players safety conscious.

In spite of all precautionary measures, however, accidents do occur in physical education classes, intramural programs and competitive interschool contests. Both their frequency and their degree of severity can be reduced by taking the following measures:

1. Play all games according to the official rules.
2. Develop skills; it is the clumsy player who is most frequently injured.
3. Allow students to participate only in those activities that are suitable to their skill maturation levels.
4. Be on the lookout for fatigue, realizing that it is the tired student who is most apt to be injured. Know that fatigue levels differ with each individual.
5. Encourage students to report all injuries to you regardless of how minor they are at the time, and see that they receive proper treatment for them.

All children injured at school should receive first aid by a qualified school nurse or teacher. In small schools the physical educator usually gives first aid and suggests the purchase of supplies to the school principal. First-aid equipment for all schools should include:

1. 1-inch compress on adhesive in individual packages.
2. Sterile gauze squares—3" by 3"—in individual packages.
3. Assorted sterile bandage compresses in individual packages.
4. Triangular bandages.
5. Sterile gauze in individual packages of about 1 square yard.
6. Picric acid gauze.
7. Burn ointment—such as 5 per cent tannic acid jelly.
8. Iodine, mild.
9. Aromatic spirits of ammonia.
10. Inelastic tourniquet.
11. Scissors.
12. 3-inch splinter forceps.
13. Paper cups.
14. 1-inch and 2-inch roller bandage.
15. Wire or thin board splints.
16. Castor oil or mineral oil for use in eyes. This should be sterile; it may be obtained in small tubes.

Teachers should remember that they are not medical doctors and can neither diagnose nor treat injuries. A complete record must be kept of all accidents. Accident reports should be filled out in duplicate or triplicate, depending upon the size of the school. The school teacher should keep one copy on file and send remaining copies to her administrators. Each accident report form might well include:

1. The name of the person injured and date of the accident.
2. The place of the accident and condition of the environment.

3. What the teacher did for first aid.
4. Names and addresses of two or more witnesses.

A suggested form follows:

SUGGESTED ACCIDENT REPORT FORM

Name of injured student _____ Sex _____

Age _____ Class _____ Address _____

Phone _____

Description of the accident _____

_____

Condition of the environment _____

What was done for first aid treatment _____

_____

Name and address of witnesses _____

_____

Additional comments _____

Final disposition of the case _____

Signature _____
Date _____

SUGGESTED READINGS

American Association for Health, Physical Education, and Recreation: *Leisure and The Schools*. Washington, D.C., 1961.

American Red Cross: *First Aid Textbook*. Philadelphia, The Blakiston Company, Current Edition.

Bourguardez, Virginia, and Heilman, Charles: *Sports Equipment: Selection, Care and Repair*. New York, A. S. Barnes & Co., 1950.

Bucher, Charles, and Reade, Evelyn: *Physical Education and Health in the Elementary School*. New York, The Macmillan Company, 1964.

Butler, George: *Community Recreation*, 4th Ed. New York, McGraw-Hill Book Co., 1967.

Carter, Joel: *How to Make Athletic Equipment*. New York, The Ronald Press, 1960.

Lederman, A., and Tracksel, A.: *Creative Playgrounds and Recreation Centers*. New York, National Recreation Association, 1960.

National Education Association: *Who Is Liable for Pupil Injuries?* Washington, D.C., 1960.

Participants in the National Facilities Conference, *Planning Facilities for Health, Physical Education and Recreation*. Chicago, Ill., The Athletic Institute, 1957.

Scott, Harry, and Westkaemper, R. B.: *From Program to Facilities in Physical Education*. New York, Harper & Brothers, 1958.

Slezak, Edward: 50 checks for a safe playground, *Journal of Health, Physical Education, Recreation,* May, 1965.

Vannier, Maryhelen: *Teaching Health in Elementary Schools*. New York, Harper & Row, Publishers, 1963.

SOURCES OF EQUIPMENT AND SUPPLIES

A. G. Spaulding & Brothers, 161 Sixth Ave., New York 13, N.Y.
American Athlete and Educational Supply Co., 13609 Normandie, Gardena, Cal.
Atlantic-Pacific Manufacturing Corp., 124 Atlantic Ave., Brooklyn 1, N.Y.
Creative Playthings, Inc., Edenburg Road, Hightstown, N.J.
Jayfro Plant, 30 Hynes Ave., Groton, Connecticut
The MacGregor Co., Cincinnati 32, Ohio
Miracle Equipment Company, Grinnell, Iowa
Nissen Medart Company, Cedar Rapids, Iowa
Paneltrol, Inc., 9 N. Colonial Ave., Wilmington 5, Del.
Peterson Mat Co., Division of Wayne Iron Works, Wayne, Pa.
Premier Athletic Corp., Riverdale, N.J.
Rawlings Company, St. Louis, Mo.
Safe Fencing Company, 21 Harrison Avenue, Glens Falls, N.Y.
W. J. Voit Rubber Corp., 45 W. 18th St., New York 11, N.Y.

Part IV

THE HOW

THUS A CHILD LEARNS

. . . Thus a child learns; by wiggling skills through his fingers and toes into himself; by soaking up habits and attitudes of those around him; by pushing and pulling his own world.

. . . Thus a child learns; more through trial than error, more through pleasure than pain, more through experience than suggestion, more through suggestion than direction.

. . . Thus a child learns; through affection, through love, through patience, through understanding, through belonging, through doing, through being.

. . . Day by day the child comes to know a little bit of what you know; to think a little bit of what you think; to understand your understanding. That which you dream and believe and are, in truth, becomes the child.

Frederick J. Moffitt, Chief,
Bureau of Instructional Supervision
New York State Department of Education

Chapter 5

How Children Learn

Children are in love with life! Watch any child having his very first "finding out about" experiences as he looks closely at a butterfly, holds a puppy ever so gently, and tries to turn a somersault, or roller skate. Such total absorption, delight, and sheer determination!

The desire to learn is a natural current in all human beings, but in youth it is a strong and forceful flood. To learn means to discover, to find ways to make a satisfactory adjustment to a new situation. It also means changed behavior in relation to achieving desirable educational goals. Children need not be driven to learn the things *they* want to learn although they sometimes must be prevented from learning or experiencing some harmful things too soon, or early in life. Our old folk saying that "you can drive a horse to water but you cannot make him drink" is truer than was once realized, for the learner, not the teacher, controls the learning situation. Pupils discover early in their school experiences how to tune the teacher out, and still give a false impression of full attentiveness.

The desire to learn spurs the child on and often gets him into all kinds of trouble, for he usually acts first and thinks later in his trial and error attempts to find out. Any child who fails to learn may be stymied by physical or emotional stumbling blocks that must be removed before any real progress can be made. Sometimes these clogs are due to an inability to see or hear, to fear of failure, or to dread of loss of parental love. A six year old in a school in Dallas who refused to take part with his class in any type of supervised activities on the playground, finally, after many tears, confessed to his teacher that he was afraid to play because he would get dirty, knowing that if he did so his "mamma wouldn't love him anymore; she hates dirty boys." Regardless of what deterring factors are present, these must be discovered and eradicated before the child will give his whole self to his trial-and-error attempt to learn.

Learning involves the entire child, for there is no separation from one's physical, mental, or emotional self. One cannot draw a picture, catch a ball, read a book, or master any learning task by only "using his head" or "learning it through his muscles." The mind of man is a central clearing house, a transfer station, a switchboard that can only function

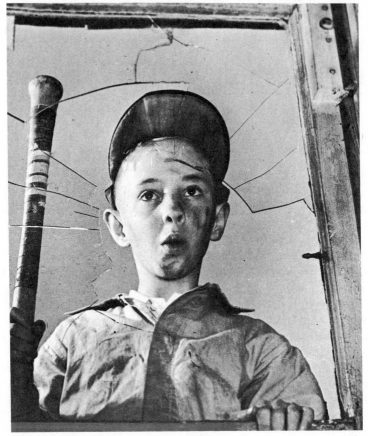

Figure 16.   Learning takes place wherever there is life. (Courtesy of AAHPER.)

as messages come to it, are received, sorted, clarified, or filed, and sent back out again. As William Kilpatrick has said, "What we live, we learn." Where we live, with whom we live, toward what ends we live—these determine what we learn. The whole community educates, but the learner teaches himself. There is great truth in George Bernard Shaw's statement, "If you teach me, I shall never learn," for *no one can really teach anyone else to do anything.* The best learning results will accrue when:

1. The activities are child-centered.
2. The individual needs, interests, and capacities of each pupil are fully understood.
3. Teachers aid children to explore and discover things for themselves.
4. Pupils are free to create their own responses in a situation.
5. Pupils are taught and guided by teachers who are really interested in them.
6. Pupils believe in what they learn and believe it will be valuable to them.
7. That which is learned will increase the pupil's power to make intelligent decisions in life.
8. That which is learned will build a greater appreciation for life, our cultural heritage, other people, aesthetics, and health.

The person who is learning does so within himself by some magical process that includes his own trial-and-error fumbling attempts. Most of our learning comes from making mistakes and then catching on how to avoid them. Without failure there can be no success. The role of the teacher is to guide the learner around pitfalls that are sure to stop him or end in failure, as well as to encourage him to keep trying until he succeeds (can ride the bicycle after falling so many times, or turn a cartwheel) and to lead him to new learning thrills and adventures he never dreamed existed. All learning can be speeded up if the learner sees its relationship to himself and to his own goals. A child's past experiences, goals, and drives are the foundation upon which his present, and often more lasting, experiences are built.

LEARNING THEORIES

Most of what children learn comes through their senses of hearing, seeing, tasting, and touching; the more these can be stimulated, the richer the learning experiences will be. A child learns when he:

1. Develops and uses new skills.
2. Forms new habits.
3. Develops new attitudes.
4. Builds new interests.
5. Gains new understanding.
6. Makes generalizations and uses learned facts.
7. Develops social skills.
8. Becomes more concerned about his environment and other people around him.

The most commonly accepted learning theories are (1) conditioning, (2) connectionism, and (3) field theory. All stress that one learns from doing, or from his own experiences.[1]

Conditioning

The simplest type of learning is conditioning, or setting a patterned reflex to the same repeated stimuli. Pavlov, in his famous dog experiments, proved that the animal could be conditioned to salivate when a bell was rung and food was expected. We all show that we have been conditioned when we automatically pick up the phone when it rings, stop at the red light, turn over and sleepily turn off the alarm on the clock at our bedside when it jars us awake, or do numerous other automatic acts to the same repeated stimuli, because within us a behavior-patterned habit has been formed. The pupil who can give back the right response when asked to spell the word C-A-T, or add 2 + 2, or name the capital of Texas, has been trained to do so.

Conditioning has many uses and values for the teacher. It is both a

---

[1]Morris Bigge: "Theories of Learning." *N.E.A. Journal,* March 1966.

great time and energy saver. However, in order to condition, the same stimuli must be given over and over again until the desired response is achieved each time. The reward of approval, praise, or other goals desired by the pupil who is being conditioned must also be given consistently in order for success to accrue. Students can be conditioned automatically to:

1. Stop and listen when the teacher is talking.
2. Wash their hands every time after going to the toilet, and before eating.
3. Move orderly and safely in squads inside the gymnasium or on the playground.
4. Keep themselves and their physical education uniforms neat and clean.
5. Develop any other health habits.
6. Develop good work and play patterns.

Connectionism

This theory, which results largely from the work of Thorndike, stresses that human beings will voluntarily select activities that bring them the most pleasure and satisfaction, and that best fill their needs. Although similar to conditioning, this theory contends that learning must be on a higher plane, and that the purpose of education is *not* to create robots or human vending machines who will give back to the teacher the sought answer upon demand, but to develop educated citizens who can solve their own problems as well as help solve group problems intelligently in many ever-changing situations.

Simply, this concept, known also as the S-R-Bond Theory of Learning, means that when a stimulated (S) response (R) is made that is accompanied by satisfied feelings, that response tends to be repeated and long remembered (Bond). The intensity of these positive feelings can produce either an advancing positive response (choosing it again, joy, satisfaction), or a retreating negative one (avoidance of choosing it again, anger, disappointment, frustration). Pleasure and annoyance become selective factors, as is seen in the case of the teacher-frightened pupil who shows visible signs of annoyance or frustration when the instructor comes near. This same child, if given the opportunity to select his own teacher, would quickly reject the one who frightens and frustrates him, and would choose instead one who is more friendly, interested in him, and makes him feel at ease.

The greater the desire the pupil has for learning, the more productive are his attempts to satisfy this need. All human beings, children and adults alike, have certain common needs. These drives make up the underlying cause of all human behavior:

1. Physiological needs (food, water, air, temperature regulation, rest, exercise).
2. Love needs (sex, mutuality, acceptance, affection).
3. Love for esteem (recognition, mastery, approval, status, adequacy, self-respect).
4. Self-actualization (desire to succeed at tasks for which one is best suited).
5. Need to know and understand.
6. Need for ambivalence (balance between love and hate, desire to destroy and build).
7. Adventure (to seek ever-greener pastures, and discover what is behind the ranges).

Thorndike's three well-known laws of learning will, if adhered to, increase the effectiveness of all teaching and the depth and breadth of all learning. These are: (1) the Law of Readiness, (2) the Law of Exercise, and (3) the Law of Effect.

The Law of Readiness.   Educators have long been aware that pupils learn best and retain concepts longer when they are ready to learn. Teachers are cognizant that there is a "reading readiness," yet few realize that there is also the right time or state of readiness for learning all things—whether it be riding a bicycle, throwing a ball, or adding or memorizing the multiplication tables. Every learner is ready when he has reached just the right stage in his development (his maturation level)—when he has not only a keen desire to learn, but is ready physically, emotionally, and mentally. Then is he most likely to succeed. Although teachers often give lip service to this vaguely-aware-of-concept, until they understand the fullest significance and truth in it, they are only wheel-spinning when they could be making real progress. The pupil is "ripe" for any learning experience when he can learn with ease, succeeds, and is spurred on to continue his efforts until he masters his task. The readiness varies with each child, yet can be generalized upon too, for just as some pears ripen and fall to the ground long before others, they all will fall within a certain season of the year.

Childhood belongs to every child. Every youngster needs this time of life to be filled with joy, wonder, and freedom. Each must have many "first-finding-out-about" experiences that are rich enough to last a lifetime and strong enough to help him endure the sorrows and tragedies that come with adulthood. All must discover the joy of solitude and have gloriously rewarding free hours to roam and explore, and to *think, feel,* and *see.* They should be encouraged to go lazily along, stopping where they will—instead of being forced by eager and often status-seeking parents to scurry along to take part in many outside-of-school activities. Patterns for adulthood and for happiness are established in childhood.

The Law of Exercise.   Practice does not lead to perfection *unless* one practices correctly, for it is harder to unlearn than to learn. According to this law, the learner must know *what* and *how* he is doing, as well as *why* in relation to what he wants to learn. Likewise, he must have a clear understanding and picture of the correct way to do the thing he is learning.

All pupils should have a feeling of success as they are learning, for nothing is as spirit-quenching as failure. Success is a spur, failure is a check-rein. Repeated failure may not only damage the ego, but may also lead to feelings of inadequacy, inferiority, or worthlessness. This connotes that the teacher must help pupils set realistic heights on learning standards for themselves.

The Law of Effect.   How the learner feels about what he is learning is of vast importance. Elementary school children especially are often much keener about learning many things *outside* of school rather than in

Figure 17. Boys respond well to exercises, for most are motivated by a desire to play on an athletic team. (Courtesy of *The Instructor*. Photograph by Edith Brockway.)

school (especially after their initial taste of school). This is but one of many reasons for their eagerness to go to camp, ride in an airplane, or have such a wide variety of other "first-time experiences." Teachers must be cognizant that there is learning wherever there is life, and that it by no means can be confined to a school or remain hidden in books. The child not only learns everywhere but is totally affected by what he learns. All learning is most fruitful and lasting when the child *has definite goals* in mind and *can be guided to select wisely* what he will learn, *to plan his method of attack* toward solving learning problems, and *to evaluate* his final results.

Motivation is the key to all learning. Just as adults are paid for their work, the child seeks his reward, too. For him, this is found in reaching desired goals, and in the elementary school, largely by pleasing adults, including his teacher. Those slower to learn must be guided to tasks in which they can find improvement (however slight it may be), security, and confidence in themselves. For the gifted and normal children, group status or self-improvement often serves as an effective motivator. An occasional pat on the back and words of encouragement are often enough to give the normal child an incentive to keep trying. Grades spur others on, but only if obtaining superior marks results from effort and brings status and recognition. Gaining even slight feelings of success often helps those having learning difficulties.

The teacher must know all students well and be able to determine what stimuli can best be used to fan each one's interest into a flame. For some this may be accomplished by praise, while for others it may require some widely different technique. The teacher, likewise, must keep in mind that when a pupil sees his own improvement, he will try even harder. Punishment in the form of ridicule, disapproval, or rejection should be avoided, for although the pupil may, finally, learn something under such treatment, he will not receive pleasure from any fleeting, unmeaningful or dreaded task, which all too soon will be forgotten anyway.

Field Theory

This theory, developed first by Koffka and Koehler, and later fostered by Hartmann and Westheimer, stresses that one learns best by grasping whole concepts. It holds that one learns from his trial-and-error attempts plus "insight"—or suddenly realizing how to do something. Anyone who has ever tried repeatedly to ride a bicycle usually was battered and bruised before he suddenly could do it! The beginner in crawl swimming has learned to do this stroke in that great moment of triumph when he *could* synchronize his arm and leg movements with his head-turning and breathing and move magically through the water using all these synchronized movements. Insight is "getting the hang" of anything we are learning, and can only result from previous trial-and-error attempts. The task of the teacher is to give the learner a pep talk so that he continues to muddle through his learning attempts until he achieves this thrill of accomplishment. Here again, the teacher must be fully aware that she must not nip learning struggles in the bud by being too much of a perfectionist or overly critical and impatient.

This concept of learning, which is also known as Gestalt psychology, places the major importance in any learning experience upon the learner, and stresses that he know more about his own values, desires, capacities, and preferences than the teacher. The instructor's main task is to help the learner to: (1) set his own goals, (2) determine his action plans, and (3) judge the results. This does not imply that the teacher is unnecessary, but does imply that her main task is that of guiding and directing, and that more learning will consequently result from doing this than from telling students what to do, for there will be less friction and more rapport, fewer failures and more success.

If the main purpose of education is to help each person increase the number of socially-approved things he can do well that will prove beneficial to him and society, teaching is more than either an art or a science, for it becomes a combination of them both, plus something else composed of a magical X quality called leadership ability by some, personality by others. The teacher must (1) provide the best kind of a warm, friendly yet controlled learning environment possible, (2) motivate pupils' desire to seek worthy goals and make these goals as attractive as possible, and (3) make even disagreeable tasks seem agreeable, or make them seem interesting to a bored, uninterested learner by changing negative attitudes to positive ones, and (4) help the learner develop finer and deeper appreciation of himself, others, and what he is doing.

Gestalt psychology also stresses that the best learning will accrue when the learning environment is used to its fullest extent. Furthermore, it emphasizes that the learner can and only will learn when *he* has a need to do so, and that he will learn best when he can do so under the friendly, consistent guidance of a firm teacher who regards him as a unique human being. It also contends that learning through mastery of whole material will come faster and be more lasting. Educators call this the whole-part-whole method of teaching and learning and are in agreement that it is usually superior and usually brings desired results quickly. A teacher should teach each class and individual in it as much as can be learned each class period.

KINDS OF LEARNING

The three kinds of learning are primary, associated, and concomitant. They are intertwined and all may occur almost at the same time. *Primary* learning means learning a specific skill, such as how to hit a baseball. *Associated* learning is marginal; it surrounds skill mastery and includes all kinds of fringe knowledge, such as the parts of a tennis racket. *Concomitant* learning is primarily concerned with attitude-shaping and character development. Almost every learning situation abounds with character-shaping and value-developing opportunities. Because character can often be best *caught* rather than taught, the behavior and attitudes of the teacher in all situations are of paramount importance, for children are eager and skilled copycats of those they admire. Leadership through example is the best way to help children develop positive attitudes and to show them how to behave in socially accepted ways as developing youngsters in a democracy.

LEARNING PRINCIPLES

Basic beliefs and action guides are educational principles. They result from experience, research, and education. The best learning accrues if the following principles are used as action springboards:

1. *Children learn experimentally.* Trial-and-error plus insight produces changed behavior, or learning. In this process, mistakes are necessary and success comes *from* failure.

2. *Learning is a "doing" activity.* Discovery results from searching. We learn from doing, not from being told or watching others perform. In order to learn, one must try out things for himself and through his own experience gain skill, understanding, knowledge, and appreciation.

3. *The learner controls the learning situation.* If the learner is in situations in which he feels secure and confident, his rate of progress becomes greater. He will be handicapped when dominated or told by adults what, when, and how he is to learn. Knowledge of his progress in relationship to that of others can be an asset or a liability, depending upon the amount of self-confidence and emotional drive the learner has, and the degree of desire to learn.

4. *Each pupil learns in his own unique way.* Every learner goes about learning tasks differently, and each develops his own unique learning progress curve that leads to victory or defeat. For the majority, this curve will rise sharply at first, taper off to a plateau, then rise again as the pupil becomes increasingly aware that he is reaching his desired goal. Learning is as personal as one's own toothbrush.

5. *Overlearning results in longer retention.* Practice of the correct pattern until what is to be learned is mastered or becomes automatic will keep it longer in the body's memory storehouse. The more a learned skill or concept is used and reviewed, the more valuable it will become. Just as unused silver tarnishes quickly, so do once-learned facts fade from memory.

6. *Emotions retard or accelerate learning.* Learning occurs more rapidly if both the pupil and the teacher are enthusiastic about and see purpose in what is to be learned. Fear and insecurity are clogs, and dam up desire until it stagnates; confidence and encouragement plunge learning on.

7. *Brief practice periods are more productive than long, drawn-out ones.* The length of each practice period should be determined by the pupil's interest level and potency of desire to accomplish the learning task. Practice will be fruitful only if it brings satisfaction to the learner and is recognized as a basic task necessary for improvement. A "cooling off" period is needed before a renewed and recharged learning pursuit can become potent enough to lead to final victory, for a learning pause can bring real refreshment, as well as desired results more quickly.

8. *Transfer will occur when situations are recognized to be alike.* The transformation of anything learned in one situation to another will take place only when the learner sees similarities in the two situations and continues to do in the second one what he did in the first. The pupil who can see and feel the relationship of the baseball throw to the tennis serve will learn the latter more quickly if he can throw a baseball correctly.

9. *Learning is an exciting and challenging adventure.* To see the truthfulness of this principle one has only to watch the happy face of any youngster who first discovers that he can swim, recite the multiplication tables, or sing *all* the way through any song without a single mistake. The child who *wants* to learn what *he* has chosen to master can have a glorious time doing so. The real teacher is one who can inspire him to want to make many new and thrilling learning discoveries.

10. *Evaluation is an essential part of learning.* Improvement and evaluation are inseparable, for one can only improve when he sees his mistakes and cares enough about what he is attempting, to avoid them. It is a difficult task for the teacher to know *when* to stop muddled learning attempts or *how* to go about it, for doing so at the wrong time and in the wrong way may destroy the pupil's zest and zeal to reach his desired learning goal to such an extent that he will give up trying, or quit. There is truth in Pope's wise statement that "only fools rush in where angels fear to tread."

SUGGESTED READINGS

Association for Supervision and Curriculum Development: *Learning More About Learning; Freeing Capacity To Learn; Theories of Instruction; The Elementary School We Need; New Curriculum Developments; Supervision in Action; Toward Better Teaching.* Washington, D.C., National Education Association.

Bigge, Morris: Theories of learning. *N.E.A. Journal,* March, 1966.

Broer, Marion: *Efficiency of Human Movement,* 2nd Ed. Philadelphia, W. B. Saunders Company, 1966.

Bucher, Charles: Health, physical education and academic achievement. *N.E.A. Journal,* May, 1965.

Cratty, Bryant: *Movement Behavior and Motor Learning.* 2nd Ed. Philadelphia, Lea & Febiger, 1967.

Humphrey, James: *Child Learning Through Elementary School Physical Education.* Dubuque, Iowa, Wm. C. Brown Company, 1965.

Metheny, Eleanor: *Connotations of Movement in Sports and Dance.* Dubuque, Iowa, Wm. C. Brown Company, 1965.

National Association for Physical Education of College Women, National Association for Physical Education for College Men: *Quest* (A symposium on motor learning—entire issue). Monograph VI, May, 1966. New York, N.Y. Board of Education of the City of New York. *Education Through Recreation: Kindergarten Experimental Edition,* 1965.

Travers, Robert: *Essentials of Learning.* New York, The Macmillan Company, 1963.

Chapter 6

The Techniques of Successful Teaching

To teach means to guide, lead, inspire, share, and discover with others. Success in this all-important profession is due largely to skill in human engineering and to one's professional preparation. Those best prepared to teach not only know something about *what* to teach but a great deal more about *how* to go about it. The latter comes from experience, experimenting and tailoring once-learned principles and the methods used by an admired former teacher to fit one's own unique situation. To teach means also to inspire others to want to seek learning treasures. To educate means bringing forth latent capabilities and to "lead forth."

Good teaching results when each instructor, through the use of teacher-guided group planning, helps individuals: (1) set up desired group goals and individual objectives to be reached, (2) select and see values in materials to be learned in order to obtain these desired ends, (3) share planned purposeful learning experiences, and (4) evaluate the final results in light of sought results. Through the use of a variety of well mastered methods of instruction, the skilled teacher will see pupils improve in skills, make positive attitude changes, deepen and broaden understanding of themselves, others, and life itself, and be able to use what they are learning in their daily lives.

TEACHING METHODS

Just as adequate professional preparation is the prerequisite for successful teaching, so also is the careful planning of each lesson. This can be done best by the whole-part-whole method, wherein the teacher begins by (1) planning the course content for a semester or a single unit, (2) devising plans for each class period of this larger whole, and (3) evaluating the results when the unit is completed.

Group plans are the prerequisites for successful group experiences. Consequently, the teacher and pupils (rather than the pupils and teacher) should set up desired individual goals and class objectives, choose the materials to be mastered, share a teaching-learning experience, and measure their success or failure to obtain their goals.

Each of the many teaching methods is valuable but there are times when one is superior to another. The best one to use depends upon ever-changing factors, which the successful instructor learns to sense. Certainly, any method is worthy of use only if desired results can be obtained through it and if it is socially approved. Also, a teaching method that has proved to be successful for one teacher may be a failure when used by another. Ways of teaching others are patterns that must be tailored to fit one's own situation. The many techniques for successful teaching include:

Chalk talks	Experiments
Drills	Class discussions
Lectures	Workshops
Questions and answers	Forums
Reports	Assignments
Demonstrations and participation	Field trips
Supervised practice	Debates
Role playing	Workbooks
Visual aids	Projects
	Combinations of all listed

The following techniques for teaching physical education are suggested for trial and each teacher's revision.[1] In each class:

1. Explain briefly what the class will do.
2. Establish a need for learning by having pupils experiment (for example, listening and moving to music to get the rhythm of the dance before teaching actual steps).
3. Demonstrate the correct way to do the whole activity. (Show the class how the complete dance looks, or the complete bat swing.)
4. Use squad leaders to demonstrate to their squads.
5. Demonstrate the correct way again to each person who is having difficulty.
6. Explain as simply as possible how to do the skill. ("Hook" elbows rather than "bend your arm and then place it through the bent left arm of your partner.")
7. Encourage pupils by praising what they do correctly so that they will keep trying until they master the skill.
8. Integrate isolated skills in a game, dance or other activity as soon as possible. (In a soccer class, for example, five minutes may be spent on learning how to kick, dribble, and trap the ball; the remainder of the period should be spent in playing a game so that these skills will be used. No class period should be devoted entirely to practicing isolated skills.)
9. Work toward 100 per cent pupil participation throughout the class period.
10. Choose, whenever possible, activities that relate to the season, weather, day or interest.
11. Keep plans flexible; overplan rather than underplan.
12. Have a high degree of expectancy for each child and stimulate him through it to do his best.
13. Analyze classes that did not go well; realize that the reason may be your fault more times than not.
14. Build skill upon skill.
15. Employ techniques that will help each child learn something new every day.

---

[1] Specific techniques for teaching various parts of the total program are given in each of the following chapters.

Pitfalls To Be Avoided

1. *Verbiage.*   Teaching is *not* telling; it is getting others to teach themselves through participation.

2. *Faulty Planning.*   Provide enough equipment or activity so that all are active. Physical education is a *doing* process, not a watching one. Ten pupils may use the baseball equipment but 100 others should not stand and watch them have all the fun. If there is insufficient equipment, use what you have to the fullest degree but add squad play and squad rotation of games that do not require equipment. Give each group a chance to use what you do have.

3. *Shot Scattering.*   Do not attempt to talk *above* groups, or while pupils are talking. Make a direct hit every time you do talk and give directions by training the pupils to be quiet when you are speaking. Insist upon observance of this rule, but be wise enough to know *when* to talk, *what* to say, and *how* to say it.

4. *Let George Do It.*   Do not pass the buck, or send an offending pupil to the principal. Handle discipline cases when they occur in a firm but fair fashion. Group pressure and group discussions can work sometimes when teacher's reprimands fail.

5. *Dressing for Class.*   Teachers should not attempt to teach physical education while wearing street clothes except in the primary grades in which the classroom teacher conducts playground activities. If pupils are required to wear special costumes, so should the teacher. Like the pupils, the instructor should be neatly dressed and clean. Soiled sweat shirts and pants are out for men, as much so as are inappropriate costumes for women. All-white shorts, shirts or blouses are recommended for both sexes.

6. *Being Too Palsy-Walsy.*   Physical educators are usually the most popular teachers in the school system. Some few gain their reputations for being "good Joes or Janes," by being back-slap happy and too friendly with pupils, especially the highly skilled ones. A leader often loses the respect of the group if and when he comes down too near the group level. All youth need to have heroes and teachers worthy of emulation. Big Brothers or Sisters or Buddies who are also their public school teachers often are not followed by children for a long period of time.

7. *Failure to Plan or See Relationships.*   Growth follows patterns. Teachers can help children build shacks or temples, make mud pies or bake cakes—but only when they utilize building blueprints. Skills must be built upon skills. Daily, weekly, monthly, and yearly plans are the blueprints of this creation.

8. *Window-pecking.*   When children have playground periods and physical education classes the teacher assigned to teach the physical education cannot do this by remote control. Some older teachers, as well as a few unprepared younger ones, believe physical education is staying in one's own warm classroom peering out of the window to watch the children playing on the cold playground, and pecking on the icy glass at them when they get into fights. Teachers of this type are gaining experience in the fine art of window-pecking, while the children are being cheated out of a real educational opportunity.

9. *Becoming Whistle Happy.*   The whistle may be used as a means of gaining group attention at the beginning of each year's work, semester, or class. Children can be trained to be quiet when the whistle is blown. But whistles can also become a nuisance, as well as a source of annoyance when used too often. Children can be taught to be automatically quiet when the teacher speaks. A gymnasium of 100 or more children *can* be a controlled teaching-learning environment. The teacher who has something exciting for children to learn has little trouble gaining their attention if she has also trained them to react to her leadership position and ability. However, whistles are recommended for playground use when the children are scattered over large areas where it may be difficult for them to see or hear the teacher.

10. *Throwing Out the Ball.*   Too often boys in elementary grades are taught physical education classes by the coach. His primary duties too often are to produce winning teams, not to teach unskilled boys how to play. Too often he is not as interested in teaching all boys as he is in training the few who are highly skilled. Coaching takes time and energy spent in after-school hours. It is easier to sit in one's office to conserve energy by drawing up plans for team practice than to teach classes. So the ball is thrown out on the gymnasium floor, like a wee bone to a pack of howling wolves, and physical education classes are taught by remote control. Luckily, such practices are diminishing in our better schools. Physical education for all in school is quite a different thing from high-pressured athletics for a few highly skilled or coordinated players.

Figure 18. Movement accuracy should precede the development of agility, speed, body flexibility, and the use of body explosive power through correct timing. (Courtesy of Elizabeth Glidden, Specialist in Elementary Physical Education, Los Angeles City Schools, Los Angeles, California.)

TEACHING MOTOR SKILLS

Every class should (1) be given a brief orientation concerning what is to be learned; (2) see a demonstration of the skills that are necessary to master the problem areas presented; (3) participate in or practice those necessary skills; and (4) evaluate progress made.

Physical educators use the previously listed teaching methods singly, in part, or in combination. The lecture method is used to some extent in explaining a skill. This may be preceded by a demonstration of that skill; the demonstration may follow a brief description of the movements being taught; or the demonstration and explanation may take place simultaneously. This procedure is followed by a period of supervised practice in which the instructor moves around the floor giving assistance to those who need it. During this practice period each one must first have a clear mental picture of the correct movement, then copy it by trial-and-error experimentation, and finally master it by gradually eliminating his mistakes. All movement skills learned should be used in a game. At first this may be in the form of drills, relays, or lead-up games such as newcomb for volleyball, hit-pin baseball for baseball, or keep-away for basketball. In using such simple activities, however, the teacher should assist each individual learner to understand the importance and meaning of the drill, relay, or game, and help him to avoid sacrificing accuracy of movement for speed—a common error made by many beginners. Movement accuracy should precede the development of agility, speed, body flexibility, and the use of body explosive power through correct timing.

The three D's of teaching motor skills are (1) demonstration, (2) diagnosis, and (3) direction. Successful physical educators have mastered all of these techniques.

DEMONSTRATION

Most of our learning comes through our eyes and ears. It has been said that one picture is worth many words, but one *experience* is superior to many pictures. This implies that when students copy what they see, they learn from this self-experience through their mistakes. The teacher should be able to demonstrate all skills as perfectly as possible, for it is vastly important that the students duplicate correct movement patterns. Mastery in a wide variety of sport and game skills should be required in the professional training period of all physical educators. If the teacher is unable to execute the skill well, however, a student leader can be trained to do it before the class instead. Although this may cause some loss of face on the part of the teacher, such a demonstration is superior to verbal instruction alone of how to do the skill correctly, or a faulty demonstration.

DIAGNOSIS

A few students in every class have skill-learning difficulties. There are many reasons for this, including emotional blocks and poor coordination, body structure, and physical condition. The teacher must be an expert in diagnosing difficulties. Some excel in this area and can direct and produce new movement patterns quickly by a few well chosen words. These master teachers say, "*Press* your left arm closer to your body," "*Glide* through the water," or give other simple directions using key words to gain quick results. The novice instructor stumbles, is unsure, and passes this uncertainty on to the student when he remarks, "I *think* your trouble is poor balance," or "Your trouble *may* be that you release the ball at the wrong time." Teachers, like physicians, should *know* what is wrong, not guess what the difficulty is. Ability to diagnose learning difficulty comes largely from (1) ability to perform the skill correctly, (2) knowledge of what each part of the correct movement pattern is, (3) experience, and (4) recognition of the fact that such detection is a vital part of the teaching-learning process which every educator must master.

DIRECTION

The teacher should next direct new movement patterns, for he or she not only must spot the learning snag but lead the student around it. Success quickens learning. Consequently, when the student follows the teacher's directions and then hits the bull's-eye, makes the basket, or hits the ball, he is eager to repeat those new movements that led to victory. However, each physical educator must realize that form is an individual matter and that each student should be assisted to discover his own most productive movement patterns.

It is impossible to isolate skill learning from attitude development or behavior change. How the student *feels* about the teacher and about what he is learning is as important as *what* he learns. The teacher's presence, encouragement, patience, and faith in the student's desire and ability to master what he sets out to do helps longed-for goals become a reality.

CLASS MANAGEMENT

The well organized, specialized physical educator, who usually teaches on the upper elementary level, dresses in uniform and conducts each class period in a formal way, in contrast to the classroom teacher on the primary level who conducts her physical education, recess, and noon-hour periods in a more informal manner. On the fourth grade level, when the two sexes should be separated and taught by a man or woman teacher, each must plan in detail regulations for the locker room, dressing for class, excuses from daily class participation, and before-class preparation. What the pupils learn, feel, or think about their physical education classes are concepts gained outside as well as inside the class instructional period on the gymnasium floor, for their locker room and showering experiences may be negative enough to counteract positive ones previously obtained in class.

Before Class. The teacher should be dressed in a costume that allows freedom of movement. If possible, she should greet each pupil by name as he enters the gymnasium or locker room. All needed equipment for the class should be ready and she should have planned well the activities she will teach.

Locker Room Regulations. Each pupil should know where he is to put his clothing when changing for class; each should lock his locker before coming into the gymnasium. A combination lock is recommended, and the teacher should have a master key for all combinations.

Costumes. Recommended costumes for girls are one-piece gym suits with a skirt or short bottom. For boys, white or dark shorts and a T-shirt are recommended. All pupils should be required to wear these costumes, with their names clearly marked on each item, plus socks and tennis shoes for each class. The teacher should require the class to appear in clean costumes periodically. Likewise, the importance of neatness, good grooming, and cleanliness should be stressed. Here again, her own example in dressing will work wonders in motivating the pupils.

Roll Call. Although roll call is generally not necessary in the primary grades, it is on the upper elementary level. It can be done speedily and accurately by using any of the following methods:

1. By squads—the squad leader is responsible for finding out who is absent in his squad.
   Advantage: Allows for leadership training. Roll is taken quickly.
   Disadvantage: Could allow for cheating. The teacher does not learn students' names and faces as quickly.
2. Seating plan—the teacher marks down names or numbers of vacant seating or standing places.
   Advantage: Fairly quick method of taking roll. The teacher is better able to coordinate names with faces.
   Disadvantage: Does not allow for leadership training. Takes more time than squad method.
3. Roll call—the teacher calls the roll with students answering if present.
   Advantage: Teacher may learn students' names with very little effort. Teacher may be assured about who is present or absent.
   Disadvantage: Too time-consuming. Allows for no leadership training.

Each teacher should develop her own system for recording absences, tardiness, excuses from daily participation, and unsuitable costume. Roll should be taken at the beginning of each class period. Requiring each pupil to wear a name tag will enable the teacher to learn each child's name more quickly, which in turn is a means of class control, because telling John Marsh to "sit up straighter and stop talking during roll-taking" is far more effective than referring to a "certain person in squad three" who needs correction.

Class Excuses. Each teacher with the approval of the principal should devise written policies regarding daily excuses because of temporary illness or for other reasons. No pupil should be excused from physical education because of a physical handicap.[2] However, when temporary excuses are needed, the school nurse or anyone else in the school health department should authorize them. Alternate plans should be devised for each pupil who cannot participate, whether this requires him to dress in the regulation uniform and observe or to take part in as much of the class as possible. Permitting the pupil to go to the library is not recommended, unless he is given an assignment related to the physical education class class activity. Some teachers have observing pupils keep score, help officiate games, or work on making an attractive class bulletin board. Regardless of what procedure is established for such cases, it must help the excused pupil spend his class time wisely in accord-

---

[2] See Chapter 20: Adapted Programs for Atypical Children.

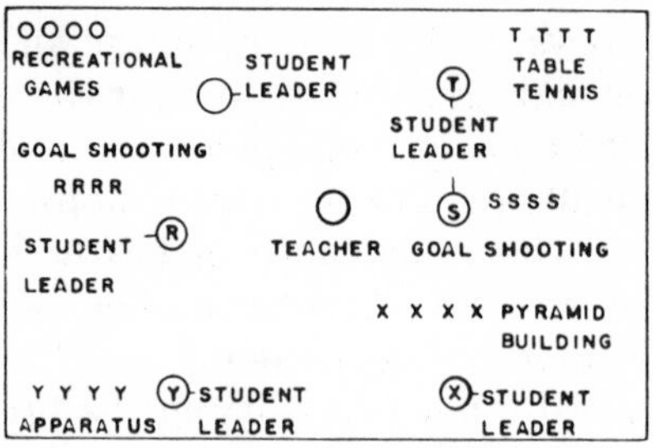

Figure 19. Diagram showing wide range of activities that can be conducted in one gymnasium. (Vannier and Fait: Teaching Physical Education in Secondary Schools.)

ance with the objectives of the physical education program. Upper class girls who have menstruation difficulties should be encouraged to take part in as much of the class as they deem possible. Requiring all to wear gym suits when they have their monthly period will encourage them to take part in milder forms of activity.

Use of Space

Although the American Association for Health, Physical Education and Recreation recommends that there should never be more than 35 students in physical education classes in elementary schools, few teachers are fortunate enough to have this ideally sized group. Probably in the near future all classes will be even larger. Consequently, teachers must devise ways to use best all available teaching stations. This plan, coupled with use of squad leaders, will enable the teacher to rotate around space-assigned groups and to supervise them all adequately. As is shown in Figure 19, a wide range of activities can be conducted in one gymnasium.

Class Time

Classes are usually one hour long. This time should be utilized to its fullest extent in light of sought objectives. A suggested time breakdown of the period includes:

Undressing	3 minutes
Roll call	2 minutes
Announcements	2 minutes
Mass calisthenics (teacher- or student-directed)	4 minutes
Teacher demonstration and instruction	8 minutes
Drill and practice of isolated skills	10 minutes
Team play, dance compositions, or other cumulating experiences	13 minutes
Dressing and showering	8 minutes
	50 minutes

Several total class periods, or major portions of time taken from a few, should be devoted to orienting the students to the purpose of the program, class planning and evaluation. Although classes are usually scheduled on an hourly basis, allowance must be made each period for passing from one class to another.

Methods of Grouping

A wide variety of student groups should be used throughout the year, for opportunities for many working groups to be squad leaders and team captains help pupils develop leadership and "followership" skills, good sportsmanship, and a widened circle of friends. Suggested means of grouping pupils include:

1. Homerooms.
2. The homogeneous or heterogeneous skilled as determined by skill tests or observation.
3. Numbering off by 2's, 3's, or 4's, depending upon class size.
4. Electing captains and having each one choose his team (although this may be used infrequently, care must be taken that those last chosen become group leaders or gain recognition in other activities.)
5. Dividing the tallest members among various squads.
6. Teacher-formed teams or squads.
7. Special skill practice groups.
8. Dividing a circle in half.
9. Asking pupils to stand behind selected team leaders, such as Jack, George, and Tom.
10. Dividing the class by numbers, the first ten going to this corner of the floor to tumble, assigning the next ten to an area, piece of equipment, and activity, and so forth.
11. The same as above, except allowing the pupils to choose the activity and equipment they wish.

Through the entire year, the teacher should stress the qualities of good democratic leadership, and the duties and responsibilities of being a team captain or squad leader.

Checking Equipment In and Out

If there is no custodian available to render this service, procedure for doing so should be established. A student should be assigned to this responsibility in each class. All equipment needed for each period must be ready before the class meets so that instruction time is not lost. This should be readily accessible so that all needed items can be gathered at once. Large laundry sacks are ideal for this purpose, and are easily carried back and forth to playing fields.

Keeping Records

Records should be functional and practical and used as a means of evaluating student progress and program content, or for recording administrative details. They should not be time-consuming or energy-

draining for the teacher. Such records include essential health information, basket or locker master sheets, cumulative physical education forms,
grades, attendance records, inventory, and accident reports. Records and
reports should be kept in a locked steel file. All recorded information
should be for present or future use and never assigned busy work, for
accurate and meaningful records and reports are as essential to good
teaching as efficient and effective class management.

Planning with Pupils

Pupils should work closely with the teacher in developing weekly
programs. The approach may well be for the teacher to have suggested
activities to present to the group, rather than asking "Well, what shall
we do today and the rest of the week?" Children tend to like most the
things they can do best, and to get into a rut consisting of old favorite
games. Weaning them away from favored activities will lead to growth.
The teacher may have to use initiative coupled with force in order to
incorporate new activities. However, she need not superimpose all her
ideas upon the group; as the adult leader she should eagerly be followed

Figure 20.   Physical education should be integrated and correlated with all other subjects in the elementary school curriculum. (Courtesy of AAHPER.)

by the pupils. She will be as long as they have enjoyable and meaningful experiences learning to master new skills.

Some techniques of evaluating outcomes are observation, comparison, questions, class discussions, analyses, and tests, both skill and written. Children can be taught to appraise what they have accomplished. So can the teacher. Evaluation, which is a method of thinking through an accomplishment so that one can revise purposes and procedures for the next effort, is an important part of teaching. When the teacher and pupils share in evaluating outcomes, democratic procedures are being used.

The process of thinking through a project is a valuable achievement in education and life. It can be used effectively with young children, for in spite of their age they have an uncanny way of seeing through things, of sizing up others as well as themselves. Their charming frankness can be utilized for individual as well as group development.

An illustration of how planning and evaluating appears in a physical education lesson follows:

Objectives. To teach children how to play "end ball."
Procedure.
    1. ORIENTATION. Give the class a preview of the game by observing an upper class play a demonstration game.
    2. PLANNING. Discuss with the class the object of the game and help them to identify skills used, team position, and the rules. Form color teams of squads and let players take assigned positions on the playfield.
    3. EXECUTING. The pupils will walk through or explore their team positions and then play the game.
    4. PUPIL'S EVALUATION. Following the playing of the game, the teacher will lead the children to consider what they should have done to play the game more effectively. They may compare the way they saw the demonstration game played with the way they played it or analyze only their play and establish their needs. The children will discover through this procedure what they need to learn or practice in order to play more skillfully. Thus they will discover their need for learning, which through increased interest will cause them to learn more rapidly than if the teacher had pointed out what she thought they needed to learn. Through such evaluation, teacher and pupils share a new purpose and agree upon objectives for the next lesson. They may have included:
        a. To practice a straight throw for distance.
        b. To practice catching while standing, while running.
        c. To play "end ball" again.

CLASS ORGANIZATION

Physical education classes are often vastly overcrowded. The ideal number of pupils per class is 20 and not more than 35. Lack of sufficient time, poor facilities, and inadequate equipment coupled with large numbers of pupils present gigantic problems to the teacher. Careful planning for the best type of class organization possible will ensure the most fruitful results. Pupils should assist the instructor in planning, conducting, and evaluating the program on each grade level. Primary children can gradually be given more responsibilities in determining what they will do, how they will learn the subject matter, and finally in evaluating their results.

Skillful organization and wise planning will assure that each period of instruction is meaningful to the learner, educationally sound and fruitful. The class should be informally conducted but well controlled. Simple games, rhythms, and quiet games by their nature allow for more freedom than self-testing or tumbling activities which are done usually to command.

The teacher should have a definite beginning and ending to each class period. She should condition the students to listen automatically when she is talking, to get into a circle or squad formation when the class starting signal is given, or to sit in assigned groups at the end of each class for a short evaluative discussion of the period. Because children experiment with each new teacher in order to learn how far they can go or how much they can get away with, it is of primary importance that from the first class to the last one in each semester the teacher be firm, fair, and consistent in her methods for controlling the group. Good class organization helps children feel secure and ready for each new challenging experience.

Formations for Instruction

Far too much precious class time can be lost by reorganizing groups for relays, teams, or skill drills. In order to eliminate such waste, students should be conditioned to form quickly into desired groups when directed to do so. Squads or teams of 6 to 10 in number usually are best. Placing each group to cover the floor area fully allows the teacher to supervise the entire class effectively. The following formations can be quickly learned and formed. In each, S.L. means Squad Leader.

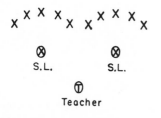

FAN

Players are spread before the leader in a fan formation. This is especially effective in skill drills for throwing, catching, and kicking balls of various sizes. The teacher works as a group supervisor.

LINE

This is the easiest of all formations for beginners to learn. It is good for relays, basket shooting, and games wherein children take turns. Not more than five should be in line if possible.

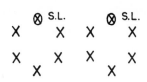

CIRCLE

Groups can get into a circle quickly from the line or fan formation by following their leader. This one is especially good for simple games and ball skill drills with the leader in the center throwing the ball to each player and correcting faulty movements when he throws it back.

SHUTTLE

This grouping is best for ball passing or kicking skill drills.

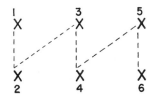

ZIGZAG

Two lines face each other. Player 1 throws to 2 who throws to 3, etc. This formation is best for soccer kicking, volleying, throwing and catching.

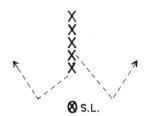

CORNER

The leader facing the line gives signal for 1 and 2 to form a V corner. The odd numbers go right; the even to the left. This grouping is ideal for skill drills and teaching response to command movements necessary for marching.

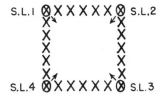

SQUARE

Have four groups form a square. Squad 1 forms West; 2 North; 3 East; 4 South. The leader stands to the left with his squad. This one is effective for ball-passing drills, and team games such as line dodgeball.

SCATTER FORMATION

A random type of formation in which students may sit or stand anywhere they wish.

Couple and Squad Formations

PUPILS FACING OUT (STANDING BACK TO BACK)

ALL FACE FORWARD

TURN AND FACE EACH OTHER

TURN AND FACE LEFT

ONE STUDENT AHEAD OF THE OTHER

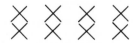

SIDE BY SIDE

DOUBLE CIRCLE FACING IN AND OUT

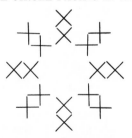

The Use of Squads

Squads can be started as early as the end of the first half of the first grade. Ideally they should be started when the pupils have reached that stage in their social development which enables them to move easily in groups. The squad leader may be selected for the first time by the teacher but the children should be given opportunities to select their own leader by the second and/or third week of each semester. The length of the leadership period can best be pupil-teacher determined. Elements of leadership are superior knowledge and skills. These take time, patience, and determination to develop. Some children are seemingly born leaders but others can be taught how to lead, too. It is important, however, that every child be given an opportunity to be in a key position in the class several times each semester, either as the squad leader or the leader of some specific activity.

Duties of the squad leader include:

1. Checking the attendance of squads.
2. Assisting the teacher in planning the daily, weekly, and semester's program.
3. Assisting the teacher with demonstrations, and helping each squad member learn each activity.
4. Assisting the teacher and squads to evaluate the program.
5. Setting patterns of good sportsmanship and fellowship as an example for the others to follow.
6. Checking equipment in and out to squad; assisting in the repair of equipment.

A real teacher becomes progressively unnecessary. After the pupils have been taught a number of games they can be given opportunities to play their favorite ones during the supervised free-play period on the playground or in the gymnasium. Suggested techniques for letting the children choose what they want to play are:

1. Assign a play space to each squad leader who will remain at the space. Each squad rotates around each leader who will lead the same game for each squad which has been assigned to him by the teacher.
2. Assign a play space to each group of 10 to 15 children who want to play a specific game. The entire squad plays the game all period. A variation of this method is to have each squad made up of three who want to play two or three of the same specific games throughout the period.
3. Assign each squad leader to a specific area and give one an opportunity to choose the game or games he would like to play. Other pupils who also want to play those games with that particular leader can join his group.
4. Assign each squad and their leader to a specific piece of equipment and have all squad groups rotate around to each piece during the period.

Use of Student Leaders

A good teacher often leads from behind. If teaching is guiding people to learn how to help themselves to become independent and to grow as citizens, then boys and girls must learn early in life how to solve their own and group problems, how to cooperate, choose leaders, how to follow, as well as how to lead others.

The use of a squad leader can produce more efficient, effective teaching. It can also enable the teacher to work more in the role of a supervisor. As soon as possile, however, the pupils should select the leader they believe to be most qualified. A Leader's Club may be organized at the fourth grade level as a means of teaching pupils how to lead. This group should meet regularly with the teacher to plan and evaluate the work to be done with the rest of the students. The group may also learn new activities to be presented later in class. Squad leaders may serve for a semester's term, or be changed more frequently. The former method adds unity to the program as well as increased leadership skill, whereas the latter passes leadership opportunities around, just as a ball is passed from one to another.

Younger children often tend to dominate rather than democratically lead others. All groups in our culture, regardless of age, must have additional training and experience in choosing leaders wisely, in leading and following others. Mankind has always felt the need for good leadership, for the history of the world shows that we have never had enough leaders in the right places at the right time. The elementary school is the rich soil in which children can develop those traits necessary for good leadership.

Class Control

Children who are happily engaged in tasks they may deem important, challenging, and fun, rarely cause difficulty, especially when they have responsibilities for planning, conducting, and evaluating their own selected activities. Those who feel secure and necessary for the group's welfare and progress rarely cause difficulty. Youth is plastic; the leader who is skilled in guiding and understanding behavior avoids, prevents, or ignores situations that could become disrupting to individual or group welfare.

Nagel suggests that in order to control children, each teacher should first make a thorough study of the following questions:[3]

1. What kind of children do we want?
2. What kind of children can best participate in a democratic society?
3. Why do children behave as they do?
4. How can we know our children better?
5. What are the normal characteristics of our children?
6. What are their likenesses and differences?
7. Why are some groups and individuals more alike than different?
8. How do we know when children are ready to learn?

Group-centered discipline should be the goal of the leader, who must realize, in turn, that this is impossible without the inner controlled actions of each group member. Class mottoes such as "We Play Fairly" or "We Believe in Everyone Having an Equal Chance" often serve as a class behavior yardstick to which the teacher can refer.

Often, reminding children of their chosen procedure ideal, and using praise, sprinkled fairly and frequently enough to be honestly earned,

---

[3] Nagel, Charles: *Methods Guidebook in Physical Education and Recreation.* Palo Alto, California, The National Press, 1956, p. 52.

will, like sugar, "catch more flies than vinegar." The teacher should be quick to sense boredom, dislike, and fatigue, as well as be ever attentive to tell-tale facial expressions, for children have not yet learned the adult's skill of concealment of frustration or unhappiness. As educators, we must know more about *why* Johnny misbehaves as well as *how best to help him* successfully cross over his present emotional stumbling block.

There are times when children lost in the crowd's shuffle will do drastic things to gain attention or to belong. Because humans are often emotionally driven rather than logically prodded into action, few can see behind or into their behavior enough to respond to questions of why they did this or that. When they say, "O, I don't know," they, indeed, speak truthfully. The wise teacher will ask *what* happened rather than *why* something did. Other questions, such as "Will what you did affect anyone else?", "What shall we do about this?", "How can we avoid making this mistake again?", often help children save face and respond in the future in positive and more self-understanding ways. The student who senses that the teacher is "agin' him" or "hates me" or "knows I'll cheat" reacts differently than the majority who do not sense these negative feelings the adult may or may not have. Consequently, the role of the teacher must change to become that of a "helper" rather than that of a director or "boss."

TEAM TEACHING

Team teaching is now being used successfully in many schools. Under this plan, two or more instructors teach the same subject to separate classes. They plan and organize together the course content for each grade and class group, and then each presents to all classes that part of the subject area (such as dance) for which she is best prepared.

Some schools are organizing teaching teams that include noncertified personnel, such as parents and older students. Through this design, in which the assistants are known as aides, many work as clerks, graders, or supervisors or perform other nonteaching duties. Such a plan, when perfected, can do much to help teachers devote most of their time to planning and conducting more individualized instruction. It can do much also to develop closer adult-parent-school relationships as well as to help older teen-agers develop leadership skills.

TEACHING BY CLOSED CIRCUIT TELEVISION

As an educational tool, television can be a powerful educational device, for what a learner hears *and* sees tends to become more meaningful.

Increasingly, in large school systems teaching physical activities through this medium is being used successfully. In Atlanta, Georgia, 1500 children from 70 classrooms are being involved yearly in preparing demonstration lessons in physical activities for television. Their viewing audience has grown from 19,000 to 47,000 in five years.

In this program teachers' guides have been developed in both elementary school health and physical education. The physical education specialists work as a teaching team, conduct workshops in health and physical education for the classroom teachers, and also go into classrooms and help children learn to do the activities they are watching other children do in each televised program. Children from different classrooms, grade levels, and schools are selected to be on programs. Those involved in this highly successful program regard teaching physical education by television as an educational medium that can be used successfully only in conjunction with other teaching tools.[4]

SUGGESTED READINGS

American Association for Health, Physical Education, and Recreation: *Professional Preparation in Health Education, Physical Education, Safety Education and Recreation Education* (A National Conference Report). Washington, D.C., 1962.

Davis, Robert: *Learning in the Schools.* Belmont, California, Wadsworth Publishing Company Inc., 1966.

Gordon, Ira: *Studying Children in School.* New York, Wiley Press, 1966.

Isaacs, Susan: *Intellectual Growth in Young Children.* New York, Schocken Press, 1966.

Klausmerier, Herbert, and Goodwin, Wm.: *Learning and Human Abilities.* New York, Harper & Row, 1966.

LaMancusa, Katherine: *We Do Not Throw Rocks at the Teacher.* Scranton, Pa., International Textbook Company, 1966.

Lee, Dorris: *Diagnostic Teaching.* Washington, D.C., National Education Association, 1966.

Miel, Alice (Editor): *Creativity in Teaching: Invitations and Instances.* Belmont, California, Wadsworth Publishing Company Inc., 1961.

Nagel, Charles, and Moore, Fredricka: *Skill Development Through Games and Rhythmic Activities.* Palo Alto, California, The National Press, 1966.

Neill, A. S.: *Summerhill: A Radical Approach to Child Rearing.* New York, Hart Publishing Company, 1964.

Polner, Murray: *The Questions Children Ask.* New York, The Macmillan Company, 1964.

Thomas, R. Murray, and Swartout, Sherwin: *Integrated Teaching Materials.* New York, David McKay Company Inc., 1964.

---

[4] For further information regarding this program write to Mrs. Gladys Peck, Atlanta Public Schools Instructional Center, 2930 Forest Hill Drive, S. W., Atlanta, Georgia 30315.

Chapter 7

The Program

THE TOTAL PROGRAM

The total program for both the lower and upper elementary grades should be a balanced one containing a wide range of activities. Broad areas around which the program should be built are:

1. Rhythmic activities
2. Games of low organization
3. Relays
4. Movement exploration
5. Camping and outing (grades 4, 5, 6)
6. Lead-up athletic team games
7. Aquatics
8. Stunts and self-testing activities

Tables 1 and 2 show the suggested time percentages for a balanced program from grades 1 through 6. Sexes should be separated at grade 4 because physical differences in boys and girls, varying interests, and performance ability become marked after the age of ten.

Table 1. TIME PERCENTAGES FOR THE PHYSICAL EDUCATION PROGRAM IN THE PRIMARY GRADES

	Grades		
	1	2	3
Rhythmic activities and movement exploration	25%	25%	25%
Fundamental play skills and daily conditioning	20	20	15
Relays	10	10	10
Mimetics and story plays	25	20	10
Athletic team games	0	0	15
Aquatics	5	5	5
Apparatus, stunts and self-testing activities	15	20	20
Total	100%	100%	100%

Table 2. TIME PERCENTAGES FOR THE PHYSICAL EDUCATION PROGRAM IN UPPER ELEMENTARY GRADES

| | Grades | | | | | |
| | 4 | | 5 | | 6 | |
	Boys	Girls	Boys	Girls	Boys	Girls
Rhythmic activities and movement exploration	20%	30%	15%	30%	15%	30%
Fundamental play skills	20	15	15	15	10	10
Relays	15	15	10	10	10	5
Lead-up athletic team games	20	15	30	20	35	30
Aquatics and camping activities	10	10	15	15	15	15
Apparatus, stunts, and self-testing activities and conditioning activities	15	15	15	10	15	10
Total	100%	100%	100%	100%	100%	100%

Some authorities in this area suggest that activity units be built around the following percentages for each grade level:[1]

Table 3. TIME PERCENTAGES BY GRADE LEVEL

Grade	Movement Skills	Ball Skills	Dance Skills
K	40%	10%	50%
1	40	20	40
2–3	40	30	30
4–6	30	50	20
7–8	30	50–60	20–10

The suggested percentages presented in Tables 1, 2, and 3 all have merit and could well be used by classroom teachers, aided by physical education specialists, to devise their own curriculum best suited to fit the needs of the children in their own school.

In as much as possible these suggested percentages should be used in order to develop a broad program. In some geographic areas where aquatics are impossible because of lack of facilities, hiking and camping may well be incorporated or used as activities suitable for children even in the primary grades.

PLANNING THE PROGRAM

Points to consider when building the daily, weekly, monthly, or semester's program in physical education include (1) the specific grade level, (2) the number of pupils in the class, (3) the age and sex, (4) the interest and needs of the pupils, (5) the carry-over value of the activities, and (6) the available facilities and equipment.

The teacher should make general and specific objectives for the class to accomplish. General objectives may be to increase (1) physical fitness,

---

[1] Anderson, Marian, et al.: *Play with a Purpose.* New York, Harper & Row, 1966, p. 475.

(2) skill range and accuracy, (3) knowledge, (4) attitudes and appreciation, and (5) better use of leisure time.

Specific objectives the teacher wishes to accomplish with the group may include to:

1. Develop in each child good health, happiness, character, and democratic spirit.
2. Develop leadership and "followership" skills.
3. Develop basic skills in as many kinds of activities as possible.
4. Develop in each child abilities to plan, conduct, and evaluate the things he can do as an individual and as a class member.
5. Develop good safety habits.
6. Develop proper attitudes toward playing, winning, losing; toward one's self and others.
7. Develop the ability to reason and to give directions.
8. Develop independence.
9. Integrate health and safety education with physical activity.
10. Develop courage and initiative.
11. Develop vigor and physical fitness.
12. Develop skills in games and activities suitable for after-school play.

Period Divisions

Children in the elementary grades should have a total of one hour daily devoted to physical education. On the primary level at least 30 minutes daily should be given to class instruction and the remainder of the time to supervised play on the playground. It is customary to have the morning time given over to the former, and the afternoon to supervised free play. Grades 4 to 6 should also have one hour daily for physical education. The suggested time division is 40 minutes for class instruction with the remaining 20 minutes for supervised playground work later. Some schools devote three 60-minute periods weekly to physical education and two 60-minute periods weekly to health instruction.

Regardless of the period divisions established by school administrators, the physical education class period should be carefully planned in order that there be a spread of activities or that more skill mastery can be accomplished. Suggested plans are:

Plan I

Primary Level (Grades 1, 2, 3)

Movement exploration	25 min.
Discussion or evaluation	5 min.
Total	30 min.

Plan II

Free play	5 min.
Ball skills	15 min.
Games	10 min.
Total	30 min.

Plan III

Free play	5 min.
Stunts and tumbling	5 min.
Lead-up team games	15 min.
Discussion or evaluation	5 min.
Total	30 min.

Plan IV

Free play	5 min.
Rhythmic activities and movement exploration	25 min.
Total	30 min.

Plan V

Upper Elementary Level (Grades 4, 5, 6)

Undressing	5 min.
Self-testing events and conditioning exercises	20 min.
Class evaluation	7 min.
Dressing and showering	8 min.
Total	40 min.

(Plans continued on following page)

Plan VI

Undressing	5 min.
Teaching new activities	20 min.
Practicing and playing	7 min.
Dressing and showering	8 min.
Total	40 min.

Plan VII

Undressing	5 min.
Review of previous day's lesson	15 min.
New games	10 min.
Evaluation	5 min.
Dressing	5 min.
Total	40 min.

Plan VIII

Undressing	5 min.
Aquatics	30 min.
Dressing	5 min.
Total	40 min.

In the primary grades, emphasis should be placed upon joyful activity; small children are not as interested in learning how to do intricate game skills as they are in being active. On the upper elementary level, however, the teacher should begin to place emphasis on skill, realizing that her pupils will receive greater pleasure from games when they can play them with better than average ability.

Figure 21.   In the primary grades, emphasis should be placed upon joyful activity. Small children are not as interested in learning how to do an intricate game as they are in being active. (Courtesy of Dr. Joan Tillotson, Plattsburgh Public Schools, Plattsburgh, New York.)

Instead of including a wide variety of activities in the beginning of the year, the teacher should start with games familiar to the pupils and gradually introduce new ones into the program. She should go from the known to the unknown, reviewing the familiar and gradually including the new.

Pupils and the teacher should evaluate together their weekly and daily progress. Time allotment for this purpose may be 5 minutes daily or 20 to 30 minutes weekly. During this period, the group should plan with the teacher the ensuing work, check progress made toward reaching desired goals and objectives, and discuss problems that have arisen during class time.

Lesson plans for each grade should be made both weekly and for the term. Activities suitable and recommended for each grade level include:

GRADE 1

Rhythmic Activities
Folk Dances
  I See You
  Shoemaker's Dance
  Danish Dance of Greeting
  Chimes of Dunkirk
  Farmer in the Dell

Singing Games
  A Hunting We Will Go
  How Do You Do, My Partner
  London Bridge
  Hokey Pokey
  Muffin Man
  Soldier Boy

Movement Exploration
  Walk to music or rhythm
  Skip to music or rhythm
  Slide to music or rhythm
  Hop to music or rhythm
  Gallop to music or rhythm
  Creative movements to changing beats

Games of Low Organization
  Have you seen my sheep?
  Crows and cranes
  Dodgeball
  Fox and geese
  Flying Dutchman
  Cat and rat
  Squirrel and trees
  I say stoop
  Slap Jack
  Circle pass ball
  Old mother witch
  Jump the brook
  Statues

Stunts, Tumbling and Self-testing
  Log roll
  Forward roll
  Push up from knees
  Running
  Jumping
  Activities on the jungle gym

GRADE 2

Rhythmic Activities
Folk Dance
  Bleking
  Kinder Polka
  Gustaf's Skoal
  Seven Jumps
  The Crested Hen
  Broom Dance
  Rovenacka

Singing Games
  Farmer in the Dell
  Hippety Hop to the Barber Shop
  Thread Follows the Needle
  I'm Very, Very Tall
  The Muffin Man
  Old King Cole

GRADE 2—*continued*

Movement Exploration
Combinations of movements
Skip-hop-glide
Changing directions
Changing tempo

Relay
Back to back
Automobile relay
Head balance relay
Rope skip relay
Passing relay
Stiff-legged relay
Gunny sack relay
Three-legged race relay
Running
Skipping
One-leg hop
Run-up, walk-back
Running backwards
Up and over
Balance relay
Up and under
Box relay
Sack relay

Mimetics and Story Plays
Rope jumping
Figure skating
Branding cows
Fishing
Bicycling
Acting out sports
Animals
Follow the leader

Building a house
The trip to the country
Cowboys and Indians
Christmas tree and Santa
Playing in the wind
Going to the grocery store
Modes of travel

Stunts, Tumbling and Self-testing Activities
Bear walk
Duck walk
Elephant walk
Seal walk
One-leg hop, changing directions
Log roll
Rope jumping
Wheelbarrow
Measuring worm
Crab walk
Leap frog
Rocking horse
Chicken fight

Games of Low Organization
Do this—do that
Midnight
Call ball
Charley over the water
Steal the bacon
Poison tag
Garden scamp
Squat tag
Red light
Wood tag
Line dodgeball

GRADE 3

Rhythmic Activities
Folk Dance
Polka
Ace of Diamonds
Green Sleeves
Indian War Dance
Norwegian Mountain Dance
Tantoli
Finger Polka

Singing Games
Jenny Crack Corn
Captain Jinks
Indian Braves
Looby Lou
Pop Goes the Weasel
Rig-A-Jig
The Needle's Eye

Dance Fundamentals
Singing

Gallop
Slides
Fox trot
Polka
Dances created to songs, poems, and stories

Games of Low Organization
Caboose
Stride ball
Bull in the ring
Three deep
Boiler burst
New York
Target throw
Last couple out
Hill dill
Circle blub bowls
Line dodgeball
Hopscotch
Loose caboose

GRADE 3—*continued*

Movement Exploration
Actions for poems and stories
Song titles
A bus ride
A train trip
The airplane
Gardening
Acting out sports

Stunts, Tumbling, and Self-testing
Knee dip
Cartwheel
Nip-up
Coffee grinder
Push-up
Cross leg stand
Foot clap
Walrus walk
Backward and forward roll
Chimney
Fish hawk dive
Twister
The swan

Team Games
Soccer keep away
Capture the flag
Kickball
Dodgeball
Boundary ball
Kick it and run
Throw it and run
Line soccer
Corner dodgeball

Relays
All four relay
Throw and sit relay
Down and up relay
Soccer dribble relay
Run and throw back relay
Automobile relay
Goal butting
Basketball pass
Horse and rider

GRADE 4—BOYS AND GIRLS

Rhythmic Activities
Folk Dance
Minuet
Broom Dance
Highland Schottische
Seven Jumps
Sellinger's Round
Sailor's Hornpipe
Maine Mixer

Square Dance
Grand March
Virginia Reel
Red River Valley
Take a Little Peek
Jump Jim Crow
Soldier's Joy

Dance, Fundamentals
Walk, run, jump, hop to even rhythm
Skip, slide, gallop, leap to uneven rhythm
Creative movements of work, play, sports
Creative dance to records
Waltz
Schottische

Games of Low Organization
Hook-on
Streets and alleys
Vis-a-vis
Animal chase
Red Rover
May I

Charades
Skin the snake
Merry-go-round
Simple pyramids
Headstand
Nip-up
Cartwheels
Running
Jumping

Camping and Outing
Hiking
Compass reading
Trail blazing
Fire building—tepee
Wood gathering
Menu planning
Outdoor cooking
Garbage disposal
Blanket rolling
Crafts from native materials
Camp project
Fishing

Team Games
Soccer dodgeball
Pin soccer
End ball
Club snatch
Bronco tag
Ankle tag
Prisoner's base

GRADE 4—*continued*

Nine-court keep away
Field ball
Skills of baseball

Relays
Rescue relay
Rope climb relay
Kangaroo relay
Leapfrog relay
Run, throw, catch relay
Goal shooting relay
Zigzag relay
Skip rope relay
Family relay
Rabbit jump relay
Soccer relay
Basketball couple passing
Goal shooting
Football pass couple relay

Stunts, Tumbling, and Self-testing
Chinning
Rope jumping
Goal shooting
Soccer kick for distance
Soccer kick for accuracy
One-leg-squat
Jump the stick

Push and pull ups
Kickball
Corner kickball
German batball
Newcomb
Captain ball
Base football
Schlagball

Aquatics (Minimum Skills)
Fear elimination
Floating
Crawl

Track and Field
25-yard dash
Standing broad jump
Pull up and/or jump and reach
Softball throw for distance and accuracy

Improvised Events

Field Events

Elementary Gymnastics
Conditioning and free exercises
Balance beam
Stall bars
Stairs

GRADE 5—BOYS AND GIRLS

Rhythmic Activities
Folk Dance
Starlight Schottische
Highland Schottische
Irish Washerwoman
Varsovienne
Kerry Dance
Troika
Sextur
Trip to Helsinki
Sicilian Tarantella

Square Dance
Oh, Johnny
Sally Goodin
Around That Couple, Take a Peek
Chase the Snake
Swing the Girl Behind You
Arkansas

Dance Fundamentals
Fox trot
Waltz Hesitation
Skip, slide, gallop
Jump and hop
Space aspects of movement
Striking and dodging
Dance creations

Games of Low Organization
Keep it up
Pinch-O
Cross tag
Fire on the mountain
Wood tag
Buddy spud
Keep away

Relays
Siamese twin relay
Jump the stick relay
Human croquet
Rope jumping relay
Running at increased distances
Squat, jump relay
Juggle relay
Pony express relay
Base running relay

Aquatics
Crawl
Backstroke
Sidestroke
Elementary diving
Elementary life saving

Stunts, Tumbling and Self-testing
Russian bear dance

GRADE 5—*continued*

Jump the stick
Hand wrestle
Human bridge
High kick
Dive
Handstand
Seal slap
Jump over stool
Track and field events
Indian leg wrestle
Stick wrestle
Rope skipping for speed and time
Bar hanging by arms, knees
Turn over on low-bar

Camping and Outing
Hiking
Compass reading
Trail blazing
Fire building—reflector oven, criss cross, travels
Wood chopping
Wood sawing
Menu planning
Outdoor cooking
Garbage disposal
Blanket rolling
Fishing-hunting
Crafts from native materials
Simple shelter construction
Camp soil conservation project
Overnight camping

Team Games
Progressive dodgeball

Volleyball
Schlagball
Base football
Softball
Touch football
Double dodgeball
Basketball—twenty-one, horse
Drop in, drop out
Circle goal shooting
Basketball pass variations
Soccer
Tennis
Speedball

Track and Field
Obstacle relays
50-yard dash
100-yard dash
440-yard run or fast walk
Broad jump
Low hurdles
Track meet

Elementary Gymnastics
Conditioning and free exercises
Swinging and traveling rings
Side horse
Rope climb
Foot and leg climb
Stirrup climb
Rolled mat activities
Still rings
Elementary flying rings
Rope climbing, single rope
Elementary horizontal bar

GRADE 6—BOYS AND GIRLS

Rhythmic Activities
Folk Dance
Kerry Dance
Sicilian Circle
Irish Song Dance
Jesse Polka
Badger Gavote
Raatikko
Cherkessia
Road to the Isles
Jarabe Tapatio
Trilby
Laces and Graces
Ranger Polka

Square Dance
Arkansas Traveler
Birdie in the Cage
Heel and Toe Polka

Cotton-Eyed Joe
Rye Waltz
Dive for the Oyster

Dance Fundamentals
Slide
Schottische variations
Waltz
Waltz variations
Congo
Lifting and carrying
Swinging
Propulsive and sustained movements
Dance creations

Games of Low Organization
Stealing sticks
Ante over
Horseshoes

GRADE 6—*continued*

Hand tennis
Box hockey
Tug-of-War
Broom hockey
Keep away
Giant volleyball
Overtake softball
Long base
Target toss

Relays
Shuttle-pass-soccer relay
Obstacle dribble relay
Dribble and pass relay
Bounce, pass, and shoot relay
Base running relays

Stunts and Tumbling
Throwing, batting, kicking for accuracy
Throwing, batting, kicking for distance
Base running
Standing broad jump
Hop, step and jump
Sprinting
The top
Knee spring
Handstand
Floor dip
Dives
Push- and pull-ups
Pyramids
Simple apparatus

Camping and Outing
Hiking
Bicycle trip camping
Use of two-handed axe
Making things with knife, with hatchet
Overnight camping utilizing all skills
learned for sleeping, playing, and cooking
in the woods

Fire building, alter fire, charcoal stove
Wood chopping and sawing
Blanket rolls
Menu planning
Outdoor cooking
Garbage disposal
Fishing-hunting-trapping
Construction of three types of shelter
Camp soil conservation
Crafts from native materials
Lashing

Team Games
Captain ball
Basketball
Fungo batting
Hit pin baseball
Soccer
Soccer dodgeball
Volleyball
Softball
Touch football

Aquatics
Diving
Breast stroke
Advanced skills in all swimming strokes

Track and Field
50-yard dash
100-yard shuttle relay
Special obstacle relays
Broad jump
Track meet

Elementary Gymnastics
Conditioning and free exercises
Fundamentals for using the back, horse,
Swedish box, Single Springboard
Intermediate skill and flying rings
Rope climbing, single and double ropes

The teacher should set up a weekly time schedule after she has chosen the broad classifications of the program and is aware of the various time percentages to be allotted to each phase. A sample weekly program for grades 1 through 6 follows:

Table 4.　SAMPLE WEEKLY PROGRAM

Grade	Monday-Wednesday-Friday	Tuesday-Thursday
1	Stunts and self-testing activities. Games of low organization	Relay and circle games
2	Rhythms and movement exploration	Supervised free play
3	Team games	Stunts and self-testing activities
4	Stunts and self-testing activities	Rhythmic activities
5	Rhythmic activities	Self-testing activities
6	Aquatics	Rhythms and movement exploration

A more detailed calendar of the activities to be included under each of the broad classifications should follow this initial plan. As the teacher becomes more skilled in planning and teaching she may gradually eliminate the initial sample weekly plan with its broad classifications, and go directly into detailed planning for each week.

The teacher should devise a daily and weekly calendar, listing under each day's column activities to be taught or reviewed. Overplanning is wiser than underplanning, for it allows for greater flexibility.

A sample weekly program for boys, grade 6, and one for girls, grade 6, follows:

Table 5. PROGRAM FOR 6TH GRADE BOYS—FORTY-MINUTE CLASS PERIOD FALL SEASON

	Monday	*Tuesday*	*Wednesday*	*Thursday*	*Friday*
First Week	Discuss class routine—dress, shower, squad, etc. Assign lockers.	Brace motor ability test.	*Circle Games* Circle tag. Circle relay. Two deep.	*Tag Games* Partner tag. Hook on. Chain tag.	Organize squads and squad leaders. Relays. Run, jump, hop.
Second Week	Discuss body mechanics. Posture test. Running relays.	*Rhythms* Fundamental rhythms: hop, skip, walk, run, jump.	*Touch Football* Instruction in passing and catching two lines practice.	*Rhythms* 1. Review of rhythms. 2. Hokey Pokey.	*Touch Football* Review Wednesday's skill. Teach punting.
Third Week	Touch football. Play.	Review rhythms. Teach Schottische.	Relay-run and throw back (football). Play touch football.	Review Schottische. Hokey Pokey.	Review of Wednesday. Teach centering ball. Play touch football.
Fourth Week	Touch football. Relay. Duck walk.	Rhythms. Teach Green Sleeves.	Teach drop kick. Skill drills.	Rhythms. Green Sleeves. Teach Gustaf's Skoal.	Review Wednesday. Squads alt. at centering, kicking, and receiving.
Fifth Week	Play touch football.	Rhythms. Teach Crested Hen Polka.	Passing to an end. Emphasize passing, catching, centering.	Rhythms. Crested Hen Polka.	Review Wednesday. Add a defensive man. Play touch football.
Sixth Week	Review running, catching, passing. Play touch football.	Review. Teach Jesse Polka.	Review rules. Play touch football.	Review all dances learned.	Test. Review of Wednesday. Add a defensive man to dodge.

Table 6. PROGRAM FOR 6TH GRADE GIRLS—FORTY-MINUTE CLASS PERIOD
WINTER SEASON

	Monday	*Tuesday*	*Wednesday*	*Thursday*	*Friday*
First Week	Physical examination.	Organization of classes.	Team game. Alley soccer. Skill drills.	Team game. Alley soccer.	Co-ed folk dance. Green Sleeves.
Second Week	Posture test. Bancroft's triple posture test.	Group games. Crows and cranes. Cock fight. Hook on.	Team game. Alley soccer. Skill drills.	Team game. Alley soccer.	Co-ed folk dance. Green Sleeves. Hokey Pokey.
Third Week	Brace motor ability test.	Stunts. Chinese get-up. Cock fight. Indian hand wrestle.	Team game. Soccer. Skill drills.	Team game. Soccer. Class tournament.	Co-ed folk dance. Jesse Polka. Dance of Greeting.
Fourth Week	Stunts. Indian hand wrestle. Jump the stick, kangaroo fight.	Team game. Soccer.	Team game. Soccer. Skill drills.	Team game. Soccer. Class tournament.	Co-ed folk dance. Road to the Isles. Sicilian Circle.
Fifth Week	Stunts. Rocking chair. Skin the snake. One over.	Team game. Soccer.	Team game. Soccer. Skill drills.	Team game. Soccer. Class tournament.	Co-ed folk dance. Review of all dances learned. Laces and Graces.
Sixth Week	Group games. Hook on. Cross tag. May I.	Team game. Soccer test. Dribble punt. Dribble pass.	Team game. Soccer test. Ability to play the game.	Team game. Soccer test. Ability to play the game.	Co-ed folk dance. Cherkessia. Badger Gavote.

Some curriculum guides only present suggested program areas for grades 1 to 7, as is shown in Table 7.

COMPETENCIES TO BE DEVELOPED

What is taught on each grade level depends largely upon where pupils are on the ladder of their social, emotional, mental, and physical development. First graders, who have been to kindergarten, are often ready for activities usually taught on the second grade level, while those who have not been are more apt to respond to activities thought best for four year old children. Likewise, pupils transferring from one school to another even in the same city often find they are ahead or lag far behind their classmates. Certainly much experimentation is needed to determine more satisfactorily (other than by expert opinion) what should be taught where. Although there is a wide gap between the skills that a first grader and

Table 7. Suggested Program Areas—Grades 1 to 7[2]

ACTIVITIES

OUTDOOR	INDOOR	TESTING	CULMINATING
Body Building Exercises (Daily)	Body Building Exercises (Daily)	Apparatus Climb	School Demonstrations
Relays	Relays	Pull-ups	1. Newcomb
			2. Serveball
Apparatus	Swimming	Leisure-time	3. Volleyball
Jungle gym		Fitness Tests	4. Foul shooting
Horizontal bars	Games		5. Basketball
	1. Circle	Kraus-Weber Tests	6. Batball
Games	2. Tag		7. Kickball
1. Circle	3. Chasing	Game Skill Tests	8. Track and field events
2. Tag	4. Bowling		Dash
3. Chasing	5. Basketball	Foul Shooting	Shuttle relay
4. Team	6. Dodgeball		Pull-ups
Batball		25 yd. Swimming Test	Hop, step, jump
Driveball	Rhythms	(4th Grade)	Potato race
Kickball	1. Fundamental		9. Rhythms
Serveball	rhythms		10. Ice skating
Newcomb	2. Creative		City-wide Demonstrations
Volleyball	3. Imitative		1. Volleyball Playday
Dodgeball	4. Round		2. Telephonic Foul Shooting
Basketball	5. Folk		3. Physical Education
Touch football	6. Square		Demonstration
Softball	7. Social		4. Physical Fitness Day
5. Track events			
	Ice Skating		

[2] Reprinted by permission of the Health, Physical Education and Safety Department, Norfolk Public School, Norfolk, Virginia.

sixth grader can do, this is not true when comparing second to third or fourth to fifth graders. Consequently, devising a list of competencies that should be developed at each grade level is wiser and leads to a sounder educational program in all grades. The following list of competencies can be used as an idea springboard for doing so:

Table 8.   COMPETENCIES TO BE DEVELOPED[3]

	Grades					
	1	2	3	4	5	6
Optimum Physical Qualities of Fitness (developed to maximum capacity)	*	*	*	*	*	*
Strength	S†	S	M‡	M	Ex§	Ex
Power	S	S	M	M	Ex	Ex
Endurance	S	S	M	M	Ex	Ex
Flexibility	S	S	M	M	Ex	Ex
Agility	S	S	M	M	Ex	Ex
Functional Skill and Coordination	*	*	*	*	*	*
Locomotion (walking, running, skipping, hopping, jumping, climbing, galloping, sliding)	M	M	Ex	Ex	Ex	Ex
Balancing	M	M	M	Ex	Ex	Ex
Rhythmic Response in Movement						
Moving to a rhythmic sound	M	M	M	Ex	Ex	Ex
Moving in simple patterns	M	M	Ex	Ex	Ex	Ex
Skip, slide, polka, schottische, step-hop, waltz, fox-trot, two-step	S	S	M	M	Ex	Ex
Patterns—honor, swing, circle, allemande, do-si-do, grand right and left balance, promenade, ladies' chain, right and left through			S	M	Ex	Ex
Ball Skills						
Rolling	S	S	M	M	Ex	Ex
Tossing	S	S	M	M	Ex	Ex
Throwing—distance and accuracy	S	S	M	M	Ex	Ex
Dribbling and juggling			S	S	M	M
Volleying			S	S	M	M
Goal shooting			S	S	M	M
Kicking, dribbling, trapping		S	S	M	M	M
Striking—hand, bat, club		S	S	S	M	M
Rope Jumping	S	M	Ex	Ex	Ex	Ex
Beginning Swimming				S	M	M
Creativity, Exploration, and Self-Expression	*	*	*	*	*	*
Efficient and Attractive Posture	*	*	*	*	*	*
Standing	M	M	M	Ex	Ex	Ex
Sitting	M	M	M	Ex	Ex	Ex
Moving	M	M	M	Ex	Ex	Ex
Increasing Emotional Maturity	*	*	*	*	*	*
Social Adaptability	*	*	*	*	*	*

† S = Some competency.
‡ M = Much competency.
§ Ex = Excellent competency.
* It is possible to play and work harder and for longer periods in the upper elementary ages.

[3] Reprinted by permission of The President's Council Program. *Youth Fitness.* Revised Ed. Washington, D.C., Superintendent of Documents, 1963.

THE NEED FOR PROGRESSION IN THE PROGRAM

Many believe that today's children are not being challenged enough educationally. Unfortunately, this is too often true of the physical education program. In the best programs there is both balance and progression through the provision of many types of learning experiences. The use of graduated size balls, games, dance, and other types of activities that call for many kinds of movement combinations should be stressed. Such progression should be within the many kinds of activities themselves and from grade level to grade level.

THE TEACHING UNIT

A teaching unit is an action blueprint plan devised jointly by the teacher and pupils. It should be based upon the needs of children and should provide them with opportunities for growth as individuals and group members. Although there are many ways to organize a teaching unit, basically each should contain a title, an overview or introductory statement, a list of objectives to be reached, an outline of content guides and possible approaches, a list of teacher and pupil activities, suggestions for evaluation, and pupil and teacher references. All plans should be kept flexible and changed, if necessary, as the teacher uses them.

Suggested topics for a unit for sixth graders in speedball include:

Brief history, nature, and purpose of the game
Safety rules
Soccer skills
  Dribbling
  Instep kick
  Kicking with the inside and outside of the foot
  Punting
  Body traps and blocks
  Sole-of-foot trap; one-leg trap; two-leg trap
  Evading an opponent
  Kicking for a goal

Basketball skills
  Catching and passing
  Overhead juggle
  Pivoting
Soccer skills
  Drop kick
  Passing
  Tackling
Speedball skills
  Pick up with one foot on a moving ball; on a stationary ball; with two feet; with one foot over a moving ball
  Lifting the ball up to pass
  Guarding
Rules
Strategy
Evaluation

THE DAILY LESSON PLAN

Careful planning is basic to good teaching every day. Although all plans should be flexible, they must be made with a definite purpose to shape all learning experiences to the needs and development of each child *and* to the society of which he is a vital part.

Lesson plans are both time and energy savers. They help to assure progression and the building of skill upon skill through a carefully planned and progressively challenging school curriculum. They also:

1. Lead to a faster setting of goals and the attainment of educational, group, and individual objectives.
2. Help keep all program offerings in a proper balance so that no one area is overemphasized (such as team relays) to the detriment of another area (such as movement exploration).
3. Make the teacher feel more secure and confident in her role as an educator who does teach something new to every child each time every class meets.
4. Spur on the learner's interest and ability to accept and master greater learning challenges.
5. Clarify thought and, through periodic review and practice, help make learning more accurate and permanent.
6. Set desirable patterns for students to follow when developing their own study and work habits, as well as when planning their own goals.
7. Insure that, during the regular teacher's absence, the substitute instructor can carry out previously-planned lessons, thus keeping learning continuous.
8. Provide for periodic measurement at times that are best for the evaluation of certain kinds of learning results.
9. Take into account pupil readiness to move on to new learning experiences.
10. Aid in making the best use of each previous class period for increased pupil learning.
11. Help teachers develop and improve teaching skill.
12. Can be used as evidence to parents, administrators, and others that educational plans have been devised and that students are being presented new materials.

Daily lesson plans enable a teacher to make the best use of each class period, are both an energy and time saver, and assure progression in the program. Each lesson should be a meaningful experience wherein the pupils learn something new as well as refine previously-learned materials and skills. *Build skill upon skill* is a motto recommended for all teachers, and most especially for physical educators.

Daily lesson plans should include objectives, needed equipment, techniques for linking yesterday's lesson with that of today, new activities to be taught with a time allotment given for each, and techniques for evaluating progress.

A well planned and conducted lesson will provide:

1. Maximum participation in meaningful activities for all pupils in the group.
2. The growth and development of each class member in accordance with stated objectives and educational goals.
3. Increased pupil interest, appreciation, and enthusiasm for physical education.
4. A variety of well selected activities that have educational value and lead toward more abundance and healthier living for the future as well as the present.
5. Opportunities to correlate and integrate physical education with health and safety education, as well as other subject areas in the curriculum.
6. Students with opportunities for self-evaluation of their daily accomplishments.

Lesson plans enable the teacher to review and relate to overall program objectives, serve as a review and help in the preparation of the coming lesson, provide an organized and progressive procedure that aids in

Teacher _____

School _____ Class _____ Date _____ Lesson _____
Unit: _____

Objectives	Methods	Time	Comments

Equipment and Materials: _____
Methods of Evaluation: _____
References: _____

Figure 22.   The achievement of optimum fitness during the formative years is basic to the education for the building and maintenance of fitness in adulthood. (Courtesy of AAHPER.)

class interest and individual motivation, often help prevent disciplinary problems from arising, help the teacher to emphasize important points and skill elements, and aid in evaluating teacher as well as pupil growth. A sample daily lesson plan is shown at the top of page 123.

COURSES OF STUDY

Although most states and local school systems have courses of study available as well as teaching guides, such materials should be used mainly as idea launching pads. An ideal physical education class is one devised and conducted skillfully for each particular class in each particular school, for no course of study or teaching guide will "fit" (or even be fit) for every child. However, such materials do have value, for from them teachers can build upon, and create, a new and better framework for their own unique teaching situation and class groups.

Every teacher is a builder—a superior, average, or poor one. The superior one will design and construct a magical place wherein children have wondrous experiences of joy and accomplishment. The average builder will stick closely to a pre-planned blueprint made for and by someone else, and her results will be about the same as everybody else's, or just another house. The poor builder is totally unaware that somewhere a blueprint does exist, or even where to start to devise her own. Her house is never built and her eager pupils who are longing to accomplish something merely mill around instead, disinterested, disillusioned, and disappointed.

Educators seldom capitalize upon their gains. They could do so by capitalizing upon what has been accomplished before, instead of going back to a starting point again and again. Already devised and obtainable courses of study, teaching guides, and other materials are, in reality, such starting points. Like medicine, they work the best miracles when taken in just the right amounts, for if a little is good, more may *not* be necessarily better.

SUGGESTED READINGS

Anderson, Marian; Elliot, Margaret; and La Berge, Jeanne: *Play with a Purpose.* New York, Harper & Row, 1966.

Barratt, Marcia: *Foundations for Movement.* Dubuque, Iowa, Wm. C. Brown, 1965.

Boyer, Madeline: *The Teaching of Elementary School Physical Education.* New York, J. Lowell Pratt and Company, 1965.

Eble, Kenneth: *A Perfect Education.* New York, The Macmillan Company, 1966.

Fabricius, Helen: *Physical Education for the Classroom Teacher.* Dubuque, Iowa, Wm. C. Brown, 1966.

Fait, Hollis: *Physical Education for the Elementary School Child.* Philadelphia, W. B. Saunders Company, 1964.

Halsey, Elizabeth, and Porter, Lorena: *Physical Education for Children.* New York, Holt, Rinehart and Winston, 1963.

Kirchner, Glenn: *Physical Education for the Elementary School Child.* Dubuque, Iowa, Wm. C. Brown, 1966.

Nixon, John, and Jewett, Ann: *Physical Education Curriculum.* New York, The Ronald Press, 1964.

SUGGESTED PHYSICAL EDUCATION CURRICULUM GUIDES

California
    Daly City. Jefferson Elementary School District: *Stunts and Tumbling for Primary Grade Children.* 1965, 42 pp.
    Redding. Shasta County Superintendent of Schools: *Physical Fitness Materials for 4–8 Grade Teachers.* 1965, unpaged (ditto).

District of Columbia
    Public Schools of the District of Columbia: *Direction Finders for Physical Education. Chart I: Warm-up Drills; Game Skills; Rhythmic Activities. Chart II: Stunts; Apparatus; Track and Field; Individual Activities; Tests.* 1965, charts, $.40 each.

Illinois
    Cook County. Arlington Heights Public Schools: *Physical Education Program and Activities Guide, (Grades One–Five).* 1965, 70 pp., $2.00.
    Hinsdale. Gower School District No. 62: *Curriculum Guide for Physical Education, (Grades Kindergarten Through Eight).* 1965, 109 pp.

Kentucky
    Louisville. Louisville Public Schools: *Physical Education: A Curriculum Guide for Grades 1 and 2.* 1965, 188 pp.
    Louisville. Jefferson County Public Schools: *Physical Education: A Tentative Guide for Classroom Teachers, (Grades 3–6).* 1956, 151 pp., $2.50.

Maryland
    Upper Marlboro. Board of Education, Prince Georges County: *A Curriculum Guide in Elementary Physical Education for Boys and Girls.* n. d., 525 pp., $5.00.

Massachusetts
    Needham. Needham Public Schools: *Physical Education Course of Study, (Kindergarten—Grade I—Grade II).* 1963, 59 pp.

New York
    Schenectady. Schenectady Public Schools: *Physical Education—Upper Elementary.* n. d., packet, $2.00.
    Spring Valley. Remap Central School District No. 2: *Boys' Physical Education, Part II, (Grades 7–12).* 1965, 71 pp., $2.00.

Oregon
    Salem. State Department of Education: *Adapted Physical Education for Oregon Schools.* 1965.
    Salem. State Department of Education: *Physical Education Scope and Sequence Chart.* 1965.

Wisconsin
    Beloit. Beloit Public Schools: *Physical Education, Elementary, (Grade 2).* 1965, various paging, $1.75.
    Beloit. Beloit Public Schools: *Physical Education, Elementary—Boys, (Grades 5 and 6).* 1965, various paging, $2.00.
    Beloit. Beloit Public Schools: *Physical Education, Elementary—Girls, (Grades 5 and 6).* 1965, various paging, $2.00.

Chapter 8

Physical Development and Youth Fitness

Because tomorrow belongs to the children of today, our very future as a nation of individuals depends upon the quality and quantity of their educational experiences during their formative years. No thoughtful adult can doubt that today's children, who will be the leaders of tomorrow, must have the brains, brawn, and belief in democracy and the values we hold precious. Tomorrow's adults must be better, stronger, and more socially sensitive than adults are now or our ancestors were. It is in the education of our present children that the future of the world will be determined for good or for evil, for man's crash into an abyss or his climb to glory.

Professional as well as lay literature is full of the results of comparative tests given to measure the components of physical fitness for body flexibility, strength, endurance, and speed of reaction time. These tests show that American children are in a poorer physical condition than those in Italy, Germany, England, Japan, and China. Although some physical educators and physicians challenge the reliability of these tests and question the sweeping conclusions drawn from them, much is to be gained from such professional critics in the further refinement of physical fitness testing devices, the accumulation of more evidence, the resulting riddance of parental apathy, and improved physical education programs for *all* children enrolled in our public schools from grades 1 to 12.

There is no doubt that in our present period of drastic change, which has no historical precedent, American parents tend to be overly indulgent and our children are sitting too much watching mediocre spectator activities. The increased mechanization of our farms, the automation in our factories, and the population explosion will in the future bring us more leisure, more wealth, more self-indulgence, and a whole set of new and challenging problems of great magnitude. Certainly there is an abundance of evidence that, in this time of shifting values, our present problem of the "soft" American who already has leisure and is throwing it away, is minute in comparison to what the problem will be in the future. Likewise, we know that although our "creature comforts" are increasing rapidly, man has not changed biologically. Children have a compulsive drive for movement; their need for it is as basic as that for sleep or food. The curtailing of vigorous activity for children of all ages can lead to faulty structural development and alarming results. There is an abundance of scientific evidence that (1) there is a strong correlation between vigorous health and educational progress and success, (2) play activities are directly related to good mental and emotional health, (3) the status of a child in school in relation to his peers is dependent to a great extent upon his motor skills and sportsmanship, (4) the problem of obesity begins early in life and is due as much to underactivity as to overeating, (5) regular activity increases the density of bones of the body and produces organic changes that increase resistance to stress and strain and greatly improve the function of the organs and systems of the body, and (6) children who are strong and energetic have fewer absences from school. Physical activity *is* essential to human growth and development.

Collectively, the fitness of all people is one of our greatest assets, for, as President John F. Kennedy said, "the physical vigor of our citizens is one of America's most precious resources. If we waste or neglect this resource, if we allow it to dwindle or grow soft, then we will destroy much of

Figure 23.   Physical activity *is* essential to human growth and development. (Courtesy of Elizabeth Glidden, Specialist in Elementary Physical Education, Los Angeles City Schools, Los Angeles, California.)

our ability to meet the great and vital challenges which confront our people." [1]

WHAT IS PHYSICAL FITNESS?

A human being, whether he is an adult or a child, is physically fit when he (1) is free from disease, (2) does not have significant deviations from normal body function or structure, (3) has sufficient strength, speed, agility, endurance, and skill to perform the maximum tasks of daily life without undue fatigue and can easily bounce back through rest when overly tired, (4) is mentally and emotionally adjusted, and (5) has high moral and spiritual concepts. Such a person is strong, healthy, and buoyant and contributes to the happiness and well-being of his family and community. Vigorous exercises, taking part in active sports and games, and positive routine health habits are the foundation upon which such fitness is built. Total fitness, which includes physical, mental, emotional and spiritual well-being, cannot be stored up like food or money, but must be maintained when once acquired and replaced when used.

ESSENTIALS FOR AN EFFECTIVE PROGRAM

Recommended essentials for an effective physical fitness program have been drawn up by the President's Council on Youth Fitness.[2] These recommendations include:

1. A school curriculum based upon the health needs of children and youth.
2. Regular instruction in health and safety education in all elementary grades with appropriate texts and materials.
3. Utilization of health resources in the community and state to strengthen the program.
4. Designation of a faculty member to coordinate the total health education program.
5. The giving of school credit for physical education, comparable to other subject-matter areas.
6. Daily physical education periods, in grades 1–6, for a minimum of 30 minutes, exclusive of recess and time spent in dressing and showering.
7. A maximum class size of 35 pupils unless there is special organization and leadership.
8. Sufficient dressing, drying, and shower rooms, and toilets for grades 4–12.
9. Adequate instructional and fitness-testing equipment and supplies.
10. Intramural sports programs for all boys and girls in grades 4–12, conducted under competent leadership.

The classroom teacher and specialized physical educator are the keystone of an effective program in the elementary school. Each should pro-

---

[1] John F. Kennedy: The soft American. *Sports Illustrated,* December 26, 1960.

[2] See the publication, *Youth Fitness,* prepared by the President's Council, available from the Superintendent of Documents, Washington, D.C., For information concerning *Operation Fitness, U.S.A.,* write the AAHPER, 1201 16th St., N.W., Washington 6, D.C.

vide opportunities for *all* boys and girls to take part in wisely selected activities that require each child to be active in games using hopping, bending, twisting, running, stretching, and other types of vigorous body movements. Likewise, each should use active games and coordination exercises (done to music)[3] that will increase vigor, strength, flexibility, endurance, and balance. Each class should begin with warm-up activities and should be varied daily with the inclusion of many games such as Up and Over, Forty Ways to Get There, and a wide variety of active group games, such as Midnight or Jump the Brook. If a gymnasium is available, the use of climbing ropes, apparatus, and tumbling is recommended, but these should be supplemented by individual and group games and exercises. If only the classroom can be used, pair the children off and mimetically do such activities as sawing wood, the "measuring worm," "trees in the wind," the "bunny hop," and so forth. In the primary grades, the teacher's goal should be to have each child play a minimum of three vigorous games daily; at least four to five should be played daily by each child on the upper elementary level, and he should also participate in more vigorous, big-muscle activities that require more strenuous and faster total body movement over a longer period of time. The teacher should take great care to stress the necessity for daily physical activity in ways that get this message across to each child so that each *does* believe in its importance throughout life and *does* take part in positive physical recreational pursuits when on his own and away from watchful adults. Because education is for use, what the learner does voluntarily when he is away from the teacher is potent information every real educator wants to know and does know.

Every effort should be made to gain parental support of the program. Showing to a P.T.A. or service groups such films as *They Grow Up So Fast* or *Focus on Fitness*[4] is a good way to stir up adult interest and gain favorable response. Parents should be concerned when they drive their children to school instead of having them get there by walking, bicycling, or roller skating, because they are actually hindering the development of those they love, as well as helping them to develop lazy, physically detrimental habits. Likewise, parents should learn the value of encouraging youngsters to (1) play out-of-doors when they come home from school, instead of watching television, (2) learn how to swim and do so daily in the summer and twice weekly or more during the winter, if possible, (3) use improvised backyard basketball goals, swings, Manila climbing ropes, stairs built to varied step heights, horizontal ladders, and slides, and (4) take part in existing swimming and physical activity programs offered in local community agencies. Above all, the parents should be aroused to the extent that

---

[3] The album, *Physical Fitness Activities for Elementary Schools,* by Ed Durlacker, Square Dance Association, Freeport, N.Y., is recommended. Also consult The Journal of Health, Physical Education, Recreation for newer materials.

[4] See the bibliography for the source of these films.

they will see to it that an adequate physical education program is provided for every child in every school in the community, and that it is conducted by a well prepared professional physical educator. Parents should be guided also into the realization that, if American school systems place an increased emphasis upon academic education at the expense of eliminating or decreasing the school physical education program, they produce mental geniuses who are physical flops and rejects. It is not a question, as they must become aware, of the mind's being superior to the body, for they are as inseparable as the two sides of a coin and one is incomplete without the other. Nor is it really a question of which type of education is superior, for they both are necessary if we are to produce strong, healthy, and intelligent human beings. A vigorous, righteous America can only be made up of all citizens who have these qualities. To this end, all adults have a tremendous contribution to make, not only for their own children, but for *all* youth.

SCREENING TESTS FOR FITNESS

Such tests should not be given until the fifth grade level. However, children in the lower grades can be tested for body flexibility and abdominal strength (which are only two of several components of fitness) by means of the Kraus-Weber test.[5] This is the test in which 57.9 per cent of the American children failed one or more of the items shown below, in contrast to 8.7 per cent of European youngsters in the same category. The six items of this test include the following:

Test I. Clasp the hands behind the neck and roll up to a sitting position as someone holds both feet on the floor.

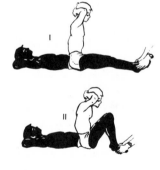

Test II. Bend the knees, clasp the hands behind the neck and roll up into a sitting position as someone holds both feet on the floor.

Test III. With hands clasped behind the neck and legs extended straight, raise the heels 10 inches from the floor. Hold this for 10 seconds or as someone counts 1 thousand and 1, 1 thousand and 2, 1 thousand and 3, and so forth.

[5] A modification of the *Junior Physical Fitness and Proficiency Test of the Amateur Athletic Union* of the U.S. is also recommended. Copies can be obtained from this organization, 233 Broadway, New York 7, N.Y.

Test IV. Lie face down with a pillow under the abdomen. Clasp hands behind the neck; then raise head, chest, and shoulders off the floor. Hold this for 10 seconds or ten counts as in Test III.

Test V. Place the hands under the head and a pillow under the abdomen. Raise both legs off the floor and keep knees straight. Hold this for 10 seconds or ten counts as in Test IV.

Test VI. Keep feet together, slowly bend forward, keeping knees straight, and see how nearly you come to touching the floor with your finger tips. Do not bend the knees or bounce down. If you can touch the floor with the finger tips for three seconds or counts of 1 thousand and 1, and so forth, you pass the test; if not, it is a failure. (This is the one item most of the American children failed.

Although some children may pass this simple test with ease, the majority will be unable to pass all six items. Again, it should be pointed out that this test measures only the minimum fitness of the trunk muscles of the body and thus is concerned with only one aspect of fitness. In order to measure the amount of fitness each child possesses, professionally trained physical educators should give tests in endurance, speed, body flexibility, and explosive power (as shown by the ability to jump certain distances in the air from a standing position), and in other areas.

At the beginning of the fifth grade, the *Youth Fitness Test* of the American Association for Health, Physical Education, and Recreation is recommended.[6] This battery of tests includes:

1. Muscular strength and endurance of arms and shoulder girdle.
2. Muscular strength and endurance of the abdominal area.
3. Leg power.
4. Arm and shoulder girdle power.
5. Speed in running.
6. Agility.
7. Flexibility.
8. Cardiovascular-respiratory endurance.

Two to five days are needed to give the entire test. The tests should be given the first and last months of the school year. All pupils should go through a conditioning program before any part of the test is taken. The test scores should become a part of each pupil's cumulative record and should be used as a guide for the construction of a physical education program based upon his needs.

Teachers must be ever cognizant that there is far more to fitness than having the ability to chin one's self or being able to run as fast as a national

---

[6]Directions and national norms are contained in the publication: *Youth Fitness Test Manual,* available for 50 cents per copy at the American Association for Health, Physical Education, and Recreation, 1201 16th St., N.W., Washington 6, D.C.

Figure 24.   A well balanced program that is well taught can and will produce physically, morally, mentally, and emotionally fit youth and adults. (Courtesy of Dr. Joan Tillotson, Plattsburgh Public Schools, Plattsburgh, New York.)

average. The underpars, the physical flops, and the weaklings, if graded only on physical fitness test scores, would often be the oldest pupils in any grade in the entire school system. These are the ones who often sour early on physical activities, are chosen last for teams, and sometimes end up as school administrators who see no place in the educational offerings for physical education, and many more become the future parents who would agree with them.

Likewise, the teacher giving such tests must realize *that children jump for joy* not merely to pass a test. This connotes that the testing program should be seen in its true perspective and that *the physical education program should be far more than a testing one.* A well balanced program that is well taught can and will produce physically, morally, mentally, and emotionally fit youth and adults.

POSTURAL FITNESS[7]

Posture, which can be changed by habits, can best be corrected, if faulty, when the child is young and his body pliable. If the child has poor

---

[7]See also Chapter 20: Adapted Programs for Atypical Children.

posture, different parts of the body are out of line. Children with marked deviations should be under the care of an orthopedic specialist. Signs of good posture are:[8]

STANDING

1. Feet parallel and about 6 inches apart.
2. Head high, as if balancing a book on the head.
3. Chest out.
4. Stomach and hips firm.
5. Abdomen and back as flat as possible.
6. Knees very lightly flexed—not locked.
7. Weight evenly distributed on each foot. Most of body weight on balls of feet.

SITTING

1. Sit back in the chair, so that hips touch the back of the chair. Feet flat on the floor.
2. Sit tall.
3. Keep chest out and neck in line with upper back.
4. When writing, lean forward from the hips. Keep head and shoulders in line.

WALKING

1. Knees and ankles limber and toes pointed straight ahead.
2. Swing legs directly forward from hip joints.
3. Lift feet off the ground—don't shuffle.
4. Shoulders and arms swing free and easy—no pulling or tension.
5. Head and chest high.
6. The heel touches the ground first in each step.

POSTURE EXERCISES

Always Stand—Sit—Walk—Think *Tall*
Always Stand and Walk with Toes Straight Ahead

Children will profit from taking part in the following activities:

RAG DOLL — Lie on back in complete relaxation. Imagine you are floating in a quiet stream; say to yourself, "float, float, float."

PUMPING — Lie on back with knees bent and pump abdominal muscles in and out in slow rhythm, keeping lower back flat on floor.

PUSH AWAY — Stand facing wall with feet 1 foot from wall, elbows bent shoulder height. Let body go forward from ankles—keep feet flat on floor. Push back into standing position.

---

[8]President's Council on Youth Fitness: *Youth Physical Fitness.* Washington, D.C., Superintendent of Documents, p. 94.

BACK FLATTENING	Stand back to wall, heels 4 inches from wall, and flatten lower back to wall. Pull up and in with abdominal muscles; down and in with seat muscles.
INCH WORM	Feet and hands on floor. Walk with hands forward away from feet. Then, with hands in place, walk feet to hands, keeping knees straight—alternate hands and feet.
ROLY POLY	Lie on back, cross ankles, cross arms across chest and lift head and feet slightly from floor. Roll to R and L side. Repeat. Try to increase the number of times doing this.
CHEST PACKING	Lie with back flat and chin in. Inhale and raise chest. Hold chest position and exhale by drawing abdomen in and up.
SELF CORRECTION AT MIRROR	Check own posture and feet in front of mirror when standing, walking, sitting, and balancing a book on head. Pull tall and hold that position as long as possible while walking. Repeat.
AN ELEPHANT	Walk on hands and feet with elbows and knees straight.
A ROOSTER	Lift chest, stand tall on tiptoes, and flap arms to look like a rooster crowing.

Figure 25.   Being an airplane helps to develop the muscles of the upper body. (Courtesy of *The Instructor*. Photograph by Edith Brockway.)

THE BIRD	Stand on a thick book with toes curled over the edge. Stretch heels high; relax. Repeat.
FOOT MARBLES	Pick up marbles with the toes and transfer them to a box. Write with a pencil held between toes.
AIRPLANE	Extend arms at shoulder level. Imitate the changing flight patterns of an airplane.
DUCKS	Tuck hands under armpits. Squat with back held straight. Walk forward like a duck, flapping your wings.
PRANCING HORSES	Prance with body erect, pulling knees up high toward chest.
ROW BOAT	Sit down and extend legs. "Row" a boat forward, backward, and in a circle. Row slowly, then as fast as you can; row as though you have heavy passengers in the boat.

CORRELATION WITH HEALTH AND SAFETY PROGRAMS

A growing child is an adult in the making who has a long way to go before he finally arrives at maturity. He can be aided in this journey by many adults, school teachers included, who can assist him during this long, slow, and sometimes painful trip. In each grade the developing child has his own individual needs in the areas of health and safety.

Health and safety education programs should provide youth with knowledge, understanding, and the properly developed attitude that good health is one of life's enduring values. Children should learn through the establishment of good health habits how to protect and improve their own health in meaningful enough ways that they will do so throughout their entire lifetime. The school program in health and safety education should include:

1. A well planned progressive health instruction program from grades 1 to 12,[9] that is skill-fully taught. Such a program should include instruction in:

Nutrition	Family life education
Value of exercise and play	Body cleanliness and grooming
The structure and function of the body	Water safety
Environmental health	Fire prevention
School bus and traffic safety	Hazards to life and health
Junior first aid	Effective and safe living at home and
Home care and nursing	school
Safety at play	Communicable disease control
Body mechanics and posture	Mental and emotional health
Safety for holidays	Care of organs and special senses

2. Health appraisal activities including a physical examination, screen tests for posture, dental, hearing, vision, and nutritional status.

---

[9] See Vannier, Maryhelen: *Teaching Health in Elementary Schools* (New York, Harper & Row, Publishers, 1963) for practical and effective suggestions for teaching health to children.

3. A remedial and follow-up program for all who need it.
4. Health protective measures to prevent and control diseases.
5. A healthful school environment, and utilizing it to teach health and safety concepts.

If we are to develop the fitness of American youth through an improved physical education program, we must do so because we, as adults and educators, feel that every boy and girl should be aided to reach his potential in life.

SUGGESTED READINGS

Books

American Association for Health, Physical Education, and Recreation: *Youth Fitness Test* (Revision of the test manual with new 1964-65 norms). Washington, D.C., 1964.

Clarke, H. Harrison: *Application of Measurement to Health and Physical Education,* 4th Ed. Englewood Cliffs, N.J., Prentice-Hall, Inc., 1967.

Clarke, H. Harrison, and Haar, Franklin: *Health and Physical Education for the Elementary School Classroom Teacher.* Englewood Cliffs, N.J., Prentice-Hall, Inc., 1964.

Cureton, Thomas: *Physical Fitness and Dynamic Health.* New York, The Dial Press, 1965.

Lowman, Charles: *Postural Fitness.* Philadelphia, Lea & Febiger, 1960.

Miller, Arthur, and Whitcomb, Virginia: *Physical Education in the Elementary School Curriculum,* 2nd Ed. Englewood Cliffs, N.J., Prentice-Hall, Inc., 1963.

Neilson, N. P.; VanHagen, Winifred; and Comer, James: *Physical Education for Elementary Schools,* 3rd Ed. New York, The Ronald Press, 1966.

President's Council on Youth Fitness: *Youth Fitness.* Washington, D.C., U.S. Government Printing Office, 1962.

Prudden, Bonnie: *Is Your Child Really Fit?* New York, Harper & Brothers, 1956.

Steinhaus, Arthur: *Toward an Understanding of Health and Physical Education.* Dubuque, Iowa, Wm. C. Brown Company, 1964.

Vannier, Maryhelen: *Teaching Health in Elementary Schools.* New York, Harper & Row, 1963.

Periodicals

Barrow, Harold: The ABC's of testing. *Journal of Health, Physical Education, Recreation,* May, June, 1962.

Espenschade, Anna: Contributions of physical activities to growth. *Research Quarterly,* American Assn. for Health, Physical Education, and Recreation, National Education Assn., May, 1960.

Halsey, Elizabeth: First steps toward fitness. *Journal of Health, Physical Education, Recreation,* November, 1958.

Hunsicker, Paul: How fit are our youth? *National Education Assn. Journal,* Vol. 48, March, 1959.

Jackson, C. O.: Challenge of fitness. *Scholastic Coach,* Vol. 28, January, 1959.

Kidder, Gene: All around fitness for all. *Journal of Health, Physical Education, Recreation,* Vol. 28, Sept., 1957.

McCoy, Mary E.: Fitness through intra-murals. *Journal of Health, Physical Education, Recreation,* Vol. 28, Sept. 1957.

Means, Louis E.: Why all this fuss about fitness? *The Instructor,* February, 1962.

Means, Louis E.: *Mimeographed Reports of Fitness Test Comparisons of American Children and Youth with those in Japan, England, Wales, Scotland, and Cyprus.* Washington, D.C., American Assn. for Health, Physical Education, and Recreation, National Education Assn., 1960. Free upon request.

Morehouse, L. E.: American living, A threat to fitness. *Journal of Health, Physical Education, Recreation,* Vol. 27, Sept., 1956.

Vannier, Maryhelen: Toward better programs in elementary physical education. *The Instructor,* February, 1963.

Vaughn, Albert: Physical fitness homework. *The Physical Educator,* October, 1965.

Physical Fitness Activities to Music

Chicken Fat: Capitol CF-1000. Instructions available—U.S. Junior Chamber of Commerce, Box 7, Tulsa, Okla. 74101, $.35 per copy.

Rhythms for Physical Fitness: R.R.2. David McKay Company, Inc., 119 W. 40th St., New York 18, N.Y.

Rhythmic Activities and Physical Fitness (Grades K through 2): LP1055. Album, manual, and wall charts available, $7.95. Kimbo Records, Box 55, Deal, N.J. 07723.

Kimbo Kids—Rhythmics: LP1066. Album, manual, and wall charts available, $7.95. Record #209—Vocal commands, Side A; Instrumental version, Side B. Illustrated teacher's instructions included. Kimbo Records, Box 55, Deal, N.J. 07723.

Primary Grades 1 to 3: Album 14; *Upper Elementary Grades 4 to 7:* Album 15. Each album contains four 78 r.p.m. records. Illustrated manual free with each album, $12.00 per album. Educational Activities, Inc., P. O. Box 392, Freeport, L.I., N.Y., 11520.

Rhythms for Group Activities: Record No. 22. *Elementary School Exercises to Music:* Record No. 4008. Record No. 4008 has vocal instructions for exercises. Voice and music, Hoctor Dance Records, Inc., Waldwick, N.J. 07463.

Primary Physical Fitness: Record RRC-803. *Intermediate Physical Fitness:* Record RRC-903. Rhythm Record Company, 9203 Nichols Road, Oklahoma City, Okla. 73102.

Music for Physical Fitness No. 1: Bowman Records 2851. Arm, shoulder, leg, and trunk development as well as flexibility and coordination, $5.95. Record Center, 2581 Piedmont Rd. N.E., Atlanta, Ga. 30324.

Suggested Films

Evaluating Physical Fitness. Athletic Institute, Room 805, Merchandise Mart, Chicago 54, Ill.

Focus on Fitness. Free of charge on a loan basis to all interested. For bookings write to: Audio-Visual Services, Eastman Kodak Company, Rochester, N.Y.

Methods of Teaching Physical Education. (Rental: $5.00), American Productions, P.O. Box 801, Riverside, California.

They Grow Up So Fast; Your Child's Health and Fitness (17 minute filmstrip explaining the parent's role in developing youth fitness). Washington, D.C., American Assn. for Health, Physical Education, and Recreation.

Chapter 9

Simple and Creative Games

FUNDAMENTAL PLAY AND SIMPLE GAMES

Although environmental conditions and standards of living change, the urge to play remains a dominant characteristic found in every race and in every country. Geographic location does not alter the original theme or idea, for games are built around age-old urges of running, jumping, hopping, chasing and fleeing, hiding and seeking, hunting, guessing and dodging. One may find hundreds of variations of these themes, with as many different names, but the original theme remains the same. Thus, we hear of Indians in Mexico playing a game which resembles the all familiar "London Bridge Is Falling Down" and of South Pacific Islanders playing an aboriginal version of "Hull Gull, Hand Full, How Many?" with sea shells.

The counterparts of the games to follow may be found of ageless vintage in many lands but are still popular with American youngsters today.

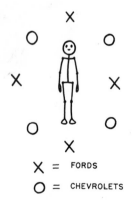

X = FORDS

O = CHEVROLETS

AUTOMOBILES OR AIRPLANES

Type: Running   Formation: Circle
Gym, playground   Players: 30 to 40
Grades: 1, 2

1. Players number off, one to four or six according to the size of the group.
2. No. 1's are Fords, No. 2's are Chevrolets, and so forth.
3. "It" calls the name of an automobile, as Ford, and all Fords run counterclockwise around the circle and return to their original place and dash to the center to touch "It."
4. The first runner to touch the starter wins the Ford race.
5. When each type of automobile has been called and the race run, the starter calls, "all winners" and this race determines the big winner.
6. Variations—Use names of race horses or airplanes.

FACE TO FACE   BACK TO BACK

BACK TO BACK

Gym, playground   Players: 12 to 16

1. "It" calls "back to back." Players must back up to partner.
2. "It" calls "face to face" and partners face and shake hands.
3. On the next call of "back to back" and each time thereafter, all players must change partners.
4. "It" tries to get a partner during the change and the player left out becomes "It."

BEATER GOES ROUND

Gym, playground, playroom   Grades: 3, 4
Formation: Circle   Players: 12 to 20

1. One player is outside the circle and carries a knotted cloth or folded newspaper. He walks around the circle and gives it to a player.
2. Receiver turns to his right and beats player lightly on back.
3. Player runs around circle to own place with beater chasing him.
4. Original starter has stepped into place of first receiver.

BIRD, BEAST, FISH

Gym, playground   Players: 18 to 24
Grades: 1, 2, 3   Formation: Circle

O – FISH
O – BEAST
O – BIRD

1. Group forms a three-deep circle.
2. Inside player is a Bird, middle player is a Beast and the outside player is a Fish.
3. "It" is in the middle; he will call a name—bird, beast or fish. The group which he names must all change places.
4. When the group is changing, "It" runs to an empty place and the person left without a place becomes "It."

CATCH THE BAT

Playground, playroom, gym   Players: 8 to 16
Grades: 2, 3, 4   Wand or bat
Formation: Circle

1. Players form a circle and number off.
2. One player stands in center and balances bat or wand with the fingertips.
3. Center player calls a number and releases the bat.
4. Number called tries to catch the bat before it falls to the floor or ground. If he succeeds, he becomes "It," and if he fails, he returns to his place in the circle while "It" calls another number.

CLUB SNATCH

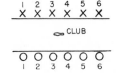

Gym, playground   Players: 12 to 18
Grades: 1, 2, 3

1. Divide players into teams, numbering each player.
2. Place an Indian club or any type object in the center between the two teams.
3. Instructor calls a number and the members of each team, corresponding with the number called, run out and try to get the club.
4. The member of the team that gets the club and gets across the restraining line without getting tagged wins the point for his team.
5. Team with the most points wins.

DOG CATCHER

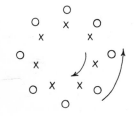

Gym, playground   Players: 20 to 80
Grades: 1 to 4

1. Name three or four kinds of dogs. Each child chooses the kind he wants to be. All go to one kennel.
2. Dog catcher calls one kind of dog. They run to opposite kennel. If caught, they are put in the pound.
3. After the dog catcher has had three turns, he tells how many dogs he has caught and chooses another to take his place until all are caught. The last one caught starts the new game.

DOUBLE CIRCLE

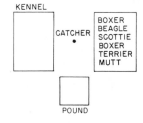

Gym, playground   Players: 8 to 24
Grades: 1, 2, 3   Formation: Double circle

1. The class is arranged in two concentric circles, one having one more member than the other.
2. On signal they begin to skip around in opposite directions until the whistle is blown or the music stops, then each player endeavors to secure a partner from the other circle.
3. One player is left without a partner. If any player is left out three times he must pay a penalty—do some stunt, sing a song, etc. Repeat.

WEAVE IN

Type: Running   Formation: Circle
Gym, playground   Players: 12 to 20
Grades: 1, 2, 3

1. One person is "It" and tags a person in the circle.
2. "It" and the tagged player start weaving in and out of the circle running in opposite directions.
3. The first one back to the empty space wins. The other player is "It" for the next game.

GIVE ME A LIGHT[1]

(Por Aqui Hay Candela—Puerto Rico)

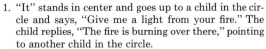

Gym, playground   Players: 10 to 20
Grades: 1, 2, 3
Formation: Circle or square with 4 ft. between players

1. "It" stands in center and goes up to a child in the circle and says, "Give me a light from your fire." The child replies, "The fire is burning over there," pointing to another child in the circle.
2. "It" goes to the child pointed out and repeats the question. In the meantime the children in the circle are changing places. If "It" finds a vacant place he stands there and the extra child becomes "It."

HAVE YOU SEEN MY SHEEP?

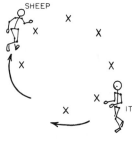

Playground, gym, playroom   Players: 8 to 12
Grades: 1, 2   Formation: Single circle

1. One player is "It" and walks around circle and asks any player, "Have you seen my sheep?" The player queries, "What does he look like?"
2. "It" describes his sheep (a player, as to eyes, hair, dress, etc.).
3. If the player guesses correctly, the sheep runs and he chases and tries to tag the sheep before he can run around the circle and return to his place.
4. "It" steps into the vacated place in the circle.
5. The player, if caught, becomes "It" and if he is not caught the chaser becomes "It" for another game.

HIGH WINDOWS

Gym, playground   Players: 8 to 12
Grades: 1, 2, 3
Formation: Single circle with "It" in center

1. "It" runs around inside of circle and tags a player.
2. "It" runs outside of circle attempting to run around the circle 3 times before being tagged by player chasing.
3. When he completes 3 rounds, players in circle raise their hands (joined) and cry, "High windows."
4. Runner comes into the circle and is safe. He continues to be "It."
5. If "It" is caught, chaser becomes "It."

PIONEERS AND INDIANS

Gym, playroom   Players: 2 equal teams
Grades: 3, 4   Any number

1. Play in two 10-minute halves.

---

[1] Miller, Nina: *Children's Games from Many Lands*. New York, Friendship Press, 1953.

2. Use slips of paper with names of supplies with numbered values. These slips are given to each pioneer.
3. Station a pioneer in the blockhouse. The object is for the pioneers to deliver supplies to the blockhouse without letting the Indians catch them.
4. If an Indian catches a pioneer, he searches him for the hidden supplies.
5. If the Indian cannot find it before 50 counts, the pioneer goes free. If he is caught again, he must surrender his supply.
6. The team with the most number of supplies wins.

HOOK ON

Playground, gym   Players: Entire class
Grade: 3

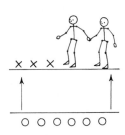

1. Pick four children to go to one end of gymnasium. Others go to opposite end. Both line up.
2. Leader blows whistle.
3. All try to hook on to one of four.
4. Try to keep back end of line away from children trying to hook on.
5. Move fast. Chain with fewest "hooks on" wins.

JUMP THE CREEK OR BROOK

Playground, gym, playroom   Grades: 1, 2, 3, 4
Players: Entire class

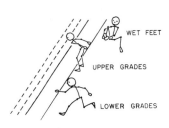

1. Two lines drawn with chalk inside, or a stick outside, represent the creek.
2. The last child over gets to draw the new line which widens the creek each time.
3. Any child who lands in the creek must take off his shoes and put them back on before he can re-enter the game.
4. For inside activity, it is suggested that third and fourth graders jump with both feet together. (Standing broad jump.)

JUMP THE SHOT

Playground, gym   Players: 8 to 12
Grades: 2 to 6   Formation: Circle

1. Knot the end of a long jump rope or attach a weight such as a beanbag or ball in a sack.
2. Teacher in lower grades, any player in upper grades stands in the center of the circle and turns, taking the rope under the feet of the players who jump over it.
3. Any player who touches the rope is out of the game.
4. The player who stays in the circle longest wins.

LOOSE CABOOSE

Playground, gym   Players: Entire class
Grades: 2, 3   Formation: Circle

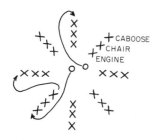

1. Players stand in groups of three in a circle.
2. First player is Engine; second is Chair Car; third is the Caboose.
3. There are two (or any number) of Loose Cabooses who try to attach themselves to the end of a line.
4. When this occurs, Engine becomes Loose Caboose and game continues.

MIDNIGHT

Playground, gym   Players: 20 to 80
Grades: 1, 2

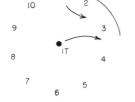

1. The Fox stands in his den and the Sheep in their fold.
2. The Fox wanders out into the meadow, and so do the Sheep.
3. The Sheep ask "What time is it?" and the Fox answers, "Two o'clock, ten o'clock," etc. The Sheep keep milling around, but when he answers "Midnight," they scamper for the fold.
4. All the Sheep that are tagged become Foxes, and the same procedure is repeated.
5. The last Sheep caught becomes the new Fox and a new game starts.

NUMBERS CHANGE

Playground, gym   Players: Entire class
Grades: 1, 2, 3   Formation: Circle

1. All players are given a number and one is chosen to be "It."
2. The players stand in a circle with "It" in the center.
3. He calls any two numbers.
4. The players whose numbers he calls exchange places, while the one who is "It" attempts to get one of their places in the circle.
5. The one of these left without a place is "It" for the next time and he calls the two numbers to change.

PLUG (An Old Broken Down Horse)

Playground, gym   Players: Entire class
Grade: 3   Rubber ball

1. Five players make Plug by locking arms around waist of player in front.
2. Others are Throwers. Thrower tries to hit Plug's tail. When hit below waist—Tail becomes a Thrower. Player who threw hit becomes Head.
3. Repeat.

POISON

Playground, gym   Players: 8 to 12
Grade: 2   Formation: Circle

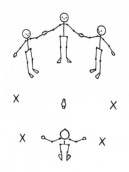

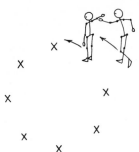

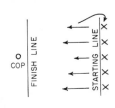

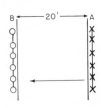

THE HOW

1. Players join hands and form circle with Indian club in center.
2. One player, chosen as the Leader, signals for the start of the game.
3. Players try to pull each other toward club to knock it down.
4. The player who knocks down the club is eliminated and the Leader replaces the club.
5. If the circle is broken, players on either side of the break are eliminated.
6. The last player to be eliminated is the winner and the leader in a new game.

COME ALONG

Gym, playground   Players: 20 to 30
Grades: 3, 4   Formation: Circle

1. One player is "It."
2. At signal, players face to right and extend right arm out in line with shoulder.
3. "It" runs around outside of circle, touches one of the outstretched arms saying, "Come along," and continues to run around circle.
4. The second player touches an outstretched arm and does the same.
5. This continues until about 10 players are running around the circle.
6. Leader cries, "Home" and players try to get to their space. Player left without a space becomes "It."

RED LIGHT

Playground, gym, playroom   Players: 20 to 40
Grades: 1, 2, 3

1. One player chosen as the Traffic Cop stands on the finish line with his back to the group.
2. The cop calls "Green Light," and the players advance cautiously while he counts.
3. The cop may call "Red Light" at any time and turn quickly and face the players. Any player in motion must return to the starting line.
4. The first player to cross the finish line becomes the traffic cop.
   This game can be used in teaching safety.

RED ROVER

Playground, gym   Players: 16 to 36
Grades: 1, 2   Formation: Line, running

1. Players join hands and form two lines facing each other, about 20' apart.
2. One player in each line is the Leader or Caller.
3. The Leader in Line B calls "Red Rover, Red Rover, let Johnny (any child) come over."
4. Johnny runs from Line A and tries to break through Line B. If he succeeds, he returns to his own line. If he fails, he stays with Line B.
5. Line A calls and so on alternately.
6. The side that finishes with the most players wins.
7. Callers should be changed at intervals.

Figure 26. Games are built around age-old urges of running, jumping, hopping, chasing and fleeing, hiding and seeking, guessing and dodging. (Courtesy of Elizabeth Glidden, Specialist in Elementary Physical Education, Los Angeles City Schools, Los Angeles, California.)

SARDINES

Playground   Players: Entire class
Grades: 3, 4

1. Sardine is a hide-and-seek game. It differs from the usual hide-and-seek game in that "It" hides and all of the other players set out to find him.
2. "It" is given time to hide and then, at a given signal, the other starts to hunt him.
3. Any player finding him must hide with him.
4. The last one finding the hiding place is "It" for the next game.

SKIP TAG

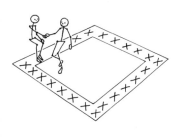

Any sizable room with seats   Players: 20 to 80
Grades: 1, 2, 3

1. Group is seated around sides of room with right hands extended.
2. "It" skips around and slaps palm of one player.
3. The chosen player skips after "It." If he is successful in tagging, he becomes "It" and the tagged player takes his seat; otherwise he returns to his seat.
4. If "It" is not tagged in three tries, he chooses a new "It."
5. In mixed groups, girls should tag boys and boys tag girls.
6. Players must skip and cannot cut corners.

SQUIRRELS IN TREES

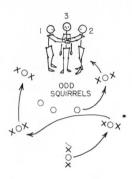

ODD
SQUIRRELS

Playground, gym, playroom   Players: 16 to 80
Grades: 1, 2

1. Number off by 3's. Nos. 1 and 2 form Tree by facing and holding hands. No. 3 is the Squirrel inside the Tree. Odd players are the Homeless Squirrels.
2. At a signal, all Squirrels must change Trees, and in the scramble the Odd Squirrels try to find a Tree.
3. Variation: In small groups play as tag with one Odd Squirrel and one Chaser (Hunter). The Odd Squirrel ducks into a Tree and the other Squirrel must vacate and find another Tree. If the Squirrel is tagged, he becomes Chaser.
4. Change positions of Trees and Squirrels often to allow running for all.

TAG IN BRIEF

Playground, gym   Players: Entire class
Grades: 1, 2, 3

Nose-and-Toe Tag

Runners cannot be tagged when holding nose with one hand, toes with other hand.

Hindu Tag

Safe when kneeling, with forehead touching ground.

Ostrich Tag

Safe when holding nose with right hand, with right arm under right leg.

Hang Tag

Safe when hanging on to something, such as tree limb or post.

Stoop Tag

Safe when stooping down.

Squat Tag

Squat for safety.

Hook-On Tag

Hook onto arm of another player to keep from being tagged.

Color Tag

Safe when touching a certain color such as red, blue, green, etc.

ARM'S LENGTH TAG

Playground, gym, playroom   Players: Entire class
Grades: 1, 2, 3

1. Two players stand each with an arm extended at full length at shoulder level.
2. Each tries to touch the other above the wrist without being touched in return.
3. A touch on the extended hand does not count.

THREE DEEP

Playground, gym   Players: Entire class
Grades: 1, 2, 3   Formation: Circle

1. Players get into double circle.
2. The chaser ("C") chases runner ("R").
3. "R" may save himself by getting in front of a group making it three deep.
4. When group is three deep, outside persons becomes "R."
5. If and when "R" is caught, he becomes "C."
6. "R" must go into circle from outside when making it three deep. When being chased, he may cut through. Variations may be made to this game by making it Two Deep, or Four Deep, depending upon number of group.

WEATHER COCK

Playground, gym, playroom   Players: Entire class
Grades: 1, 2, 3

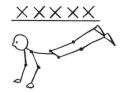

Children should know directions North, East, South and West.

1. One player represents weather bureau and stands in front of others and tells the way the wind blows.
2. Weather bureau says, "The wind blows north," the players turn quickly to the north, etc.
3. When he says "whirl wind," the players spin around three times on right heel.
   Play rapidly for interest.

COPYCAT

Gym, playground, playroom   Players: 10 to 12
Formation: Line with "Cat" in front   Grades: 1, 2, 3

1. Cat performs. He may imitate a frog, a rabbit, a bear, a crab, a mule kicking, or a bird pruning its feathers.
2. Players in line imitate movements and sit.
3. First player to guess what the Cat was imitating becomes the Cat.

CHARLIE BROWN

Gym, playground   Players: 12 to 20
Grades: 1, 2, 3   Soft rubber ball

Charlie Brown in the comic strip is well known for his teams that never win and his luck of always falling on his face if a ball comes near him.

1. Charlie rolls out ball and lies down.
2. Players walk in slow motion to recover the ball.
3. Player who recovers ball throws to hit Charlie. If he misses, he takes Charlie's place. If he hits, the game goes on with the same Charlie.

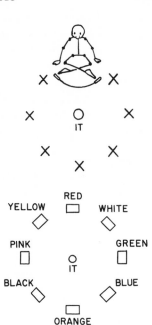

FASTEN SEAT BELTS

Gym, playroom, playground   Players: 10 to 30
Grades: 1, 2   Jump rope for each player
Formation: Single circle

1. "It" (stewardess) stands in center of circle.
2. Players stand in circle with a jump rope in front of each player.
3. Stewardess calls "Board plane." Players move clockwise.
4. Stewardess calls "Find your seats." Each child sits back of rope.
5. Stewardess calls "Fasten seat belts." First child to tie rope around body becomes the next stewardess.

COLOR ME

Gym, playroom   Players: 8 to 12
Grades: 1, 2   1 package of construction paper
Formation: Single circle

1. "It" stands in center of circle.
2. Players march clockwise.
3. "It" says, "Color me red."
4. "It" tries to get to red before the other players. If he does, the last player to get behind a color is "It."

BLAST OFF!

Gym, playground   Players: 20 to 30
Grades: 1, 2, 3   Formation: Two lines

1. Players squat on line 1.
2. Captain does "count-down" from ten to zero as players gradually rise to standing position.
3. As Captain counts "zero" players run to opposite line 2. First player across becomes Captain.

CONSTRUCTED CREATIVE GAMES

In the average school an inventory of games would include checkers and boards, Chinese checker boards, marbles, and a few bingo sets. Private schools would rate higher, for student bodies and staffs are smaller, and often there is more money left from the equipment budget to buy new games. Active Parent-Teacher Associations in the public schools have felt the need for more equipment and have raised money to buy ping-pong tables and shuffleboard sets. They could, likewise, help establish game libraries. The game library functions as any library. For example, a child who is giving a party could check out a number of games and return them at a designated time. Such a library should include puzzles of metal or wood, magic tricks, manufactured table games such as dominoes, checkers, monopoly, and larger constructed games.

Actually, there is no point for having a poverty game program in any school, for children are interested primarily in play and are creative enough to make their own games if given encouragement. The rag bag, the button box, the attic, the garage or the grocery store yields adequate materials for constructing a multitude of games. Building contractors are Santa Clauses for enterprising youngsters who really want to help build permanent games for their schools. Cheese boxes, fish buckets, apple and orange crates, and hundreds of feet of beaver board, sheet rock, moulding, plyboard and lumber go each day into junk heaps that would supply the demands of game-hungry children.

There are numerous manufactured games available to schools with money allotted for such purposes. The games described below can be made by the children in the upper elementary grades; they are as inexpensive and expendable as the resourcefulness of teacher and pupils. The actual outlay of money should be for the purchase of nails, tacks, paint, thinner, and paint brush. Few homes exist where one could not find small amounts of usable enamel that will eventually harden. Paint is essential—the attractiveness of the finished game will depend largely on the eye appeal of bright, clear color.

PITCHING GAMES

Board Games

Because the bulletin board type of game has many uses, it will be as much at home in the classroom as in the playroom. The classroom teacher will find such games most helpful in checking absorption of subject matter which cover states, capitals, terrain, industries, foodstuffs, etc. The inserts can be made in art class. Manila, tag board, wrapping paper or detail paper are satisfactory. The design may be done in water color or tempera paint. Rubber darts are cheap and available at five and ten stores.

Molding, lath,
or board
1″ x 2″

Window glass
36″ x 36″
or
24″ x 36″

BULLETIN BOARD

Frame as for a picture. Back with heavy paste board, beaver board, or wall board. Secure on three sides, leaving an opening at the top to permit removal of game inserts.

Maps

Integration of subject matter using a map of the United States is shown in the following game. The room may be divided into two teams by numbering off by seat rows, or by sex, if the boys and girls are equally divided. First three rows are Blue team, second three rows form the Red team. A member of the Red team throws a dart at the map and must name the capital of the state the dart hits. If his identification is correct, the Red team scores one point. The Blue team throws next. The team scoring ten points first wins.

SKILLS AND RULES RELATED TO TEAM AND INDIVIDUAL SPORTS

Knowledge of team games and individual sports may be gained through games that use miniature playing courts or fields and correct game terminology. In all of the following games the players are divided into two teams. It is better to have a legal number of players necessary for the prescribed game and positions designated by the team captains. This procedure familiarizes the students with playing positions and duties of specific players, and provides for turns as in the batting order for baseball, etc.

Each player, in turn, is given 8 darts and allowed to throw until a score or out is made. A coin may be tossed to see which team has the first turn. Two players should be chosen as score keepers. Regulation score pads may be used or dittoed or mimeographed sheets modified to suit the indoor game. The abbreviations used should be self-explanatory but modifications of rules are indicated.

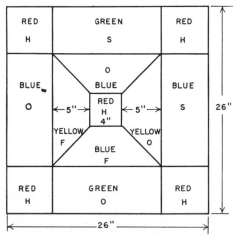

BASEBALL[2]

H—Home Run
O—Out
F—Foul Ball
S—Strike

Colors for the divisions are suggested. Any available paint may be used.

---

[2] Modification of a game by O'Keefe, Patric, and Aldrichin, Anita: *Education Through Physical Activities.* St. Louis, The C. V. Mosby Co., 1955, p. 197.

BASEBALL

RED S	GREEN O	RED T
H BLUE	B BLUE	F BLUE
	D YELLOW — H RED — S YELLOW	
F	O BLUE	H
ST	T GREEN	ST

B—Ball   D—Double (2 Base)
F—Foul   T—Triple (3 Base)
H—Home Run   O—Out
S—Single (1 Base)   ST—Strike

FOOTBALL

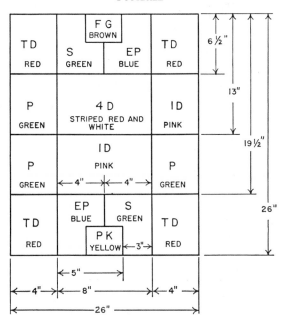

TD—Touchdown—6 points   EP—Extra Point—1 point
FG—Field Goal—3 points   1D—First Down—gets another throw if
PK—Place Kick—3 points   last dart hits this square
    S—Safety—2 points   4D—Fourth Down—gives up darts
                          P—Penalty—gives up darts

BASKETBALL

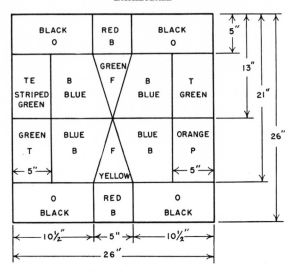

B—Basket—2 points
F—Free Throw—1 point
O—Out of Bounds—loses dart
T—Travel—loses darts
TE—Technical Foul—opposing team gets one throw
P—Personal Foul—opposing team gets two throws

SOCCER

LAVENDER SD	RED FG	GREEN O
F YELLOW	PK	FG BLUE
FG BLUE	P K STRIPED GREEN	F YELLOW
O GREEN	F G RED	SP BROWN

PLACE KICK ORANGE

FG—Field Goal—2 points
PK—Penalty Kick—1 point
O—Out of Bounds—loses darts
Pl K—Place Kick—continues to throw

SD—Successful Dribble—continues to throw
SP—Successful Pass—continues to throw
F—Foul—opposing team gets darts

VOLLEYBALL

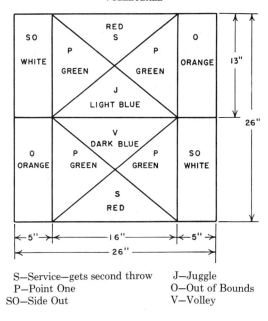

S—Service—gets second throw   J—Juggle
P—Point One   O—Out of Bounds
SO—Side Out   V—Volley

TARGET SKILLS

Most of these games may be done individually on cork, plywood, or different types of ceiling or wall board. Storage space is an item to be considered. Vacuum darts will adhere easily to glass but will not stick to uneven surfaces. Plyboard must be painstakingly sanded and heavily coated with varnish or shellac. Metal darts will stick in any soft wood or heavy cork but are taboo in most school systems because of the safety hazards.

BOMBS AWAY!

Paint a salt box. Cut a round hole in one end the size of a quarter. Teach pupils how to drop five marbles accurately, one at a time, into the box. The best scorer out of each five tries wins. A cigar box may be used in place of a salt box.

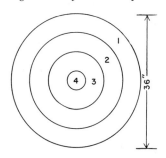

TARGET THROW

Use overhand throw
Inside: Beanbags, rubber or tennis ball
Outside: Tennis or softball

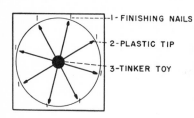

WHEEL OR DIAL WITH NUMBERS

1 - FINISHING NAILS

2 - PLASTIC TIP

3 - TINKER TOY

Class is divided into two to four teams and each team numbers off one through ten. A selected leader spins the dial and asks a question. Teams may alternate or the first one who raises his hand after the number is called may answer the question. The questions may be made by the class or teacher on any desired subject. This is also a good party game.

PEG BOARD

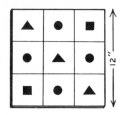

12″

This board has holes for round, square, and triangular pegs. This game is suitable for the first and second grades and is excellent for children with poor manual coordination. Couples may make the play more interesting by counting the length of time it takes to get each peg in its proper place. The boards and pegs can be made in the manual training shop. The board should be painted a light color and the pegs dark red, blue and green.

FINGER SHUFFLEBOARD

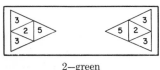

2—green
6—blue
5—red

Board may be painted on wrapping paper for table use or painted on wall or plyboard. Use checkers or bottle tops for pucks and thump with middle finger. Four may play as for horseshoes and the game point may be set by the players.

There are many pitching games that may be made at little expense. Rings may be tenniquoits of rubber or may be made in class from rope, tubing, or rubber fruit-jar rings. Boards may be made to hang on the wall, stand as an easel, or lay on the floor.

HORSESHOES FOR INSIDE

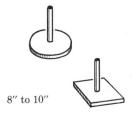

8″ to 10″

Set stakes a certain distance apart according to age level. Use regular rules for pitching horseshoes. Small rope rings, 6 inches in diameter, are suitable. The rings are secured with string and Scotch or bicycle tape. If tenniquoits are used, lead washers should be imbedded in the bottom of the board for weight.

WALL BOARDS

Floor boards that lie flat may be made any desired size from 12" x 12" to 36" x 36". Nails or dowel stakes are vertical. The size of the ring will be indicated by the size of the board and stakes.

Eye screws   Finishing nails slanted
12" x 12"   Fruit-jar rings

SCHNOZZLE

Beaver board
Molding or lath frame
Dowel pin

Large numbers of children can be entertained in true carnival spirit while developing skill in pitching accuracy. Small rubber balls or beanbags may be pitched into wastebaskets, nail kegs, syrup buckets or shallow cheese boxes. The bags or balls can be pitched through holes cut in boards in different shapes such as circles, squares, triangles or half circles. Faces or any design may be painted on the board to fit the need. The underhand pitch should be used and the holes should be large enough to permit easy passage of the bag or ball.

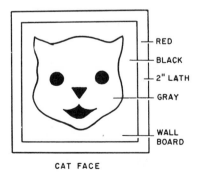

CAT FACE

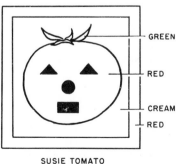

SUSIE TOMATO
(USE IN UNIT ON FOODS)

PITCHING

EASEL

Equipment. 4 rubber balls, 2″ in diameter, or 4 beanbags, 5″ square filled with beans, peas, or gravel. Duck is the most durable of fabrics but colored Indian Head domestic is attractive and is available in all colors to tie in with the color scheme of the board.

Rules. The teacher or players can set the game. One point for eyes, two for nose and three for mouth. It is suggested that the children set and draw their own pitching line and set up penalties for stepping over this line.

PUT A SPOOK IN A HAUNTED HOUSE

A box is decorated to look like a haunted house. Ghosts are made of white cloth with beanbag heads. Each ghost has a number written on it. If the first grader is able to give the correct number, he may throw the spook in the haunted house.

Santa Claus's sleigh or pack, the Easter Bunny's basket and other seasonal characters with their unique equipment may be used. Jack-o'-Lantern toss game made from a scooped-out pumpkin and played with numbered beanbags is also a good seasonal game.

OTHER SUGGESTIONS

ALPHABET GAME

Individual letters painted on construction paper may be mounted on detail paper, heavy cardboard, or a very light wall or plyboard. Letters may be sawed out and painted a bright color. Number of sets depends on the size of the class, a different color being used for each team. Word lists are secured for each grade, and teacher or pupils calls out the word. Children with the letter rush to the floor and the team that spells the word correctly first wins. Two cards should be made of letters that commonly appear twice in a word.

BOX HOCKEY

Players: 2 to 4

Equipment. The frame illustrated in the diagram consists of two sides, two ends, and a middle partition. It may or may not have a bottom. Dimensions of the frame are 3½ feet in width, 7 feet in length, and should be made of 2-inch material. Other equipment needed includes a ball or piece of wood 2 inches in diameter and hockey sticks or any stick 3 feet in length.

Rules. The players stand facing each other on opposite sides of the box. Each player's goal is the hole at the end of the box on his left. The object of the game is to hit the ball through this hole with the stick. To start the game, the ball is placed in the groove at the top of the middle partition. The two players place their hockey sticks on the floor on opposite sides of the partition, raise them, and strike them together above the ball. This is done three times and after the third tap, the ball is hit. If the ball is knocked out of the box, it is put in play by tossing it on the floor

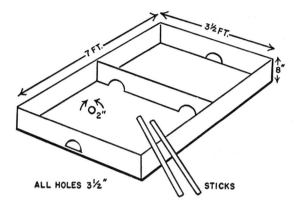

of the box opposite the point where it went out. Resume play after each score with a *face off*. Players may not step inside the box. One point is scored each time a player puts the puck through the hole in the end of the box. Game—5 points.

TIN CAN WALKERS

Cut two holes in each of two large tin cans. Run a string through each hole in each can and tie it together at waist height through both cans.
Use can to walk on.

STILTS

Use two 2 x 4 boards. Nail a footrest block on each board about 10 inches from the floor. Use the stilts for balancing while walking with them.

BOWLING GAME

Take 10 one-quart cartons, round type, and paint each a different color. Make a half-inch slit in top of each and insert ice cream paddles. Color each differently. Number each paddle. Place cartons four, three, two and one in a row like bowling pins. Tennis balls can be used and rolled various distances depending upon the grade. Various scoring methods can be used. Added scores are suggested.

HOOP OBSTACLE COURSE

Set up an obstacle course of boxes, draw parallel lines, etc. Paint a barrel hoop or make one from wire. Each pupil rolls the hoop over the course.

SUGGESTED READINGS

Carlson, Bernice, and Ginglend, David: *Play Activities for the Retarded Child.* New York, Abingdon Press, 1965.

Carter, Joel: *How To Make Athletic Equipment.* New York, The Ronald Press Company, 1960.

Donnelly, R. J.; Helms, W. G.; and Mitchell, Elmer: *Active Games and Contests.* New York, The Ronald Press Company, 1958.

Forbush, William B., and Allen, Harry: *The Book of Games for Home, School, and Playground.* Revised Ed. Philadelphia, The John C. Winston Co., 1954.

Hindman, Darwin: *Handbook of Active Games.* Revised Ed. New York, Prentice-Hall, Inc., 1951.

Hunt, Sarah, and Cain, Ethyl: *Games the World Around.* New York, A. S. Barnes & Co., 1950.

National Recreation Association, 315 Fourth Avenue, New York:

    No. 332, *Make Your Own Games*

    No. 258, *Outline Guide in Arts and Crafts*

    No. 277, *Homemade Play Apparatus*

    No. 272, *Table Football Game*

    No. 240, *A Folding Table for Table Tennis*

Pelton, B. W.: *How To Build Games and Toys.* New York, D. van Nostrand Co., Inc., 1951.

Peter, John: *McCall's Giant Golden Make-It Book.* New York, Simon and Schuster, 1953.

Sehon, Elizabeth L.; Anderson, Marian H.; Hodgins, Winifred W.; and VanFossen, Gladys R.: *Physical Education Methods for Elementary Schools.* 2d Ed. Philadelphia, W. B. Saunders Company, 1953.

Squires, John: *Fun Crafts for Children.* Englewood Cliffs, N.J., Prentice-Hall, Inc., 1964.

Chapter 10

Relays

Relays are a boon to the teacher who has oversized classes. A large number may participate with a minimum of organization but the end results are manifold. Most children enjoy this activity and learn skills and team co-operation while developing large muscles and coordination.

ORGANIZATION OF TEAMS

Boys and girls on the primary level should compete on the same teams. On the upper elementary level it is best, generally, to have the boys compete with boys and the girls with girls. However, when there is an equal sex distribution and class members do not wish to be separated, mixed competition is highly desirable. Other helpful suggestions are:

1. Permanent teams, in which there is an equality of skill and size, are organizational time savers.
2. Change team captains at regular intervals.
3. Train and assign student officials.
4. Divide your class by counting off 1-2, 1-2, and so forth, all the 1's being in one line and all the 2's in another line. It is unwise to let the children choose their team members too often, for one child always tends to be the last one chosen. Another way of dividing the class is to have on one side all children whose name begins with A–L, and all whose name begins with M–Z on the other. Or have all whose birthday is from January–June on one team and all whose birthday is from July–December on the other.

TRUE RELAY

1. Establish the type of formation, starting line, turning line, method of touching off, signal for starts, and objective of relay. (Right hand to right hand is most accepted touch-off.)
2. Possible fouls should be discussed and a penalty set. A team should not be disqualified because a member commits a foul, but a point for each foul should be subtracted from the place won.

Team	A	B	C	D
Place	1st	2nd	3rd	4th
Points	5	3	2	1
Fouls	3	0	1	1
	2	3	1	0
Score	2nd	1st	3rd	4th

3. Start relays by a signal, whistle, or oral command. (1–2–3 go! Emphasize the word *go!*)

4. Completion of relay may be indicated by the first member of each team raising hands high, by sitting down, or the whole team may squat or sit down.

MODIFIED RELAYS

The modified relay can be used with primary grade children where the details of the true relay seem too complicated. This type of relay is run in heats and each child who comes in first in his heat wins a point for his team. The team scoring the most points wins the relay. Otherwise, directions for the true relay may serve as an adequate guide for organization. Relays that use the line or file formation are

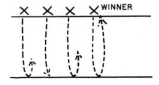

more suitable and the type will be governed by the skill of the group.

RELAY FORMATIONS

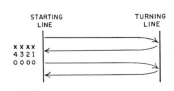

SHUTTLE

16 to 24 per team

No. 1 runs to opposite line and touches off No. 2 and goes to foot of line. No. 2 runs, and so forth. All runners end up on opposite sides.

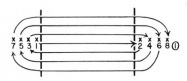

SINGLE FILE OR DOUBLE LINE

8 to 16 per team

No. 1 runs, turns, runs back and touches off No. 2 and goes to foot of line. No. 2 runs, and so forth.

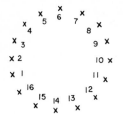

CIRCLE

8 to 16 per team

No. 1 runs around circle clockwise or counterclockwise and returns to place. Nos. 2, 3, and so on, run circle until all have run.

TYPES OF RELAYS

Most of the relays listed below use a parallel line or file formation. Distance indicates the number of feet from the starting line to the goal or turning line. The grade level for which relay is best suited is also given. The types of relays described include:

1. Relays using skills and stunts learned in self-testing activities.
2. Relays using locomotor skills.
3. Relays requiring equipment.
4. Relays related to team sports
5. Obstacle relays.
6. Novelty relays suitable for special event days and parties.

Relays Using Skills and Stunts Learned in Self-testing Activities

Grades: 1 to 6   Distance: 15 to 20 feet

Children race, using the prescribed stunt from the starting line to turning point and back. These stunts are described fully in the chapter on stunts and tumbling.

Bear Walk	Kangaroo Hop	Log Roll
Crab Walk	Lame Puppy Walk	Double Line Formation
Duck Walk	Monkey Run	Wheelbarrow Relay
Frog Jump	Rabbit Hop	

Figure 27. The crab relay is great fun for children. (Courtesy of *The Instructor*. Photograph by Edith Brockway.)

Relays Using Locomotor Skills

Grades: 1 to 6   Distance: 20 to 40 feet

Galloping.

Hopping—Hold one foot at front or back.

Jumping—Feet close together. Take small jumps with little knee flexion.

Skipping—Low and High Skip.

Sliding.

Running.

These locomotor movements are described fully in Chapter 12: Rhythms and Dance.

RUNNING RELAY

Race using command for start: On your mark, get set, go!

First through third grade use standing start.

Fourth through sixth grade use crouch start.

LINE RELAY

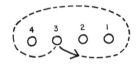

Grades: 4 to 6

Teams number off consecutively from front to back. Teacher or leader calls a number. This child steps out of the line to his right and runs counterclockwise around his team, returning to his original place in line. Winner scores a point. Team with the highest score wins.

RESCUE RELAY

Grades: 3 to 6   Distance: 30 to 50 feet

A leader stands behind a goal line facing his team which is lined up behind the starting line. On a signal, the leader runs to the first player of his team, grasps him by the wrist and runs back to the goal line. The rescued player then runs back and gets another player, and so forth, until all have been rescued.

Walking: Grades 1 to 6. Arms are bent and elbows are held close to sides.

Relays Requiring Equipment

ALL UP RELAY

Grades: 4 to 5   Distance: 20 to 40 feet

Equipment: 1 to 3 Indian clubs for each team

Chalk two circles the desired number of feet from the starting line. Place one, two or three Indian clubs in one circle. First in line runs and takes the club out of one circle and places it in the second circle, and runs back and touches off the second player who returns the club to circle No. 1. If a club falls over, the player must return and stand it upright.

BALANCE RELAY

Grades: 2 to 6   Distance: 20 to 30 feet
Equipment: Beanbags, erasers, or books

Walk erectly, arms at side, balacing one of the listed objects on top of the head. If the object falls off, the player must stop in his tracks and replace it, then continue.

BOWLING

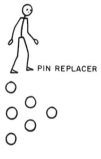

PIN REPLACER

Grades: 4 to 6   Distance: 20 to 40 feet
Equipment: 6 Indian clubs and one baseball for each team

Assign one child on each team to replace pins and call out score. Place pins 6 inches apart in a triangle. Roll the baseball and knock over as many pins as possible. A player gets one point for each club knocked over. Each bowler retrieves the ball and passes it to next in line.

CAP TRANSFER

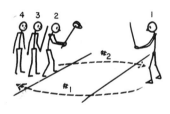

Grades: 4 to 6   Distance: 20 to 40 feet
Equipment: 3 sticks and one cap for each team

The first three children on a team are given sticks. No. 1 is stationed at the turning point. No. 2 places a cap on the end of his stick and runs to No. 1 and transfers the cap to his stick. No. 1 returns to the starting line, transfers the cap to No. 3, gives his stick to No. 4 and goes to the foot of the line, and so on, until all have run. The team regaining its original position first wins. If a cap falls off, it must be picked up with the stick without the aid of hands.

CIRCLE RELAY

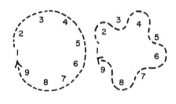

Grades: 2 to 6
Equipment: Handkerchief or beanbag for each team

Give starting player handkerchief. On signal, player runs around the circle and passes the handkerchief to person in front of him. First circle to finish wins.
Variation: Zigzag in and out between members of team.

DRIVING THE PIG TO MARKET

STILE

Grades: 4 to 6   Distance: 20 feet
Equipment: Wand and dumbell for each team, chair or stool

Dumbell must be rolled up to and around stile (stool). Dumbell is controlled by sliding the wand back and forth along the hand grip.

FETCH AND CARRY

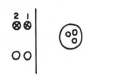

Grade: 4   Distance: 20 feet
Equipment: 3 beanbags

Draw a 15-inch circle about 5 feet in front of each team's starting line. 20 to 30 feet from the starting line draw 3 crosses about two feet apart. No. 1 picks up beanbags one at a time, making three trips to place them on the crosses, and runs back and touches off No. 2 who returns the beanbags to the circle in three trips. 3 does as 1, and 4 as 2, and so forth.

GOAT BUTTING

Grades: 3, 4   Distance: 20 feet
Equipment: Any large ball, as a basketball

Start in crouch position with ball on starting line, butt ball to turning line and back over starting line.

HOOP ROLLING

Grades: 4 to 6   Distance: 40 to 50 feet
Equipment: Hoop and flat board for each team

Roll hoop to turning line, pick up, roll back.

MERRY-GO-ROUND OR DIZZY-IZZY

Grades: 3 to 6   Distance: 30 to 50 feet
Equipment: Baseball bat for each team

First player stands bat up straight, places palms down on top and head on back of hands. Walks around bat 8 times, drops it and runs to turning line and back to foot of line. No. 2 picks up bat as soon as it is dropped and repeats action of No. 1.

OVER AND UNDER

UNDER

OVER

Grades: 2 to 6
Equipment: Volleyball, soccerball or basketball

Stand in stride position, about 14 inches apart. No. 1 passes ball over head to No. 2 who passes it through his legs to No. 3, etc. No. 4 runs to head of line and starts ball overhead to No. 1. When No. 1 returns to head of line, relay is finished.

PUSH BALL

Grades: 5, 6   Distance: 20 feet
Equipment: Any large ball, 6 inches in diameter or over

Push ball with stick over goal line, pick it up and carry back to next player.

SKIP ROPE RELAY

Grades: 1, 2, 3   Distance: 30 to 50 feet
Equipment: Short rope

Skip to turning line and back. Children learning to jump a short rope find it much easier to run than to stand still.

STRIDE BALL

Grade: 4
Equipment: Volleyball or
soccerball for each team

Teams stand in deep-stride position and pass or roll the ball between legs to the back of the line. Last player in line carries the ball to the head of the line, passing the team to the left, and starts the ball again through the legs.

Relays Related to Team Sports

SOCCER RELAYS

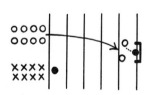

SOCCER RELAY

Grade: 6   Distance: Soccer field
Equipment: Soccerball   Formation: Double line

On signal, couples pass the ball back and forth to each other down the field, make a goal and pass the ball back to the starting line. Only the feet may be used and neither player shall play the ball twice consecutively.

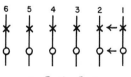

LINE RELAY

Grades: 5, 6

Divide group into teams of six. Draw parallel lines 10 yards apart. Teams line up on parallel lines with one team player on each line. On signal, No. 1 runs to the first 10-yard line and catches the hand of No. 2 who runs and catches the hand of No. 3. When No. 5 has the hand of No. 6 all continue to the starting line. The team that crosses the starting line first wins.

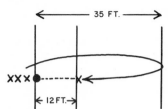

RUN AND ROLL RELAY

Grade: 4   Distance: Total 35 feet, 12 feet to first line
Equipment: Soccerball for each team

First player runs to and across the turning line, returns to the 12-foot line and rolls the ball to No. 2. If the waiting player cannot reach the ball, No. 1 must retrieve the ball, return to the 12-foot line and roll it again.

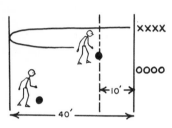

SOCCER RELAY VARIATIONS

Grades: 4 to 6   Distance: 40 feet

Dribble to turning line and back to within 10 to 12 feet of line and pass with the inside of the foot. In the fourth grade the waiting player is allowed to stop the ball with his hands. In the fifth and sixth grades the waiting player traps the ball.

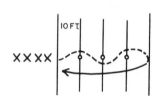

ZIGZAG RELAY

Grades: 4 to 6   Distance: 40 feet
Equipment: Soccerball for each team, 3 Indian clubs

Space Indian clubs 10 feet apart between starting and turning lines. Dribble in and out between clubs to turning line, pick up ball and run straight back to team.

FOOTBALL RELAYS

Refer to *Cross Over* and *Baseball Relay* in softball section of relays.
Refer to *Circle* and *Zigzag Volley* in volleyball section of relays.

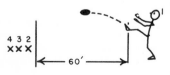

RUN AND PUNT RELAY

Grade: 6   Distance: 60 feet
Equipment: Football for each player

First player is given a ball. On signal, he runs to turning line and punts to waiting player and moves back to make room for him. The team that gets all team members to the opposite side first wins.

CENTER PASS RELAY

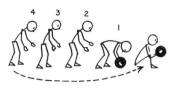

Grade: 6   Distance: 10 feet
Equipment: Football for each team

Teams line up on parallel lines spaced about 8 to 10 feet apart. The first player places the ball on the ground and on signal passes the ball between his legs to the player behind him. Number 2 places the ball on the ground and repeats the action. The last player to receive the ball runs to the front of the line and sits. The line that finishes first wins.

VOLLEYBALL RELAYS

THROW AND CATCH

Grade: 4   Distance: 30 feet
Equipment: Volleyball for each team, long rope and jump standards

In front of teams, stretch a rope across standards at a height of 6 to 8 feet. On signal, the first player runs forward, tosses the ball over the rope, catches it on the other side and returns to his team, hands the ball to player No. 2 and, passing to the right, goes to the foot of the line. *Fouls:* Failure to throw ball over rope; failure to catch ball after it has cleared the rope.

CIRCLE VOLLEY RELAY

Grade: 6
Equipment: One volleyball for each team

Divide group into teams of eight; each team forms a circle with 7- to 9-foot space between players. No. 1 starts the ball by throwing it in a high arch, slightly above the head of No. 2 who receives the ball and hits it to No. 3. Each player may play the ball as many times as is necessary to get it into a favorable position for passing. If a player drops the ball, he retrieves it, takes his position and throws it to the next player. Groups that are more advanced in skills may put the ball in play by hitting the ball up in the air, then hitting it to the next player. The team that gets the ball back to No. 1 first, wins. *Fouls:* Holding and throwing except in cases mentioned.

ZIGZAG VOLLEY

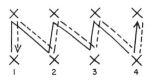

Grade: 6

Team may be divided equally into parallel lines facing each other. The ball is volleyed back and forth down the line and back. The team that gets the ball back to the starter first, wins.

BASKETBALL RELAYS

BASKET SHOOTING RELAY

Grades: 5, 6   Distance: 15 to 20 feet from goal
Equipment: Basketball for each team

On signal, the first player runs to shooting position and
tries to make a basket. He shoots until a basket is made
and runs back to the line and gives the next player the
ball. Team finishing first wins.
Variation: Dribble the ball into position and try for a
basket and pass the ball back to next in line. Run to foot
of line. Determine pass to be used before relay starts. It
may be overhead, side, two arm, shoulders, etc. See
Basketball Skills.

POST BALL

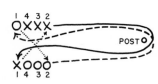

Grades: 4 to 6   Distance: 30 to 40 feet
Equipment: Two volleyballs, one post or base

Only two teams should use one post. On signal the first
player runs around the post, to the foot of the opposing
team's line and throws the ball to No. 2 on his team, who
repeats the action of No. 1 and throws the ball to No. 3.
The last player who reaches the end of the opposing line,
raises the ball high above his head to indicate that his
team has finished.

BASKETBALL PASS RELAY

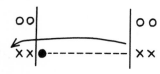

Grades: 3 to 6   Distance: 10 to 15 feet
Zigzag Pass   Players: 10 feet apart
Shuttle Pass

Player may take one step before passing, runs to end of
opposite line, moving to the right. Stipulate type of pass.

ARCH GOAL BALL RELAY

Grades: 4, 5   Distance: 15 to 20 feet
Equipment: One basketball for each team

On signal, the first player passes the ball over his head to
the player behind him, and so on down the line. When
the last player receives the ball, he runs forward past the
line and attempts to shoot for a goal, using a chest or
shoulder throw. He is allowed 3 tries. Whether he is
successful or not, he takes his position at the head of the
line and passes the ball overhead. To determine the winning team, score one point for finishing first and two
points for each goal. Deduct one point for each foul.

SOFTBALL RELAYS

POST OR BASEBALL RELAY

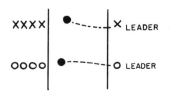

Grades: 4 to 6   Distance: 10 to 12 feet
Equipment: Baseball or beanbag

Choose a leader for each team. Leaders stand about 10 to 12 feet in front of teams in parallel lines. On signal, the leader throws the ball to the first player using the underhand throw. The first player catches the ball, throws it back to the leader and immediately squats in line. The leader throws to the second in line, etc. Game continues until all players are squatting. The winning team finishes first with the fewest errors. *Errors:* Failure to catch ball, dropping ball.

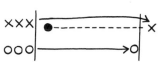

Variation: *Pass and Squat.* Grades 4 to 6. This relay is played in the same manner except for the formation. Players line up side by side.

CROSS OVER RELAY

Grades: 4, 5   Distance: Determined by the skill
                               of the players, 15 to 20 feet
Equipment: Softball for each team

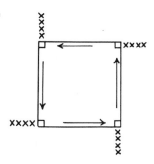

Give a ball to the first player on each team. On signal, No. 1 runs to the goal line, turns and throws the ball to next player in line and steps back. No. 2 catches the ball and repeats the action of No. 1, and steps in front of No. 1. The team that finishes first with the fewest fouls wins.

ROUND THE BASES

Grades: 3 to 6   Players: 10 to 36, two to four teams

Two teams: One team lines up at second base, the other team lines up at home plate. If there are enough teams, line up behind all bases. On signal, No. 1 starts around the four bases, touching off No. 2 at the base he started from. Side finishing first wins. Fouls: Running over 3 feet outside base line; failure to touch each base.

Obstacle Relays

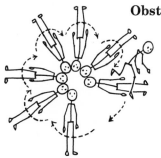

HUMAN HURDLE OR SPOKE RELAY

Grades: 5, 6

Each team forms a circle and all lie on floor with heads touching in the center. One player is designated as starter. On signal, he jumps up and hurdles (clockwise) each player and when he reaches his place, he touches off the next player and takes his original place on the floor.

HUMAN OBSTACLE

Grade: 5   Distance: 20 to 30 feet

Place 4 children between starting and turning lines, spaced several feet apart. No. 1 stands upright, No. 2 stands in stride position, No. 3 stoops in leapfrog position, No. 4 stands upright. The first player runs around No. 1, crawls through the legs of No. 2, leaps over No. 3, runs around No. 4 and returns in a straight line to his team.

LEAPFROG RELAY

Grades: 4, 5

Each team forms a circle and bends over in leapfrog position, facing the same direction. Player designated as the starter, leaps over each player, returns to original position and touches off the player in front of him.

SERPENTINE

Grade: 4   Distance: 20 to 40 feet
Equipment: Indian clubs for each team

Place clubs about 2 feet apart, starting 2 feet from the turning line. Player zigzags between clubs and runs straight back to line.

STOOL HURDLE

Equipment: 3 stools   Distance: 20 feet

Place stools 5 feet apart. Player straddle hops the first, does a flat-footed jump over the second and leaps over the third, runs to turning line and returns in a straight line to his team.

Novelty Relays

(Suitable for special days and parties)

BALLOON OR FEATHER RELAY

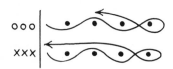

Grades: 4 to 6   Distance: 10 to 15 feet
Equipment: Balloon or feather for each team

Blows balloon or feather to turning line and back. If it falls to floor must be picked up at that point and put in air again before proceeding.

Box Relay

Grades: 1 to 6   Distance: 10 to 20 feet
Equipment: 2 shoe boxes

Players divide into two teams. Each leader runs to the turning line and back wearing two shoe boxes. If any player steps out of a box he must begin again from the starting line.

Bronco Relay

Grades: 1 to 6

Lines number off by two's to form couples. First couple in each line straddles a broom stick and races to the turning line and back. Second couple takes the stick and repeats action of couple 1, etc.

Paper Bag Relay

Equipment: Paper bags for all participants

Blow up bag at starting line, run across turning line, pop bag and return.

Pilot Relay

Grades: 3 to 6   Distance: 30 to 50 feet

No. 1 faces turning line and grasps hands of 2 and 3 who face in opposite direction. No. 1 runs forward to turning line and 2 and 3 run backwards. On the return, No. 1 runs backwards and 2 and 3 run forward.

Sack Relay

Grades: 1 to 6   Distance: 20 to 50 feet
Equipment: Sack of burlap or duck

Players jump with sack pulled up well above the hips.

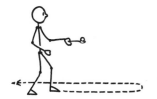

Spoon and Ping-pong Ball Relay

Grades: 2 to 6   Distance: 20 feet
Equipment: Tablespoon and ping-pong ball for each team

Balance ball in spoon and walk rapidly to turning line and back. If the ball rolls off, it may be replaced with the free hand of the player and returned to the place where it rolled off. The relay is more interesting and difficult if the ball is picked up without aid from the free hand.

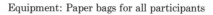

SWEEP UP RELAY

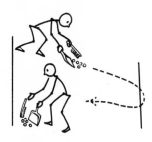

Equipment: 5 ping-pong balls, a broom and dust pan for each team
Distance: 15 to 20 feet

Five ping-pong balls are placed directly in front of the starting line. On signal, the first player sweeps the balls into the dust pan with a whisk broom and races to the turning point and back, dumping the balls gently to floor so they will not scatter. Second player repeats action of first, etc.

THREE-LEGGED RELAY

Grades: 2 to 6   Distance: 20 to 40 feet

Team forms a double line. With inside legs tied together, first couple run to turning line and back; then second couple do the same, etc.

TOOTHPICK AND RING RELAY

Grades: 3 to 6   Distance: 15 to 20 feet
Equipment: Toothpick for each team member and a ring for each team (small celluloid curtain ring is light and suitable)

No. 1 puts toothpick in mouth and places ring on toothpick, runs to turning line and back and transfers ring to toothpick in mouth of No. 2.

PAUL REVERE RELAY

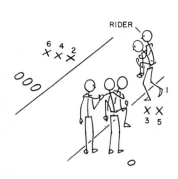

Grades: 3 to 6   Distance: 20 to 30 feet

This is a shuttle relay. After each team selects a rider the players number off, the even numbers standing on one side and the odd numbers on the opposite side. On signal the rider mounts the back of No. 1 who carries him to No. 2 where the rider, without touching the ground, exchanges mounts and No. 2 carries him to No. 3. Continue until the last man carries the rider across the finish line. If a rider falls off he must mount again at the point of the fall. If he falls off in changing mounts, he must get on his original mount again before making the change.

SUGGESTED READINGS

Bancroft, Jessie: *Games (A Treasury of 600 Delightful Games for Children of All Ages)*. New York, The Macmillan Company, 1937.

Donnelly, Richard; Helms, William G.; and Mitchell, Elmer D.: *Active Games and Contests*. New York, The Ronald Press Company, 1958.

Geri, Frank H.: *Illustrated Games and Rhythms for Children.* New York, Prentice-Hall, Inc., 1955.

Hindman, Darwin: *Complete Book of Games and Stunts.* New York, Prentice-Hall, Inc., 1956.

Kraus, Richard: *Play Activities for Boys and Girls.* New York, McGraw-Hill Book Co., 1957.

Latchaw, Marjorie: *A Pocket Guide of Games and Rhythms for the Elementary School.* New York, Prentice-Hall, Inc., 1956.

Macfarlan, Allan and Paulette: *Fun with Brand-New Games.* New York, Association Press, 1961.

McVicar, Wes: *Eight to Eighteen.* 15 Spadina Rd., Toronto, Canada, National Council of YMCA's of Canada, 1955.

Chapter 11

Basic Skills and Lead-up Games to Team Sports

Skills required in team games taught from the first grade through the sixth grade will gradually increase proficiency in relays, lead-up games, modified team games, as well as formal drill or practice. The desire to play team games, often manifested in the third and fourth grades, can be fulfilled in the fifth grade where interest has become sustained, instead of sporadic, and the participants have reached a level of understanding and skill necessary to thorough enjoyment of games involving group cooperation and complicated rules. When primary level children start asking for team games, let it be remembered that there is no substitute for skill when the child is ready, as judged by the teacher, for progressive instruction.

In the primary grades one can teach games that introduce simple skills with the ball, such as catching, throwing, kicking, and dodging. These give a general background of mechanics that carries over into all types of games where a ball is used.

SUGGESTED GAMES LISTED ACCORDING TO DEGREE OF DIFFICULTY

Call Ball   Hot Ball
Ball Toss   Circle or Line Dodgeball
Ball Puss   Square Ball
Stride Ball

Suggested ball technique games include:

BALL PUSS (Target Ball)

×   ×   ×

×   (IT)   ×

×   ×   ×

Gym, playground   Players: 9 to 10
Grades: 2, 3

1. Each player stands on a base while "It" is in center with ball.
2. At signal, all change places and "It" tries to hit someone with the ball.
3. A player who is hit becomes "It."

174

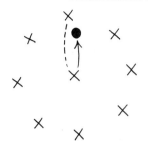

Ball Toss

Playground, playroom, gym
Grades: 1, 2   Players: 8 to 12
Formation: Circle   Large ball

1. Ball is thrown around circle.
2. Player in center throws to each player in circle who returns ball to thrower.
3. Concentrate on throwing and catching, and as skill improves, increase speed.

Boundary Ball

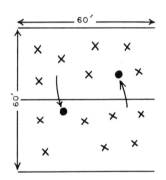

Gym, playground   Players: 20 to 40
Grades: 3, 4   Volleyball or soccerball

1. Draw two parallel lines 60 feet long and 60 feet apart. Draw a center line.
2. Divide players evenly and place teams at opposite ends of the field facing center.
3. The line back of each team is that team's goal.
4. Give each team a ball. At a given signal each tries to throw the ball so as to cross the other team's goal.
5. The ball must bounce or roll across the goal.
6. Players move freely in their own end of the field trying to keep opponents' ball from crossing the goal.
7. Team that gets the ball across goal first wins.

Bowling

Gym, playroom   Grades: 1 to 6

This increasingly popular sport may be enjoyed from the first through the sixth grade. You may use milk cartons or oatmeal boxes filled with sand and gravel and soft balls or the real pins and bowling balls.[1] It is suggested that no bowling technique or scoring be taught through the third grade. In the fourth through the sixth grade, regulation bowling technique and modified scoring may be taught.
Hold: Pick up ball in both hands. Insert third and fourth fingers on one side and thumb in single hole on top. Support ball in left hand with thumb up.
Stance: Feet together.
Progression: 3 step—Step forward with left foot, push ball forward, step on right, carry ball back of hip, step left, slide and release ball in front of left foot.
Progression: 5 step (for the highly coordinated)—Step left, push ball forward, step right, left, right, ball backward, step left, *slide* and release.
Scoring: Play three games (frames). One point for each pin knocked down.

---

[1] Cosom Corporation Ltd., 2514 11th Ave., Regina, Saskatchewan, Canada.

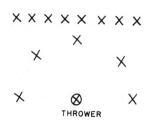

⊗ THROWER

THROWER

CALL BALL

Playground, gym   Players: 8 to 12
Grades: 1, 2   8″ rubber ball or volleyball
Formation: Line or circle

1. One player is *Thrower.*
2. Thrower calls name of a player and tosses ball in the air.
3. Player whose name is called attempts to catch the ball. If he succeeds, he changes places with the Thrower.
4. If a player misses, the Thrower calls names until the ball is caught.
5. In a new and unacquainted group, number off and call a number or call colors of clothing.

CIRCLE KICK BALL

Gym, playground   Players: 18 to 30
Grades: 2 to 5   Formation: Circle
Number off by twos to form teams

1. Each player attempts to kick ball between the legs of two opposing players. Score one point for a successful kick.
2. If a player kicks the ball over the heads of the opposing team, the opponents score one.

CIRCLE KICK BALL

Gym, playground   Players: 16 to 24
Grades: 2 to 5   Two teams, two captains
Formation: Circle   Rubber volleyball

1. Ball is put in play by kicking toward opponent.
2. While the ball is in play all players must stay in their half of the circles, except the captains who may move out of position to kick balls which have stopped out of reach of their teammates.
3. One point is scored for a team each time: Player kicks ball through opponents' half circle; player kicks ball out over shoulders.
   Opponent kicks ball out on his own side.
   Opponent plays ball with hands (except girls using hands to protect face or chest).
4. Player who receives the ball when it goes out puts it into play again.
5. This game may allow heading as skill permits.

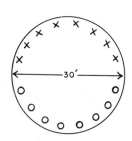

CIRCLE CLUB BOWLS

Playground, gym   Players: 12 to 24
Grades: 2, 3   Indian clubs, softball, volleyball
Formation: Circle

1. Form a circle. Place a club back of each player who stands in stride position.
2. Each player tries to throw the ball through the legs of another player.
3. Player whose club is knocked down is out of the game.

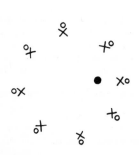

CORNER SPRY

Playroom, gym   Players: 30 to 40
8" rubber ball   Formation: Line relay with 3 feet
of space between each player

1. Divide the class into four teams with a captain at the head of each team.
2. The captain throws the ball to each player, who returns it. As soon as the last player catches the ball, the captain calls, "Corner spry" and runs to the head of the line and the last player becomes captain. The first team that gets back to its original position wins the game.

HOT BALL

Gym, playground, playroom   Players: 12 to 20
Grades: 2, 3   Any kind of ball
Formation: Circle or double line

1. Players pass ball as rapidly as possible around circle. Players who drop ball must drop out of game.
2. Variation 1—"It" in center of circle may try to touch the ball as it is passed from one player to the next. If he succeeds, he changes place with the player who had the ball when it was touched.
3. Variation 2—Group forms double lines facing each other. On signal, balls are passed to the end of the line and back. The line finishing first wins.

LINE DODGEBALL

Grades: 2, 3   Players: 12 to 24
Gym, playroom, playground   Volleyball

1. Two lines are drawn about 20 feet apart. Halfway between lines a box about 4 feet square is drawn.
2. One player stands in the box. Half the players stand on one line and half on the other.
3. Players on both lines take turns throwing and trying to hit the center player below the waist.
4. The center player may dodge but must never have both feet out of the box at any time. If hit, the center player changes places with the one who threw the ball.

PALM THE BALL

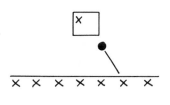

Gym, playground   Players: 12 to 18
Softball, tennis ball or small rubber ball
Formation: Circle

1. Players stand in circle with hands at back, palms up, forming a cup.
2. "It" places the ball in a player's hands.
3. Player receiving ball turns and runs in opposite direction and each tries to get back to the vacant place first.

SQUARE BALL

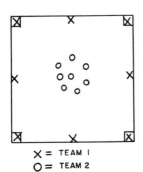

X = TEAM I
O = TEAM 2

Gym, playground   Players: 16
Grades: 2, 3, 4   Volleyball or 8″ rubber ball

1. Team 1 takes places on bases, team 2 in center of square.
2. Players on bases begin passing ball around the square.
3. Unexpectedly, a player on base tries to hit an inside player with the ball.
4. If the center player is missed, the ball continues around the square. If the player is hit, team 1 runs around the bases until the player hit picks up the ball and calls, "Halt."
5. Player with the ball tries to hit one of the halted players.
6. Game: Score one for each player hit and score one for the opposing team for each miss. Set game at 10. Teams change places at end of game.

STRIDE BALL

Gym, playground   Players: 12 to 16   Soccer or volleyball
Grades: 2 to 4   Formation: Circle

1. Players stand in circle with legs in stride position.
2. "It" stands in the circle and tries to throw or bat ball between the legs of other players.
3. If the ball is out of reach a player may retrieve it but must return to the circle before he puts it back into play.
4. If the ball goes through a player's legs three times he must drop out of the game.

CLASS ORGANIZATION

DIVISION OF TEAMS

Some teachers divide classes into teams and keep the same teams through the entirety of a sports unit. This procedure saves time and offers the participants the opportunity to become thoroughly familiar with teammates and the way they play. Others divide teams each week. The latter method has the advantage of exposing the participants to more and differing playing situations, hence, develops alertness and versatility to meet the unexpected. A teacher must judge which method best meets the situation and needs in that particular school but it is recommended that teams be divided with an equalization of skill. Selected teams may wear distinguishing colors or pinnies given to them by their squad leaders. Skill segregation makes for dull competition. Then, too, a child with poor motor ability or skill weakness often improves more rapidly while playing with others more highly skilled.

CHOICE OF LEADERS

Leaders or team captains should be chosen because of their sportsmanship and knowledge of the game. Weekly rotation of captains is advisable in order to develop leadership and acceptance of responsibility within the whole group.

Student officials must not only be grounded in the rules of the game but also must remain fair and impartial in their decisions. Daily rotation of officials permits each equal playing time. Student officials will require frequent advice from the teacher; this help should be exact and consistent. Surprisingly enough, fifth and sixth graders can become quite technical in their insistence that games be played according to the rules. Emotionally some become more touchy about inconsistencies than do high school students.

TEACHING SKILLS

There are three commonly used methods for teaching skills: (1) the part method, (2) the whole method, and (3) the part-whole method. The first consists of teaching each skill through formal drill until a fair degree of proficiency has been reached. In the second, the teacher briefs the children on the rudiments of the game, demonstrates the fundamental skills, places the players on the field or court and starts the game, stopping it when necessary to correct errors in form or strategy. In the third, one combines the elements of the first and second method.

Children in elementary grades, as a rule, take a dim view of formal practice. Because they are primarily interested in the game itself, drill should be held to the minimum. Each skill should be explained briefly, demonstrated, then tried individually in a race, relay or lead-up game. Relays are particularly effective in motivating the learning process, for competition serves as a means of stimulating and holding interest while skills are being mastered.

FUNDAMENTAL SKILLS RELATED TO TEAM GAMES

Soccer Skills

SIDE

FRONT

Dribble

Tap ball with the inside of the right and left foot alternately, keeping the ball close to the feet and always under control. Beginners are prone to kick the ball then run to catch up.

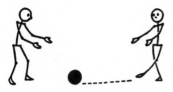

Passing

Take weight on right foot and swing left leg back and forward, hitting the ball with the inside of the left foot. To pass forward left, reverse action hitting ball with inside of right foot.

Kicking

Swing leg back and contact ball at instep. Keep the toe pointed down.

Trapping

Slow balls may be stopped with a raised foot, toes up. As contact is made, the toes are lowered to secure the ball. Fast balls are trapped with the leg. If the ball is on the right, take a small step sideways to the left and at the same time roll the right instep in toward the ground and trap the ball with the knee and the inside of the calf.

Heading

Get under ball, lower the head slightly, stiffen the neck and meet the ball with an upward and forward movement to control direction. This skill is too advanced for the majority of elementary children.

CIRCLE KICK SOCCER

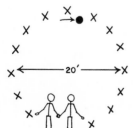

Playground, gym   Players: 16 to 20
Grades: 3, 4   Equipment: Soccerball
Formation: Single circle, hands joined

1. Ball is rolled into center of circle and players pass the ball around the inside of the circle.
2. Players trap, block and pass with feet and legs, but keep hands joined.
3. If the ball goes outside the circle, the players between whom it passed are eliminated from the game.
4. When all but five are eliminated, the game is over.

BASE FOOTBALL

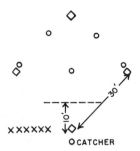

Playground   Players: 10 to 20
Grades: 1 to 6   Equipment: Football, bases

1. Kicker punts (kicks from hands) and tries to make all bases without getting put out.
2. May run until ball is held by catcher at home plate or is played to base at which he is running.
3. Score one point if runner completes circuit.
4. Kicker out if: (a) Ball doesn't go over 10' line. (b) Ball caught on fly. (c) Touched by ball when in hands of opposing team.
5. Player may stay on base and advance on next kick.
6. Kicking team has 3 outs, then changes places.

KICK BALL

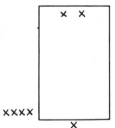

Playground   Players: 10 to 24
Grades: 2 to 6   Equipment: Baseball, diamond, bases 30' apart, soccerball or basketball

1. Seven innings make a game.
2. Pitcher rolls ball to batter who kicks it into the field.
3. The general rules of baseball apply, with the following exceptions: (a) The base runner may be tagged out or "thrown out." (b) A runner must be tagged with the ball held in the hand. (c) "Thrown out" means the base is tagged with the ball or touched by some part of body of baseman or fielder while the ball is in his hands, before the runner reaches base.
4. There may be from 5 to 12 on the team.
5. Use soccerball or basketball.
6. Pitchers box 15' to 20' from home plate.

KICK FOR DISTANCE

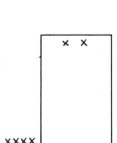

Playground   Players: Any number
Grades: 3 to 6   Equipment: Football, soccerball

1. Line up behind kicking line—two players stand at end of field to recover kicks.
2. Each player given definite number of tries.
3. Longest kick recorded—player with longest kick is winner.

KICKOVER BALL

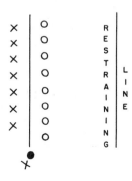

Playground, gym   Players: 12 to 24
Grades: 3 up   Equipment: Soccerball

1. Players are divided into two teams and placed in parallel lines facing each other. Teams alternate putting ball in play.
2. A space is left between the feet of the teams. By superior kicking, one team tries to kick the ball over the heads of the other team.
3. After the ball is kicked over one team's head, the two end players jump up and try to retrieve the ball and run over a restraining line.
4. The team with the most points wins. Game may continue until all get a chance to retrieve the ball.

LINE SOCCER

Playground: 30' x 30' field   Players: Two teams,
Grade: 4   8 to 12 players each
Equipment: Soccerball

1. Teams number off and take positions.
2. On signal the soccerball is rolled in from the sideline and the No. 1's on each team run out and try to dribble and kick the ball over the opponent's goal line.
3. Guards and linesmen try to stop the ball with feet or hands. If hands are used, the ball must not be held or moved.
4. Score two points for kicking the ball across the opponent's goal line. Score one point for a successful free kick.
5. When one player kicks the ball out of bounds, it is given to the other player in the center of the field.
6. A free kick is awarded for: runner using hands, pushing, blocking, or holding.
7. Free kick: Ball is placed in center of field and player tries to kick it over the opponent's goal line. Neither linesman nor the opposing player must interfere with the kick. Free kick must not pass over the heads of linesmen.

Baseball Skills

Catching

Cup relaxed hands, closing firmly when contact is made and give with the ball. Balls above the waist are caught with fingers up, thumbs together; balls below the waist are caught with hands down, little fingers together.

Throwing

Underhand. Hold ball in the hand palm up, weight on the right foot. Swing arm backward then forward keeping arm close to body. Simultaneously step forward with the left foot and release the ball at hip level and follow through with weight on right foot. This is a legal pitch.

Overhand. Hold ball in hand with palm down with fingers spread easily around the ball. Draw arm backward with elbow bent; swing arm forward using hand, wrist, elbow and shoulder to deliver ball as weight is shifted to the left foot and follow through with entire arm and body.

Batting

Stand facing plate with body parallel to the flight of the ball. Hold the bat in both hands close to the end with right hand on top. Weight is evenly divided on comfortably spread feet, bat is held over the plate, back and at shoulder level. The distance from the box to the plate in softball is short so it is important to get set to hit every ball. As the pitcher releases the ball, put weight on right foot shifting to left as the bat is swung parallel to the ground. Drop bat and step off on the right foot for the run to first base.

Fielding

Stand with feet spread to allow movement in any direction. Ground balls often bounce, so fielder steps forward with fingers down and fields the ball off of his toes.

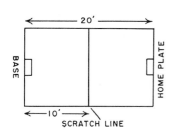

Base Running

Weight is on the left foot as the pitcher starts the throw. Step off on right foot as the pitcher releases the ball or batter gets a hit. Run close to the base line and touch each base.

Bat Ball

Playground, gym   Players: 10, 24
Grades: 3, 4, 5
Equipment: Volleyball or 8″ rubber ball

1. Divide into two teams, one in field, one at bat.
2. Batter strikes ball with hand or fist. If his hit is successful, he runs to the base, tags it and returns to home plate.
3. A fielder tries to hit the runner. He may only take two steps and can pass the ball to teammates.
4. A player is out when (a) a fly is caught, (b) he is hit by a ball, (c) he does not tag the base, or (d) he does not hit the ball beyond the scratch line.
  Game may be timed or played by innings. Score 2 points for each completed run and 1 point for a foul made by fielder.

Beat the Ball

Playground, gym   Players: 2 teams
Grades: 2, 3   Equipment: Volleyball

1. Play on playground ball diamond.
2. Batter throws ball into field and runs the bases; keeps going until he reaches home or is put out.
3. Fielders field ball and throw it to first base; first baseman throws it to second, and on around bases.
4. If runner reaches home before ball does, he scores one point. Otherwise, out.
  Variation. Hand beatball: Same except pitcher pitches ball and the batter bats it with open hand.
  Variation. Bowl beatball: Same except pitcher rolls ball and batter kicks it.

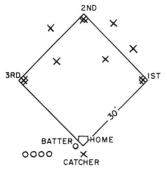

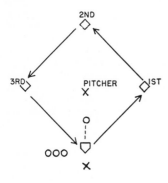

DIAMOND OR BOX BALL

Playing field   Players: Two teams of equal size
Grades: 3 to 6
Equipment: Volleyball or soft rubber ball

1. "Box" or square made by 3 bases and home base for lower grades. Baseball diamond may be used for upper grades.
2. The pitcher throws the ball so that it bounces once before crossing home plate. The batter strikes the ball with his open hand, or clenched fist, out into the field. The ball must first strike within the box or diamond for the batter to be safe. If the ball strikes outside the diamond the batter is out. All other baseball rules apply. One point is scored for each successful runner. Nine innings make a game.

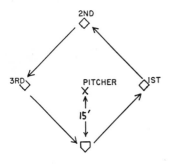

HAND BASEBALL

Baseball diamond   Players: 2 teams, 9 on each
Grades: 3, 4, 5
Equipment: Volleyball or soft rubber ball

1. Pitcher delivers ball to batter with under hand throw, 15′ from home plate.
2. Batter hits the ball with open hand or fist.
3. A runner may be put out by hitting him with a ball any time he is not on base.
4. Game: Nine innings. Score one for each completed run.

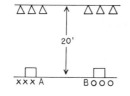

LINE BOWLING

Playroom, gym   Players: 8, 12
Grades: 4, 5
Equipment: 3 Indian clubs, 6″ to 8″ ball

1. Two parallel lines, 20′ apart, with boxes at opposite ends from the court.
2. Alternate teams try to knock down the pins from their respective boxes.
3. The bowling player on team "A" replaces the pins in a triangle, 12″ apart, and goes to the foot of his line.
4. Team "B" player retrieves the ball and bowls from his box.

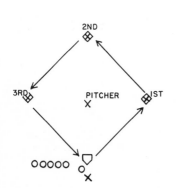

BASEBALL OVERTAKE CONTEST

Baseball diamond   Players: 8, 12
Grades: 3, 4, 5   Equipment: Softball

1. All positions of the infield are occupied except short-stop. Pitcher holds softball.
2. Runner stands on home base and at signal runs the bases.
3. At same time, pitcher throws the ball to catcher on home base and from there it is thrown around the bases.
4. One point is scored for each base the runner reaches ahead of the ball.

5. After all the running team have run, the teams change positions.
6. Runner throws ball to any player on the opposite team. The fielder throws ball to catcher, etc.

PROGRESSIVE BAT BALL

Gym, playground
Players: 10 players to a team—any number to 150
Grades: 4, 5, 6   Equipment: Volleyball

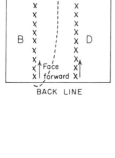

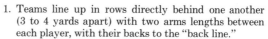

1. Teams line up in rows directly behind one another (3 to 4 yards apart) with two arms lengths between each player, with their backs to the "back line."
2. The team farthest from the "back line" turns and faces the rest.
3. A player tosses a ball and bats it with his hand, then runs to the "back line." The ball must go within the square, and the other players attempt to hit the runner before he reaches the line.
4. The runner is out if the ball is caught in the air or if it hits him. If the runner reaches the "back line" safely, he must return to his team on the next play. Players must maintain their positions and advance the ball by passing only.
5. A batted ball striking outside the square is a foul and the batter is out.
6. One point is scored for each player who reaches the "back line" and returns to his team.
7. Three outs retires a team which then moves to the "back line" and the next team in line moves into play.

LONG BASE

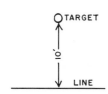

Playground   Players: 14, 20
Grades: 1 to 6   Equipment: Bat and softball

1. Divide into 2 teams.
2. Pitcher throws ball to batter who bats.
3. Runner runs to long base and remains if he arrives before ball.
4. Next runner does same and runner No. 1 comes in.
5. Fielders catch ball and try to put either one out.
6. Runner may make home run if he has time.
7. Out if doesn't hit in 3 times.
8. When team has 3 outs they change places.

TARGET

Playground, gym   Players: 8, 12
Grades: 1 to 6
Equipment: Target, soccerball or volleyball

1. Target suspended on wall, fence, tree, 10' away from thrower.
2. Thrower attempts to hit bull's-eye with soccer or volleyball.
3. Each has 3 successive turns and best of three scores is counted.

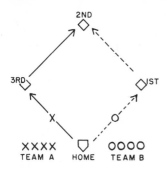

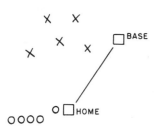

RACE AROUND THE BASES

Playground   Players: 12, 24
Grades: 2, 3, 4

1. Two players start from home plate.
2. One player runs to first, second, third and back to home. The second player runs to third, second, first and home.
3. Player who reaches home plate first wins.
4. If a player fails to touch a base, he must go back and do so.

THROW IT AND RUN

Playground, gym   Players: 10, 18
Grades: 3, 4   Equipment: Softball or volleyball

1. Thrower scores run by throwing softball (or rubber volleyball) out into playing field, running to first base and back to home plate.
2. If a fielder catches fly ball or returns ball to catcher before thrower returns home, thrower is out.
3. Team scoring most runs wins.

Volleyball Skills

Service

The underhand serve is the simplest to teach, easiest to learn, and most practical for use in placement of the ball. Stand facing opposite court with ball in left hand. Weight is on the right foot as right arm swings backward to shoulder height. Shift weight to left foot as right arm swings forward, knocking the ball out of the left hand. Follow through with the whole body as the ball leaves the right hand. The ball may be struck with the open palm, palm side of the closed fist, or thumb and forefinger side of the closed fist. The assist is generally used in elementary grades.

Receiving the Ball

Take a stance with knees slightly flexed. If the ball is high, flex elbows with hands up, take a small step forward, and meet the ball with fingers relaxed. If the ball is low, flex knees more deeply, step forward, and meet the ball with fingers down and palms forward. Children should be taught from the start to keep their eyes on the ball and be ready to receive a volley, or a pass, from a teammate.

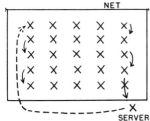

Passing the Ball

Try to give upward impetus to the ball and direct it by turning the hands and body toward the desired objective. A high ball can be handled more easily and gives a good background for teaching the "set-up" and juggle (girls) which is taught in junior high school.

Rotation

Snake or "S" type rotation is used because of its simplicity and the fact that generally 30 to 40 play on each side.

KEEP IT UP

Playground   Players: Entire class
Grades: 2, 3, and up

1. Divide into as many groups as there are volley and basketballs.
2. Pitch the ball up in each group and see which group can keep the ball up the longest without it touching the floor.
3. If you have to use basketballs, be sure to alternate the basketball among the groups.

FIST FUNGO

Playground, gym   Players: 12, 16
Grades: 3, 4   Equipment: Volleyball
Formation: Scattered

1. Batter faces scattered players and bats ball toward them with open hand or fist.
2. A fielder who catches the ball exchanges with the batter.
3. A player who fields the ball but does not catch it on the fly, tries to hit the batter. The batter may not move his feet.
4. If the batter is hit, he exchanges places with the fielder. If he is not hit, he has another turn.

SHOWER BALL

Volleyball court   Players: 20, 50
Grades: 2 to 6
Equipment: Net and 1 ball for every 10 players

1. Ball may be batted or tossed over the net. Only one player on each side may handle the ball, and it cannot be held over 3 seconds.
2. A player may only take one step with the ball.
3. Points are given for violations and each time the ball touches the ground.

CAGE BALL

Playing field: 30' to 80' according to age groups
Grades: 2 to 6   Players: 10 to 50
Equipment: Large ball and volleyball net

1. The net is placed at 8', and the area is marked into 3 playing divisions.
2. Each player must stay within his assigned area.
3. The server stands back of the line and tosses or bats the ball to a player who assists it over the net.
4. Players rotate for service, and only the serving team can score.
5. When the ball is not assisted on service, dropped, goes into net, or out of bounds, it goes to the opposing team.

NEWCOMB

Playing field: Tennis court or volleyball court
Grades: 4, 5, 6   Players: Any number to form 2 teams
Equipment: Volleyball or soccerball and net

1. The ball is thrown back and forth over the net, and each team attempts to keep it from touching the ground on their side.
2. Any number of players may handle a ball on one side, but it must not be held over 3 seconds.
3. A point is scored when the ball touchs the ground or goes out of bounds.

Basketball Skills

Stance

Stand with feet apart, knees slightly bent to permit shifts in all directions.

Passing

Concentrate on accuracy, passing with just enough momentum so that the ball may be caught easily. Step in the direction of the pass in order to back up teammates.

Overhead

Two Arm. Arms above head, elbows slightly bent. Propel ball straight forward.

Overhead

One Arm. Same as above, except ball is balanced on one hand.

Chest

Ball is held to chest with elbows bent. Push ball forward and upward, as arms are extended, and release when arms are straight.

Side-Arm

Balance ball on hand, arm back, weight on the foot on the same side. Transfer weight to other foot as ball is thrown.

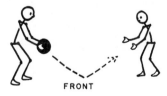

FRONT

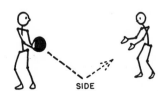

SIDE

Bounce

Arms in position as for chest pass. Keep ball low, as high bounces are easily intercepted. Ball is held to side, one arm across chest, both elbows bent. Throw ball as arms are extended.

Roll Pass

Allow children who have not advanced far in skills to roll the ball on the floor as in bowling.

Catching

Receive high balls with fingers up, low balls with fingers down. Relax hands and give with the ball. Always keep your eye on the ball.

Shooting Baskets

Arch. Hold ball slightly to the front about chin level, with fingers up, elbows bent. Look at the basket, straighten arms and push the ball in a high arch.

Lay-Up Shot. Player receives ball under or close to basket, jumps into air and tries to lay the ball so that it will enter just over the rim of the basket.

Dribble

Body in crouch position, head up so that the player can look over the court. Bounce the ball low by flexing the wrist back and hitting the ball with the fingers. Elementary grade children do not develop a high degree of skill in dribbling as they lower their heads to watch the ball.

Foul Shots

Arch. Same as high arch shot, but knees are flexed more and toes must not cross the foul line.

Scoop. Small children find it easier to shoot a foul shot by catching the ball with fingers down and throwing it underhanded in a high arch.

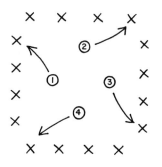

CATCH, THROW, AND SIT

Playground, gym, playroom   Players: 12, 16
Grade: 3
Equipment: Softball, football, or volleyball

1. Divide group into teams of 8 to 12. Line up against walls of gym or in a hollow square.
2. Captain faces his team and must keep one foot in a 3-foot circle.
3. Captain stands 15′ from team.
4. At signal, he throws ball to first player on right, who catches it, throws it back and then sits down. This is repeated down the line.
5. If any player or captain fails to catch the ball, he must recover it and return to position before throwing it.
6. Team wins which has all players seated first.

KEEP AWAY

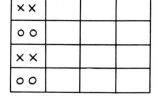

Playground   Players: 8 to 32
Grades: 1, 2, 3, and up
Equipment: Baseball or basketball

1. Draw court of four rectangles about 6′ x 10′.
2. Place 2 pupils in each rectangle. The alternate rectangles are partners and try to keep the ball away from the other two.
3. When a player steps on or out of the line, the ball goes to the opposite team.
4. This can be played either with baseball or basketball.

TWENTY-ONE

Basketball court   Players: 2 to 12
Grades: 4, 5, 6   Equipment: Basketball

1. Players take a long shot (15′ to 20′) at the basket, and a short shot.
2. Long shot scores 2 points and short shot 1 point.
3. Players take turns and the first to score 21 points wins.
4. Variation: Players may shoot from the foul line, retrieve the ball and take a short shot. Small, light ball may be used for primary children.

SIDE LINE BASKETBALL

One-half regulation basketball court
Players: Two teams, 6 to 8 per team
Grades: 5, 6   Equipment: Basketball

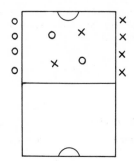

1. Two members of each team play on the floor and players line up on side.
2. Regulation basketball rules are followed except the ball may be passed to teammates on the side lines.
3. Both teams play the same basket.
4. The defensive team becomes offensive by throwing the ball to a player on the side lines.
5. The center line is out of bounds, and stepping over any line gives the ball to the opposing team on their side line.
6. Ball may be put into play by center toss up, or by giving the ball on the side lines to the team scored against.
7. Players on side lines rotate with players on floor.
8. Score 2 points for each basket made and 1 point for free throw after a foul.

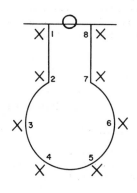

KEYHOLE BASKETBALL

Area around basket   Players: 2 to 10
Grades: 4, 5, 6   Equipment: Basketball

1. Chalk eight marks around basket.
2. No. 1 player shoots from the first mark.
3. If he makes the basket, he moves on and shoots from the No. 2 mark, and on around until he misses.
4. The other players shoot in turn and advance counter-clockwise.
5. The first player who reaches his original position wins.

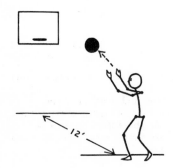

FREEZE OUT

Basketball court   Players: 8 to 10 to a basket
Grades: 5, 6   Equipment: Basketball

1. Players scatter out and take turns at shooting for the basket.
2. The first player shoots a long shot, then a short shot. If he misses the first but sinks the short shot, the next player must make a long shot that would cover the short shot, or a short shot. If he does not succeed, he is frozen out of the game.
3. Each player in turn must try to make the same shots as the preceding player.
4. The last player to remain in the game wins.

NINE COURT BASKETBALL

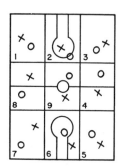

Basketball court: Divide court into 9 equal areas
Grades: 5, 6   Players: Two teams of 9 each
Equipment: Basketball

1. Played as basketball except each player is assigned an area and must stay within that boundary.
2. Players advance the ball toward their goal by passing and may dribble one time. Only forwards may shoot at the goal.
3. Ball is put in play by a center toss up.
4. Unguarded free shot, worth one point, is awarded for fouls, as blocking, holding, etc.
5. Ball is taken out of bounds for infractions as crossing line, traveling, etc.

SUGGESTED READINGS

American Association for Health, Physical Education, and Recreation: *Football Skills Test Manual* (Boys); *Basketball Skills Test Manual* (Boys) (Girls); *Softball Skills Test Manual* (Boys) (Girls). Washington, D.C., 1966.

American Association for Health, Physical Education, and Recreation, Division of Girls' and Women's Sports:

Guides: *Aquatics*, 1965-67; *Archery, Riding,* 1966-68; *Bowling, Fencing, Golf,* 1964-66; *Field Hockey, Lacrosse,* 1966-68; *Gymnastics,* 1965; *Outing Activities and Winter Sports,* 1965-67); *Soccer, Speedball,* 1966-68; *Softball,* 1966-68; *Tennis, Badminton,* 1966-68; *Track and Field,* 1966-68; *Volleyball,* 1965-67. (These guides contain official rules for players and officials, and selected articles. Guides are published biannually except the basketball guide. $1.00 per copy.)

Reprint Series: *Selected Aquatics Articles,* 1964; *Selected Basketball Articles,* 1964; *Selected Field Hockey-Lacrosse Articles,* 1963; *Selected Soccer-Speedball Articles,* 1963; *Selected Softball Articles,* 1962; *Selected Tennis-Badminton Articles,* 1963; *Selected Volleyball Articles,* 1960. (All $1.00 per copy.)

Technique Charts: *Aquatics—Swimming and Diving* (18 charts), $2.00; *Badminton* (12 charts), $1.50; *Basketball* (12 charts), $1.50; *Bowling—Ten Pin* (9 charts, boys and girls), $1.00; *Softball* (11 charts), $1.00; *Speedball* (8 charts), $1.00; *Tennis* (12 charts), $1.50; *Volleyball* (11 charts), $1.50.

Blake, William: *Lead-up Games to Team Sports.* Englewood Cliffs, N.J., Prentice-Hall, Inc., 1964.

King, Eleanor (Editor): *How We Do It Game Book,* 3rd Ed. AAHPER, Washington, D.C., 1964.

Vannier, Maryhelen, and Poindexter, Hally Beth: *Individual and Team Sports for Girls and Women,* 2nd Ed. Philadelphia, W. B. Saunders Company, 1968.

Wadsworth Press, Belmont, California: (Each of the following recommended booklets in the Wadsworth Sports Skills Series can be obtained directly from the above address.)

Beginning Archery—Roy Niemeyer.
Beginning Badminton—John Friedrich.
Beginning Bowling—Donald Cassady and Maria Liba.
Beginning Golf—Ben Bruce and Evelyn Davis.
Beginning Handball—Richard Robertson and Herbert Olson.
Beginning Swimming—Marlin MacKenzie and Betty Spears.
Beginning Tennis—Peter Everett and Virginia Dumas.
Beginning Volleyball—William Odeneal and Harry Wilson.

Chapter 12

Rhythms and Dance

Rhythm has been described as ordered movement that runs through all beauty. It is seen in a lace pattern that has design repeated on different levels or in architecture in which beams, arches and windows balance in harmony. In nature one observes plant life following a prescribed rhythm in symmetry and growth. All body movements tend to be rhythmic. Watch for rhythm in the following:

> A man raking leaves.
> Metalsmith raising a bowl.
> Pitcher winding up and delivering a baseball.
> Tumbler executing a roll or a flip.
> Housewife using a mop, broom, or vacuum cleaner.
> Child transferring sand from pile to bucket.

Rhythm in dance is unlike rhythm found in sports or daily chores in that it serves no utilitarian purpose but is simply expressive movements made with or without music. In teaching children, one starts with the familiar and progresses as skill and perception increase.[1]

RHYTHMS

How to Introduce Rhythms

TIME

Have children recite and clap in rhythm familiar nursery rhymes such as Pat-a-cake, Little Bo Peep (Nursery Rhymes—Frank Luther, Decca Records, CU 100, CU 101, and 75522–3). Clap to known songs such as Yankee Doodle. From the third grade on, the rhythm pattern and underlying beat can be explained; the groups can clap the two parts and

---

[1] Murray, Ruth Lovell: *Dance in Elementary Education.* 2d Ed. New York, Harper and Brothers, 1963.

then do it in rounds. Most children above the first grade know a number of radio commercials and enjoy clapping out the rhythm.

Example 1.

Ha - lo everybody ha - lo

Ha - lo is the shampoo that glorifies the hair, etc.

Example 2.

Row, row,/ row your/ boat

Gently/ down the/ stream

Mer ri ly,/ mer ri ly,/ mer ri ly,/ mer ri ly/

Life is/ but a/ dream.

Rhythm pattern 3

Underlying beat 4

3
4

BOUNCING BALLS

    a. Bounce balls to music.

    b. Bounce balls to each other in couple or circle formation.

    c. Children act as balls and bounce around the floor as music indicates.

    d. Form couples: one child is the ball; the other the bouncer. Bounce to music, alternating as ball and bouncer.

    e. Combinations of bounces to music.

    f. Rhythm combinations by Ruth Evans—Record 203–204.

JUMPING ROPE

This may be introduced as a self-testing activity or offered along with rhythms because it requires skill and timing. In any case it is a must in any elementary program. Long ropes of 12 to 16 feet are more practical but additional individual ropes can be used to good advantage.[2]

GAMES

RHYTHMIC LIMBO
Caribbean

Grades: 3 to 6   Double line

Record: Hoctor Dance Records, Inc.—1608B

    A light standard with 6 penny nails may be used, or two children may hold an 8-foot bamboo cane. Two students may walk under the pole at the same time. Each time the entire group has gone under, the pole is lowered 2 inches.

---

[2] See Chapter 21 for specific directions on teaching this activity and for jump-rope ditties.

Position: Knees flexed, pelvic girdle tilted back, hips and shoulders dropped, and head back. Knees turn out and ankles roll in as knees come closer to the floor. Go forward with rhyme, with the bar set at shoulder height of the smallest in the class.

Wiggle the ankle,
Wiggle the knee
Under the bar
Like a willow tree.

LEMME OR LUMMI STICKS
Indian Game

Gymnasium, playroom   Grades: 2 to 6

Equipment: One set of sticks for each player. These are made of ¾″ dowel rods cut 18″ long. Paint half of the sticks one color and half another. Educational Activities, Inc., sells a kit with 24 sticks, instructional record, and illustrated instruction sheets.

Rhythm: 1 – 2 – 3 – 4   Rhythm background may be played by a drum.

Position: Players sit in cross-legged position on floor, facing each other. Sticks are held in the center; thumb next to body; four fingers on opposite side; fingers spread slightly. To match sticks simply strike together. In throwing the sticks, hold them perpendicular and throw straight across and catch on the diagonal.

Position 1: Heads of sticks rest on floor.
1 – 2 – 3   Strike heads of sticks on floor in rhythm.
– 4   Match sticks with partner. (Repeat 4 meas.)
Position 2: Stand sticks upright.
1 – 2 – 3   Strike sticks on floor in rhythm.
– 4   Match sticks with partner. (Repeat 4 meas.)
Position 3: Sticks in position 1.
1 – 2   Strike sticks on floor.
– 3   Hold sticks off floor and cross the right over the left.
– 4   Match sticks with partner. (Repeat 4 meas.)
Position 4: Return sticks to position 2.
1 – 2   Strike sticks on floor.
– 3   Partners exchange right sticks by throwing to each other.
– 4   Strike floor with sticks.
1 – 2   Strike sticks on floor.
– 3   Partners exchange left sticks by throwing.
– 4   Strike floor with sticks. (Repeat 8 meas.)
Position 5:
1 – 2   Strike sticks on floor.
– 3   Partners exchange *both* sticks by throwing.
– 4   Strike sticks on floor. (Repeat 8 meas.)
Note: One partner throws both sticks to the inside and the other throws toward the outside.

Repeat movements 3, 2, and 1; as a finale cross sticks.
For the primary grades it would be wise to use only positions, 1, 2, and 3.

TINIKLING OR BAMBOO HOP

Gymnasium, playroom, playground   Grades: 3 to 6

Educational Activities, Inc. sells a kit that includes the record, 12 instruction sheets, music, and six 5-foot bamboo poles.

MARCHING

This is an excellent way to introduce and review time and floor spacing without a self-consciousness that often exists among children. First and second graders like to march but are indifferent to left and right feet and complicated directions, so this phase of rhythms should be confined to the upper elementary grades, if any measure of excellence in performance is expected. There is no need to motivate this activity because older brothers and sisters in bands and drill teams have already created an enthusiastic acceptance.

Previous training in the fundamental locomotor movements, i.e., walking in rhythm to cadence, should make the following easy:

Music

Any good march with a sound beat is suitable. Record BOL 54, available from Record Center, 2581 Piedmont Rd. N.E., Atlanta, Georgia 30324, contains five marches and 15 theme charts, giving a wide range of feeling and themes.

Fundamentals in Marching

1. Clap hands to rhythm of march music or drum.
2. Take steps in place, stepping first on left foot in time to march music or drum beat.
3. Maintain good posture; eyes straight ahead; rib cage pulled up.
4. March forward in time to music; let arms swing easily at the sides in opposition to the feet.
5. Try to keep an even spacing in relation to the person in front.
6. Keep in step and learn to do a rapid step-close-step if you get out of step.

Marching Patterns

First and Second Grades

1. In a circle formation march single file; by 2's; by 3's.

2. In a square formation march single file; by 2's; by 3's. Make square turns at corners; then by 2's and 3's; those on the outside pivot around inside marcher.

Third Grade

1. Up center by 2's; boys left; girls right.
2. Up center by 2's; all single file left.
3. Up center single file; all left by 2's. Boy marks time as girl marches to his right side. Both turn and march to corner.

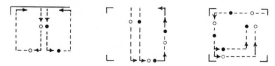

Fourth Grade

1. Up center by 2's; first couple left; second couple right; third couple left; fourth couple right.
2. Up center by 4's; form single file left and right.
3. Diagonal cross. Repeat.
4. Up center by 2's.

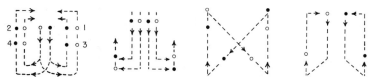

Fifth and Sixth Grades: Sequence

1. Up center by 4's; first four left; second right; third left; fourth right; at foot single file.
2. Up center by 8's; left and right as in figure 1.
3. Up center by 8's; lines 1 and 3 complete circle to left. Lines two and four complete circle to right. Leave enough space between lines of eight and take small steps on the turn to keep lines straight.
4. Break into single file and spiral inward.
5. Serpentine. Boys wind in and out (serpentine), passing left and right of girls, who remain stationary. As boy reaches last girl all form circle and march off single file.

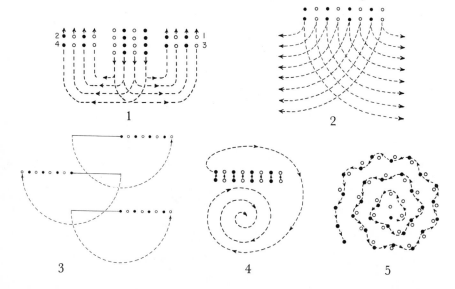

In the fifth and sixth grades, according to the proficiency of the group, many figures may be worked out using the diagonal cross by 2's, double circles moving in opposite directions, and a combination of the various figures done in sequence. The figures do not have to be complicated because, if the marchers maintain correct time and proper spacing, the movements are effective. This type of controlled rhythm is enjoyable when introduced at intervals with free-flowing movements.

FUNDAMENTAL MOVEMENTS

Even movements are walking, running, hopping, and leaping. Uneven movements are skipping, sliding, and galloping. Each movement should be defined and demonstrated without and with the drum beat. If the space is large, the whole class may execute the movements in unison. Where the space is limited, as in a playroom, take the class by couples, lines, or waves. The use of records adds interest. Book sources for all the following dances can be found at the end of this chapter. Record references, listed alphabetically, are also to be found at the end of this chapter.

Locomotor Movements[3]

1. Even movements—walk, run, jump, hop, and leap.
2. Uneven movements—skip, slide, and gallop.
3. Define and demonstrate each:

    a. *Walk*—shifting of weight from one foot to the other at a moderate rate of speed.
    b. *Run*—same as walk but faster and remaining in air longer between shifting of weight.
    c. *Hop*—leave floor on one foot and return to floor on same foot.
    d. *Jump*—leave floor from both feet and return on both feet.
    e. *Leap*—same as walk and run, only more height and in air longer.
    f. *Skip*—combination of walk (or run) and hop-step; hop on right foot; step; hop on left foot.
    g. *Slide*—step to side on left foot; slide right foot to left. Step lf.; close rt. When time is accelerated, a tiny hop accompanies the step-slide.
    h. *Gallop*—leap on left foot; step with right, bringing it beside left. Leap; step, etc.

Formations and floor patterns can be introduced at this time that will lend interest and variety to the simplest locomotor movements. On the primary level, children are inclined to lump themselves in a knot as a bunch of sheep and it will be necessary at times to chalk formations on the floor such as:

WEDGE   CIRCLE   OBLIQUE   ARC   SQUARE

---

[3] Record Reference Q, T.

ACCOMPANIMENT

1. Hand clapping (refer to section 1 on how to introduce rhythms).
2. Drums.
   a. Manufactured—A small snare-type drum open on one side and played with a large lamb's-wool hammer is fairly inexpensive and will last a long time, if properly cared for. The closed leather drum made in India or China is played with a small, hard hammer. This type of drum requires careful handling, is expensive, but does have a good, decisive tone.
   b. Homemade drums:
      (1) American Indian—Buckskin stretched tightly and tacked to a hollowed-out piece of wood such as a tree limb, stump, or mixing bowl.
      (2) Cheese box—Remove lid, stretch tightly, and attach with tacks or staples a piece of unbleached muslin. Wet the muslin and allow to dry thoroughly. Decorate box and muslin and apply one or two coats of white shellac.
      (3) Oatmeal box or similar round container of paper. A two-pound coffee can may be used but the sound is not as pleasing. Cut two circles of leather or inner tube. With a leather punch place holes 1 inch apart. Lace top and bottom together with leather or plastic thongs or strips cut from an old inner tube. This type of drum is not durable but is easily made and gives out a resonant tone when played with the hand.
3. Hard sticks or paddles.
   a. Round doweling or 1 x 1 sticks, 12 inches long, of hard wood such as maple, oak or teak wood.
   b. Paddles of any wood cut out a half of an inch thick give a sharp sound.
4. Vocal accompaniment.
   a. Half of the class recites a poem and the other half follows cadence or suggested thought.

Example[4]

> This is the way the lady rides,
> Gentle and slow, gentle and slow
> This is the way the lady rides
> All on a pleasant morning. (*Slow easy run*)
> This is the way a gentleman rides. (*High-stepping spirited* horses)
> This is the way the farmer rides. (*Clumsy gait and gallop of* farm horses)

   b. Singing—Song indicates movement.

Example: With Your Hands[5]

> With your hands go clap, clap, clap;
> Now with your feet go tap, tap, tap;
> Join your fingers in a ring with me
> And jump in the circle one, two, three.

---

[4] Salt, Benton, and Fox, G. I.: *Teaching Physical Education in Elementary Schools.* New York, A. S. Barnes & Co., 1942, pp. 215–216.

[5] Record Reference J, No. 1184.

Formation: Single circle

Children face toward inside of circle and execute action indicated in the song. On the last line all join hands and move clockwise with the movement in the words of the song which may be a hop, skip, run, gallop, etc.

5. Piano.

a. The piano is excellent for accompaniment because the teacher can accent each beat, stop at any time, and take up again at the same place. The use of the piano requires special talent, aside from the ability to play, because instruction and demonstration must be interwoven with the accompaniment, requiring a great deal of change from piano to floor. It is ideal in schools where an accompanist is available.

6. Record player.

a. The record player has become standard equipment in most schools and the supply of available records is becoming more complete each year. The most satisfactory machine has a speed regulator and will play 33, 45, and 78 r.p.m. records.

b. Best use of records.

(1) Buy records that carry 6 to 8 rhymes, singing games, or dances. Albums seem expensive but are actually economical because of the number of recordings on each record. The playing time on a standard 78 record is too long for elementary grade children.

(2) Play record and clap rhythms lightly, accenting change of phrasing with a heavy clap.

(3) Dance with prescribed steps. Listen to music. Do first step without music, then with music. Master and proceed to second step. Do first and second, etc.

7. Tape recorder.

a. The tape recorder is a reasonably expensive piece of equipment but has many advantages and pays for itself many times over a period of years. A small school system can build a record library, tape the records and allow teachers to check out tape and machine as they do films. The teacher can tape drum beat sequences for the teaching of fundamental movements and creative experiences and be left free to observe, demonstrate, suggest or correct.

SINGING GAMES

There is a variance of opinion as to the best method of presenting singing games and dances. Some teach children to listen for phrasing; some describe a step in rhythm with the music as step, close step; still others count as for the waltz, one, two, three. Few teachers will be blessed with classes that can progress, to a child, with the first method. A combination of all three reaches the monotone and the child with two left feet.

Come Let Us Be Joyful

(German) Educational Dance Recordings, FD-1

Formation. Three pupils in a line around a circle, like the spokes of a wheel.

1. Each group of three, with inside hands joined, walk three steps forward and bow to opposite group on the fourth count. Walk back to place in four steps. Repeat.

2. Center child turns partner on right with right elbow turn in four skips. He turns partner on left with left elbow turn, with four skips. He repeats all of this.

3. Each group of three takes three steps forward, bows and takes four steps backward. All walk forward, drop hands, and pass through to face new group of three, without turning.

CAPTAIN JINKS

Record—Victor 20639 (American)

    A. I'm Captain Jinks of the Horse Marines
       I feed my horse good corn and beans,
    B. I swing the ladies in their teens,
       For that's the style in the army!
    C. I teach the ladies how to dance, how to dance,
       How to dance, I teach the ladies how to dance,
       For that's the style in the army!
    D. Salute your partner, turn to the right,
       And swing your neighbor with all your might,
       Then promenade with the lady right,
       For that's the style in the army!

Formation. Start with partners in a single circle facing clockwise.

Action. Verse 1. All march forward to music.

      Verse 2. Partners face and do two-handed swing skipping clockwise.

      Verse 3. Form double circle, girls on inside, boys on outside; join inside hands and skip forward.

      Verse 4. Face partner; boy bows (boy may salute) while girl curtsies; boy moves to his right to swing his neighbor two times around and promenades his new partner (boy stays on outside of circle).

WAY DOWN IN THE PAW PAW PATCH

Record—Victor 45-5066B (American); Folkraft 1181

    1. Where, oh where is dear little (Betty)?
       Where, oh where is dear little . . . . ?
       Where, oh where is dear little . . . .?
       'Way down yonder in the paw paw patch.
    2. Come on boys and let's go find her,
       Come on boys and let's go find her,
       Come on boys and let's go find her,
       'Way down yonder in the paw paw patch.
    3. Pickin' up paw paws, puttin' them in a basket,
       Pickin' up paw paws, puttin' them in a basket,
       Pickin' up paw paws, puttin' them in a basket,
       'Way down yonder in the paw paw patch.

Formation. Five or six couples form a double line—

    Boys: X X X X X X
    Girls: O O O O O O

The first name of the girl is sung as each new lead couple takes their place.

Action. Verse 1. First girl turns to her right and skips clockwise around the entire group.

      Verse 2. Girl encircles group again and line of boys follow her and come back to original place.

      Verse 3. Partners join hands and skip clockwise. When the head couple reaches the foot of the line, they hold joined hands high to make an arch and the other couples skip under it. The second couple is now the head couple. The game is repeated; singing out the name of the new girl continues until all couples have been at the head of the line. On the last verse, the children act out the motion of putting paw paws in a basket.

HERE WE GO OVER THE MOUNTAIN TWO BY TWO[6]

1. Here we go over the mountain, two by two
   Here we go over the mountain, two by two
   Here we go over the mountain, two by two
   Rise up, Sugar, rise.
2. Show us a lively motion, two by two
   Show us a lively motion, two by two
   Show us a lively motion, two by two
   Rise up, Sugar, rise.
3. That's a very lively motion, two by two
   That's a very lively motion, two by two
   That's a very lively motion, two by two
   Rise up, Sugar, rise.

Formation. Single circle of partners, facing in. One couple stands in the center.

Action. Verse 1. Children sing and walk counterclockwise while the center couple thinks of some movements to perform.

Verse 2. The center couple performs the chosen movements.

Verse 3. Entire group imitates action demonstrated by couple in center. The center couple chooses a couple to take their place and the game is repeated.

HOKEY POKEY

Record—Capitol 1496 (American)

1. You put your right hand in,
   You take your right hand out,
   You put your right hand in,
   And you shake it all about,
   You do the Hokey Pokey and turn yourself about,
   That's what it's all about—Yeah!
2. You put your left hand in, etc.
3-10. You put your right and left elbow, shoulder
   and hip, head, and whole body.
11. You do the Hokey Pokey,
    You do the Hokey Pokey,
    You do the Hokey Pokey,
    That's what it's all about.

This singing game is a modernized version of Looby Loo and finds favor in primary through adult groups.

Formation. Single circle facing in.

Action. Players follow calls by performing action indicated.

Verses. When the song calls for the "Hokey Pokey" the elbows are bent, the hands are up (palms out) and are wig-wagged backward and forward in front of the face. The player takes a quick turn clockwise and claps out the rhythm of the song, thrusting the right hand toward the center of the circle at the conclusion.

Last Verse. Hands are held high and waved in a trembling motion. Players kneel, slap the floor with both hands, and rise and shout as the music finishes.

---

[6] Barnett, Cecile Jean: *Games, Rhythms, Dances.* 22 W. Monroe St., Chicago, Illinois, Arrow Business Service, 1950.

RIG-A-JIG

Record—Disc 5038; Childhood Rhythms, Series VI, Record 602; Folkraft 1199

As I was walking down the street,
Heigh-o, heigh-o, heigh-o, heigh-o
A little friend I chanced to meet
Heigh-o, heigh-o, heigh-o.

Chorus

Rig-a-jig-jig, and away we go
Away we go, away we go,
Rig-a-jig-jig, and away we go
Heigh-o, heigh-o, heigh-o.

Formation. Single circle facing center. One player stands inside circle.
Action. The child in the center walks around the inside of circle until the words "A little friend" are sung. He chooses a partner and skips around circle. As the chorus is repeated, each child inside the circle chooses a partner until all have been chosen.

BLUEBIRD (AMERICAN)

Record—Folkraft 1180

Bluebird, bluebird, in and out my windows,
Bluebird, bluebird, in and out my windows,
Oh! Johnny, I am tired.

Chorus

Take a little boy and tap him on the shoulders,
Take a little boy and tap him on the shoulders,
Oh! Johnny, I am tired.

Formation. Single circle facing center with hands joined and held high to make arches. One child, the Bluebird, stands in the center of the circle.

Action. LINES 1 AND 2.   Bluebird walks around circle weaving in and out under the arches.
        LINE 3.   Bluebird stops behind boy.
        CHORUS.   Bluebird places hands on shoulders of child and taps lightly through chorus.

The dance is repeated with the boy becoming the leader and the girl following behind with hands on his shoulders. Continue the game until all are chosen. Substitute "Jenny" for Johnny when girls are chosen.

JINGLE BELLS

Any recording of this tune with a lively rhythm, such as Folkraft 1080 (American) *Grades 3 to 6*

Formation. Double circle facing counterclockwise.

PART I.

Dashing thru the snow	With hands in skating position, partners slide forward four slides with right foot leading.
In a one horse open sleigh	Leading with left foot, repeat above.
O'er the field we go Laughing all the way. Bells on bob-tail ring Making spirits bright, What fun it is to ride and sing A sleighing song tonight!	Continue this "skating step" alternately leading with right foot and left foot.

PART II.

Jingle bells! Jingle bells! Jingle all the way!	Partners face and clap in rhythm to words.
Oh! What fun it is to ride In a one horse open sleigh.	Partners link right arms and skip about each other eight skips making two complete circles.

PART II. (Repeated)

Jingle bells! Jingle bells! Jingle all the way!	Partners face and clap.
Oh! What fun it is to ride	Link left arms and skip four skips.
In a one horse open sleigh!	Boy moves forward to next girl.
Repeat all.	

SAFETY AND OTHER SINGING GAMES

Singing games may be created by the children to make them more aware of what is expected of them in the school community. These games can pertain to citizenship, safety, special events or good manners and can be adapted to well known melodies or, with the help of the music teacher, can be written to tunes of their own.

EXAMPLES

1. *Swing* (Set to original tune)

> I swing high a bit, and low a bit.
> But when I swing, I always sit.
> Swinging sideways, and swinging double.
> Is not for me; it means trouble.
> Up, up I go into the sun,
> Swinging safely makes swinging fun.

2. *Trapeze* (Sung to *Rock-A-Bye Baby*)

Formation. Single circle, facing clockwise.

I am a monkey, I swing so free,	Children walk while swinging arms.
You may see bars, It's really a tree,	Stretch arms high.
I hang by my knees,	Squat with hands on floor.
I cut di do-es,	Jump around.
I look when I drop, And land on my toes.	Take big jump toward center of circle and land lightly on toes.

3. *Lunch Room* (Sung to *Old MacDonald Had a Farm*)

Formation. Single circle facing forward.
Action. Children sing and march, making the motions of taking a tray, eating food and cleaning off their tables. On the last line, they stop, turn, and point to three children in the circle.

We wait for the bell to sound, To the lunch room we are bound, In a line so straight with tray and plate, We move and never crowd. The food is good,	The milk is fine, We slowly chew, And take our time. Our plates are clean, our tables too, Did you, did you, did you?

SQUARE DANCE

Folk dancing has been enjoyed by limited groups in the larger cities of the United States for a long period of time. The repertoire of these groups has been composed chiefly of international dances.[7] The past ten or fifteen years have seen a revival of square dancing which has enthusiastically swept the whole country, cities, small towns, and hamlets alike. The eagerness of these groups has given a tremendous boost to all folk dancing, for they gradually added to their "know-how" couple and group dances from all countries.

Square dancing patter and calls vary in different parts of the country and even in towns in the same state. However, the fundamental formations and steps are the same.

A teacher may start square dancing in the third or fourth grades using circle or round dances. In the fifth or sixth grades the children should be able to execute a number of simple round, square, and longways dances.

Teaching Suggestions

1. Choose a square dance record that is moderately slow and do your own calls. Records with calls move too fast for children to follow.

[7] Book Reference 14, p. 1.

Figure 28. By the sixth grade children should be able to do well a number of simple round, square, and longway dances. (Courtesy of AAHPER.)

2. Call in a modulated voice, keeping the words of the call in time with the music and spaced to give the dancers time to follow instructions. Beginners will require more time to execute any call, but teach them from the start to LISTEN to the calls. Keep the patter simple to avoid confusion.

3. Teach the shuffle step emphasizing smoothness and grace and discouraging any tendency to bounce, skip, or hop. The proper performance of this one step in square dancing makes the difference between a movement of fluid beauty and a comical, grotesque caricature of a jumping jack.

4. Keep the square symmetrical and snug so that the dancers can progress easily from one call to the next. Children are inclined to spread out into a ragged circle; this causes them to break the rhythm and run to the next figure that is called.

5. Practice each call until the children know *where* they are going.

6. Be patient and accept enthusiastic participation as your goal rather than letter-perfect execution.

Teaching Progressions

THE CIRCLE[8]

Form a single circle alternating boys and girls. The boy's partner is on his right; his corner on his left. The following terms and figures may be taught in the circle:

Honor Your Partner. Boy bows from the waist with his right arm in front and left arm in back (avoid stomach-clutching and head-ducking). Girl does a simple curtsy by placing one foot behind the other and flexing knees slightly. She may hold her skirt at the side.

Honor Your Corner. Same as above to corner. (The boy turns and bows to the girl on his left.)

Circle Left. All join hands and move forward around the circle.

Circle Right. Move to right as above.

PROMENADE

Couples move counterclockwise around the circle; the girl is on the boy's right. The boy has the girl's right hand in his right hand and her left hand in his left hand; his right arm is crossed over girl's left arm.

GRAND RIGHT AND LEFT

Partners face, touch right hands and pass on to the next, touching left hands, and on around the circle, weaving in and out until partners meet

---

[8] Book Reference 23, pp. 43–55; Record Reference G.

again. The boys move counterclockwise; the girls clockwise. It may be necessary to have the children hold on to partner's hands until they can touch the left hands, release, hold left hands, and so forth.

SWINGS

Two-Handed Swing. Partners face, clasp both hands and swing around. This swing is recommended for children up to the sixth grade.

Elbow Swing. Hook right or left elbows and swing around once. Use alternately with two-handed swing.

Waist Swing. Boy takes girl in social dance position and swings her around to the right, stepping left, right, left, etc. Usually a waist swing calls for two turns.

Allemande Left. Boy and corner face, join left hands, walk around each other and return to home position. Practice this figure a few times and add the Allemande left to the grand right and left and end up with the promenade home.

THE SQUARE[9]

Break the large circle into small circles of eight each which constitute a set. Teach the sets to "square up." Each couple in the set forms one side of the square which should be large enough to allow free movement and tight enough to prevent running back to home position. First couples have their backs to the Caller or music. Proceeding counterclockwise are couples two, three and four. First and third are called "head couples" and second and fourth are called "side couples." A couple's starting position is "home." Have the couples identify themselves by raising their hands. Review all fundamentals learned in the circle and you are ready to teach a dance.

Rᴇᴅ Rɪᴠᴇʀ Vᴀʟʟᴇʏ[10]

There are a number of good recordings of this tune.

Grades 4, 5, 6

This simple version is a favorite among the youngsters of the Southwest. Many groups sing as they dance, which helps them know what steps to do next. Different versions may be found in the listed references.

Formation. Squares of eight.

The first couple lead down the Valley,
And you circle to the left and to the right.
Then you swing with the girl in the Valley,
And now you swing with your Red River Girl.

First Couple moves to Couple No. 2 and all form a circle. Move to left; move to right. Each boy swings his opposite girl one and a half times around. Each boy swings his partner one and a half times around. Couple No.

---

⁹ Book Reference 25, p. 3.
¹⁰ Book References 16, 25.

Then lead right on down the Valley,
And you circle to the left and to the right.
Then you swing with the girl in the Valley,
And now you swing with your Red River Girl.
Then you lead on down the Valley,
And you circle to the left and to the right.
Then you swing with the girl in the Valley,
And now you swing with your Red River Girl.

2 should be in home position and Couple
No. 1 in the center of the square.
Couple No. 1 moves on to Couple No. 3 and
repeats action of first verse.

Couple No. 1 moves on to Couple No. 4 and
repeats action of first verse.

Repeat all with Couples 2, 3 and 4 leading
out.

The square dance has four parts: (1) an introduction or opener, (2) the main figure, the trimmings, (3) fill-ins or mixers and (4) the ending. Numerous examples of patter for all dances may be found in the references listed at the end of the chapter.[11] There is no doubt that the Allemande left and grand right and left take on color when called as, "On your corner with the old left hand, why in the world don't you right and left grand," but calls at this level should be kept simple with just enough variation to avoid monotony.

Examples of Introductions:

Honor your partner, the lady by your side (*corner*)
All join hands and circle wide (*move to left*)
Break and swing and promenade home.

All eight balance, all eight swing,
Now promenade around the ring.

Examples of Endings:

Bow to your partner, bow to your corner,
Bow to your opposite, and there you stand.

Promenade (add girls' names) two by two,
Take her home like you always do.

TAKE A LITTLE PEEK[12]

Grade 6
Formation.   Squares of eight.

First couple, balance and swing,

Out to the couple on the right, and take a little
peek.
Back to the center and swing your sweet.

Out to the side and peek once more.
Back to the center and swing all four.

Holding inside hands, couple faces, takes
two steps away from each other, then waist
swings.
Couple 1 moves to Couple 2, divides and
they peek at each other around Couple 2.
Couple 1 swings once around with a waist
swing in center of square. Peeks again.
Couple 1 waist swings in the center while
Couple 2 does same in home position.

---

[11] Book References 14, 23, 25.
[12] Book Reference 25, p. 23.

Circle four in the middle of the floor.

Do-si-do, and a little more do,

Grab your partner, on to the next, and take a little peek.

Back to the center and swing your sweet.

No. 1 boy picks up Couple 2 and all join hands and circle to the left.

Do-si-do—left to partner and swing; right to corner and swing.

Take partner and move on to Couple 3.

Couple returns to home position.

Repeat action above.

Repeat entire call with Couples 2, 3 and 4 leading out.

COWBOY LOOP[13]

Grade 6
Formation. Squares of eight.

First couple, balance and swing.
Out to the couple on the right,

And circle four in the middle of the floor.
Two hold up, and four trail through.

Turn right around and go back through.

Tie that knot like the cowboys do.

Circle six and all get fixed.

Now, two hold up, and six trail through.
Turn right around and go back through.
Tie that knot like the cowboys do.
Circle eight and all get straight.
Round and round and round you go.
Break that ring with a do-si-do.

And promenade home.

Two steps backward, bow and swing.
Lead out to Couple 2. Boy joins hands with girl in Couple 2.
Form a circle and move clockwise.
No. 1 boy drops his corner's hand and leads the line under the joined and raised hands of Couple 3 who walk forward as the line passes under the arch.
Couple 3 drops hands, pivots, and forms an arch with other hands. No. 1 boy turns his line and leads it back under the arch. Couple 3 walks down the line, as it passes under the arch, back to home position.
The line has passed under the arch. No. 1 boy moves to the right and leads the entire line under an arch formed by Couple 2. Couple 3 waist swings in home position.
No. 1 boy picks up Couple 3 and all circle to the left.
Couple 4 forms the arch.
Repeat action above.
Repeat action above.
All circle to the left.
Continue circling.
Left to partner, swing once around, swing corner once around with the right hand, and come back to partner.
Promenade counterclockwise back to home position.
Repeat: Couples 2, 3, and 4 lead out.

ADDITIONAL SUGGESTED DANCES AND SOURCES

1. All Hands Across (Ref. 23, p. 200)
2. Sisters Form a Ring (Ref. 14, p. 30; 25, p. 19)
3. Wagon Wheel (Ref. 14, p. 41; 25, p. 44)
4. Texas Star (Ref. 14, p. 59; 25, p. 33)

[13] Book Reference 23, p. 31.

LONGWAYS FORMATION

There are two types of longways formations used in dances. The type shown in Fig. 1 is formed by a double line with partners facing forward. This formation is used in the party game, "Way Down in the Paw Paw Patch." The type shown in Fig. 2 is used in the "Virginia Reel" which remains one of the most popular of American folk dances among all age groups. It serves as an excellent introduction to square dancing as a number of the basic movements are learned. Third and fourth graders prefer the skip as the basic step but fifth and sixth graders show a preference for the shuffle step, which is less strenuous and more dignified.

FIG. 1	FIG. 2
O X	O→X
O X	O X
O X	O X
O X	O X
O X	O X
O X	O→X

Head of Set
O—girls
X—boys

VIRGINIA REEL

(American) Folkraft 1249, with calls; Folkraft 1312, no calls.

Formation. Six to eight couples longways, partners facing.

Action. In the first six steps the head boy and girl move forward to the center to execute the movement and move backward to places. The head girl and foot boy repeat the same action by moving to the center of the set and returning to their places.

STEP 1. Boys bow to corners, girls curtsy to corners   Measure: 1–4
Head boy and head girl move to center, bow and return to places
Head girl and foot boy repeat action   Measure: 5–8

STEP 2. Hook right arms and swing around once clockwise   Measure: 1–4
Repeat   Measure: 5–8

STEP 3. Hook left arms and swing around once clockwise   Measure: 9–12
Repeat   Measure: 13–16

STEP 4. Join both hands and turn clockwise   Measure: 9–12
Repeat   Measure: 13–16

STEP 5. Dos-a-dos, passing right shoulders   Measure: 17–20
Repeat   Measure: 21–24

STEP 6. Dos-a-dos, passing left shoulders   Measure: 25–28
Repeat   Measure: 29–32

STEP 7. Head couple faces, joins hands and moves sideward to the foot of the set with four slides and returns to the head of the set with four slides.   Measure: 1–4

STEP 8. Head couple hooks right elbows and turns around one and a half times until the boy is facing the girls' line and the girl is facing the boys' line. The boy hooks left elbows with the second girl as the girl hooks left elbows with the second boy. They swing halfway around counterclockwise and meet back in the center, hook right elbows and turn half clockwise. This is repeated down the line with the head couple turning each dancer with the left arm and turning each other with the right arm. When

they have turned the last dancer at the foot of line, they
turn around one and a half times, join both hands and
slide back to the head of the set.   Measure: 5–16

(If there are more than six couples, the 12 measures
may not provide sufficient music to complete the action.
Repeat if necessary.)

STEP 9. All face head of set; head boy turns outward
and leads the line toward the foot of the set with a slow   Cast
shuffle. At the same time the head girl turns outward and   off
leads the girls to the foot of the set with the same step.   Music

STEP 10. Head couple joins hands high to form an
arch and all couples pass through. The second couple is
now the head couple and the dance is repeated until all
couples have been at the head of the set.

Variation. Some groups that like more action stand
farther apart and all dance the first six steps, first dancing
with their partners then with their corners.

Couple Dances

JESSE POLKA

Record—Beer Barrel Polka, RCA Victor: 25–1009-B; Folkraft 1071; 1263 (American-
Bohemian). Any good polka.   *Grade 6*

Formation. Couples in varsovienne position. Boy and girl on same foot.

STEP 1. Touch left heel forward and take weight on
left foot. Count 1 and   Measure: 1

STEP 2. Touch right toe back. Count 2. Step beside
left foot without taking weight, and touch right heel forward and step back; count 3, taking weight on right foot,
and   Measure: 2–3

STEP 3. Touch left heel forward: lift left foot; cross
toe in front of right foot (cut) and   Measure: 4

STEP 4. Four two-steps, beginning left.   Measure: 5–8
Repeat the entire dance.

COTTON-EYED JOE

Record—Columbia 37658—Foot N' Fiddle, Sept., 1947; Folkraft (calls) 1255 (American-
Texas).   *Grade 6*

Formation. Partners in social dance position. Boy begins on left foot; girl on right foot.

STEP 1. Touch heel to front; touch toe to back by right foot—step, together—step (two-
step). Repeat in reverse direction.

STEP 2. Turn away from partner (to boy's left; to girl's right) with three two-steps. Complete circle and face partner with three stamps.

STEP 3. Four slides to boy's left. Repeat in reverse direction.

STEP 4. Four two-steps in social dance position. Repeat all.

This vigorous Texas frontier dance usually follows the description in steps one, two and
four. In step three, one finds many variations, two of which are:

1. Boy and girl go in opposite directions, clapping and sliding for four counts, returning to
original position in four counts.

2. Push or paddle step to boy's left for four counts, and to boy's right for four counts.

VELETA

Record—Michael Herman (American-British); Folkraft 1065. *Grade 6*

Open Position

STEP 1. Partners join inside hands. Starting with outside foot (boy's left; girl's right) take two waltz steps forward. Measure: 2

Face partner, change hands and do two draw steps to left. Measure: 2

Repeat in opposite direction. Measure: 4

Closed Position

Start backward; boy on left foot; girl follows on right. Do two waltz steps. Measure: 2

Two draw steps; boy with left foot; girl with right. Measure: 2

Four waltz steps. Measure: 4

Repeat entire dance.

MIXERS

Teachers who are working with children who have had rhythmic training from the first grade up will encounter little trouble in directing or teaching mixed groups. However, where groups are new to each other or shy, it is well to warm up with a Grand March, a group dance or a mixer to get everyone acquainted and relaxed. A child should not be allowed to "sit out" too often. If there is an odd dancer, make a game of the mixer and let the boy or girl try to get a partner as a change is made. The children should be allowed to choose their own dance partners at intervals but if they get in a rut, partners should be juggled with a mixer. Mixers are fun and an excellent method of juggling partners in shy groups.

MAINE MIXER

Record—Glowworm, Imperial 1044 (American). *Grades 4, 5, 6*

Formation. Double circle facing right (counterclockwise). Join hands with girl or boy's right. Group sings or chants instructions until mixer is learned.

Everybody goes to town
You pick 'em up, you lay 'em down
Back away and say adieu

Eight steps right.
Take one step away, face partner and wave.

And balance to the right of you.

Boy and girl balance to opposites to their right. This is their new partner.

Dos-a-dos and watch her smile

New partners circle back to back and return to original place.

Step right up and swing her awhile
Give that girl an extra swing

Boy swings girl with waist swing.
Boy twirls girl and takes promenade position.

And promenade around the ring.

MEXICAN MIXER

Record—Labios de Coral, Imperial 119 (American). *Grades 5, 6*

Formation. Couples in social dance position form a circle: boys facing counterclockwise; girls facing clockwise.

STEP. 1. Do grapevine to inside of circle. Boy steps back of left foot with right, to the outside with the left foot, forward right and swings the left leg out. Girl does same, starting on left foot.

Repeat same to outside of circle.

Step left back; right side; left forward; right swing.

STEP. 2. With a wrist hold, couple turns to right with four step-hops—right, left, right, left.

STEP. 3. Boy claps while girl moves away to right (step 1) with a step right; left; right; swing; four step-hops, turning with hands on hips.

Repeat, moving left to partner.

Girl claps and boy does same; girl moving to inside of circle and back. As he does the step-hops, he turns to his left (counterclockwise) and moves on to the next girl.

INTERNATIONAL DANCES

Increasingly, educators are teaching children that other countries are not foreign if one knows enough about them. In any metropolitan city, a teacher has a wealth of material in one class whereby world fellowship could be taught with live authenticity. The mores, habits and folklore of a people cease to be strange when explanations throw light on their origin.

Folk dancing is one phase of education for international understanding that should not be tampered with if one desires a true picture of a people. A way of life and the very character of a people is expressed in its folk music and dance. Hence, if we use these dances they should be taught as near the original as possible, giving the student a rich background in the country, costume and reason for the dance. The Czechs take on new stature when one has seen the *Beseda*. A Slav is a person to be admired once the intricate and subtle steps of a *Kolo* have been mastered. The child who has been taught the *Ländler* will think of the Germans as a noisy, lusty, fun-loving people who like to "stomp" out a good tune. Likewise, the beautiful strains of *Alexandrovski* remind one that Russians love beauty in movement. The close-knit barrier of race falls limply as one joins in a circle to dance the friendly *Cherkessia* which is both joyous and sad with its undercurrent of the tragic Jewish past. Folk dancing can be an invaluable adjunct to the teacher who is trying to present world geography in an honest way. While the child is learning through the dance how his "world-neighbors" feel, the time is ripe to develop a project whereby he can learn how they look in festive costumes. Children may bring dolls to school dressed in native costumes or may dress them as an art or social studies subject.

There are other facets to folk dancing. Coordination and skill can be developed that carry over into all dancing, particularly social dancing.

Children need to learn how to do social dancing as much as they need to know almost any other subject taught in schools. Folk dance develops in one the ability to move to rhythm and to coordinate hands and arms with feet and legs. Often our most polished social dancers of the high school level have been the best dancers in a fourth grade folk dance class.

The European and American folk dances that appear in published form have been acknowledged in this book. The sources of a number of American dances are unknown, for a dance will pop up in one community and a visiting folk dance devotee who is present will take it back to his own group with slight changes. Credit has been given to known individuals who have introduced dances to folk dance groups. In many folk dances the music practically calls the steps. In describing these simpler dances in which the music phrasing speaks for itself, counts and measure have been excluded.

KALVELIS

Record—Sonart Folk Dance Album I—Folkraft 1051A (Lithuanian-Blacksmith).
Grades 5, 6

Formation. About eight couples form single circle facing counterclockwise.

STEP 1. All polka (without hop) eight steps right.	Measure: 1–8
All polka (without hop) eight steps left.	Measure: 1–8
CHORUS: Clap own hands; partner's right; own hands; partner's left. Double hand grasp and skip to left four times; skip to right four times.	Measure: 9–16
Repeat	Measure: 9–16
STEP 2. Girls do four polka steps into circle, turn, and four polka steps back to place. Boys do same.	Measure: 1–8
	Measure: 1–8
	Measure: 9–16
CHORUS—twice.	
STEP 3. Girls weave around circle going back of the first dancer and in front of the next, etc.; sixteen polka steps. Boys do same.	Measure: 1–16
	Measure: 1–16
CHORUS.	
STEP 4. All do grand right and left.	Measure: 1–16
CHORUS—twice.	Measure: 1–16
STEP 5. All join hands and polka eight times right as in Step 1.	Measure: 1–8
Polka eight times left.	Measure: 1–8

TANTOLI

Simple Version—Crampton, The Folk Dance Book—Record—(Scandinavian). *Grades 3, 4*

Formation. Couples in double circle facing counterclockwise with inside hands joined and free hands on hips.

STEP 1. With outside foot, place heel to floor forward, and toe on floor backward. Polka step hopping on inside foot. Repeat three times, beginning on inside foot, outside, and inside.	Measure: 1
	Measure: 2
	Measure: 3–8

STEP 2. Partners face, join hands at shoulder level and turn clockwise with sixteen step hops, boy starting on left foot; girl on right.   Measure: 8

(This step has been called the "Windmill" as the arms are lowered toward the foot that the hop is taken on and raised on the opposite side.)

Repeat dance.

TANTOLI

Advanced Version—Folk Dancer, July–August, 1946—(Swedish) Scandinavian Album—Victor.   *Grades 5, 6*

Formation. Double circle facing counterclockwise; boy places arm around girl's waist; girl has left hand on boy's right shoulder. Free hands on hips.

FIGURE 1. Couples move forward with two step hops on outside foot (boy's left; girl's right). Couples turn clockwise with two hop steps.   Measure: 1
                                                          Measure: 2
Repeat three times.   Measure: 3–8

FIGURE 2. Moving counterclockwise, take one Schottische step forward: Boy's step: left, right, left, hop on left. Girl's step: right, left, right, hop on right. Couples take   Measure: 9
one Schottische step backward, beginning on inside foot. Measure: 10
Couples turn twice around in place (clockwise) with four step hops. Face in slightly.   Measure: 11–12
Repeat measures 9–12.   Measure: 13–16

FIGURE 3. Facing counterclockwise, couples do heel-toe polka as described in simple version, without hop. Boy's step: heel of outside foot (left) forward; toe back- Measure: 1
ward. Step left, close right, and step left. Girl does same, Measure: 2
starting on right foot.
Repeat measures 1–2 beginning on inside foot.   Measure: 3–4
Repeat measures 1–4.   Measure: 5–8
Lean backward as heel is forward, and lean forward as toe is backward. Chorus: "Windmill" step described as simple version. Sixteen hop steps, alternately raising and lowering arms. Boy begins on left foot; girl on right.   Measure: 9–16

FIGURE 4. Couples form a double circle facing each other; boy on the inside of circle; girl on outside; hands on hips. Both move counterclockwise with four side steps.
Side step: Boy takes a step to the side, swinging the foot in an arc, and brings the right foot to the left.
Repeat three times, and on the third time, he steps on the left foot with a stamp and swings the right leg across. Girl does the same, starting on right foot.   Measure: 1–2
Repeat measures 1–2 in opposite direction, moving clockwise.   Measure: 3–4
Repeat measures 1–4.   Measure: 5–8
Repeat chorus, in open position as in Figure 3.   Measure: 9–16

FIGURE 5. Face counterclockwise as in Figure 1 and• take one Schottische step forward beginning on outside foot. Boy: left, right, left, hop. Girl: right, left, right, hop. One Schottische step backward, beginning on inside   Measure: 1
foot.   Measure: 2
Bend knee (outside) and brush foot forward and backward on floor twice.   Measure: 3
Carry foot back and tap toe on the floor three times.   Measure: 4
Repeat measures 1–4.   Measure: 5–8
Repeat chorus as in Figure 3.   Measure: 9–16

Csebogar

Record—Victor 20992; Folkraft 1196 (Hungarian). *Grades 2, 3*

Formation. Partners form single circle facing in; girl on boy's right; hands joined.

step 1. All move clockwise with eight slides. Measure: 1–4

step 2. All move counterclockwise with eight slides. Measure: 5–8

step 3. Hands still joined and held high; take four skips toward center of circle. Measure: 9–10

Lower hands; skip backward to original places. Measure: 11–12

step 4. Partners face and place right arm around partner's waist and raise left arm high, with elbow straight. Skip eight times turning clockwise. Measure: 13–16
(Variation. Upper grades may use eight paddle steps, or the Hungarian. Turn twice, around with a hop right, step left, and step right.)

step 5. All face partners; join both hands and step sideways toward center of circle, closing with opposite foot in four slow slides, or draws. Measure: 17–20

Repeat to outside of circle. Measure: 21–24

step 6. Repeat action of Step 5 with two draw steps. Measure: 25–28

step 7. Repeat Step 4. Measure: 29–32

Gustaf's Skoal

Record—Victor 20988; Folkraft 1175 (Swedish). "Skoal" means formal greeting.

Grades 2, 3

Formation. Square—Four couples.

1. Head couples—3 steps forward and bow on 4th count. Measure: 1–2

2. Head couples—3 steps backward and feet together on 4th count. Measure: 3–4

3. Side couples do same. Measure: 5–8

4. Repeat all. Measure: 1–8

5. Side couples join inside hands and form arch. Head couples skip toward each other, take new partners. Skip through arch, girls go to right, boys to left. Leave new partners and return to original positions meeting own partners. Measure: 9–12

6. All clap hands, join both hands with partner and make one complete turn. Measure: 13–16

7. Side couples repeat Step 5 with head couples forming arch. All repeat Step 6. Measure: 9–16

Danish Dance of Greeting

Record—Victor, 17158; Folkraft 1187. *Grades 1, 2*

Formation. Single circle; dancers facing the center with hands on hips.

Action.

step 1. Clap hands twice; turn to partner and bow. Clap hands twice; turn and bow to neighbor. Measure: 1–2

STEP 2. Stamp right; stamp left; turn in place four running steps.   Measure: 3-4

Repeat measures 1 and 2.   Measure: 1-4

STEP 3. All join hands and take sixteen running steps to right.   Measure: 5-8

Repeat to left. Repeat entire dance.   Measure: 9-16

CHIMES OF DUNKIRK

Record—World of Fun Series, M 105 (French, Flemish, Belgian).   *Grades 1, 2*

Formation. Double circle of partners facing each other; boys with back to center of circle.

Action.

STEP 1. Clap three times; pause.   Measure: 1-4

STEP 2. Partners join both hands and walk around circle in eight counts.   Measure: 5-8

STEP 3. Partners join right hands and balance. Repeat.   Measure: 9-12

STEP 4. Partners walk around each other once and boy moves on to his left to the next girl.   Measure: 13-16

ACE OF DIAMONDS

Record—Victor 20989; World of Fun Series, M 102 (Danish).   *Grades 2, 3*

Formation. Double circle; partners facing; boys with back to center of circle.

Action.

STEP 1. Partners clap hands once; stamp foot once; hook right arms and swing around once.   Measure: 1-4

Repeat using left arm.   Measure: 5-8

STEP 2. Girl puts hands on hips and moves backward toward center of circle with a step, hop. Step left; hop left; step right; hop right. Repeat. Boy follows with arms crossed on chest: step right; hop right; step right; hop right. Repeat. Return in reverse.   Measure: 9-16

STEP 3. Polka—skating position, going counterclockwise.   Measure: 1-16

TROIKA

Record—Kismet S112; Folkraft 1170 (Russian).   *Grades 5, 6*

Formation. Groups of three facing counterclockwise. Center dancer is a boy; outside dancers girls. Hands are joined; free hands on hips.

FIGURE I

STEP 1. Four running steps forward diagonally to right.   Measure: 1

STEP 2. Repeat diagonally to left.   Measure: 2

STEP 3. Eight running steps forward around circle.   Measure: 3-4

STEP 4. Hands still joined, the girl on the boy's right runs under arch, made by boy and girl on left, in eight steps. Other two run in place.   Measure: 5-6

STEP 5. Girl on left runs under arch and back to place in eight steps.   Measure: 7–8

FIGURE II

STEP 1. Each group of three joins hands in a circle and runs to left (clockwise) for twelve steps, beginning on left foot.   Measure: 9–11

STEP 2. Stamp in place—left; right; left. Repeat Steps 1 and 2 running to right (counterclockwise).   Measure: 12
                                                        Measure: 13–16

Release hands and repeat entire dance with same partners. Partners may change in measure 16. Girls raise outside hands to make an arch, release boy and he runs with four steps to next group while girls stamp in place.   Measure: 16

GREEN SLEEVES

Record[14] (English)—Folk Fun Funfest (Dick Kraus) Educational Dance Recordings, P.O. Box 6062, Bridgeport 6, Connecticut.   *Grades 3, 4, 5, 6*

Formation. Double circle in sets of two couples, numbered 1 and 2, facing counterclockwise; girls on right.

STEP 1. Holding hands, walk forward sixteen steps.

STEP 2. Form a star in sets. Man No. 1 gives hand to girl No. 2 and man No. 2 to girl No. 1. Walk clockwise eight steps; change to left hands and walk back to place counterclockwise.

STEP 3. Couple No. 1 join hands and back under arch made by couple No. 2 who walk forward four steps, then walk backward while No. 1 makes the arch. Repeat.

Repeat entire dance.

TROPANKA

Folk Dancer Record—Disc Album 635 (Bulgarian stamping dance).   *Grades 3, 4, 5, 6*

Formation. Single circle; little fingers joined.

Stamping step—cross foot over in front in ballet position with heel turned out.

STEP 1. Beginning on right foot, take five running steps to right and stamp twice with left foot. Turn and run to left five steps and stamp twice with right foot.   Measure: 1–2
                                                                                      Measure: 3–4
Repeat first four measures.   Measure: 1–4

STEP 2. Facing center, all step on right foot, hop on right foot and swing left foot in front. Step; hop; swing; starting on left foot.   Measure: 5

Step on right foot; cross left foot over and stamp twice.   Measure: 6

Repeat measures 5 and 6, starting on left foot.   Measure: 7–8
Repeat measures.   Measure: 5–8

STEP 3. Moving toward center of circle, all starting on right foot, step, hop right, step, and hop left. Step right and stamp twice with left foot. (Arms raised high shout "Hey!")   Measure: 5
                                                                                      Measure: 6

Repeat action of measures 5 and 6, dancing backward, starting with left foot. Gradually lower arms.

Repeat measures 9 through 16 as in measures 1 through 8.

---

[14] Record Reference M, T, V.

CHERKESSIA

Sonart Folk Dance Album M8 (Jewish).   *Grades 5, 6*

Formation. Single circle, hands joined.

Teaching Suggestions. There should be quite a bit of bending backward and forward and swing of joined hands as the dance progresses. On the verse the circle moves to the right; on the chorus the circle moves to the left.

Action.

CHORUS. The dance begins with the chorus and is repeated after each figure.

Circle moves to the left. All leap on right foot across and in front of the left (ct. 1); step to the side with left foot (ct. 2); step across and behind left foot with right foot (ct. 1); step to side with left foot (ct. 2).   Measure: 1–2

Repeat first two measures three times.   Measure: 3–8

Bend forward on steps to the front and lean backward on steps to the back.

FIGURE 1. Circle moves to the right with sixteen steps. All step to the side on the right foot, extending the left leg to the side (ct. 1); place left foot behind the right and bend both knees slightly (ct. 2).   Measure: 9

Repeat seven times.   Measure: 10–16

CHORUS   Measure: 1–8

FIGURE 2. Step hop—all turn to right and step on the right foot with the left leg (bent at knee) extended backward; hop on the right foot (ct. 1). Same on the left foot (ct. 2).   Measure: 9–10

Repeat measures 9 and 10 for remainder of music.   Measure: 11–16

CHORUS   Measure: 1–8

FIGURE 3. Feet are held close together. All move toes to the right (ct. 1); all move both heels to the right (ct. 2). Repeat.   Measure: 9–16

CHORUS   Measure: 1–8

FIGURE 4. All kick alternately feet forward 16 times, beginning right.   Measure: 9–16

CHORUS   Measure: 1–8

FIGURE 5. All kick alternately feet backward 16 times. Lean forward.   Measure: 9–16

CHORUS   Measure: 1–8

FIGURE 6. All turn to the right and move forward in the circle with 16 shuffle steps done in a semi-crouch position. The shuffle is a step right; close left; step right; etc. End dance by raising joined hands high in the air.   Measure: 9–16

BROOM DANCE

Victor Record—20448 (German).   *Grades 2, 3*

Formation. Couples form double circle facing counterclockwise. One child is left in the center of the circle with a broom.

Action.

PART 1. Couples march around the room to the music

and the child in the center gives the broom to someone in the circle and takes his place. This one gives the broom to another quickly and takes his place, and so on for 8 measures.

Measure: 1–8

PART 2. The child who has the broom at the end of the eighth measure must dance with the broom in the center of the circle while the couples skip around singing Tra, la,·la through 8 measures and the dance begins again with the center dancer passing the broom on.

Measure: 9–16

The verse and music may be found in the listed reference.

THE CRESTED HEN

Folkraft 1194 (Danish).[15]   *Grades 2, 3*

Formation. Sets of three, one boy with a girl on either side.

STEP. The hop-step is done through the entire dance. Step on left foot on count one; hop on left foot; swing right foot in front of it on count two, keeping the knee bent. Reverse and step-hop on right foot; swing left foot to front.

FIGURE 1. All sets of 3's join hands to form circles. Moving to left (clockwise) stamp left foot and do eight step-hops. Dancers lean back as they circle.

Measure: 1–8

Repeat measures 1 to 8, moving counterclockwise with eight step-hops.

Measure: 1–8

FIGURE 2. Girls release hands and place free hands on hips. Boy never releases the hands. Girl at the left of boy dances (step-hops) in front of him and under the arch made by raised hands of the boy and the girl on the right.

Measure: 9–12

Repeat same action with girl on the right, passing through arch.

Measure: 13–16

MAYIM[16] (Water)

Record—Folkraft 1108a (Israelian).   *Grades 4, 5, 6*

Formation. Students stand in circle facing center, hands joined and down.

Action.

1. Four circasia combinations to the left. For each circasia combination:
   a. Place right foot in front and across left (accent right foot).
   b. Bring left foot alongside right foot.
   c. Place right foot back, across left foot, to left.
   d. Hop on left foot alongside right foot.

2. All take 8 steps toward center of circle, lifting hands gradually, accentuating first step by raising right knee.

3. All face left and take four walking steps toward left, starting with right foot.

4. While hopping on right foot, tap with left foot over right foot. Then tap with left foot to the left side. This combination is done 4 times.

5. While hopping on left foot, tap right foot over left foot. Then tap with right foot to right side. Slap hands on odd beat. This combination is done 4 times.

This dance is supposed to convey the movement of water, of waves, of going toward the well, and the joy of discovering water in an arid country.

---

[15] N. P. Neilson and Winifred Van Hagen: *Physical Education for Elementary Schools.* New York, A. S. Barnes & Co., 1929.

[16] Maine Folk Dance Camp. Contributed by the Michael Hermans.

RAATIKKO

Folk Dancer Record—Scandinavian: 1123 (Finnish Polka—Old Maid's Dance). *Grades 5, 6*

Formation. Couple; social dance position.

STEP 1. Eight polka steps, turning clockwise.

STEP 2. Four draw steps. Boy has girl by one arm pulling and girl moves reluctantly toward rock.

STEP 3. Eight slide steps away from rock.

STEP 4. Repeat steps 2 and 3.

Repeat all.

Background. On the coast of Finland, there is a large rock close to the beach. According to the story, if a boy succeeds in pulling a girl behind the rock, she will be an old maid.

GIE GORDON'S

Beltona Record—BL-2455; Folkraft 1162 (Scotch—The Gay Gordons).   *Grades 5, 6*

Formation. Couples in varsouvienne position.

Action.

STEP 1. Both start on left foot. Take four walking steps forward. Reverse and take four walking steps backward, but continue in the same line of direction.

Repeat.

STEP 2. Boy holds girl's right hand high with his right hand and polkas forward as girl does four polkas (clockwise) turning under boy's arm.

STEP 3. In social dance position, do four polka steps turning clockwise.

Repeat entire dance.

FINGER POLKA

Standard Record—2001A (Lithuanian).   *Grades 3, 4, 5, 6*

Formation. Couples form double circle, facing counterclockwise; boys on inside of circle.

Action.

STEP 1. Eight polka steps in open position (hold inside hands, starting hop on outside foot, etc., back to back and face to face).

STEP 2. Eight polka steps in closed position turning clockwise.

STEP 3. Drop hands and face partner. Stamp three times; clap own hands three times. Repeat. Shake right finger at partner; make turn on own left, slapping right hand against partner's right hand as turn is taken. Stamp three times.

Repeat entire dance.

ROAD TO THE ISLES[17]

Record—Imperial 1005A (Scotch).   *Grades 5, 6*

Formation. Couples in varsouvienne position.

---

[17] Book Reference 16.

STEP 1. Point left toe forward and hold. Grapevine | Measure: 1
step moving to right. Step left foot back of right foot; step | Measure: 2-3
right to side; step left foot in front of right foot and hold.

Point right toe forward and hold, and grapevine to | Measure: 4
left stepping right, left, right and hold. | Measure: 5-6

Point left toe forward and hold. | Measure: 7

Point left toe backward in deep dip and hold. | Measure: 8

STEP 2. Schottische forward diagonally to left, begin-
ning on left foot—left; right; left; hop. | Measure: 9-10

Schottische forward diagonally to right, beginning on
right foot—right; left; right; hop. On hop, in measure 12,
half turn to right facing in opposite direction, keeping
hands joined. | Measure: 11-12

Schottische, beginning on left foot.
On hop, take half turn to left facing original direction. | Measure: 13-14
In place, step right; left; right; hold. | Measure: 15-16

BLEKING

Record—Victor 20989; Folkraft 1188 (Swedish). | *Grades 2, 3, 4*

Formation. Partners face with both hands joined.

STEP 1. Bleking (Blē-king): Jump lightly to left foot,
placing right heel to floor—count 1.

See-saw arms by extending right arm forward with
elbow straight and left arm backward with elbow bent.
Reverse arms and jump lightly on right foot, placing left
heel to floor—count 2. | Measure: 1

Repeat Bleking step three times in quick time—
count 1 and 2. | Measure: 2

Repeat measures 1-2 three times. | Measure: 3-8

STEP 2. Extend arms sideward and turn in clockwise
direction with sixteen step-hops, alternately raising and
lowering arms and kicking free leg to the side of the hops. | Measure: 9-16

Repeat entire dance.

JAMAICA HOLIDAY

There is a rhythm and a sound and it is Ska-lip-so. The accompanying
arm and foot movements are so simple in telling a story that a four year
old or an octogenarian can do them and they are fun. The provocative
rhythm dictates a simple beat and you just listen and follow through.
A 4/4 beat on the drum will suffice. The suggested record will add more
flavor because the music indicates the steps.

Record—Calypso Dance 44a (Stepping Tones). Second half of record. (Available from
Record Center, 2581 Piedmont Rd. N.E., Atlanta, Ga. 30324.

Movements:

1. Arms swing to time backward and forward. With fourth through the sixth grades, put feet forward and backward on the split count (half-time).

2. The Dove—This is the theme and the bird flies, flies away. Arms are held high overhead and starting from left the arms move to right and back with hands fluttering.

3. Chicken Peck—Imitate a chicken pecking, with the head and neck extended sharply and drawn back.

4. Wash—The women wash down by the stream and the motion is done by the hips with a down, down scrubbing motion, palm against palm, right against left. First on the right side, then on the left.

5. Knee Bump—In a semi-crouch position arms are crossed in front of body, knees about 12 inches apart. Arms go out to side as knees bump, return to first position and repeat.

6. Elbow Touch—This is a samba movement. Bend arms and touch left elbow with right fingers, right elbow with left fingers. Left, right left. *Count:* 1, 2; 1, 2, fast 1, 2, 3 pause. Repeat. *Feet:* Step left, right, left, right, left. Repeat starting with right and taking tiny steps.

7. Horse Ride—Crouched as on a horse, the rider pulls reins and flexes knees as if riding and occasionally slaps the flank of horse.

8. Lariat—With the weight on the left foot, the rider tosses a lariat overhead in right hand with a circular movement, keeping the left leg straight and flexing the right knee.

SOCIAL DANCING

Children who have advanced progressively through fundamental rhythms, singing games, and creative, folk, and square dancing find themselves ready in the sixth grade for social dancing. Because this is the type of dancing the majority will be doing as they grow older, it is well to expose them to at least the simple fundamentals before they enter Junior High School. Basic steps learned in group and couple dances pave the way to

Figure 29. Pupils who have progressed successfully through fundamental rhythms, singing games, and creative, folk, and square dancing are ready by the sixth grade for social dancing. (Courtesy of AAHPER.)

this more restrained type of movement; the desire to emulate adult patterns serves as a useful motivating force. The children will get some practice at parties in their own homes but it is suggested that at school affairs the social dancing be interspersed with folk dances as mixers, couple and group dances. In this way the future Fred Astaires, Gene Kelleys, and Arthur Murrays get an opportunity to "let off steam" and are less likely to become tense in this new field of experience.

Basic fundamentals such as body position, leading, following, turning, the fox trot and the waltz adequately introduce sixth graders to social dancing. Teachers who desire additional information will find it worthwhile to read the listed references.[18]

If you have seen the latest in the Frug, the Twist, the Jerk, and the Watusi and wonder where one should start with social dancing, you are not exactly alone. True, the text is Victorian by comparison but we cannot help feeling that with a little aging the young ones will come around to a more sedate form of dancing. In the meantime, let them shake, rattle, roll, and jerk. We do not feel that instructions are necessary. As a substitute we offer Jamaica Holiday in the section on International Dances.

Teaching Suggestions

BODY POSITION

The boy's arm is around the girl's waist; fingers together and palm toward the body. His left arm is extended to the side at a comfortable height and he holds the girl's right hand lightly with his palm down. The girl rests her hand lightly on the boy's right shoulder or arm, depending upon his height. Both face with toes pointed directly forward, stand a comfortable distance apart to allow freedom of movement, and hold the body erect with heads up.

WRONG

WRONG

RIGHT

LEADING

The boy leads by pressure with the right hand, arm and the upper part of the body. His lead should be firm and indicate positively to his

---

[18] Book References 14, 20.

partner what he intends to do. The girl must anticipate the next step or change of direction by being alert and following the indicated directions. The boy generally steps off on his left foot and the girl follows on her right. A good leader mixes his steps, going forward, backward and sideward so that the girl does not have to go backward all the time.

BASIC STEPS

DANCE WALK

Walk forward and backward in time with the music, keeping the feet in contact with the floor and close together, swinging the legs from the hip with knees relaxed. Stress the importance of moving smoothly as if the bodies were "lighter than air." (Note: Young boys are prone to duck their heads and in an earnest manner plow the west forty with a flat-footed "clomp" or to bob up and down energtically with bent knees, forcing their partners to do likewise.)

TWO-STEP

Step forward left and take weight.	Ct. 1
Bring right foot to left and take weight right.	Ct. 2
Step left and take weight.	Ct. 3
Pause with the weight still on the left and move right foot forward.	Ct. 4
Finish the step forward and take weight on right.	Ct. 1
Bring left foot to right and take weight.	Ct. 2
Step right and take weight.	Ct. 3
Pause with weight on right and move left foot slowly forward.	Ct. 4
Continue alternating left and right.	Ct. 4

This step is executed in the same manner forward, backward and sideward.
Direction: Step, together, step, and step, together, step, and.

FOX TROT

The fox trot is danced to 4/4 time and is the step most used in social dancing. Lack of body control at this level eliminates the dip, rock and hesitation for the average pupil. It is well to concentrate on combinations of the dance walk, two-step and turns. The turn presents quite a problem to the beginning leader who generally progresses in a wide arc or finds himself facing a wall and awkwardly backs away. Turns to the right seem to come more easily to both boys and girls and, because the pivot turn is generally done to the right, it may be taught first.

Pivot Turn. Boy steps backward on the left foot;	Ct. 1
pivots to R as he steps forward on the right foot.	Ct. 2
Two-step Turn.	
Step left sideward	Ct. 1
Bring right foot to left	Ct. 2

Step left forward; take quarter turn to left	Cts. 3–4
Step right sideward	Ct. 1
Bring left foot to right	Ct. 2
Step right backward; take quarter turn to left	Cts. 3–4
Repeat above to make complete turn.	

The leader will develop step patterns that form, in time, his own individual style but in the beginning it is helpful to teach a few set routines that can be learned by the entire group.

SIMPLE PATTERNS

DANCE WALK

1. Forward fast—Step L (ct. 1); R (ct. 2); L (ct. 3); R (ct. 4)
   Forward slow—Step L (cts. 1–2); R (cts. 3–4)
2. Forward step L (ct. 1); R (ct. 2); L (ct. 3); pivot R (ct. 4)
3. Backward step L (ct. 1); R (ct. 2); L (ct. 3); pivot R (ct. 4)
4. Combinations—Step forward L (ct. 1), R (ct. 2), L (ct. 3), pivot R (ct. 4); step backward L (ct. 1), R (ct. 2), L (ct. 3), pivot R (ct. 4); step forward L, R, L, pivot R; step backward L (cts. 1–2), R (cts. 3–4). Repeat all.

TWO-STEP

1. Dance as described on page 210: forward, backward and sideward.
2. Dance with two-step turn.
3. Combine with dance walk as: Step forward L (ct. 1); close R to L (ct. 2); step forward L (cts. 3–4); step forward R (cts. 1–2); step forward L (cts. 3–4).

WALTZ

The popularity of the waltz has waxed and waned but still remains today in America as an integral part of our dance. The slow tempo waltz is preferred in the United States to the faster Viennese waltz or the more heavily accented waltz of the Germans. Waltz music is played in 3/4 time and there are three beats to each measure. The two-step waltz will not be included here.

TRUE WALTZ

Move forward—Step L	Ct. 1
Step R	Ct. 2
Bring L to R, weight on L	Ct. 3
Step R	Ct. 1
Step L	Ct. 2
Bring R to L, weight on R	Ct. 3

BOX WALTZ

Step L forward	Ct. 1
Step R sideward	Ct. 2
Bring L to R, weight on R	Ct. 3

This step is a good lead-up to teaching turns. On the first beat the dancer steps diagonally forward on the left foot and takes a quarter turn to the left and repeats the box step as decribed above. If the turn is made each time the left foot goes forward, a complete turn is accomplished in four times.

TEACHING SUGGESTIONS FOR THE WALTZ

Have the children line up across the end of the gymnasium. Take a position in front of the class so that each child can see your feet, turn your back to the group and demonstrate the forward waltz. Lead the class slowly down the floor repeating at first: Step L, step R, close L, step R, step L, close R and later: step, step, close, step, step, close. Practice until the pattern is set, stressing the weight transfer on the third count which permits the step left and then right. Now play a slow waltz and repeat the above directions to music. Teach the backward and box waltz in the same manner. When the children have mastered these steps *alone* let them practice the same routine with partners.

DANCING TERMINOLOGY

Allemande Left.   Boy and corner face, join left hands, and walk around each other and back to place.

Allemande Right.   Partners join right hands, and walk around each other and back to place.

Balance.   Step forward left; step forward right beside left; rise slightly on toes. Step backward on right, step back left beside right and rise slightly on toes. In square dance, take two steps backward and bow to partner.

Break.   Release hands (used in square dances).

Corner.   The girl is on the boy's left; the boy is on the girl's right.

Dos-a-dos.   Boy and girl circle each other passing right shoulder to right shoulder and back to back returning to original position.

Do-si-do.   Boy faces partner; both join left hands and walk around (counterclockwise) until each is facing their corner; join right hands with their corner and walk around (clockwise) to original positions.

Draw Step.   Step to side on left foot and draw right foot to left, shifting weight to the right foot.

Elbow Swing.   Hook right or left elbows and swing around once.

Foot Couples.   Last couples in a longways set.

Fox Trot.   See page 227.

Gallop.   See page 199.

Grand Right and Left.   Partners face, touch right hands and pass on by to the next, touching left hands and on around the circle until partners meet again. The boys move counterclockwise; the girls clockwise. In square dancing, an Allemande left usually precedes the Grand Right and Left and partners Promenade home when they meet.

Grapevine. Step left to side; step right behind left; step left to side; step right in front of left.

Head Couples. First and third couples in a set.

Home Position. Original position of each dancer in the set.

Marching. Walking in a military or dignified manner with even steps.

Paddle Step. Weight is on the left foot. Pivot on left, turning clockwise, stepping around with the right.

Polka. Weight is on the left foot. Hop on left; step on right; bring left to right and transfer weight to right foot. Hop on right, etc. (very often in folk dancing the hop is left off). Hop; step; close; step.

Positions

Closed Position. (Ballroom or social dance position.) Partners face; boy has his right arm around girl's waist; girl has left hand on boy's right shoulder. Boy holds girl's left hand in his right hand at about shoulder level, elbow slightly bent.

Open Position. Partners are side by side facing the same direction. Boy has his right arm around girl's waist and the girl has her left hand on the boy's right shoulder. The free hands may, as the dance demands, hang loosely or be placed on the hips.

Skater's Position. See Promenade.

Varsouvienne Position. Partners face in same direction, girl slightly to front of boy. Boy holds girl's left hand in his left hand at shoulder level and extends his right arm across the girl's shoulders and holds her right hand in his right hand.

Promenade. Each boy takes his partner in skater's position, and all couples move counterclockwise around the circle. Partners stand side by side; girl is on the boy's right. The boy takes his girl's left hand in his left hand, and her right hand in his right. His right arm is over her left arm.

Schottische. Step left; step right; step left; hop left—run, run, run, hop, or one, two, three, hop.

Shuffle. A flowing one-step with feet in contact with the floor. This is the principal step in square dancing and when done properly gives the impression that the dancer is moving without any apparent effort.

Side Couples. Couples two and four in a set.

Slide. See page 199.

Step-hop. Step on left; hop on left; step on right; hop on right.

Step-swing. Step on left, swinging right leg forward in front of left. Step right and swing left leg over.

Two-step. Step forward left; bring right to left; step forward left. Step forward right; bring left to right; step forward right. Teach: Step, close, step.

Waltz. Step forward left on count one; step forward right on count two; close left to right on count three. Step right; step left; close right to left.

SUGGESTED READINGS

1. Ainsworth, Dorothy, and Evans, Ruth: *Basic Rhythms: A Study in Movement.* New York, Chartwell House, Inc., 1955.
2. Andrews, Gladys: *Creative Rhythmic Movement for Children.* New York, Prentice-Hall, Inc., 1954.
3. Bauer, Lois M., and Reed, Barbara: *Dance and Play Activities for the Elementary Grades.* Vol. I and II. New York, Chartwell House, Inc., 1954.
4. Burger, Isabel: *Creative Play Activity.* New York, A. S. Barnes & Co., 1950.
5. California Folk Dance Federation: *Folk Dances from Far and Near.* Berkeley, California, The California Book Company Ltd., 7 volumes, 1945, '46, '47, '48, '49, '50, '51.
6. Duggan, Anne; Schlottman, Jeanette; and Rutledge, Abbie: *Folk Dance Library.* Four volumes, New York, A. S. Barnes & Co., 1948.
7. Durlacher, Ed: *Honor Your Partner.* New York, The Devin-Adair Co., 1949.
8. Eisenberg, Helen and Larry: *And Promenade All.* 2403 Branch Street, Nashville, Tennessee, 1947.
9. Evans, Ruth; Bacon, Mary E.; Bacon, Thelma I.; and Stapleton, Joie F.: *Physical Education for Elementary Schools.* New York, McGraw-Hill Book Co., Inc., 1958.
10. Farwell, Jane: *Folk Dances for Fun.* Rural Recreation Service, Recreational Helps to Leaders, Dodgeville, Wisconsin, 1954.
11. Folk Dance Federation of California: *Let's Dance.* Vols. A, B, C. 420 Market St., Room 521, San Francisco, California.
12. Geri, Frank H.: *Illustrated Games and Rhythms for Children: Primary Grades.* Englewood Cliffs, New Jersey, Prentice-Hall, Inc., 1955.
13. Halsey, Elizabeth, and Porter, Lorena: *Physical Education for Children.* New York, Holt, Rinehart and Winston, 1963.
14. Harris, Jane A.; Pittman, Anne; and Waller, Marlys: *Dance A While,* 2nd Ed. Minneapolis, Minn., Burgess Publishing Co., 1966.
15. H'Doubler, Margaret N.: *Dance: A Creative Art Experience.* New York, Appleton-Century-Crofts, Inc., 1940.
16. Herman, Michael: *Folk Dances for All.* New York, Barnes & Noble, Inc., 1947. Publication, *Folk Dancer,* Community Folk Dance Center, P.O. Box 201, Flushing, Long Island, N.Y. Back copies available.
17. Kulbitsy, Olga, and Kaltman, Frank L.: *Teacher's Dance Handbook.* (Kindergarten through sixth grade), Bluebird Publishing Company, Folkraft, 1161 Broad Street, Newark, New Jersey, 1960.
18. Latchaw, Marjorie, and Pyatt, Jean: *Folk and Square Dances and Singing Games for Elementary Schools.* Englewood Cliffs, New Jersey, Prentice-Hall, Inc., 1966.
19. Monsour, Sally; Cohen, Marilyn; and Lindell, Patricia: *Rhythm in Music and Dance for Children.* Belmont, California, The Wadsworth Press, 1966.
20. Murray, Ruth L.: *Dance in Elementary Education.* 2d Ed., New York, Harper & Brothers, 1963.
21. Royal Academy of Dancing and Ling Physical Education Association: Seven books in a series: *Dances of Czechoslovakia, Sweden, Netherlands, Austria, Finland, Greece and Switzerland.* 41 E. 50th Street, New York, Chanticleer Press, Inc., 1949.
22. Saffron, Rosanna: *First Book of Creative Rhythms.* New York, Holt, Rinehart and Winston, 1963.
23. Shaw, Lloyd: *Cowboy Dances,* 1943. *Round Dance Book,* 1948. Caldwell, Idaho, Claxton Printers, Inc., 1942.
24. Shurr, Gertrude, and Yocom, Rachael D.: *Modern Dance Techniques and Teaching.* New York, A. S. Barnes & Co., 1949.
25. Smith, Raymond: *Square Dance Hand Book and Collection of Square Dances and Mixers.* 1038 Cedar Hill, Dallas, Texas.

26. Stuart, Frances R., and Ludlam, John S.: *Rhythmic Activities, Series I and II.* Minneapolis, Minn., Burgess Publishing Company, 1955.
    ———, ——— and Gibson, Virginia: *Rhythmic Activities, Series III.* Minneapolis, Minn., Burgess Publishing Company, 1961.
27. Vernazza, Marcelle: *Making and Playing Classroom Instruments.* Fearon Publishers, 2263 Union St., San Francisco, Cal., 1959.

RECORD REFERENCES

A. Bowman Records: 4921 Santa Monica Blvd., Los Angeles 29, Cal., *Holiday Time Album,* No. 302.
B. Bowmar, Stanley Company: Burns, Joseph, and Wheeler, Edith: *Creative Rhythm Album.* (Visit to a farm, park and circus.) 12 Cleveland Street, Valhalla, New York.
C. Burns Record Company, 755 Chickadee Lane, Stratford, Conn.
D. Capitol Records, Sunset and Vine, Hollywood, California.
E. Childhood Rhythms, Vols. I, II, VI. 326 Forest Park Avenue, Springfield, Massachusetts.
F. David McKay Co., Inc., 119 W. 40th St., New York 18, N.Y. Rhythms for primary and intermediate grades, folk dances and social dances.
G. Decca Records: *Ye Old Time Night, Cowboy Dances.* Called by Lloyd Shaw. Book of instructions included. Decca Album A-524.
H. Durlacher, Ed: *Honor Your Partner.* Square Dance Associates, 102 N. Columbus Avenue, Freeport, New York.
 I. Educational Activities, Inc., P.O. Box 392, Freeport, N.Y. 11520.
J. Folkraft Record Company: *Library of International Dances,* 7 Oliver Street, Newark, New Jersey.
K. Folkways: *Rhythms of the World.* 117 W. 46th Street, New York, New York. "Birds, Beasts, Bugs and Little Fishes."
L. Henlee Record Company: Texas Square Dance Music (without calls), 2404 Harris B., Austin, Texas.
M. Herman, Michael: Folk Dance Records, Box 201, Flushing, Long Island, New York.
N. Hoctor Dance Records, Waldwick, N.J. 07463.
O. Imperial Records: Square Dances (without calls), Jimmy Clossin.
   Square Dances (with calls), Lee Bedford, Jr.
   American Folk Dances, Russian Folk Dances, Baltic Folk Dances.
P. Israeli Music Foundation, Israeli Folk Dances (Direction book included), 731 Broadway, New York.
Q. Kimbo Records, Box 55, Deal, N.J. 07723.
R. Le Crone Rhythm Record Co., 9203 Nichols Rd., Oklahoma City, Okla. 73120.
S. MacGregor Records, 2005 Labranch, Houston, Texas.
T. Methodist World of Fun Series, Methodist Publishing House, Nashville, Tennessee. Singing Games, Folk Dances, Couple Dances, etc.
U. Phoebe James Products: *Creative Rhythms for Children.* Box 134, Pacific Palisades, California .
V. *Playtime Records:* These records are non-breakable, cost twenty-five cents and are found in most drug stores or record shops. Each contains a simple rhyme or singing game.
W. Radio Corporation of America. RCA Victor Division, Camden, New Jersey. *RCA Victor Record Library for Elementary Schools,* which includes: Music of American Indians with instructions and suggestions for sixteen dances; Rhythmic Activities, 5 volumes for primary and upper grades; Singing Games.
X. *Rainbow Rhythms.* Piano recordings, arranged and recorded by Nora Belle Emerson, edited by Thomas E. McDonough; 4 series 78 r.p.m. with instructions included in each set. P.O. Box 608, Emory University, Atlanta 22, Georgia.
Y. Record Center, 2581 Piedmont Rd. N.E., Atlanta, Ga. 30324.
Z. Rhythms Productions: Capricorn Records, affiliates of Woodcliff Productions.
   Folk Dances from 'Round the World, Series I through V, Instructions included. Records LP—A 106-A 110.
   Railroad Rhythms—Musical score by Ruth White, Instructions. Record AF 101.
   Activity Songs—Facts, fancies and experiences of children. Record A 102.

AA. Scandinavian Folk Dance Album, Michael Herman, Box 201, Flushing, Long Island, New York.
BB. Shaw, Lloyd—Recording Company, Box 203, Colorado Springs, Colo.
CC. Square Dance Albums—Capitol, Disc, Keystone and others.
DD. Square Dance Associates, 102 N. Columbus Ave., Freeport, Long Island, New York.
EE. Sonart Folk Dance Album M-8, Sonart Record Corporation, 251 W. 42nd Street, New York. May order from Michael Herman.
FF. Swiss Folk Dance Album M-8, Columbia Recording Company, Bridgeport, Connecticut.
GG. Ultra Records—Jewish Folk Dances, Vols. I and II. New York City. Also available from Michael Herman, Box 201, Flushing, Long Island, New York.
HH. Windsor Records—5528 N. Rosemead Blvd., Temple City, California.
II. Folk Dance Funfest (Dick Kraus), Educational Dance, FD-1, FD-2, FD-3, FD-4. David McKay Company, 119 W. 40th Street, New York 18, N.Y.
JJ. *Living With Rhythms Series*—Basic Rhythms for Primary Grades; Animal Rhythms; Rhythms and Meter Appreciation; Rhythms for Physical Fitness (Dick Kraus), David McKay Company, 119 W. 40th Street, New York 18, N.Y.

VISUAL AIDS, WORDS, AND MUSIC

a. Bertail, Inez: *Complete Nursery Song Book.* New York, Lathrop, Lee and Shephard Company, 1947.
b. *Building Children's Personality Through Creative Dancing:* Extension Dept., Bureau of Visual Instruction, University of California, Berkeley, California (film).
c. Durlacher. Ed: *Honor Your Partner.* New York. The Devin-Adair Co.. 1949.
d. Gomez, Winifred Loerch: *Merry Songs for Boys and Girls.* New York, Follett Publishing Company, 1949.
e. Lomax, John and Alan: *The 111 Best American Ballads, Folk Songs, U.S.A.* 2d Ed. New York, Duell, Sloan and Pearce, 1947.
f. *Materials for Teaching Dance,* Vol. III, Selected Visual Aids for Dance. Washington 6, D.C., National Section on Dance by the AAHPER, 1201 16th Street, N.W.
g. Wilson, John: *Children's Pieces.* 56 Jane Street, New York 14, N.Y. Book I, six pieces," Book II, 8 pieces; Book III, 7 pieces. Include such as: "Night Magic," "The Sick Lamb," "Early Morning Song," and "The Lost Balloon."

SUGGESTED RECORDS FOR CREATIVE MOVEMENT EXPERIENCES

Available from: Educational Department, R.C.A. Victor Records, 155 E. 24th St., N.Y., N.Y.
Dance Me a Story
Little Duck
Noah's Ark
The Magic Mountain
Balloons
The Brave Hunter
Flappy and Floppy

Chapter 13

Movement Exploration

To move is to live! Movement, learning, and living are closely linked experiences through which we, regardless of age, are constantly learning more about our ever-changing selves and the world of which we are a vital part. Movement itself is the foundation upon which all educational experiences are built. It is at the very heart of every good physical education program in which each student should have opportunities to learn to master through his own experiences a wide variety of movement problems of ever-increasing complexity in sports and games, rhythms and dance, aquatics, and self-testing activities that require body control and flexibility, strength, quick reaction time, accuracy, and the ability to make quick decisions.

Through movement, the child can improve his health and fitness, gain an understanding of how his own body works, as well as acquire better control of it, develop a better understanding of himself and others, communicate his own feelings and creative ideas, and learn how to respond to challenges that he has set for himself or that have been set by others.

THE TEACHER'S ROLE

The teacher should strive to utilize best all available space in this exploratory program and should plan for progressive program activities that will take children from what they can already do well to new movement discoveries and challenges that they must strive hard to master. Often the same movement problems can be presented in many different ways. The children should be encouraged to express their own ideas for new problems and should be increasingly exposed to greater challenges. As one authority in this field suggests:

Basic to the success of the program is the willingness and eagerness of the teacher to experiment with movement. The teacher truly seeking individual expression from children will usually avoid moving herself or giving demonstrations. This attitude will prevent children from imitating her patterns and restricting exploration on their part. Carefully planned sequences for building a vocabulary of movement, for establishing a comfortable emotional climate, and for

Figure 30. To move is to live! To live is to learn! (Courtesy of the Detroit Public Schools, Detroit, Michigan.)

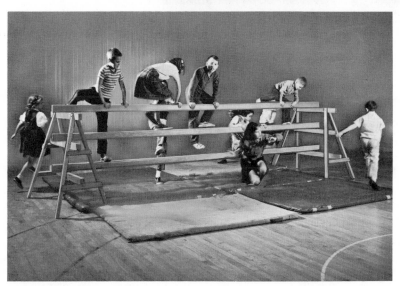

Figure 31. Children delight in learning how to control their bodies through a wide variety of challenging movement experiences. (Courtesy of the Lind Climber Corporation.)

understanding children's movement potential create an ideal setting for the encouragement of movement expression.[1]

TEACHING TECHNIQUES

It is only from creative teaching that creative movement experiences for children can evolve. The following suggestions, however, can help make these richly shared educational experiences valuable to both the teacher and the learner:

CLASS CONTROL

Scattered formations with plenty of space available for children to run, skip, and move freely about are needed for this program. From the beginning the teacher should condition the children to stop, look, and listen when they hear a given signal, such as a drum beat, piano chord, or even a whistle.

PROBLEM POSING

Although each teacher should develop her own technique for presenting problems, suggested ones are: "Can anyone . . . ?" "What can . . . ?" "See if you might do this . . . ?" "Who can do it in a better, faster, louder, quieter (etc.) way . . . ?" or "Who wants to make up a game using this . . . ?"

SAFETY

Often, since herein the element of competition is removed, few children will overtax their limits and most will set the more difficult tasks for themselves. However, it is suggested that having the children all run clockwise or counterclockwise in a circle, start to move at the same time, or play in a designated area will help them to become more safety conscious.

DISCIPLINE

Authorities agree that far too many school discipline problems are teacher caused. Be sure, then, that your children are working to achieve

---

[1]Hussey, Delia: *Exploration of Basic Movement in Physical Education.* Publication 4-322 TCH, Detroit, Michigan, Detroit Public Schools, 1960, pp. 6–7.

Figure 32. As wide a variety of equipment as can be had should be utilized. (Courtesy of the Detroit Public Schools, Detroit, Michigan.)

social behavior goals or to learn mottos, such as "We take turns in this class," that they are not kept waiting too long for the "go" signal when they are given equipment to use, or that they really *do* feel they can explore or express themselves freely in this class.

SUGGESTED EQUIPMENT

Use as wide a variety of equipment as possible in this program. Suggested are:

Many ropes of varying lengths
Balls of all sizes
Tossing games
Blocks of all sizes
Bars, ropes, jungle gyms
Wands, broomsticks
Parachutes
Horizontal and window ladders
Benches
Telephone poles, large tree trunks
    for climbing
Tumbling mats

Hoops
Barrels to roll
Car and bicycle tires, inner tubes, hula hoops
Balance beams and boards
Boxes of all sizes and weights
Climbing steps and ladders
Beanbags (one for every one or two children)
Low turning bars
Teeters
Many 2 x 4 boards to be used in balancing
    and jumping activities
Stilts and tin can walkers

SUGGESTED ACTIVITIES

Locomotor Activities

WALKING

1. How many tiny or giant steps does it take you to cross this room?
2. Can you change your direction and still keep walking? Level? Speed?
3. Can you express joy when walking? Sorrow? Anger?
4. Can you walk on only your toes? Heels? Inside of your feet? Outside?
5. Discover how many ways you can walk.

RUNNING

1. Run and stop fast when you hear the whistle.
2. Who can run in the greatest number of different ways?
3. Can you combine a run with any other kind of movement, such as a jump?
4. If you can run forward, how many other ways can you run?
5. Can you run using your arms in a way other than by swinging them forward and backward?

HOPPING

1. Hop as fast as you can on one foot.
2. Jump as lightly as you can on both feet.
3. Combine a hop with another movement.
4. If you can hop in a circle, see in how many other patterns you can hop.
5. Jump as high as you can five times; then lower your body every time you hop for five more times. Who can hop lowest to the floor?

SLIDING

1. See how many ways you can slide other than forward.
2. Combine a slide with any other kind of movement.
3. Slide around in a circle with a partner.
4. Slide in a big circle with two others. Can you find a way to go in and out of a circle while sliding?
5. Can you slide face to face then back to back with a partner?

SKIPPING

1. Skip forward, skip in a big circle, then on a diagonal.
2. Can you skip holding hands with a partner?
3. How many others can skip with you holding hands?
4. How fast can you skip? How slowly?
5. Can you change from a skip to a slide or a gallop?

JUMPING

1. How many times can you jump up and down on one foot? On both feet?
2. Can you jump going around in a circle? In a square? Forward? Backward?

3. Who can jump first on one foot and then on the other for the longest time?
4. Can you jump from the top of this box or table to the mat below?
5. Can you jump, run, jump, skip?

GENERAL LOCOMOTOR ACTIVITIES

1. Choose a corner in this room. Run to it fast when I say "go!" Now do it very slowly.
2. Bend as far as you can forward, backward, and to the side as you walk forward.
3. Make yourself squat as low to the floor as you can. Stretch high as near to the ceiling as you can.
4. Raise your right arm and left leg, then your left arm and right leg while marching in place. Now march around the room.
5. As you run forward change from being a tall giant to a tiny mouse, but keep moving.

Using Equipment

TURNING BAR

1. Can you make a circle over this bar?
2. Who can chin himself on the bar?
3. Can you circle the bar using just one leg?
4. Who can "skin the cat" using this bar?
5. Can you reach behind you and by grasping the bar make a circle over it with your body?

THE CLIMBING LADDER

1. See how fast you can go up and down the ladder.
2. Can you climb up the ladder without using your feet?
3. Can you weave in and out of the rungs to go up and come down the ladder?
4. Can you skip any rungs while climbing it?
5. What else can you do using this ladder?

THE STAIRS

1. Who can go up and down the stairs without holding onto a railing?
2. Can you go up and down them by hopping on two feet? One foot?
3. Can you go up and down backward? Jump up and down them facing sideward?
4. Can you walk up and down them balancing yourself by your hands?
5. Can you go up and down by moving over one, two, or more steps?

SAWED-OFF BROOMSTICKS OR WANDS

1. Can you balance the stick in the palm of your hand? On two, then on one finger?
2. Can you throw it up into the air, spin around, and catch it before it hits the floor?
3. Can you play pitch and catch with it with a partner, using the same hand you catch it with to throw it to her?
4. Can you balance the stick while kneeling on one knee? Both knees? While slowly lying down and getting back up?
5. Can you twirl the stick while pretending to be a drum majorette?

Figure 33.   Exploring ways of turning. (Courtesy of the Detroit Public Schools, Detroit, Michigan.)

TIRES

1. See how fast you can roll the tire.
2. See if you can roll it in a circle. In a straight line. Backward.
3. Jump in and out of it moving around in a circle if the tire is flat on the floor.
4. Can you crawl through it when someone holds it up?
5. Can you throw a volleyball through it? A baseball?

CREATIVE PLAY

The beginning of the century found a child with few toys and the capacity to play for hours on end with "findings." A pile of sand, a few bits of broken glass or china and twigs furnished materials for full-scale villages complete with houses, barns, schools, and churches. Tea parties of mud pies were served with great formality from a pedestal table made of dirt. From large leaves and twigs young designers fashioned hats, capes, skirts and dresses which were modeled with an amusing exactness of adult patterns. Labor-saving devices were few and mothers kept too busy, except to call children for meals, naps and baths.

Figure 34. Exploration of pushing movements. (Courtesy of the Detroit Public Schools, Detroit, Michigan.)

Today, the infant lies in a toy-bedecked crib and collects more toys as birthdays and Christmases pass. Sand is to be had by the load, and woe to the child who dares pluck a leaf from a guarded and nurtured tree. Labor-saving devices have left mothers leisure time to play nurse-maid, a job made easier by access to parks, well equipped libraries, recreation centers, nursery schools, neighborhood movie houses, radio, and television sets. Urban children are gradually being deprived of all stimuli which once enabled them to play without direct instruction and supervision, and mothers complain that the children cannot amuse themselves over a thirty-minute period without being bored.

Today's teacher is completely aware of the short span of attention present in the newly acquired pupil, which is characteristic of the age level, but not entirely physiological or psychological. The classroom teacher and the special teachers have tried to remedy this and to give the child a measure of security and self-sufficiency by equipping him with the tools for living. It cannot be said that real effort has not been made to develop the "whole" child mentally, physically and emotionally, but how near have we come to meeting this objective? Paté de fois gras is palatable, but is the process good for the goose? We still stuff children and expect magic results in the way of initiative. How many of us ask, "Is there a child in the class

Figure 35.   Creative play is not new, but its possibilities are comparatively untouched. (Courtesy of Elizabeth Glidden, Specialist in Elementary Physical Education, Los Angeles City Schools, Los Angeles, California.)

who could create from his own background of experience an enjoyable period of play acceptable to his classmates?" It is far easier with age, poise and experience to direct play than to develop in one child the ability to do the same thing "free hand." The art teacher can take potential talent and draw from it the maximum in imagination, reality, or originality. Play is laughter, high spirits, and joy unlimited. In this field where sheer enjoyment is the key it would be shameful if teachers did not meet the challenge of the children's needs and at least give them the CHANCE to be ingenious leaders.

Creative play is not new but its possibilities are comparatively untouched. There are several reasons which explain this fallow corner in a field rich with all the newest trends in progressive education, the most prevalent being overcrowded conditions which exist in the majority of public schools. The average teacher finds it difficult to deal with a class two to four times the normal load without assuming full or partial leadership. Creative play calls for small, intimate groups, managed in the most informal manner. The ideal group would not exceed 20 and each child would have frequent chances for expression, but creative play can and has been developed in many schools, in recreation centers, and on playgrounds. A certain amount of regimentation is required in all large schools, especially where the platoon system is used, and, while it is necessary, the routine subdues latent creativeness. The time element is another reason why creative play has not flourished. Creativeness cannot be nurtured by bells. It takes a gifted teacher to hold on to a vision gained and to reproject it into the minds of the participants with sustaining and refreshing enthusiasm the next day.

There can be no static method for developing creative play. The group, its individual characteristics and dominant field of experience, will dictate to the resourceful teacher the plan of procedure. An imaginative six year old child may invent a game that will keep a class engrossed for thirty minutes. There are also people who play a piano by ear, while others must learn scales and notes before tackling the simplest of piano selections. Thus, one may find a group of fourth graders who must be re-introduced to the fundamentals of play, i.e., chase, flee, tag, seek, dodge, guess, follow, and so forth, before one child comes forth with an original game. However, we, as teachers cannot complain too loudly, since we have leaned with monotonous regularity on tried and true game books for years. One must face innumerable presentations of questionable originality. Tact and patience will reward the persistent teacher. In any case, the reward will be adequate when the child can competently lead a game—the day Jimmie teaches a game that he calls, "I Gotcha." It *is* different! All of the children eye Jimmie with open admiration slightly tinged with envy, and one even wisecracks, "Watcha know, right out of his little pointed head." On this day you, teacher, have arrived and can take proper pride in your fledgling.

This does not mean that every child will immediately burst forth with new and exciting games. The neo-dubious will still crop up, but the group will become more discriminating and take the criticizing chore out of the hands of the teacher by observing, "Ah, I learned that at Daily Vacation

Figure 36. These primary children are enjoying imitating animals through exploratory movement activities. (Courtesy of *The Instructor*. Photograph by Edith Brockway.)

Figure 37.   Exploration of stretching and bending. (Courtesy of the Detroit Public Schools, Detroit, Michigan.)

Bible School," or "We learned that at camp." The hard sledding is over. From then on original ideas will start appearing with encouraging regularity. Do not be too critical and, above all, try to gear your evaluation to the grade level.

Children are innately creative but the current, consuming interest will always be reflected in games. At present the "Spaceman" and "Batman" are "It." Children from Spokane to Los Angeles, Dallas to Duluth, and New Haven to Key West are make-believe "cowboys," roping, cutting calves,[2] chasing rustlers, packing six shooters, slapping leather,[3] and addressing playmates as "podner." Sex does not enter into the picture. There is an "Annie Oakley"[4] for each "Astronaut."[5] Even now cowboys are becoming "old hat," for youthful "prospectors" are industriously beginning to search out atomic materials with 5 and 10 Geiger counters, or fly to the moon in a rocket. This does not make any difference as long as the child is creating a type of play which includes mental and physical activity, and is guided into democratic channels.

Creative play involving movement fundamentals will be found in its most productive form from the first through the fourth grades. New games will still appear which concern themselves largely with skills in lead-up games, but the interest has shifted to team sports, and creativeness is

---

[2] Round-up—Separation of calves from stock ready for market.

[3] Hitting leather chaps with bridle reins to urge on horses and cattle.

[4] Real life character who was crack shot.

[5] Current space hero.

manifested through methods for improving offensive and defensive play. However, games related to subject matter may be created through the eighth grade and on into high school as a method for motivating learning.

Numerous European physical educators are experimenting successfully with providing educational and creative play situations for children. The child is challenged to perform a movement but is not told how to do it, for each must create his own solution to the challenging problem posed by the teacher or group. Special emphasis is given to tasks which strengthen the trunk and feet, increase body flexibility and elasticity, develop a "feel" for movements such as bending and stretching which will develop good posture, perfect movement skills in running, jumping, throwing, and supporting activities, and develop rhythmic beauty for movement. Foremost exponent and leader of this new and creative elementary physical education is LiselottDiem of Germany. From her work, as well as from that done experimentally in other European countries, the new approach to elementary physical education, known as "Movement Exploration," has developed.[6]

Examples of the movement tasks posed as creative problems for children to solve which Mrs. Diem has found to be the most successful and satisfying for children are:

Who Can (*using a box*)
Run the most lightly, land on the top of the box, then jump off?
Jump from the box and touch the floor for the briefest time with his finger tips?
Place his hands on the box, jump upright on it and take a flying jump down, doing it the most gracefully?

Who Can (*using no equipment*)
Stretch his legs the highest while turning a cartwheel and land on his feet softly like a cat?
Skip forward, turning sideways, alternate running with skipping, first alone, with partner, then in rows?
Skip backwards with long reaching skips, next with a basketball on his head, then with arms crossed behind the back, then skip facing and away from a partner in unison?
Roll backwards and forwards quickly and quietly; sit touching his knees with his forehead?
Walk like a little man, a giant, and change the fastest from these?
Sit on the floor alternating a toe and heel change the fastest while sitting the tallest?
Frog jump from a squat position?
Bounce up and down into the air, turning and spinning?
"Merry-go-round" with a partner changing from high to low, slow to fast?
Run on hands and feet forward, backward, sideward?

Who Can (*with broomsticks or wands*)
Run like a big snake with 10 others around the sticks, then run the fastest alone over the sticks?
Walk forward, backward, sideward on the stick?
Stand the stick upright, turn around quickly and catch it before it touches the ground?
Run, walk, and skip forward, backward, and sideward juggling the stick on the palm of his hand?

---

[6]A copy of her book translated into English, entitled *Who Can*, is available at $1.60 per copy (plus 12 cents mailing charge) from Mrs. Paul Dunsing, George Williams College, Downers Grove, Illinois, 60515. A wonderful film of her experimental work with primary children is available from Robert Freeman, Metropolitan YMCA, 19 S. La Salle St., Chicago, Illinois, 60601.

Juggle the wand on his finger, sit down and stand up still balancing it?

Who Can (*with a hoop or tire*)
Roll the hoop forward, backward and around in a circle while walking, running, skipping?
Pick the hoop up with his toes?
Roll the hoop and run through it?
Use the hoop like a skipping rope and jump through it?

Who Can (*with a telephone pole, skinned tree trunk or beam*)
Walk upright up the inclined pole, walk on all fours?
Walk across the pole when it is 3–4–5 feet above ground in horizontal position?
Walk halfway across, sit down and get up without using his hands?
Travel on the underside while hanging by his hands and feet?
Walk across throwing and catching a ball, rolling a hoop or doing something else?

Who Can (*with a ball*)
Skip forward and backward while bouncing the ball?
Turn around and catch it while skipping?
Sit like a tailor and roll the ball around him the fastest?
Lift his legs high into the air and roll the ball under, around, and over them?
Start from a sitting position, throw the ball up and catch it standing?
Serpentine run first around five balls in squads without touching any ball?
Jump like a bunny over five balls one at a time?
Bounce the ball completely around himself without turning his whole body or moving his feet?
Sit on the floor and dribble the ball around himself, do the same while stretched out on his stomach or on his back, or get up from any of these positions while still dribbling the ball?

What Mrs. Diem and other European physical educators have done, as illustrated above, can be used as a pattern by any creative American teacher and can be enlarged upon with the help of his students. The carry-over values of such creativeness are vast. A physically educated individual is one who can use his whole body wisely with the maximum of output and the minimum effort in our ever-changing and problem-ridden world. Children will gain skill in movement and problem solving through this type of creative play which can have great carry-over value into their own adulthood.

GAMES CREATED BY CHILDREN

Below are listed games which have been presented by elementary children and show creativeness influenced by background experience.

JUNGLE JIM

Grade 3

(Jungle Jim is a comic-strip character read by many children.)

Twelve children form a hollow square. Leader winds in and out of the square tapping children who identify themselves as certain animals or birds. As each child is tapped he follows the leader in a snake-like line until the entire group is drawn into a circle. The group sings, "We Went to the Animal Fair." The leader then calls upon each child to give an imitation of the animal he represents. The child who gives the best imitation becomes the next leader.

RADAR SCREEN

Grade 5

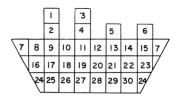

Class is divided into two teams who make out questions on any subject. Teacher reads and directs questions or, better, team leaders do same. When a question is answered correctly, a block is hung on that team's screen. The team that fills its screen first is the winner. Colored blocks hung on eye screws, 2 half squares equivalent to one whole square.

WASH DAY

Grade 2

CLOTHES PINS		LAUNDRY
10	5X	
20	6X	
30	7X	
40	8X	

Numbers 5, 6, 7 and 8 decide what piece of laundry they will represent as: sheet, towel, shirt. Number 1 pin gets two guesses as to what he is holding on the line. If the guess is correct, he changes places with Number 5. The questioning goes on down the line. If a clothes pin misses three times he must drop out of the game and a new player takes his place. The players representing the wash decide on a different article after each round of questioning.

PROGRESSIVE PRESENTATION

Mimetics

Mimetics can be presented in the first through the sixth grades. A child loses self-consciousness quickly in interpreting the suggested subject. At first the movements will be actual imitations of the toy, machine, or animal. Later the movements can become more subtle and suggestive rather than purely imitative. Mimetics serve as a smooth lead-up to creative dance. An accompaniment is not always necessary for mimetics but will be suggested when there is a need for music in each of the following activities.

1. Mechanical[7]
   Bicycle—Series I, Ruth Evans
   See-Saw—Series I, Ruth Evans
   Airplane—Series I, Ruth Evans
         Rhythms for Children—Vic. 20162
   Jumping Jack—Series II, Ruth Evans
   Fire Engine—No music—pantomime—sirens, driving through the streets, unwinding the
         hose, etc.
   Train—Series I, Ruth Evans
   Dolls[8]—Dance of Chinese Dolls, RCA Victor 22163-A
   Tops—Series I, Ruth Evans

---

[7] Record Reference D.
[8] Record Reference X.

Figure 38.   Exploration of percussive movement to different kinds of accompaniment. (Courtesy of the Detroit Public Schools, Detroit, Michigan.)

       Clocks—Series II, Ruth Evans
       Elevator—Series II, Ruth Evans
       Swing—Series I, Ruth Evans
       Railroad Rhythms[9]
       Windmills[10]
  2. Animals[11]
       Horse—Series I, Ruth Evans
       Bear—No music—pantomime—walk in slovenly, rolling gait, looking for honey. Bear in the zoo sits, claps paws, and catches a thrown piece of bread.
       Elephant[12]—Series I, Ruth Evans—Arms form the trunk which swings from side to side; elephant sits up, eats, drinks water and sprays water on the crowd.
       Puppy—Does tricks: rolls over, plays dead, sits up, covers face, prays, and walks on hind feet and then on front feet.
       Kitten—Plays with a ball of yarn, retreats, stalks, and pounces on prey.
       Kangaroo—No music—pantomime—hop
       Deer—No music—pantomime—being chased by hunters and hounds
       Squirrel—No music—pantomime—short jerky movements, hiding nuts
       Beasts[13]
       Puppy[14]
       Cat stretches—Stanley Bowman—206
       Rabbit—Stanley Bowman—203

---

  [9] Record Reference Z. [AF 101].
 [10] Record Reference X.
 [11] Record Reference D., Vol. I; B.
 [12] Record Reference X.
 [13] Record Reference K.
 [14] Record Reference X.

3. Insects[15]
   Butterfly—Butterfly Dance—Indian Rhythms, RCA Victor 22174, Ponies and Butter-
       flies—RCA Victor 22079
   Bee—The Flight of the Bumblebee
   Cricket—No music—pantomime—lively jumping movements, rubbing arms together
   Firefly—No music—pantomime—quick flitting movements, interspersed with pauses
4. Miscellaneous
   Birds[16]—Rhythms for Children—20401
   Witch[17]—Series I, Ruth Evans
   Giant—In the Hall of the Mountain King—Victor 11835, The Giants—Victor 20743
   My Shadow[18]
   Bubbles[19]
   Snowflakes and Skating[20]
   Little Fishes[21]
   Elf[22]—Gnomes and Dwarfs—Victor 19882

Creative Movement

Creativity can often be best expressed in movement. It is an activity
that releases seeds of creative ability that grow with great abandon when
sown at an early age. The child on the primary level is full of energy and
free of inhibitions. This provides an opportunity to develop innate creative ability at a productive age.

Every child intensely feels his surrounding environment and is
acutely conscious of change or new additions. Each child would naturally
react in a different way to these stimuli; this is as it should be, but such is
not the case when creative dance is introduced. There will always be the
more aggressive leader who sets a pattern that will be followed sheep-like
by other less imaginative children. Participation may be accepted as a goal
but is an inadequate one. Aping should be discouraged from the first and
differences pointed out to develop pride in the originality of individual
expression.

Whether the exercise involves abstract feeling or a story or theme, a
picture should be painted by the teacher to fire the imagination. The instructor may select one group and accompany their rhythm with a drum
beat, accenting exciting moments with a heavier beat.

1. *Story or theme*—The use of a story or theme offers excellent transition from mimetics
and story acting to creative rhythm.
   Story Example: Little Red Riding Hood
                    Divide the class: Girls are Little Red Riding Hood and the boys
                    are the wolves. Little Red Riding Hood skips through the forest

---

[15] Record Reference K.
[16] *Ibid.*
[17] Record Reference D.
[18] Record Reference X.
[19] *Ibid.*
[20] *Ibid.*
[21] Record Reference K.
[22] Record Reference D.

Figure 39A. Creativity can often be best expressed through movement. (Courtesy of Elizabeth Glidden, Specialist in Elementary Physical Education, Los Angeles City Schools, Los Angeles, California.)

with her basket. She arrives at her grandmother's and is tired and out of breath. In her encounter with her strange-looking grandmother, she shows surprise, bewilderment and horror. The boy (wolf) shows pleasure, satisfaction and greed.

The Three Bears

Divide the class into groups of four. Go through the story, letting Goldilocks run and skip, eat the food, and lie down to sleep. The bears enter and show chagrin and anger as they find their porridge eaten. They discover Goldilocks who awakens and flees with the bears close behind.

Snow White and the Seven Dwarfs

Divide the class into groups of nine. To the slow beat of the drum the dwarfs march with Snow White who is in the center in a trance as a sleepwalker. The prince releases her from her sleep by tapping her on the shoulder. Sadness gives way to joy as the entire group leaps, jumps and leaps.

Figure 39B.   Movement exploration in the elementary school curriculum is vital to the child's development of body control, expressiveness, and creativity. (Courtesy of Mr. Ray Sacker, Victor Record Division, Radio Corporation of America.)

Theme Example: Circus Day[23]
            Clown
            Marionettes—RCA Victor 22163
        Transportation
            Walking
            Bicycling
            Riding in cars
            Trains
            Plane
            Horse

Other People at Work
    Eskimos
    Indians
    Dutch
    Sailors
    Farmers
    Big game hunters
Special Days
    Halloween
    Easter

[23] Record Reference B.

Valentine's Day	Swimming
Christmas	Football
Thanksgiving	Skating
School's Out!	Track
Songs	Fishing
Peter Cottontail	Parade
Rudolph the Red	Horses
Nosed Reindeer	Elephants
Santa Claus Is	Dancing Bears
Coming to Town	The Seasons
Stories	Visit to the Park[24]
Three Little Pigs	Visit to the Farm[25]
Billy Goat Gruff	Seasonal Characters
Jack and the	Witch
Beanstalk	Santa Claus
Sport Movements	Holiday Rhythms[26]
Rowing	

2. *Free feeling*—Examples
   a. Walk in the leaves—The first frosts have painted the leaves with many colors and they lie in a heavy carpet on the ground. The leaves are dry and crackle underfoot; a kick sends them sailing into the air.
   b. Wind in the trees—The wind sighs in the tall pines as they sway back and forth. The limbs of the large oaks sway more gently while the leaves of the elm, aspen, and cottonwood quaver and chatter at an excited pace.
   c. Fire—The freshly built fire crackles and the flames leap high, gradually dying down to coals and then embers.
   d. The world is big, big

   And I am small, small

   But you should see me
   When I stand tall, tall.

   Giants don't scare me
   I can climb to the stars.

   Jack used his beanstalk,
   I prefer a moonbeam by far.

   Sometimes I'm a puppy
   Who rolls, leaps and barks.
   Sometimes I'm a fierce tiger
   Who slinks through the parks.

   My mom say I'm a tomboy,
   With springs here and there,
   For making like a pogo stick,
   But she's really not fair.
   For at the end of the day
   It's still in our house,
   I put my dolly to bed
   And we're quiet like a mouse.

---

[24] *Ibid.*
[25] *Ibid.*
[26] Record Reference F.

Anger   Strength   Power

Joy   Happiness   Contentment

Sorrow   Sadness   Weakness

e. Growing things—The planted seed swells, sprouts and pushes through the ground to take on leaves, buds and flowers.
f. Feeling for color—Using the primary level for observation, the following reactions were recorded.[27] (Construction paper was used for colors.)
Red—exciting; pugnacious; challenging.
Blue—calm in light shade; intriguing in intense shade.
Green—soothing; restful; lazy.
Yellow—happy; delightful; uplifting.
Black—depressing; still; quiet.
If these exercises seem too abstract, the color may be tied in with tangible things such as:
Red—bullfighter's cape; football jersey; rubber ball; shoes.
Blue—sky; water; eyes; bluebird; glass.
Green—grass; trees; moss; fish.
Yellow—sun; light; canary bird; fire; gems.
g. Balloon—The balloon is released and soars through the air, rocking with the blasts of wind until it hits a thorn on a tree and slowly deflates.
h. Emotions—The instructor sets the scene and uses the drum cadence which the students follow.
   1. Anger, strength, and power require a strong drum beat with an occasional resounding drum beat.
   2. Joy requires a light and quick drum beat that invites skipping, leaping and jumping.
   3. Sadness, sorrow, weakness and disappointment require a low, slow beat that finally dies away as an echo.
i. Adult activities—The following adult activities in the house and yard are suggested for first grade boys and girls. The boys have seen all of these activities and enjoy imitating their mothers' and fathers' familiar chores. In the second or third grades the boy balks at doing women's work and is interested only in the manly chores.
   Half of the class may do the activities and the other half guess what they are

---

[27] Foster, Mildred: Original Unit on Creative Dance taught at Margaret B. Henderson Elementary school, Dallas, Texas.

doing. The teacher should suggest some activities and lead the class into making up their own.

Cleaning house: running the cleaner, sweeping, mopping, and dusting.
Washing and ironing, folding clothes, and putting them away.
Making beds, baking a cake. and putting baby to bed after bathing.
Washing dishes, putting them into the drainer, drying them, and placing them on the shelves. Setting the table and clearing.
Father barbecues a steak, hamburgers, and corn.
Father paints the house and washes and waxes the car.
Father mows the lawn, edges, prunes, and waters.

j. Space adventures—Today we are all concerned with space, and our children have seen space shots, missile launchings, and simulated landings on the moon. Let us see what we can do with these stimuli. We know that the air is very rare and light, so let us get off the earth first and imitate the possible locomotor movements used in outer space where the body is weightless.

Missile shot—Squat position, head bowed, arms close to body. Start rotating hands toward body. Gradually increase the size of rotation and slowly rise until the arms are making huge circles and a standing position is achieved. Raise arms straight overhead and jump into the air and run, run, run.

Space walk—All movements seem to be in slow motion. Slowly jump from space craft. Arms wave slowly to maintain balance as body bends sideways, backward, and forward.

Moon trip—We have landed on the moon. Our boots are weighted. Forward hop as in slow motion, backward hop, slow walk forward with legs raised high and stretched forward. Slow forward roll, slow backward roll, slow jumps toward objects or classmates.

3. *Importance of imagination*

Imagination is innate in all children. It flowers richly in some but must be extracted with consummate skill from others. An idea presented may bring an alert look, a sparkle in the eye, or the dead look of flat unconcern. An idea must fit the known field of experience, or ground must be spaded previously to prepare the soil for growth. Fundamental activities, such as chasing, fleeing, dodging and reaching, are accepted by all children. Known games succeed; this is also true of rhythms. A child who has been raised on the prairie is unable to feel the wind in the pines, but he has a definite feeling for a whining wind that blows sand into dunes of ever-changing patterns or rolls tumbleweeds crazily across vast, open spaces. The child from the north has visions of the soft fall of snow that is feather light, the drifts, and the eerie cry of the blizzard. Smudge pots often darken the skies of California and Florida, but more familiar is the smell of orange blossoms, the waxy white of the trees, and the fruit-laden abundance of a warm climate. There is the beach with scampering waves; the sun by day and the moon by night painting the ripples. There is also the hard, cold winter of northern days and nights, frozen with a hard pristine sparkle; the stream that runs through great canyons and moves later at a sedate pace by flat, shallow banks. The sun shines on maple, aspen, fir, cottonwood, spruce and pine; on corn, cotton, tobacco and wheat our land over. These things children see, and can express if teachers guide and help them to release their feelings.

SUGGESTED READINGS

Andrews, Gladys: *Creative Rhythmic Movement for Children*. New York, Prentice-Hall, Inc., 1954.

Cameron, W., and Pleasance, Peggy: *Education In Movement*. Oxford, England. Basil Blackwell Company, 1965. (Available from: The Ling Book Shop, 10 Nottingham Place, London, England.)

Fleming, Gladys; Sanborn, Jeannette; and Schneider, Elsa: *Physical Education for Today's Boys and Girls*. Boston, Allyn and Bacon, 1965.

Hackett, Layne, and Jenson, Robert: *A Guide to Movement Exploration*. Peek Publications, 982 El Cajon Way, Palo Alto, California, 1966.

Halsey, Elizabeth, and Porter, Lorena: *Physical Education for Children,* Rev. Ed. Holt, Rinehart and Winston, 1963.

Johnson, Leo: Parachute play to exercise. *Journal of Health, Physical Education, Recreation,* April, 1967.

Mosston, Muska: *Development Movement.* Columbus, Ohio, Charles Merrill Books, Inc., 1965.

North, Marion: *A Simple Guide To Movement Teaching.* London, England, Werner Studios, 1964. (Available from: The Ling Book Shop, 10 Nottingham Place, London, England.)

Popen, Sharalyn: Go parachuting. *Journal of Health, Physical Education, Recreation,* April, 1967.

Saffron, Rosanna: *First Book of Creative Rhythms.* New York, Holt, Rinehart and Winston, 1963.

Shurr, Evelyn: *Movement Experiences for Children.* New York, Appleton-Century-Crofts, 1967.

Vernazza, Marcelle: *Making and Playing Classroom Instruments.* Fearon Publishers, 2263 Union Street, San Francisco 23, California, 1959.

SUGGESTED FILMS

Movement Education (Available from: University Elementary School, Audio-Visual Department, University of Iowa, Iowa City, Iowa.)

    Movement Education in Physical Education. 15 min., sound bl. & w. Rental or sale. (Joan Tillotson and Lorena Porter)

    Movement Education: Time and Space Awareness. 7 min., sound, bl. & w. Rental or sale.

    Movement Education: Guided Exploration. 7 min., sound, bl. & w. Rental or sale.

    Movement Education: The Problem-solving Technique. 9 min., sound, bl. & w. Rental or sale. (Joan Tillotson and M. Gladys Scott) 1965.

Movement Education—German Films (Available from: Physical Education Supply Associates, P. O. Box 292, Trumbull, Connecticut.)

    Bewegungserziehung im ersten und zweiten Schuljahr. (Movement Education in the First and Second School Year) 22 min., 2 reels, silent, bl. & w. (Liselott Diem).

    Bewegungserziehung im dritten und vierten Schuljahr. (Movement Education in the Third and Fourth School Year) 20 min., 2 reels, silent, bl. & w. (Liselott Diem).

    Bewegungserziehung im der Landschule. (Movement Education in the Rural School) 25 min., silent, bl. & w. (Liselott Diem).

Basic Skills (Available from: Charles Cahill and Associates, Inc., 5746 Sunset Boulevard, Hollywood, California.)

    Physical Education Basic Skills.

    "Unit A: Softball, Tumbling, Soccer."

    "Unit B: Football, Basketball, Apparatus."

    8 or 16 mm., silent films, detailed instruction booklets included.

RECORD REFERENCES

See list at the end of Chapter 12, page 232.

Chapter 14

Graded Stunts, Self-testing Activities, Tumbling, and Trampolining

A program that excludes self-testing activities, stunts, and tumbling has missed a golden opportunity in aiding the development of the whole child. The abundant use of large muscles in these activities, plus the development of fine coordination, flexibility, balance, and timing, round out the muscle-building process in a most satisfactory manner. The resultant body control gives a sureness of movement and confidence to the child which cannot be gained through any other aspect of the total physical education program.

Physical and social end results more than justify the inclusion of this activity. The pleasure derived from viewing one's progress gives stature to all, but particularly to the boy or girl who does not take naturally to sports, i.e., the frail or obese child. Individual disciplined control necessary for good performance in class carries over into play and social life.

Elementary school children do not have to be sold on this part of the program if it is scaled to their age and skill level. The majority will look forward with enthusiasm to periods spent learning stunts and tumbling. The cause for the small percentage of holdbacks can be traced generally to family objections, where the word tumbling is used in a general way to include all self-testing activities. Parents have visions of their children hurtling through space with resulting neck and back injuries. This fear is inevitably transferred to the child. Public demonstrations of grade-level accomplishments coupled with thorough explanations of each activity will give parents and children alike new appreciation of the program. People support things in which they believe!

Figure 40. The majority of elementary school children look forward with enthusiasm to periods spent learning stunts and tumbling. (Courtesy of Dr. Joan Tillotson, Plattsburgh Public Schools, Plattsburgh, New York.)

UNIFORMS

Boys and girls enjoy working together in these activities through the fourth grade; consciousness of body is absent, in most groups, through the second grade. However, there are parents who object to mixed classes in this activity. Usually this problem can be eliminated by having the girls wear slacks, jeans, or shorts in class.

EQUIPMENT

The size of the budget is always a deciding factor in the purchase of equipment. However, many stunts require only limited space and little equipment, and can be done inside or outside the school. Wands are inexpensive but a sanded mop or broom handle serves the same purpose. Mats are comparatively expensive equipment but, with proper care, will last for years. Ingenious instructors have used cotton mattresses with good results. These may be purchased at Army-Navy surplus stores or from local mattress factories. The cotton filling will lump in time but washable covers hold the mat firm. Athletic firms make mats of all sizes. A 5' x 7' mat is small enough to be handled by four children and heavy enough to hug the floor. Foam rubber is being used as a filling but hair felt is more commonly used in mats because it offers resistance plus the necessary resiliency.

The heavy canvas mat cover is the least expensive and the most durable. Its drawback is that it soils easily. Some mats are backed with plastic on the floor side. There are all types of detachable covers available in washable cotton, plastic, and rubberized materials. They not only aid in cleanliness but add years to the life of the mat.

If storage is available, it is best to store mats flat. Where mats must be hung from the walls, safety brackets are best, as they push flush against the wall preventing sagging, thus eliminating a safety hazard. *Never* allow a mat to be pulled or dragged across the floor and *never* allow hard-soled shoes on a mat. Canvas-covered mats should be beaten often and cleaned with a vacuum cleaner. Cotton covers should be laundered frequently and plastic-covered mats should be washed weekly with a mild soap and rinsed with a cloth wrung out in clear water.

SAFETY PRECAUTIONS

Safety instruction should be given by the instructor but children become more aware and cooperative when they write and post their own version of precautionary safety measures. A fourth grade group worked out the following list of suggested directions.

FOUR ON A MAT—Do not move mats that are too heavy.
PLACE MATS clear of walls, bars and benches.
LEADERS CHECK mats before and during class to see that they do not separate.
DO NOT walk, jump or play on mats except in class periods when a teacher is present.
LINES should stand a good 12 inches from the mat and ALWAYS move in the same direction.

GET OFF the mat as soon as the stunt is completed.
DO YOUR clothes keep you from moving or get in your way?
ARE YOUR pockets EMPTY?
DO YOU have on sox or tennis shoes?
GIRLS, have you taken off all bobby pins, hair ornaments and jewelry?

Alert teacher spotting is necessary through the elementary grades to anticipate and forestall accidents. Men are physiologically better equipped as spotters but women can work safely with most children on this level if they will observe a few simple suggestions. A spotter should assume a position that permits easy, quick assistance and rapid shifts to avoid hampering the activity and to escape flying arms and legs. The stronger arm (generally the right) should receive the weight of the child and slightly flexed knees allow quick movements in any direction. Kneel on the knee away from the performer. It is not wise to give too much assistance as it is frustrating and robs the child of the feeling of accomplishment. In less difficult stunts the presence of the spotter is all that is necessary to instill confidence. Two pupils standing on either side of each mat can be trained as assistant spotters.

CLASS ORGANIZATION AND PRESENTATION

Each stunt should be analyzed and all possible risks eliminated by:
1. Explanation and demonstration from start to finish.
2. Teacher spotting.
3. Teaching progressive skills to permit easy transition from known to unknown.
4. Being sure in couple stunts that the two pupils are approximately the same size and of the same skill.
5. Having classes prepare posters with rules and regulations for procedures with safety and the best learning conditions in mind.
6. Taking into consideration physical limitations. *Watch* for fatigue and do not allow tired children to continue the activity. Do not allow children recuperating from recent illnesses to participate. Allow only minimum participation and watch carefully children with chronic sinusitis, bronchitis, asthma, epilepsy, and heart conditions.

Activities that follow have been graded as near as possible to pupil ability level but the teacher must be guided by the skill of the group, for some stunts listed for the first grade would be enjoyed by sixth graders and are not repeated in the list of suggested stunts. It is important that interest be held by introducing enough material each period to challenge the more proficient and by organizing the class in squads to allow frequent individual turns at trying. In large groups of the lower elementary level, simple stunts may be done in double lines on either side of the mats. Only one child should be allowed to a mat when more advanced stunts are taught for the first time.

SIMPLE STUNTS   DIFFICULT STUNTS

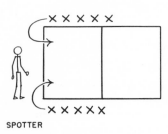

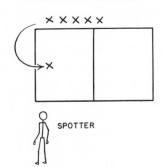

After a variety of stunts have been taught, each child may be allowed to call the stunt to be executed.

Try to develop a group feeling of pride in good execution and discourage laughter or critical remarks directed toward poor performers. Place praise and attention on the ones who *try* as well as on those who show excellent form.

It is wise to keep the activity on the ability level of the group, as adventurous youngsters will try to do stunts they have observed that are too difficult for their background of experience.

SUGGESTED LESSON PLAN

Class: third grade, third month of instruction
Period: 30 minutes   Number: 20 to 40

Entire Class

(Spaced about floor to permit free movement)
Sit-Ups
Turk Stand

Tumbling

Cartwheel
Forward Roll (Standing Position)
Backward Roll

Individual Stunts

Monkey Run
Crab Walk
Seal Crawl
Rabbit Hop
Measuring Worm

Couple Stunts

Wheelbarrow
Rocker

GRADED STUNTS

GRADE 1

Elephant Walk	Tight Rope Walking	Weather Vane
Monkey Run	Chicken Walk	Log Roll
Rabbit Hop	Seal Crawl	Sit-Ups
Frog Hop	Lame Puppy Walk	Somersault
Duck Walk	Human Ball	Bear Walk

GRADE 2

Turk Stand	Spanker	Step Over the Wand
Egg Roll	Backward Kick	Jump and Slap Heels
Crab Walk	Bent Knee Hop	Forward Roll
Jumping Jack	Knee Lift	Backward Roll
Inch Worm	Kangaroo Hop	Cartwheel

GRADE 3

Free Standing	Mule Kick	Egg Sit
Full Squat	Bear Dance	Thread the Needle
Wicket Walk	Dip	Knee or Stump Walk
Balance Stand	Frog Dance	

COUPLE STUNTS

	Grade		Grade		Grade
Bouncing Ball	1	Chinese Get Up	4–6	Cock Fight	2–6
Wring the		Rocker	4–6	Rooster Fight	1–6
Dishrag	1–3	Churn the Butter	3–6	Hand Wrestle	2
Row Boat	1	Wheelbarrow	1	Pull Across	3–5
Leapfrog	1–6				

GRADED SELF-TESTING ACTIVITIES

Individual Stunts

GRADE 4

Stiff Leg Bend	Under the Bridge	Up-swing
Stiff Knee Pick Up	Long Stretch	Up-spring
Folded Leg Walk	Jump and Reach	Human Rocker
Bells or Clicks	Knee Dip	Jump Foot
Knuckle Down	Cut the Wand	Coffee Grinder
Knee Mark	Backward Jump	
Stoop and Throw	Palm Spring	

GRADES 5–6

Grasp the Toe	Forearm Head Stand	Hand Stand
Fish Hawk Dive	Jump Over the Stick	Double Forward Roll
Tripod	Corkscrew	Through the Stick
Head Stand	Crane Dive	Dive Over One

GRADE 6

Head Spring	Shoulder Mount	Shoulder Stand
Hand Spring	Rising Sun	

Figure 41. In teaching self-testing activities it is important that interest be built and increased by introducing varied material in each class to challenge the more proficient children. (Couresy of Public Schools of Lincoln, Nebraska.)

Couple and Group Stunts

GRADES 4, 5, 6

Leapfrog	Bull Dog Pull	Toe Wrestle
Skin the Snake	Hog Tying	Elephant Walk
Wand and Toe Wrestle	Walking Chair	Eskimo Roll
Indian Wrestle	Merry-Go-Round	Back-to-Back Roll
	Pull Across	

DESCRIPTION OF STUNTS[1]

BACKWARD JUMP—4

Stand on mat with toes at the edge, heels toward center. Jump backwards as far as possible swinging arms forcibly. Land lightly.

---

[1] The number following the name of the stunt indicates the grade for which the stunt is best suited.

BACKWARD KICK—2

Jump in place on both feet four times. On fourth jump, kick both heels backward. Land lightly on toes.

BALANCE STAND—3

Stand on either foot, bend body forward to right angle with body, supporting free leg slightly bent from knee, head up, arms to side horizontal.

BEAR DANCE—3

Squat on one heel, other foot extended forward. Draw extended foot under body and shoot other foot out to front. Arms are folded across chest.

BEAR WALK—1

Place hands on floor with arms and knees straight. Body sways from side to side as a lumbering bear would walk.

BELLS—4

Hop on left foot, extend right leg to side and bring left heel to click with right heel.

BENT KNEE HOP—2

Child squats and takes a tuck position (arms and hands wrapped around knees). Walk on balls of feet.

COFFEE GRINDER—4 TO 6

Child places one hand on floor, other in upright position. He straightens his legs and arms and walks around using the hand on the floor as a pivot.

CORKSCREW—6

Stand with feet 15 inches apart. Place piece of paper at toe of right foot. Swing left arm across body and go between legs to pick up paper.

CRAB WALK—3

Hands and feet on floor, face up, back straight. Walk backward, using right arm and right leg, then left arm and left leg.

CRANE DIVE OR NOSE DIVE—5

Toe a line. Place a piece of folded paper, at least 6 inches high, 6 inches in front of feet. Bend forward, raising one leg to rear and pick up paper.

CUT THE WAND—4

Hold a wand about 3 feet long vertically in front of the body, grasping one end and resting the other end on the floor in front of the feet. Release the wand and lift right leg over and catch before it falls.

DIP—2 to 6

Place crumpled paper 12 inches in front of body. Kneel with hands behind back, bend and pick up paper with teeth.

DOG RUN—1 to 3

Place hands on floor in front of body. Knees and arms lightly bent. Imitate a dog walking and running.

DUCK WALK—1 to 6

Squat position with knees wide, hands under arm pits. Swing feet wide to the side with each step and flap wings. First graders love to bring the arms to the back and make a tail by placing the hands together.

EGG ROLL—2 to 6

Cross legs and kneel. Wrap arms across chest. Roll using arms and knees to start.

EGG SIT—2 to 6

Sit on floor with knees bent close to chest. Grasp ankles, rock back and extend legs.

FISH HAWK DIVE—5

Kneel on one knee with the other leg entirely off the ground. Bend forward and pick up an object which is directly in front of the resting knee.

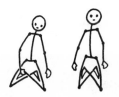

FOLDED LEG WALK—4 TO 6

Sit on mat. Take left foot and place it as high as possible against the right thigh. Cross right leg over the left and place high on the left thigh. Fold arms or extend to side for balance. Rise to kneeling position and walk across mat on knees.

FREE STANDING—3

Lie on back on mat with arms folded across chest. Come to standing position without unfolding arms or using elbows.

FROG DANCE—3 to 6

Squat, keep back straight, and fold arms across chest. Hop on left foot and extend right leg to side. Hop again on left foot and draw the right leg under body and extend left leg to side.

FROG HOP—2 to 6

Squat position, arms between legs, hands on floor. Take short hops by placing hands ahead of feet and bring feet up to hands.

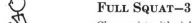

FULL SQUAT—3

Clasp wrist with right hand behind the body. Keep back straight and bend knees deeply and touch floor with fingers. Knees are spread wide.

GRASP THE TOE—5

Stand on one foot, grasp the other foot at the arch with two hands. Bend forward and at the same time lift the foot, attempting to touch the toe to the forehead.

HUMAN BALL—1 TO 6

Sit on mat with knees up and feet together. Reach arms under inside of legs and lock fingers over ankles. Roll over.

HUMAN ROCKER—4 TO 6

Lie face down, bend knees, arch back and grasp right foot with right hand and left foot with left hand. Rock forward on chest and back on thighs. Rock in open position, holding arms and legs together tightly.

Figure 42. Children learning the human rocker. (Courtesy of Dr. Joan Tillotson, Plattsburgh Public Schools, Plattsburgh, New York.)

INCH WORM—2 TO 6

Lean prone position. Keep hands stationary and walk feet to hands and walk back with hands to starting position keeping legs straight.

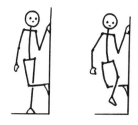

JUMP FOOT—4 TO 6

Stand with one foot against wall, about 12 inches from floor and in front of inside leg. Spring from inside foot and jump over leg.

JUMPING JACK—2 TO 6

Take a squat position, arms across chest. Spring to erect position, weight on heels, back straight, arms horizontally to sides.

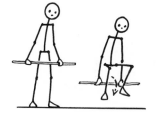

JUMP OVER THE STICK—5

Hold wand in horizontal position in front of body, palms down. Swing wand forward and back, jumping over wand.

JUMP AND REACH—4

Stand facing wall. Without lifting heels reach high with both hands and mark with chalk highest point reached. Stand with side to wall. Start from crouch position, jump and mark point reached with chalk held in nearest hand.

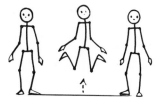

JUMP AND SLAP HEELS—2 TO 6

Jump into air, bring heels up to side. Slap heels.

KANGAROO HOP—2 TO 6

Squat with arms folded over chest. Spring into air and come back to squat position with knees flexed to prevent jar.

KNEE DIP—3 TO 6

Stand on one foot and grasp the other foot behind the back with opposite hand. Bend down with arm outstretched for balance, touch knee lightly to floor and return to standing position.

KNEE LIFT—2

Stand with feet apart and hands extended forward at hip level. Jump up and try to touch the knees to the palms. Repeat, raising hands higher.

KNEE MARK—4 TO 6

Kneel on both knees behind a line on the floor. Place one hand behind the back and reach forward with a piece of chalk and mark point reached.

KNEE WALK OR STUMP WALK—4 TO 6

Kneel and grasp ankles or toes with hands. Walk on knees, leaning forward slightly to maintain balance.

KNUCKLE DOWN—4

Place toes on line. Without moving toes from line or using hands, kneel and rise.

LAME PUPPY WALK—1 TO 4

On all fours, raise one foot in air and walk as a dog on three legs.

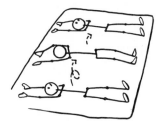

LOG ROLL—1 TO 6

Lie on back with arms extended over head, legs straight, roll slowly over to end of mat. The body must move as "one piece" to keep direction straight.

LONG STRETCH—4 TO 6

Stand with feet together, toeing line. Hold piece of chalk in one hand. Bend knees deeply and place free hand on floor. Walk forward on hands as far as possible without moving toes from line, and mark on floor. Walk back to squat position and stand.

MONKEY RUN—1 TO 6

On all fours scamper agilely, imitating monkey. Put down hands, then feet.

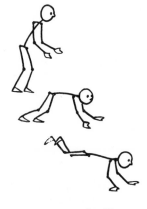

MULE KICK—3 TO 6

Bend forward, place hands on floor, bend knees and kick into air as a mule.

PUSH-UPS—3 TO 6

Get on hands and knees with arms below shoulders and shoulder distance apart. Extend legs backward until hips and knees are straight. Lower body, by bending elbows until nose touches floor. Raise body and repeat.

RABBIT JUMP—1 TO 6

Squat with hands in front of feet. Push with feet and lift hands from floor. Catch weight on hands and bring feet to hands.

SEAL CRAWL—1 TO 3

Prone leaning position with fingers turned to side as flappers. Keep legs together, weight on toes. Drag body along by walking on hands and let hips swing.

SINGLE SQUAT—5 TO 6

Stand on mat, raise arms to side for balance. Raise one leg in front, knee straight. Squat, keeping weight well over supporting leg. Return to standing position without losing balance.

SIT-UPS—1 TO 6

Lie flat on floor with arms extended above head, legs straight and together. Come to sitting position and keep legs tight to floor. Lie down slowly.

SOMERSAULT—1 TO 2

Stand on floor at end of mat with feet astride. Place hands on mat between feet without bending knees. Touch back of head to mat. Body will roll forward and somersault will be completed.

SPANKER—2 TO 6

Take position as for Crab Walk. Raise both feet in the air and slap seat with right hand, then left hand. Advanced: Hop and extend right leg and spank with left hand, hop and extend left leg and spank with right hand.

STEP OVER THE WAND—2 TO 6

Grasp a wand at both ends with the backs of the hands toward the ceiling. Keep wand close to floor, bend forward, and step over the wand first with one foot, then with the other. Stand straight. Back over in same manner. Stand.

STIFF KNEE PICK-UP—1 TO 6

Stand with feet together, bend forward, and pick up article placed 3 inches in front of toes, without bending knees.

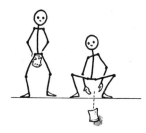

STIFF LEG BEND—1 TO 6

Stand with heels together and arms at side. Bend forward and touch floor with fingertips.

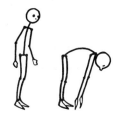

STOOP AND THROW—4 TO 6

Stand in stride position, toeing a line. Hold beanbag behind back with both hands. Bend knees deeply and throw beanbag between legs, using both hands. Keep a record of distance for competition.

THREAD THE NEEDLE—3 TO 5

Clasp the hands in front of body, bend the trunk forward, and step through clasped hands with right foot, then left foot. Return with stepping backward with right, then left foot.

THROUGH THE STICK—4 TO 6

Grasp a wand behind the back, palms forward. Bring wand over head to position in front of body without losing grasp. Swing right leg around right arm and between the hands from front, over stick. Crawl through head-first and back over with left foot.

TIGHT ROPE WALKING—1 TO 3

Walk a line drawn on the floor (10 feet long). Use arms to balance.

TURK STAND—1 TO 6

Arms folded across chest. Sit cross-legged on floor. Stand without using hands or changing position of feet.

UNDER THE BRIDGE—4

Stand toeing a line with the feet about 12 inches apart. Have chalk in one hand. Squat, and with the hand holding the chalk reach forward between the legs to mark the floor as far forward as possible.

UP-SPRING—4 TO 6

Kneel, ankles extended, toes flat. Swing arms back, then forward vigorously, pushing with the feet at the same time. Bring body to erect position.

UP-SWING—3 TO 6

Kneel with the weight on the balls of the feet. Swing arms back, then forward, coming to standing position.

WEATHER VANE—1 TO 3

Stand with feet apart, hands on shoulders, elbows up. Turn from side to side.

WICKET WALK—3 TO 4

Simple: With knees straight, bend forward touching floor with hands. Walk forward and backward with small steps, keeping legs and arms close together. Advanced: Grasp ankles and walk without bending knees.

COUPLE STUNTS–PRIMARY

BOUNCING BALL–1 TO 2

One child is ball and other the bouncer. Try to achieve feel and rhythm of bouncing ball.

CHURN THE BUTTER–3 to 6

Back to back, elbows locked, No. 1 bends forward from the hips. No. 2 springs from floor, leans back and lifts feet from floor. Repeat action with No. 2 bending forward.

DOUBLE WALK–2

Couple face and grasp upper arms. No. 2 steps diagonally across insteps of No. 1 who walks forward. No. 2 shifts weight as No. 1 walks.

HAND WRESTLE–2 to 6

Two children face and join right hands and each raises one foot behind him. On signal, each attempts to cause the other to touch either the free hand or foot to floor.

PULL ACROSS–5

Divide class into two equal groups. Draw line on floor and have teams stand on opposite sides of the line. On signal, each child grasps his opponent by the right hand and attempts to pull him across the line. Limit bout to two minutes.

ROCKER—3 to 6

Partners sit facing each other and extend legs so that each child sits on feet of other child. Grasp upper arms and rock. One leans backward and lifts other child up. Alternate.

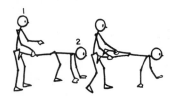

ROOSTER FIGHT—3 TO 6

Couple face with arms folded across chest and weight on one foot. On signal, each tries to throw the other off balance by pushing with his arms. First one to lose balance, by putting down a foot, loses.

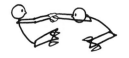

WHEELBARROW—1 TO 3

No. 1 grasps legs of No. 2 at knees and walks as guiding a wheelbarrow. No. 2 walks on hands and keeps back straight.

ROW BOAT—2

Facing partner, sit cross-legged on mat. Grasp partner's hands. When one child leans back, he will pull the other child forward.

Figure 43. Sawing wood is a good dual activity for developing the upper body. (Courtesy of *The Instructor*. Photograph by Edith Brockway.)

WRING THE DISHRAG—1 to 3

Partners face and join hands. Lower arms on one side and turn away from each other and under the raised arms. Stand back to back. Raise other pair of arms and turn under.

COUPLE AND GROUP STUNTS—UPPER ELEMENTARY

BULLDOG PULL—5

Number of participants: 10 to 20. Equipment: Rope 3 to 5 feet long. Two Indian clubs. Place rope on floor between two clubs. Divide group into two teams. Line up facing and parallel to rope. Two opponents step forward and grasp ends of rope. On signal each pulls rope and tries to pick up Indian club. One- to two-minute bouts. Keep score.

COCK FIGHT—5 to 6

Sit on floor facing partner. Draw up knees close to body and have toes touching partner's toes. Clasp hands in front of knees. Place wand under knees and over arms at elbows. Try with toes to lift partner's feet so he will roll over backward.

CHINESE GET-UP—4 to 6

Partners stand back to back with elbows locked. Sink to floor and rise by taking small walking steps and pressing against backs.

ELEPHANT WALK—4 TO 6

Couple face. No. 1 stands in wide stride. No. 2 springs forward and upward around waist of No. 1. No. 2 bends backward and crawls between legs and grasps ankles. No. 1 bends forward and walks with swaying motion.

HOG TYING—5 TO 6

Two face kneeling on hands and knees with a four-foot rope each in hands. On signal, each tries to tie the opponent's ankles together. Any fair wrestling hold is permissible.

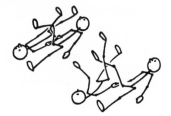

INDIAN LEG WRESTLE—5 to 6

Two children lie side-by-side, facing opposite directions. Place hips at opponent's waistline. Hook inside legs, hook inside arms. Raise inside legs to count 3 times. On the third count bend knees, hook them and try to force the opponent into a backward roll.

LEAPFROG—4 to 6

Base takes wide stance, bends forward from the hips, and braces hands on knees. Top runs forward and jumps both feet over base's back. Place hands on base's shoulders and push, extending legs to side. Land on both feet, knees and ankles relaxed.

MERRY-GO-ROUND—5 to 6

Group of 8 to 10. Form circle and take double wrist lock. 1, 3, 5, 7 sit on floor with knees straight and feet together in the center. On signal, 2, 4, 6, 8 take a step outwards and 1, 3, 5, 7 raise hips until body is in inclined position with back straight. 2, 4, 6, 8 walk around circle and the center group are the spokes of a wheel.

SKIN THE SNAKE—6

Forward. All line up directly behind the other in stride position. All bend forward and reach right hand between knees to person behind and reach forward with the left hand and grasp right hand of person in front. Last person in line crawls through and assumes stride position. Next in line follows until all have crawled through.

Backward. Line up as before. Last one in line lies down flat and the rest of the line moves backward. As each person reaches the end he lies down. The last performer to lie down rises and walks forward, straddling the line, and pulls the next performer to feet. Continue until all return to original position.

TOE WRESTLE—5 to 6

Same as Cock Fight but instead of using a wand, the arms are wrapped around knees.

WALKING CHAIR—4 to 6

Line up behind each other. Hold hips of person in front. All sit back so the legs touch the thighs of the one behind. Each supports own weight. On signal, all move forward in step.

TUMBLING STUNTS LISTED AS TO DIFFICULTY AND GRADE LEVEL

	Grade		Grade
Forward Roll Progressions	1–6	Handstand	4
Cartwheel Progressions	2–6	Dive Over One	4
Backward Roll Progressions	2–6	Handspring	5
Tripod	3	Headspring	5
Headstand	4	Eskimo Roll	6
Forearm Headstand	4	Back-to-Back Roll	6

DESCRIPTION OF TUMBLING ACTIVITIES

All of the following stunts require "Spotters."

BACK-TO-BACK ROLL

Review "Churn the Butter" as a lead-up stunt. Base and top stand back to back, lock elbows, base's on outside of top's. Base stands with one foot forward and one foot backward for better balance, bends knees, gets hips in small of top's back. On signal top springs from mat, brings knees to chest, throws head well back to lean over base. Top at same time bends forward slightly, pulls up on arms to roll top over back and head.

BACKWARD ROLL PROGRESSIONS

Basic. Start in sitting position. Place hands at shoulders, palms up, thumbs toward neck. Roll back, pushing with the feet, tuck head forward and bring knees close to chest. As hips are vertical to shoulders, push with hands. Land on toes in squat position.

Stand to stand. Start in standing position. Sit, keeping feet as close to body as possible. Roll back, pushing forcibly with hands, and extend legs in a vigorous snap to finish in a standing position.

CARTWHEEL PROGRESSIONS

1. No hip extension. Stand with right side to mat. Bend sideways and place both hands in line on the mat. Push off with feet, first right, then left. Swing legs over arms and push with right hand, then left hand. Finish in crouched position.

2. Alternate, starting from right, then left.

3. Hip extension: Elbows and legs straight, head up, back slightly arched.

4. Click heels in air: As performer reaches vertical position, quickly click heels before lowering one leg.

5. Cartwheel on one hand: Free hand on hip, make push from mat more vigorous. Give this only to those with excellent arm and shoulder development.

DIVE OVER ONE

1. Place obstacle close to edge of mat. This may be rolled mat or child in tuck position or kneeling on all fours. Take a short run and when one foot from obstacle, extend arms, duck head and forward roll to standing position.

2. Dive over person kneeling on hands and knees.

3. Dive through spread legs of child doing a headstand.

ESKIMO ROLL

Forward. Base lies on mat, legs raised, knees flexed. Top stands behind base's shoulders, reaches forward and grasps base's ankles with fingers to outside, thumbs to inside. Base grasps top's ankles in same grip. Top does a forward roll between base's legs, and pulls top to feet. Continue to roll changing positions.

Backward. Same position as above. As top rolls backward base pushes forcibly against top's ankles and against mat with head and shoulders. Stay close together.

FOREARM HEADSTAND

Kneel and place forearms, palms down, on mat. Place forehead between hands. Walk up and kick up one leg, secure balance and raise other leg slowly to vertical position.

FORWARD ROLL PROGRESSIONS

1. Squat to Sit (Somersault): Squat with weight on toes and hands on mat just ahead of toes. Round back by tucking head between knees. Push with hands and feet and roll over to sitting position. Keep body in tight ball to prevent slapping back.

2. Stand to Stand: Execute as in No. 1. Bend forward and place hands on mat. Finish in standing position.

3. Run and take off from one foot.

4. Spring from both feet.

5. Continuous forward rolls.

6. Forward roll with arms folded across chest.

HANDSTAND

Stand on hands, feet raised straight in air with head and hands making a triangle. Arch back slightly for balance. Walk on hands. Shift weight gently and keep over hands.

HANDSPRING PROGRESSIONS

1. Over back: Do handstand about 1 foot from base, arch back, drop legs to floor, pushing forcibly with hands.

2. Handspring with assistance of base.

3. Handspring over base's arms.

4. Handspring over two rolled mats.

Figure 44. Learning to do a handstand is a challenging activity which, when mastered, brings delight to children. (Courtesy of Dr. Joan Tillotson, Plattsburgh Public Schools, Plattsburgh, New York.)

HEADSTAND

Start with tripod position. Gradually raise legs high in rear, keeping legs and ankles together.

HEADSPRING PROGRESSIONS

Place two rolled mats in center of mats. Place head and hands on top. Spring from feet, push hard with head and hands, arch back and snap legs down toward mat. Land in squat position and rise to erect position. Headspring from one rolled mat. More spring and body snap required.

TRIPOD

Form a triangle by placing hands on mat, fingers forward and bend elbows to form a shelf. Place right knee above right elbow and left knee above left elbow. Lower one leg at a time or go into a forward roll.

PYRAMID BUILDING

Pyramid building offers excellent training in body control and group adjustment but it also has a dual value in its salesmanship. The simplest of pyramids, if executed in a clean-cut and decisive manner, is showy. Pyramid building is the cherry that tops a sundae. The part below may be more filling and nutritious, and definitely it required more work, but the bright red has eye appeal. Physical educators should not overlook showmanship in selling their program to the public even though they are completely aware that there is no substitute for hard-earned skills, learned with slow, patient, and sometimes monotonous, repetition.

The basic requirements for simple pyramid building are:
1. Strength
2. Balance
3. Timing
4. Knowledge of fundamentals
5. Ability to work as a team

The last requirement explains why this activity is postponed, gen-

Figure 45. Pyramid building offers excellent training in body control and group cooperation. (Courtesy of C. G. White, Director, Kanakuk Kamp.)

erally, until the sixth grade. Many fourth graders who have progressed through a well-planned program show excellence in performance in individual stunts but are not interested in working as a team. However, the teacher working with small and skilled groups would be justified in introducing this activity at a lower level.

Finished pyramids should meet the requirements of good design, namely, balance, proportion, and interest (varying levels). The structure may start from a line, circle, square, rectangle or triangle, but all units, whether they are composed of two, three or five performers, should give the whole a feeling of continuity. This should not be dependent upon physical contact. In the most commonly used pyramids one finds the high point in the center, but the sides can be higher if symmetry is maintained. In simple elementary pyramids the base looks and is more secure if the ends taper to the floor.

The teacher or a pupil may give the counts or signals vocally, with a whistle, a snapper, or by a sharp clap with the hands. All move to the edge of the mat in a formation arranged to enable first positions to be taken with a minimum of walking.

Count 1: Bases move to positions on mats
Count 2: Tops move to positions
Count 3: All tops mount
Count 4: Tops dismount
Count 5: All return to place

The pyramid is good if:

1. Performers have moved quickly with good posture and precision to positions.

2. Movements have been executed in unison to count.

3. Completed pyramid is maintained until steadiness is attained. (Rhythm of building is impaired if held too long.)

4. Dismounted in positive and orderly manner.

On the following pages are suggested stunts that may be used in typical pyramids. Once the feel has been attained, classes should be encouraged to create their own pyramids.

Grade level indicated and listed according to difficulty.

Stunts Suitable for Pyramid Building

	Grade		*Grade*
Shoulder Rest	3	Stand on Partner's Knee	5
Triangle	4	Sitting Balance	5
Stand on Partner	5	Angel Balance	5
Horizontal Stand	5	Mercury	5
Thigh Mount	5	Knee-shoulder Stand	6
Sitting Mount	6	Handstand Archway	6
Handstand Supported at Hips	6	Shoulder Stand on Base's Feet	6
Handstand on Partner's Knees	6	Standing Mount	6
		(if children had a continuous self-testing program)	

Description of Stunts for Pyramid Building

ANGEL BALANCE

Base lies on floor with legs raised, knees slightly bent and places feet diagonally alongside of top's pelvic bones. Grasps hands. Top springs forward and base straightens legs. Base lowers arms, and top arches back, and raises arms as in a swan dive.

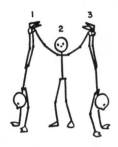

HANDSTAND ARCHWAY

No. 2 is base. On signal, Nos. 1 and 3 do handstand and base catches at ankles.

HANDSTAND SUPPORTED AT HIPS

Base lies down, places feet across lower abdomen of top who puts hands to floor. Base places hands on top's shoulders. Top springs and base extends legs and supports base's hips with feet.

HORIZONTAL STAND

Base grasps top's ankles, with thumbs on inside of legs. As top springs and shifts weight to hands, base straightens arms.

KNEE-SHOULDER STAND

Handstand on knees of base with shoulder support.

MERCURY

Base clasps hands at back, palms up. Top places right foot on base's hands and springs from left foot. Secures balance and extends arms and free leg, brace supporting leg from knee down on top's back.

SHOULDER REST

Extend legs straight above head and support hips with hands. Weight on shoulders and elbows.

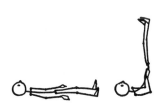

SHOULDER STAND

(See knee-shoulder stand.) Grasp hands. Top does handstand with support of feet at shoulders.

SITTING BALANCE

Base lies on mat, legs in air and slightly bent. Top sits on base's feet, extends arms backward and grasps top's hands. Base straightens legs and releases hands. Top extends arms to side.

SITTING MOUNT

Base stands in stride position, top stands directly behind. Base kneels on one knee and places head between top's legs. Top places legs under base's arms and behind back. Top rises, straightening knees slowly. Stands erect.

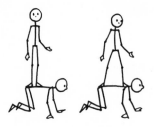

STAND ON PARTNER

Stand on lower back with feet placed diagonally or one foot on lower back and one foot on shoulders.

STAND ON PARTNER'S KNEE

Base aids balance by support at knee.

STANDING MOUNT

Top stands directly behind base. Base stands in deep-stride position with arms raised up and back. Top grasps base's hands and places right foot on base's thigh, then left foot on left shoulder, right foot on right shoulder. Gradually straightens knees, releases hands and stands tall, arms extended. Base supports top with hands at back of knees.

THIGH MOUNT

No. 2 mounts thigh of No. 1 with right foot and mounts thigh of No. 3. Stands erect and extends arms to side. Nos. 1 and 3 support at waist.

TRIANGLE

Base lifts one of top's legs to shoulder. Top springs and places other leg on base's other shoulder.

POSES FOR PYRAMIDS

Ends—Single

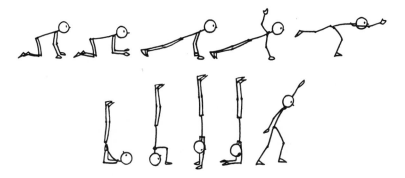

Centers—Couples and Groups

Sides

Pyramids

REBOUND TUMBLING (TRAMPOLINING)

Fifteen years ago the trampoline was a piece of equipment found in circuses, athletic clubs and colleges. It was used by a limited number of skilled tumblers, gymnasts and divers. Today, one encounters the trampoline in the gymnasiums of many schools and recreational centers, in the back yards of private homes, and in recreational parks where small children and adults may practice from thirty minutes to an hour for a fixed price.

The trampoline is fun and exciting and gives the child a feeling of being "lighter than air"; consequently, it lends to the simplest routine a sense of power in excelling. With proper spotting and clear instructions, this equipment is quite safe. The following routines are recommended for the elementary school. More difficult routines are eliminated for obvious reasons. Safety factors must be considered at all times. Although training rigs are expensive and time consuming to use in large classes, they are recommended if the school can afford to buy them.

Figure 46. With proper spotting and clear instructions, trampolining can be safe, fun, and exciting. (Courtesy of the Nissen Corporation, Cedar Rapids, Iowa.)

Procedure

1. One student at a time on the trampoline.
2. Jump in stocking feet to protect the bed and to give traction.
3. Follow explicitly routine set by instructor.
4. Instructor stands at the side and places a spotter at the other side and ends. If the student loses his balance, a light push with both hands sends him back to the middle of the bed. Spotters should place hands on the frame and keep hands off the suspension system.
5. Class counts off by fours. No. 1 on the trampoline. Numbers 2, 3, and 4 take their turn at spotting and on the trampoline. Upon finishing, No. 1 takes spotting station of No. 4, and No. 4 moves to station of No. 3, etc.

Routines

I. MOUNT

1. Mounting ladders or small tables covered with mats are excellent and speed up the safe and orderly procedure of getting on and off the trampoline.

2. Place hands on the frame and crawl on and off.

3. Skilled students in the upper elementary grades may take a short run, place hands on the frame and do a forward roll onto the bed.
4. *Never* allow a student to step on the suspension system.

II. DISMOUNT

1. In dismounting, *never* allow a student to jump from the bed to the floor. The more skilled may place their hands on the frame and vault to the floor, or jump with flexed knees from the frame to a mat.

III. FUNDAMENTAL BOUNCE

1. Stand in the middle of the bed, rib-cage pulled high and eyes forward on the frame or end of bed.

2. Arms lift forward and upward in a circular motion as you leave the bed and return to sides as you come down.

3. Feet are shoulder width apart on landing and together in the air.
4. Students should be taught that control is more important than height.
5. Mount, bounce ten times, dismount.

IV. KNEE DROP

1. Kneel in center of bed with legs and back straight, arms at side.
2. Pull arms hard forward and upward and come to standing position.
3. Three bounces to knee drop. Repeat twice. Dismount.

V. Hands and Knee Drop

1. Start in erect position.
2. Bounce 3 times.
3. Land on bed with hands and knees.
4. Push with hands to come back to erect position.
5. Repeat twice and dismount.

VI. Seat Drop

1. Bounce 3 times.
2. Go to seat drop. Legs are straight, toes pointed and hands are close to side of hips.
3. Push with hands as you return to erect position.
4. Repeat twice and dismount.

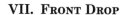

VII. Front Drop

1. Three low bounces and land in prone position.
2. Keep head up and arms extended forward.
3. Push up with arms to return to standing position.
4. Repeat routine twice and dismount.

VIII. Back Drop

1. Three low bounces.
2. Land on back with chin pulled in close to chest, arms extended forward.
3. Kick forward and up with legs to return to standing position.
4. Repeat routine twice and dismount.

IX. Mixed Routines

1. 3 bounces, knee drop, 3 bounces, seat drop. Repeat.
2. 3 bounces, hands and knee drop, 3 bounces, front drop. Repeat.
3. 3 bounces, seat drop, 3 bounces, back drop. Repeat.
4. 3 bounces, knee drop, 3 bounces, back drop. Repeat.

SUGGESTED READINGS

Bailey, James: *Gymnastic Activities in the School.* Boston, Allyn and Bacon, 1965.

Borkowski, Richard: Rough and tumble; A guide to physical toughness activities in boys' physical education. *Journal of Health, Physical Education, Recreation,* April, 1967.

Burns, Ted, and Nicoleau, Tyler: *Tumbling Techniques.* Illustrated, New York, The Ronald Press Company, 1957.

Department of Education: *Junior Division Physical Education,* Grades 4, 5, 6. Ontario, Canada, 1966.

Frey, Harold, and Keeney, Charles: *Elementary Gymnastic and Apparatus Skills.* New York, The Ronald Press Company, 1964.

La Due, Frank, and Norman, Jim: *This is Trampolining,* 2d Ed. Cedar Rapids, Iowa, Nissen Trampoline Co., 1956.

Loken, Newton: *Beginning Tumbling and Balancing.* Athletic Institute, Chicago, Ill., 1951.

Loken, Newton, and Willoughby, Robert: *Complete Book of Gymnastics,* 2nd Ed. Englewood Cliffs, N.J., Prentice-Hall, Inc., 1967.

McClow, L. L., and Anderson, D. N.: *Play Gymnastics* (850 informal play exercises and 40 arrangements of gymnastic apparatus). New York, F. S. Crofts and Co., 1940.

Pond, Charles: *Tumbling in Total Gymnastics.* Champaign, Illinois, Stipes Publishing Company, 1965.

Szypula, George: *Tumbling and Balancing for All.* Dubuque, Iowa, William C. Brown Company, Publishers, 1957.

INSTRUCTIONAL AIDS

Nissen Trampoline Co.
215 A Ave. N.W.
Cedar Rapids, Iowa

Nissen Training Kit—Illustrated
wall charts, lesson plans, and
progress charts.

Gym Master—Chart of basic
trampoline skills.
3200 S. Zuni St.,
Englewood, Colorado

National Sports Company—Basic
tumbling chart.
360–370 N. Marquette St.
Fond du Lac, Wisconsin

Chapter 15

Elementary Gymnastics

Elementary gymnastics is gaining an increasingly important place in American physical education programs on all educational levels. Free exercises and stunts are the foundation upon which all gymnastic activities are built. The former are made up of improvised patterns of movement that include vertical and horizontal balances, usually done to music. The latter are composed of the headstand, forearm stand, handstand, handspring, and flip. It is important that a spotter (preferably the teacher) stand by the side of the performer in such activity to help him learn desired skills more quickly and to prevent injury by anticipating which way he is most likely to fall, should he lose body control. The best assistance the spotter can give is pushing, lifting, catching, or holding, depending upon the particular activity the pupil is doing and his movement errors.

WARM-UP EXERCISES

OBJECTIVE

Ultimately, these exercises should enable the individual to execute any body movement with relaxed ease while expending a minimum of energy. Maja Carlquist[1] believes that "it is essential that we teach ourselves conscious relaxation of muscles; conscious contraction of muscles." This process gradually becomes unconscious and natural as short periods of relaxation and contraction are used alternately and followed by longer periods.

The following exercises are simple, but try to follow the principle mentioned above. They do not have to follow as a unit, and may be freely interspersed with exercises on apparatus, but it is suggested that a short period of walking, running, skipping, bending and stretching releases the tension from sitting in a classroom and, consequently, improves performance in which more complex coordination is demanded.

---

[1] Carlquist, Maja: *Rhythmical Games*. London, Methuen & Co., Ltd., 1955.

Figure 47.   Elementary gymnastics is gaining an increasingly important place in American physical education programs on all educational levels. (Courtesy of the Nissen Corporation, Cedar Rapids, Iowa.)

1. Walk using normal steps, body held in a relaxed posture while arms swing naturally at sides. Gradually increase the stride, extending knees and insteps until a run with giant strides is achieved.

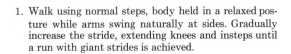

2. Pedal in place, alternately shifting weight from one foot to the other. Strengthens feet and gives flexibility to knees.

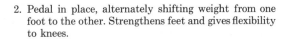

3. *Skip:* Start with a free, loose skip, arms at side. Gradually increase height until arms are used to pull, knees are high and the feet are used in a springlike motion.

4. *Swings:* Swing arms forward and sideward stopping sideward swing at the point where tension begins. Swing arms forward, sideward, and describe a circle in front crossing arms.

Swing arms forward and backward using entire body. Flex knees and straighten both forward and backward swings. With feet spread wide, swing can be carried backward through the legs.

Swing both arms horizontally from side to side. Bend over with body relaxed and start a low swing alternately transferring weight and gradually increasing the perimeter of the swing until the body is in an erect position.

See how many ways the children can swing their arms, legs and body, setting their own rhythm.

5. *Stretching:*
Standing position: Extend arms at shoulder level, stretch, relax. Let body fall forward; head and arms down; knees relaxed. Raise body and stretch arms high, coming up on tiptoes. Vary with bobs up and down and stretch upwards.

With feet comfortably apart, left arm at shoulder level, right arm curved over head, bend toward left with soft stretches.

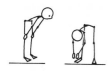

Hands on knees, spine straight, head up. Bounce up and down letting hands slide down legs until fingers touch toes. With back rounded, bob and touch toes forward and bob sideways, alternately touching right and left ankles.

Kneeling position: Trunk stretch. Arms at side, bend left and right. Lower head, sit with arms curled around head, return to kneeling position.

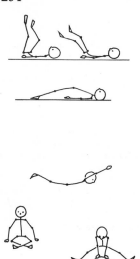

Floor positions: On back, hands at side, lift hips and legs and bicycle pedal in air and lower toward floor, stretching knees and insteps.

On back, make an arch of the body using back, neck and leg muscles.

Body in prone position, arms extended shoulder width, in relaxed position. With feet and arms together, arch body and rock backward and forward.

On back, arms above head, stretch left arm up and right leg down. Now, right arm up and left leg down.

6. *Cross-legged sit:* Stand erect, cross legs and sit down. Come back to original position.

7. *Leap-frog:* Straddle vault over child longways and sideways.

APPARATUS USED IN GYMNASTICS

Side Horse	Vertical and Oblique Ropes	Swedish Box
Long Horse	Horizontal Bar	Single Springboard
Buck	Balance Beam	Rolled Mats
Rings	Stall Bars	Stairs

IMPROVISED EQUIPMENT

Vaulting boxes, built in a pyramid shape, with three detachable boxes and covered with padding may be substituted for the side horse, long horse, and buck. A buck may be made from a tree trunk cut to size. It should be heavily padded with mats. A balance beam may be made from a railroad rail or a board twelve feet long and two inches wide. It should be made stationary and so constructed that it can be raised to various heights from the floor.

Equipment should be checked daily to insure longevity, operation and safety.

SAFETY

1. Provide adequate spotting.

2. Teach students to "give" with a fall.

3. Teach students to land always on floor or mat with relaxed and flexed knees.

4. Follow progression in learning *gradually* and *thoroughly,* being sure that simple techniques are mastered before proceeding to the more difficult.

5. Place mats under rings, ropes and bars and on the mounting and dismounting sides of all vaulting devices.

ROPE CLIMBING

Rope climbing looks difficult but can be fun and safe. At the start, students should only travel a few feet and descend. Never slide down a rope, because severe rope burns can result in permanent injury.

1. Stand close to rope and grasp with both hands, one above other. Place one foot on top of other and grip rope between calves and shins. Hips are now in a sitting position and arms are straight. Practice until climber can hold position securely without slipping.

2. Straighten legs and bend elbows.

3. Reach up with hands and draw legs up to position 1. Repeat twice.

4. Descend by taking position 3 with body close to rope. Alternately lower hands on rope as the leg grip is released to allow a slow descent. The feet clamp to control the downward movement.

Chinning:
1. Grasp rope high above head.
2. Hang.
3. Pull up until elbows are bent, and lower body to mat.

Figure 48. Rope climbing is recommended for girls as well as boys. Here we see that a climbing pole can be used with equal results. (Courtesy of the Nissen Corporation, Cedar Rapids, Iowa.)

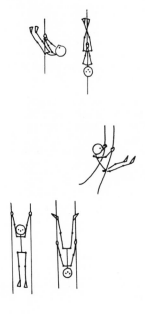

Inverted Hang:

    1. Grasp rope above head.

    2. Swing feet forward and upward.

    3. Secure position on rope with one foot in front and one in back.

    4. Descend by releasing leg grip and lower feet to mat.

DOUBLE ROPES

Free ropes: Run forward, grasp ropes, and swing feet forward and land on mat with flexed knees.

Stationary ropes:

    1. Jump and grasp ropes, hang, drop.

    2. *Inverted hang:* Hang by hands, draw knees up, drop head back and extend feet upward, one foot in front of rope, the other back of rope.

    3. *Skin the Cat:* From inverted hang position, bring feet down to rear, hang, drop to mat. See Still Rings, page 298.

BALANCE BEAM

The balance beam can be one of the most rewarding pieces of equipment in the gymnasium. It provides excellent opportunities to develop balance and presents an enjoyable challenge to the child. In earlier days, children in small towns spent hours walking on railroad rails. The beam may range from 18 inches to 3 feet above the floor. The latter may be used for vaulting.

    Suggested Activities:

    1. Travel in straddle seat.

    2. Travel sideways across beam.

    3. Walk forward and backward.

    4. Walk forward and backward on heels.

    5. Monkey walk forward on all fours.

    6. Duck walk forward.

    7. Duck walk sideward.

    8. Sideward, stepping over front foot.

    9. Sideways, stepping over back foot.

    10. Squat on one leg, free leg forward.

    11. Stand, sit on beam, stand.

Figure 49. Use of the horizontal bar can add another challenging activity to the program. (Courtesy of the Nissen Corporation, Cedar Rapids, Iowa.)

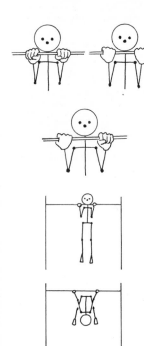

HORIZONTAL BAR

Adjust height of bar for the average in a class so that no child will have to jump higher than 12 inches.

1. *Front grasp:* Grip bar with fingers forward and thumbs under the bar.

2. *Reverse or rear grasp:* Grip bar with fingers turned toward performer and thumbs under the bar.

3. *Combined grasp:* Left hand using reverse grasp, right hand using forward grasp.

4. *Chin:* Place hands on bar, shoulder width apart, using either grasp. Pull body up until chin is level with bar. Lower body. Repeat until tired.

5. *Skin the Cat:* With front grasp and fingers away from performer, pull bent knees up to chest and carry through arms. Drop feet to mat and release bar.

Figure 50. The use of rings can be an integral part of both the playground and the gymnasium program. (Courtesy of Elizabeth Glidden, Specialist in Elementary Physical Education, Los Angeles City Schools, Los Angeles, California.)

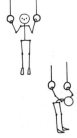

STILL RINGS

Adjust rings to shoulder height.

1. *Chin:* Take front grasp as used on horizontal bar. Pull body up until the head is even with the rings. Keep rings close to the chest.

2. *Skin the Cat:* Follow instructions for this stunt on horizontal bar.

3. *Inverted hang:* Spring from mat and raise hips and knees to chest. Extend legs upward, body arched, head back and feet together with toes pointed. Keep rings close to sides.

STALL BARS

Floor exercises that generally require spotters, corrective exercises for specific weaknesses such as spinal curvature, and numerous stunts can be performed on the stall bars. The child with a poor sense of balance develops muscles with a sense of security because he has something solid from which to work.

The teacher sets up a unit of exercises, demonstrates, and checks as they are executed by students. It is a good idea to draw stick figures of the unit and tape them to the wall. Then the teacher may supervise other floor activities while the students perform prescribed activities. A few exercises are suggested.

1. Hang, using reverse grasp. Raise right leg; lower. Raise left leg; lower. Raise both legs with bent knees. Keep body flush against bars. Raise both legs until they are in horizontal position.

2. Squat in front of bars with hands on a rod at a comfortable height. Jump to first rod. Shift hands and jump to second, etc.

3. *Side lean:* Stand with left side close to bars, elbow bent. Gradually straighten left arm and extend right arm and leg. Repeat from right side.

4. Lie on back and tuck toes under first bar. Arms above head. Pull to sitting position and return to supine position.

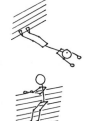

5. *Side swing:* Face stall bars, feet on 2nd wall bar with knees bent and hands at a comfortable height. Swing to right side stretching knees. Swing to left.

6. *Pendulum swing:* Hang facing bars. Swing from side to side, lifting alternate hands.

7. *Climb upward:* Place feet on 2nd wall bar. Grasp bar above and, using alternate hands, climb until body is flush against the bars. Dismount by springing backward, landing with flexed knees.

8. *Headstand:* Place mat in front of bars. Do head and handstand following instructions on pages 278 and 279. Face bars and allow feet to rest against the bars for steadiness.

9. *Handstand:* See page 278 for instructions. For children who have difficulty in balancing, the bars give a steady point of reference.

VAULTS

Vaults may be done using the side horse, long horse, buck, low parallel bars covered with a mat, Swedish box and the balance beam. The vaults should be adapted to the size and ability of the elementary age. Vaults on the long horse generally require a beat board or springboard and their use should be limited to the well coordinated student in the fifth or sixth grades.

General Hints

1. Make approach with a short run.
2. Take off from both feet.
3. Push hard with the hands.
4. Keep head up.
5. Always land on mat with flexed knees.
6. Use double thickness of mats on the dismount side.

SWEDISH BOX AND BUCK

1. Jump to box, jump to floor.

2. *Squat vault:* The legs are between the arms, and knees are pulled up to chest. Push hard with hands and kick feet forward.

3. *Straddle vault:* Use the same technique as in leap-frog. Push with hands as legs are extended to side.

4. *Flank vault right or left:* Both hands on buck, transfer weight to one hand as the legs swing to the side with body straight, legs and trunk in line. This vault may be executed on a low horizontal bar or balance beam.

SIDE HORSE

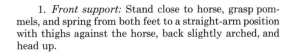

1. *Front support:* Stand close to horse, grasp pommels, and spring from both feet to a straight-arm position with thighs against the horse, back slightly arched, and head up.

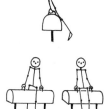

2. *Left and right leg half circle:* From front-support position, swing left leg over the horse and across the pommel. Shift weight away from swinging leg to supporting arm.

Grasp pommel again. Keep legs straight. Swing right leg over in the same manner. Grasp pommel again. Dismount with a light spring or return to front-support position by swinging legs back over the horse.

3. Jump to a squat, stand in the saddle, knees to chest. Release pommels and dismount.

Figure 51. Some children are ready for more advanced activities before others. (Courtesy of the Nissen Corporation, Cedar Rapids, Iowa.)

4. *Squat vault:* Jump, grasp pommels with hips high, knees to chest; push hard with hands and release pommels as the body moves upward.

5. *Straddle vault:* Spring from both feet, hips high, legs straight, head up. Release pommels on upward movement.

SINGLE SPRINGBOARD

In using this equipment, the pupil should run on the board in quick steps, making the last step about 1½ feet from the end of the board for the spring. Stress gaining height on the forward swing. In most of the activities shown below, pupils should follow each other in rapid succession. A mat should be placed under the take-off part of the board, and should extend out in the area where pupils will land. A Spotter should stand at the side of the mat ahead of the performer. The following stunts are for upper elementary pupils who have had previous lessons in stunts and tumbling:

Plain Jump and Hand Clap

1. Run up the board.

2. Jump high into the air on the take-off at the end of the board.

3. Clap hands overhead.

4. Land in balanced position, knees bent.

5. Repeat, clap hands behind back.

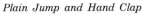

6. Jump, clap hands above head, behind back, land.

7. Repeat, clap hands under one leg.

Swan Jump

1. Jump high on the board.
2. Swan with arms extended sideward, arch body, keep head back.
3. Land with arms forward, knees bent.

Jump and Turn

1. Run, jump on board.
2. Run, jump on board, quarter turn.
3. Run, jump on board, half turn.
4. Run, jump on board, full turn.

Jump and Heel Click

1. Jump high off the board.
2. Click heels together in the air, land with bent knees.
3. Repeat, click heels together twice before landing.
4. Repeat, click heels together three times before landing.

Jump and Kick

1. Run, jump high, kick buttocks, keep head back, back arched, thighs extended.

2. Run, jump, quickly flex thighs, keep knees straight, bend body slightly forward, touch toes in jack-knife position, extend body, land with knees bent.

3. Run, jump high, bring knees to chest with both hands.

Jump and Dive

1. Reach for mat with hands, keep body straight, make a slight spring jump, land on back of neck and shoulders.

2. Dive for height by springing high, reach arms out, extend body in mid-air, use hands and arms for landing.

Figure 52.   The trampoline has become an increasingly popular part of the physical education equipment. (Courtesy of the Nissen Corporation, Cedar Rapids, Iowa.)

ROLLED MATS

Large groups can readily use a rolled mat, for two or three performers may use the same one, depending upon the stunt being learned. Simple activities such as running and jumping over the mat are recommended for the younger children, while more advanced stunts appeal greatly to older pupils. The rolled mat, 15 to 20 feet in length, which should be placed on top of a large flat mat, can also be used for teaching elementary dives, cartwheels, handstand, armstand, and somersaults for tumbling. Spotters should watch each performer carefully and anticipate faulty movements.

Run and Cross Over

1. Run, jump over the mat, taking off with one foot forward in a stride jump.

2. Run, jump over the mat, taking off with both feet at the same time.

3. Run, hop over, hold left foot momentarily in right hand; repeat, reversing hand and foot.

4. Run, jump over, clap hands over head.

5. Run, jump over, kick buttocks.

6. Run, jump over, facing sideways.

7. Run, jump, turn complete circle in the air, land with bent knees.

Dive Over the Roll

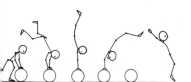

(Beginners should stand at near side and reach over, doing a forward roll.)
1. Dive over roll.
2. Jump, dive higher over the roll.
3. Swan dive over, arch body, arms sideward, tuck, and recover.

Hand Balance on the Roll

1. Stand near the roll.
2. Hand balance by leaning well forward on the kick up.
3. Arch, keep body extended, arch forward, bend over, come to erect position.

STAIRS

This type of equipment can be made easily. Any two sets of stairs can be used when placed back to back and made stationary and/or secure. When only one set of stairs is available, the stunts can be done by having the pupils go up doing the activity and then jump off onto a mat on which the stairs should be placed. This type of equipment is intriguing to elementary children and is especially good for teaching them proper jumping and landing skills. A Spotter should stand where he can best assist those who have faulty body movements. Wide stairs will enable two or more children to use this equipment safely at one time. The following stunts are to be done in an upstairs and downstairs fashion.

Go Up and Down

1. Run up and down, using one foot at a time.

2. Jump up and down, changing feet at the top.

3. Jump up and down zigzagging by jumping to left side on the first step, to right on the next one, etc.

4. Run up and down at full speed.

5. Run, jump off at the top, and land with bent knees.

6. Hop sideward upon left foot; hop down sideward on right foot.

7. Jump up the first two steps backward; turn; hop up rest frontward; hop down frontward; turn and hop down the last two steps backward.

8. Walk up steps, do a handstand on top, and walk down the steps in handstand position.

SUGGESTED READINGS

American Association of Health, Physical Education, and Recreation: *Gymnastic Guide,* Latest Edition. Washington, D.C.

Diem, Liselott: *Who Can?* Wilhelm Limpert Publisher, 1955, Copyright U.S.A. by George Williams College, Chicago, 1957.

Hughes, Eric: *Gymnastics for Girls.* Englewood Cliffs, N.J., Prentice-Hall, Inc., 1963.

Loken, Newt: *How To Improve Your Apparatus Activities.* The Athletic Institute, 209 S. State St., Chicago 4, Ill., 1960.

Loken, Newton C., and Willoughby, Robert J.: *Complete Book of Gymnastics.* Englewood Cliffs, N.J., Prentice-Hall, Inc., 1967.

McVicar, Wes: *Eight to Eighteen.* National Council of YMCA's of Canada, 15 Spadona Rd., Toronto, Canada, 1955.

Mosston, Muska: *Developmental Movement.* Columbus, Ohio, Charles Merrill Books, Inc., 1965.

O'Quinn, Garland: *Gymnastics for Elementary School Children.* Dubuque, Iowa, W. C. Brown Company, Publishers, 1967.

Vannier, Maryhelen, and Poindexter, Hally Beth: *Physical Activities for College Women,* 2nd Ed. Philadelphia, W. B. Saunders Company, 1968.

Loop films: Available from The Athletic Institute, 805 Merchandise Mart, Chicago, Illinois 60654.

Boys	*Girls*
Parallel bars (14 loops)	Free calisthenics (6 loops)
Tumbling (8 loops)	Balance beam (6 loops)
Rings (12 loops)	High–low bar (6 loops)
Vaulting (5 loops)	Side horse (6 loops)

Chapter 16

Track and Field

The American Association for Health, Physical Education, and Recreation has presented a program called "Operation Fitness U.S.A." in cooperation with former President Eisenhower's Council on Youth Fitness. The fundamental games, lead-up games and relays teaching skills provide an excellent preparatory background for the suggested program for boys and girls in the 4th, 5th and 6th grades. It is essential that a thorough conditioning precede this program, if maximum performance is expected, and each child should be watched carefully for overexertion.

This program can be adapted for class use and the scoring can be kept for individuals or, when numbers permit, classes can be broken into teams for competition. The teacher of physical education can decide the advisability of intramural and inter-school competition. If an inter-city meet is planned, official forms, reports, certificates and instructions may be secured from the office of the AAHPER.[1]

SUGGESTED INDOOR ACTIVITIES

Boys	*Girls*
25-Yard Dash	25-Yard Dash
100-Yard Shuttle Relay	100-Yard Dash
Standing Broad Jump	Standing Broad Jump
Rope Climb[2]	Special Obstacle Relay
Special Obstacle Relays	Softball Pitching Accuracy
Pull-up or Jump Reach[2]	Other Improvised Events
Other Improvised Events	

In elementary schools without gymnasiums junior-senior high school gymnasiums or community recreation centers can be made available for these indoor activities.

---

[1] American Association for Health, Physical Education, and Recreation, 1201 16th St., N.W., Washington 6, D.C.

[2] Instructions for the rope climb and pull-up may be found in Chapter 15, Elementary Gymnastics.

SUGGESTED AND OFFICIAL OUTDOOR EVENTS

Boys	Girls
25-Yard Dash	25-Yard Dash
50-Yard Dash	50-Yard Dash
60-Yard Dash	60-Yard Dash
240-Yard Relay	240-Yard Relay
Standing Broad Jump	Standing Broad Jump
Running Broad Jump	Running Broad Jump
High Jump	High Jump
Softball Throw for Distance	Softball Throw for Distance
Softball Throw for Accuracy	Softball Throw for Accuracy
Obstacle Relay (Suggested)	Obstacle Relay (Suggested)

NEEDED FACILITIES AND EQUIPMENT

1. Gymnasium.
2. Playground with 100-yard straightaway or track.
3. 8′ × 20′ pit for broad and high jump, filled with sand or sawdust.
4. Standard for high jump with bamboo pole.
5. Softball.
6. Targets.
7. Whistle or starting pistol.
8. Lime for marking outside starts, finishes and curved lanes.
9. Tempera for marking starts, finishes and curves in the gymnasium.
10. Steel tape for measuring.
11. Take-off board, 2 to 3 feet square for running broad jump. (Optional—lime marker may be used.)
12. Batons—9 inches. Can use bamboo pole, doweling, broomstick or mailing tubes.
13. Officials.
    Starter.
    Judges—one for each place to be given.
    Scorers.
    Referee.

The equipment and facilities listed above meet minimum requirements. At a scheduled track meet on an official track, starting blocks, stop watch, timers, and so forth, would be present.

DASHES

I. *Standing start:* This start is recommended for elementary school children as the majority will be running in tennis shoes. The runner places the feet in a comfortable position, one foot slightly back of the other, and arms in opposition. The runner leans forward slightly and, at the gun signal, takes off with the back foot.

II. *Crouch start:* Starting must be adapted to each runner because body measurements vary as to trunk, legs and arms. The following instructions are basic.

THE HOW

On Your Mark:

1. Squat about a foot from the starting line.
2. Place the hands, shoulder width, back of the line with weight on thumbs and fingers.
3. Kneel on right knee, and the left foot should be even with the right knee. Adjust width.

Get Set:

1. Rock forward and upward, hips down, head up and weight on the hands and front foot.

Go:

1. Whip arms.
2. Push with front leg.
3. Step forward on back leg.
4. Straighten up gradually.

STANDING BROAD JUMP

1. Toe the line with both feet.
2. Crouch low with knees bent and arms back of hips.
3. Jump forward carrying arms and feet forward and upward.
4. Land on both feet.

RUNNING BROAD JUMP

This event includes the approach, jump and landing.

1. *Approach:* Run 16 to 20 strides. Take off on one foot from the board.
2. *Jump:* The hitch kick is used by many older jumpers. The feet cycle in the air. The tuck jump is simpler. Jump high in the air, tuck the body as if sitting in a chair, bring feet together.
3. *Landing:* Legs are forward and arms back. As heels hit the pit, arms are thrust forward so the body will fall forward.

HIGH JUMP

All children enjoy jumping, but the child with long thighs and limber hips will excel in this event. The scissors jump will be enjoyed most by this age level, though it has been replaced in high school and college competition by the western roll and the straddle roll.

Scissors Jump

1. *Approach:* The child should be allowed and instructed to follow his natural urge to approach the bar from either the left or the right. The jumper stands at a 45-degree angle to the bar and runs to gain momentum. The number of steps required will depend upon the size of the jumper, i.e., 7, 9, or as many as 11 steps.

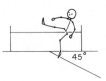

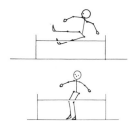

2. *Jump:* The jumper approaches with his right side to the bar and takes off from the left foot, swinging the right leg up and over the bar. The left leg follows over the bar in a scissors movement. Legs are kept straight.

3. *Landing:* Land on both feet in the pit, facing in the same direction as at the begining of the jump.

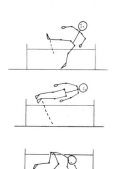

Western Roll

1. *Approach:* Come in from the left and approach as in the scissors jump. The left shoulder is toward the bar at the take-off.

2. *Jump:* Take off on the left foot and swing the right leg forward and over. The left leg tucks at the side of the right and the jumper rolls over the bar.

3. *Landing:* The jumper lands on his left foot and hands.

RELAY: 240-YARD

The shuttle relay as described on page 160 is suited to gymnasiums and can be used with the shorter distances as a training event. A baton may be passed or the runner may touch off the next runner. The 240-yard relay is run by a team of four, each running a distance of 60 yards and passing a baton to the next runner.

The baton, in official relays, must be passed within a 20-yard space. The visual exchange is recommended for the elementary level. When the approaching runner is 5 to 7 yards away, the receiver should start running, looking back with the right arm extended backward, hand open and palm up to receive the baton.

The initial runner may use the standing or crouch start and carries the baton in the left hand.

SOFTBALL THROW

Distance: Look at page 182 for baseball skill of overhead throw. Throw at a 45-degree angle because this trajectory provides the maximum distance.

Accuracy: Throw at a target made up of colored circles of various sizes, or at an archery target face. Give number values for each colored circle.

SUGGESTED READINGS

Armbruster, David, et al.: *Basic Skills in Sports,* 4th Ed. St. Louis, C. V. Mosby, 1967.

Doherty, Kenneth: *Modern Track and Field,* 2nd Ed. Englewood Cliffs, N.J., Prentice-Hall, Inc., 1963.

Fait, Hollis, et al.: *A Manual of Physical Education Activities,* 3rd Ed. Philadelphia, W. B. Saunders Company, 1967.

Miller, Kenneth: *Track and Field for Girls.* New York, The Ronald Press, 1964.

Provaznik, Marie, and Zabka, Norma: *Gymnastic Activities with Hand Apparatus for Girls and Boys.* Minneapolis, Burgess Publishing Company, 1965.

Scott, Phebe, and Crofts, Virginia: *Track and Field for Girls and Women.* New York, Appleton-Century-Crofts, 1964.

Seaton, Don Cash, et al.: *Physical Education Handbook,* 5th Ed. Englewood Cliffs, N.J., Prentice-Hall, Inc., 1967.

Chapter 17

Aquatics

There is a great need for aquatics on the elementary level. One finds the most apt pupils in the pre-school and six year old child. At this age level the child can listen, reason and take instruction in the basic elements of swimming. Fear of water, in the majority of cases, is absent, and the learning process is far quicker than at a later period when a "tightening up" occurs which slows up this process.

Death comes to many small children by drowning because of ignorance of the simplest forms of water safety and swimming techniques. Various organizations are doing a splendid job of eliminating these unnecessary deaths, but they have their limitations. A summer program of three months cannot be as satisfactory as a nine-month program where continuous progress is made in an environment conducive to learning.

Aquatics in the elementary school will be limited for a problematical number of years because of facilities, but increasing numbers of schools are including pools in their new plans. The newer unit building that uses one plot of land for senior, junior, and elementary schools permits sharing one pool built for teaching and competition. In warmer climates, pools adjacent to school buildings can be used during the spring and fall months and in some cases, if the water and decks are heated, such pools can be used during the entire year. In some cities the city recreation or park departments have cooperated with the board of education by building pools on the school campuses.

The six year old does not have a high degree of muscular coordination so that skill expectancy should be correspondingly low. This condition will exist up to the third grade and sometimes into the fourth. The fifth grader has acquired coordination, poise, balance and timing which enable him to acquire proficiency in strokes. Individual differences in classes will always determine the speed in teaching new techniques. The suggested methods of teaching follow the steps in progressive learning which, with repetition, on different grade levels, lead to the expected skill.

CLASS ORGANIZATION

The organization of a swimming class is of utmost importance on any level, but doubly so with young children where the attention span is short.

Figure 53.   Learning to swim is easy for the pre-school and six year old because at this age fear of water, in the majority of cases, is absent. (Courtesy of Elizabeth Glidden, Specialist in Elementary Physical Education, Los Angeles City Schools, Los Angeles, California.)

Deck space, the size and shape of the pool and the depth of the water will indicate the best formation, but in arranging a class for demonstrations or practice, the teacher should keep the following in mind:

1. Safety factors.
2. The teacher should be able to see each student.
3. Each student should be able to see and hear the instructor.
4. Formations should give adequate space for practice without interference, and should allow maximum participation.
5. If possible, the students should not have to face the sun.

FORMATIONS FOR DEMONSTRATIONS

In deck demonstrations, a circle or arc may be used in *A* or *B* with small groups and *C* with large groups. Formation *D* is ideal for pool demonstrations with small groups, while *E* and *C* may be used for large groups.

FORMATIONS FOR PRACTICE

Static   Fluid[1]

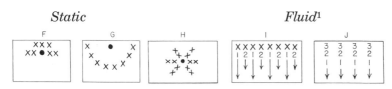

For static drill in bobbing, breathing, etc., use *A, B, F* and *G*. The double circle, as in *H,* is a good formation for static drill as the class progresses, especially in large groups. The stronger students from the outside circle help the weaker students in the inside circle.

For drill in skills such as the prone float, leg strokes, and so forth, use formation *I* for small groups. The number ones go as a group and are followed by the number twos. *J* is best for large groups and each numbered group progresses in waves. The same formation may be used for distance swimming in the upper elementary, and lanes should be observed.

METHOD AND CONTROL

From the beginning, students must be taught to *listen* and follow instructions. Short, simple commands should be repeated until a pattern is

---

[1]*Water Safety Instructor's Manual:* The American Red Cross, Washington, D.C., 1961.

Figure 54. All elementary children should learn how to swim. (Courtesy of Flint Community Schools, Flint, Michigan.)

set up in the mind of the student. Teachers are able to reach the students through repetition of key words such as: *Heads down!* for diving; *Squeeze* when the legs are brought together; *Push* when the soles of the feet are to push against the water; and *Press* when the palms are down and propelling the body forward.

Repetition is the essence of all learning, but pure drill can become very boring; therefore, diversified activities better accomplish set goals. The whistle should be used sparingly and secure absolute and instant attention. The instructor must have control at all times. There will always be one or two students who wander out of line and do not respond to instruction, but when the lack of attention becomes general, it is best to end the class with a game or relay and clear the pool.

PRELIMINARY SKILLS

ENTRY

It is imperative that the water in which beginners are taught be warm. A child or adult who is cold and shivering will become tense and learn little. Splashing of wrists, arms and back of neck breaks the shock of entry. Jumping up and down helps increase circulation and tempers the body to the temperature of the water which should be 82 to 84 degrees. Remember that your one big job is to build confidence in the pupil which means confidence in you as an instructor and confidence in his own ability to learn. At this point there can be no hurry, and play must be mixed freely with instruction. Keep in mind the attention span of your charges and keep in mind that *confidence* and *relaxation* are prime essentials.

DUCKING

Hold gutter with one hand and nose with the other. Squat and submerge head.

BREATH-HOLDING

Compare the chest to a balloon. Demonstrate by gasping in breath and showing that the air is held in the chest cavity and not in puffed-out cheeks. Hold breath above water and later submerge.

Opening Eyes

Hold breath, submerge and open eyes under water. Count fingers or pick up toys, washers or pebbles from the bottom. This not only gives confidence but eliminates the habit of wiping water from the eyes which slows up teaching.

Exhaling

Strangling frightens a child, so breath control is of utmost importance. Exhalation should be easy and relaxed. Forcing the breath out through the mouth and nose under pressure, as if you were blowing out a candle, hurries the process at first but later the exhalation would more nearly resemble a sigh. Hold to the gutter for the first trials. Later, stand in shallow water, bend at the waist and repeat inhaling and exhaling five times in succession.

Bobbing

Inhale above the water, submerge with knees flexed, and exhale. Shoot the body above water and repeat. This is fun and gives excellent practice in rhythmic breathing. This technique is used later as a safety device in progressing from deep to shallow water.

Relaxing

Take a deep breath, bend at the waist and drop head into water. Let arms hang loosely and allow knees to buckle.

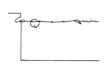

Prone Float

Place finger tips lightly on the gutter, take a breath, submerge face and stay under water long enough to allow feet to float to top. Tap gutter four or five times with fingers.

Tuck Float

Once the child has learned to relax, the most needed information is the fact that the water will support the body. There are a few who cannot float easily because of weight displacement and you will find this type in the wiry, lean children rather than in the well padded ones, but propulsion of the body through the water will take care of this handicap later.

Bend forward at the waist, take a quick breath, go into a tuck, drawing the knees to the chest, chin to knees and clasp arms around the legs. To recover footing simply straighten the legs and stand up.

PRONE GLIDE AND RECOVERY

Glide back to the side of the pool; one foot flat against the side wall 10 to 12 inches from the bottom; arms and hands on top of the water. Inhale, submerge face, and give a gentle shove away from the bank with the raised foot. The body is in a straight line from the outstretched arms to toes. When the forward glide is spent, tuck legs, as sitting down in a chair, press hands down through water toward the knees and stand.

BACK GLIDE AND RECOVERY

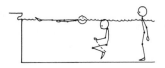

Face side of pool and place both hands in the gutter. Put one foot against the side of the pool, inhale, and shove into glide. As the forward motion is spent bend knees, drop arms palms up and vigorously pull arms in an arc toward the surface, lower feet and stand.

METHODS OF STAYING AFLOAT WITH MINIMUM EFFORT

HORIZONTAL FLOAT

Divide the class into couples (1 and 2). Number ones will face the side of the pool in waist-deep water with number twos standing directly behind them. Number one assumes a semi-sitting position with knees bent and hands in gutter. He inhales and lays back on the water by gradually straightening the legs and extending the arms obliquely. Number two assists, if needed, by placing the finger tips or the palm of the hand in the small of the back or on the back of the head.

FINNING

Check and see how many children have seen fish swim and then imitate the motions of the pectoral fins with the right hand, the left hand and both hands. Do this first above the surface and then on the surface to get the feel of the water resistance. Lower the arms to sides, flex wrists, and push the water toward the feet. Now, get in the horizontal float position and repeat this motion. Better propulsion is obtained if the arms are kept fairly close to the sides.

SCULLING

Imagine that the water is sand. With the arms extended and resting on top of the water, pull hands toward each other until the thumbs touch. There is a mound of sand between the hands. Turn the thumbs down and spread the sand out pushing to the side. Repeat these motions until it becomes easy and rhythmic. The process of pull-in and push-out resembles that of frosting a cake, only it is done with both hands. Make a figure eight in the water with both hands. Lay back in float position and repeat motions.

TREADING

Hold to the gutter with one hand and keep body erect and at right angles to the side of the pool; use free hand in finning or sculling motion and at the same time employ galloping, bicycling or scissor action of the feet and legs. As skill progresses, release hand from gutter and employ both hands instead of one.

STROKES

ELEMENTARY BACKSTROKE

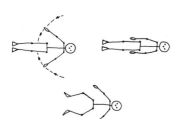

Arms. Start from back float to glide position, arms along side. Drop elbows toward bottom of pool, slide hands along sides of the legs and body until hands reach the chest, turn fingers outward, extend arms to full length, grasping water with the palms of both hands and press parallel with the water until hands have reached the sides of the body.

Legs. Simultaneous with the action of the arms, spread knees slightly and, as arms are extended, step with feet into a "V" position. Catch the water with the soles of the feet, squeeze legs together to back glide position. Arms and legs work in unison followed by a glide.

SIDE STROKE

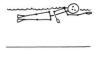

Shove off in lying position on either side with arm on underneath side fully extended above head and the other arm lying along side of the body, legs together and extended. Grasp the water with the underneath hand and press backward and downward at a 45° angle to a point directly in front of the chin. The side arm comes forward in rhythm with the lead arm to retrieve the water and is pushed toward feet and side.

The leg action is coordinated with the movement of the side arm. Pull knees up slightly, step forward with the top leg, reach backward with the other leg to a wide arc, squeeze legs together and glide.

BREAST STROKE

Breast stroke can be taught with the face above water or with rhythmic breathing, submerging face during the glide. Shove off in prone glide position. Grasp the water with the palms of the hands, press backward and downward until hands are parallel with the shoulders, pull elbows to sides of body, palms down, fingers pointing forward. Extend arms to starting position.

As the arms are pressed backward and downward, drop knees, the outer edges of the feet are turned upward, toes outward. Push with the soles of the feet in an arc, outward and backward until the legs meet. Arms are extended as the leg action is completed, followed by a glide. Errors in timing may be avoided by allowing the child to do only one complete stroke at a time until a perfect pattern has been set.

BACK CRAWL

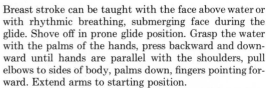

In the back crawl the major part of the propulsive force comes from the legs which at full extension whip up and down, traveling 10 to 14 inches. The knees, feet and ankles are relaxed and the emphasis is placed on the upward lift of the top of the foot. Shove off in back glide and begin rhythmic leg action. Lift arms alternately and swing upward, outward and backward, dropping relaxed hands and catching water when arms have reached a "V" position. Press water with a full arm swing toward the feet. The legs whip up and down six times during completed cycle of both arms. Raise the head slightly and look at the feet in order to keep the leg movement constant.

FRONT OR COORDINATED CRAWL

The crawl can and should be taught from the beginning of swimming instruction. The modified stroke with the head out of the water and a rapid and sporadic arm and leg action has been called the "human stroke" by the American Red Cross and the "dog paddle" by others. This stroke is gradually molded into the true crawl as the mental set and muscular coordination matures to the point where the child can cope with the highly coordinated combination of leg thrash, arm cycle and rhythmic breathing.

Legs. The leg action is the same as that used in the back crawl except that the downward pressure with the instep and the upward lift with the sole of the foot is equal.
Arms. Lift the elbow, using the shoulder muscles and letting forearm and hand hang relaxed; lead forward with the elbow and extend arm fully; cup hand and pull water to hip. Alternate right and left arms.

Breathing. The right hand is usually dominant, so the majority of swimmers will inhale from the right side, but breathing from the left side is equally acceptable if it comes more naturally to the child. Turn the chin to the side until the mouth is clear of the water line and quickly inhale through the mouth; then turn the face to the front, submerge and exhale through the mouth and nose. Watch carefully to check any tendency to lift shoulders and roll the body, as the movement executed properly with the head and neck will not alter the horizontal body position.

The body lays on the water with a slight arch in the back. The arms revolve and the swimmer inhales as one arm is ready for the recovery and exhales as the opposite arm executes the downward pull. The legs thrash out three beats to each arm or six beats to the complete cycle of both arms.

DIVING

Entry into the water by a dive gives the child a sense of achievement and builds confidence. Instruction can be started as soon as the student is able to push up from the bottom. Teaching progressions are:

Sitting Dive. Sit on the side of pool placing feet in gutter, arms above head, hands together, and elbows pulled close to ears. Bend forward until balance is lost, inhale, and shove into water. Turn hands up and push or swim to the surface.

Kneeling Dive. Kneel on one knee with one foot at the edge of the pool, toes over the edge, and arms in position as for sitting dive. Keep head down; give a slight push and enter water; keep legs and arms fully extended.

Standing Dive Progressions. It is easy to progress from the kneeling dive to the standing dive. Place one foot on the side of pool and one leg extended to the rear. Bend in the middle and lean over until balance is lost. The instructor may assist by holding the lifted leg, being sure the child breaks at the waistline and keeps the head down. Later, the student may lift the leg without assistance. As soon as the child has learned to keep the head down, he may place both feet on the deck and dive into water by flexing knees, bending over, pushing with arches and ankles and straightening the knees.

Plunge. Stand with the toes hooked over the edge of the deck, feet hip-width apart. Assume a crouch position, knees slightly flexed, body leaning forward and arms hanging loosely. Whip arms backward and forward, shove with feet, and hurl body out on water, going about 12 inches below the surface.

TEACHING AIDS IN SWIMMING

For many years teachers have used teaching aids in developing form in the various strokes. These aids are the old-fashioned water wings, harness and inner tube, and more recently flutter boards, floats and fins. Some claim that the use of any aid delays the acquisition of confidence. Others feel that in mass teaching the metal or rubber float is an invaluable aid and will be put aside readily when the child has reached a stage of learning that includes confidence and a muscular coordination which enables him to stay on top of the water.

AQUATIC FUN TIME

A "Fun Time" of 5 to 10 minutes is the perfect ending for a learning period in the water. The student leaves the pool relaxed and with a sustained enthusiasm that carries over to the next teaching period. The games and races utilize the simplest to the more advanced skills and give impetus to the desire to master these skills in the formal teaching period.

It is recommended that for the first, second and third grades this period be used purely for play. In the fourth, fifth and sixth grades, when the competitive spirit begins to run high, teams may be selected for a semester and a running score kept on the contests. Relays may be used instead of races when the groups are large.[2]

Shallow Water

See how many can hold their breath and sit on the bottom of the pool.
See how many can submerge, holding their breath, and count their fingers.
Blow small sailboats, balloons or ping-pong balls across the pool.
Poison Tag: "It" tries to tag a player who is safe while floating, finning or sculling.
Corks: Throw in 10 corks. See who can collect the most.
Retrieving: Throw smooth rocks, lead washers, pucks and tin plates into the pool. See who can collect the most objects in a prescribed time.
Water Dodgeball: This promotes ducking, because the player is safe under water.
Tunnel Ball: Divide into teams and pass ball between the legs.
Can You Do It: Divide into two groups, selecting a leader for each group. The leader of one group performs a stunt. If the opposing team can not do it, he receives a point for his team. Teams alternate in performing stunts.
Drop the Puck: The players form a circle and "It" drops the puck behind a player who must retrieve it and try to catch the player before he returns to the vacant place. If he does not catch him, he becomes "It."
Life Line: Divide into teams. One member takes his position on the opposite side of the pool. At the whistle, one at a time drops into the pool and advances, joining hands with numbers 2,

---

[2] See pages 159–160 for relay formations.

3, 4, etc. Upon reaching the lone player, they see how fast they can get him back to their starting post. This is not only a game but a device for rescuing weak swimmers who have stepped over their depth.

Leap Frog: Line up teams as for the game on land. The No. 1 player who returns to the head of the line first, wins the game for his team.

Races using finning, sculling and elementary strokes; limiting distance to proficiency of swimmers, i.e., 10 ft., 20 ft., 30 ft.

Underwater Race: 10 to 20 feet.

Bobbing Race: Use bobbing technique and lunge body forward as body shoots to surface.

Flutter Board Relay: Use flutter board with the flutter or whip kick. This may also be used for advanced swimmers.

Deep Water

The game program, for swimmers who can handle themselves in deep water, can be as varied and as interesting as the ingenuity of the instructor. Many land games and team games can be adapted to use in the water. Life buoys or floats with lead anchors become floats; hula hoops or old basketball hoops serve as goals; wooden beads float on ropes and describe the playing area, and old volleyball nets may be stretched across the pool with short standards and improvised vises attached to the scum gutters.

Water Baseball: Use bat and plastic ball. The diamond may be limited to shallow water, deep water or both. Use regulation baseball rules.

Water Volleyball: Use water polo ball. Anchor net three feet above water. Mark limits with floating beads. Follow regulation volleyball rules.

Water Basketball: Place goals on sides of pool, if width permits. Play as in land basketball.

Modified Water Polo: Because water polo requires a great deal of stamina, its use must be limited to the fifth and sixth grades, and the play area should be limited. The goals of two 3-foot uprights and a crossbar 10 feet wide may be made of ½ inch galvanized pipe and anchored to the sides and scum gutters. The goal should clear the water by 3 feet.

Two teams of 7 to 10 line up in front of their respective goals.

Action
1. The ball is put in play in the center of the play area.
2. The ball may be thrown or carried.
3. A point is scored when the ball passes between the uprights and below the crossbar.
4. The game is divided into two halves of 5 to 8 minutes and teams change goals at the half.
5. A ball that goes out of bounds is brought back by the team that was not in contact with the ball. If the ball goes out over the goals it is brought back at a corner.
6. If a team holds or interferes illegally with the progress of the ball, a foul is called and a free throw is allowed from a designated line 10 feet from the goal.

Games, Races and Relays

Front and Back Flutter Kick: Front with face in water and back with head raised, chin on chest and hands by sides.

Underwater Race: Start with racing dive and swim under water for distance or in shorter distance for time.

Medley Relay: Use back crawl, breast stroke and front crawl. Push balloon or water polo ball with breast stroke.

Carrying Relays: Race, carrying a lighted candle, umbrella, a spoon holding an egg or a ping-pong ball or flag.

Tandem or Centipede Relay: 4 to 6 swimmers work as one body and stroke as a crew.

Front Crawl: Swimmers hook feet around waist of swimmer back of them and stroke in unison.
Racing Back: Hook toes in armpits of swimmer in front and stroke as crew.
Will-o'-the wisp: Divide into groups of 6 or 8. Blindfold all players except "It" who has a bell or
    whistle. He swims under water and each time he surfaces he rings the bell or blows the
    whistle and the players try to catch him. If he is caught, he joins the group and the captor
    becomes the Will-o'-the-wisp.

TESTING PROCEDURES

Testing, (1) gives the instructor a record that aids in pointing out weaknesses to be corrected, and (2) provides potent motivational aid. Someone once observed that the man does not live who does not like to see his name in print. Children are not different from adults in this respect and, while a good mark is a reward for effort, a poor mark may for some be a spur that challenges them to try harder.

The American Red Cross has graded sheets that are available to Water Safety Instructors. They give a card to a child upon the successful completion of each test, i.e., Beginner, Intermediate, Swimmer and Advanced Swimmer.

The tests that follow have been made simpler and graded down to young children, and, while they require the same skill, the reduced distances demand less stamina. The suggested names for the tests could be changed to fit the need and the last test could be divided into two if it is too difficult for the group. Small fish made of felt, in school colors, with the size increasing for graded tests would be proudly stitched on bathing suits or trunks. Certain days should be set aside for testing and a routine followed; a child should be given credit for any completed skill whether it is in sequence or not.

FINGERLING TEST

1. Breath-holding—take deep breath, submerge, and pick up four objects in a 12-inch radius.
2. Bobbing—executed 10 times in a deliberate manner. Should not finish gasping for breath.
3. Prone Float—horizontal position if possible. If feet sink to bottom, grading should be done on relaxation of swimmer.
4. Prone Glide and Recovery—body should plane through water and after the glide is spent, the recovery should be unhurried.
5. Back Glide and Recovery—same as front except head raised slightly.
6. Back Float—horizontal; semi-horizontal; knees bent or vertical position acceptable.
7. Finning—hands close to sides.
8. Sculling—described figure eight. Definite propulsion through water.
9. Crawl—dog paddle; arms may be under water or out. Rhythmic breathing not required. Distance only requirement.
10. Elementary Back—fair amount of form expected as coordination is simple.
11. Dives and Jump in Shoulder-depth Water; level off and swim 10 feet.

FINGERLING TEST	BREATH HOLDING 4 OBJECTS	BOBBING 10 TIMES RHYTHMIC BREATHING	PRONE FLOAT & RECOVERY	PRONE GLIDE & RECOVERY	BACK GLIDE & RECOVERY	BACK FLOAT	FINNING	SCULLING	CRAWL 15 FT.	ELEMENTARY BACK 15 FT	SITTING DIVE	KNEELING DIVE	JUMP (SHOULDER DEPTH) LEVEL OFF & SWIM								TOTAL POINTS
GRADES 1 & 2	1	2	3	4	5	6	7	8	9	10	11	12	13								
NAME	5	5	5	5	5	5	10	10	10	10	10	10	10								100

KEEPER TEST	BOBBING 20 TIMES	ELEM. BACK 25 FT.	FLOAT ½ MINUTE	TREAD WATER ½ MINUTE	SIDE STROKE 25 FT	UNDERWATER SWIM	JUMP INTO DEEP WATER	STANDING FRONT DIVE	SCULLING 20 FT.	CRAWL 25 FT.	SURFACE DIVE	TURN OVER	KICK GLIDE ON FRONT	KICK GLIDE ON BACK	3 MINUTE SWIM						TOTAL POINTS
GRADES 2 - 5	1	2	3	4	5	6	7	8	9	10	11	12	13	14	15						
NAME	5	10	5	5	10	5	5	5	5	10	5	5	5	5	15						100

FISH TEST	ELEM. BACK 25 YDS.	RACING DIVE	25 YDS SIDE STROKE	FLOAT 1 MIN.	25 YDS BREAST STROKE	TREAD WATER 1 MIN.	RACING BACK 25 YDS	TURNS	CRAWL 25 YDS	FRONT DIVE	SWIM 5 MIN										TOTAL POINTS
GRADES 5 - 8	1	2	3	4	5	6	7	8	9	10	11										
NAME	5	5	10	5	10	10	10	5	10	10	20										100

GRADING SHEET FOR SWIMMING STROKES	ELEMENTARY BACK					SIDE					BREAST					CRAWL					BACK CRAWL
	ARMS	LEGS	BODY POSITION	COORDINATION	TOTAL																
	1	1	1	2	5																

KEEPER TEST

1. Elementary Back—good form required.
2. Tread Water—hands allowed.
3. Side Stroke—fair form, grade 3 (on swimming stroke sheet) should be a passing grade.
4. Underwater Swim—two body lengths.
5. Jump into Deep Water—level off and swim to bank of shallow water.
6. Standing Front Dive—do not grade for form. Head-first entry only requirement.
7. Sculling—in good form and relaxed.
8. Crawl—arms should clear water and fair degree of coordination expected in arms, legs and rhythmic breathing. 3 passing grade.
9. Surface Dive—toes should go under water without swimming assist.
10. Turn Over—change from back to side or front and continue to swim for several feet.
11. Kick Glide—flutter kick for 20 feet on back or front without use of hands or arms.
12. Three-minute Swim—use any stroke and sculling or finning.

FISH TEST

All strokes should be done in good form. If a board is available, the front dive should be done from it, otherwise from the bank.

SUGGESTED READINGS

American Red Cross: *Swimming and Diving,* Revised Ed. Washington, D.C., 1962.

American Red Cross: *Water Safety Instructor's Manual.* Washington, D.C., 1962.

Armbruster, D. A.; Allen, R. H.; and Billingsley, H. S.: *Swimming and Diving,* 4th Ed. St. Louis, C. V. Mosby Co., 1963.

Barr, Alfred S.; Grady, Ben F.; and Higgens, John: *Swimming and Diving.* New York, A. S. Barnes & Co., 1950.

Cureton, T. K.: *Fun in the Water.* New York, Association Press, 1957.

Gabrielsen, M. A.; Spears, Betty; and Gabrielsen, B. W.: *Aquatics Handbook.* New York, Prentice-Hall, Inc., 1960.

Kauffman, Carolyn: *How To Teach Children To Swim.* New York, G. P. Putnam's Sons, 1960.

Lukens, Paul W.: *Teaching Swimming.* Minneapolis, Minn., Burgess Publishing Co., 1952.

Mackenzie, M. M., and Spears, Betty: *Beginning Swimming.* Belmont, Calif., Wadsworth Publishing Co., 1963.

Official Aquatic Guide, latest edition. National Section for Girls' and Women's Athletics, American Assn. for Health, Physical Education, and Recreation, Washington, D.C.

Smith, Hope: *Water Games.* New York, The Ronald Press Company, 1962.

Vannier, Maryhelen, and Poindexter, Hally Beth: *Individual and Team Sports for Girls and Women,* 2nd Ed. Philadelphia, W. B. Saunders Company, 1968.

Chapter 18

Classroom and
Quiet Games

GENERAL TECHNIQUES

Adverse weather conditions create few problems to the master teacher who has learned to utilize the classroom for active games and contests during stormy, unpleasant days. This emergency period can be one of bedlam for the novice and one of boredom for the pupils. Scheduled playground play need not be canceled during cold, wet days. Instead, the classroom, corridors, lunchroom, or other space can be used. However, this makeshift period of classroom play should never be substituted for rugged outdoor activity or daily instruction in physical education. Rather, it can be an addition to the total program. Although children must learn how to run, skip and jump and use their bodies in other types of the fundamental big-muscle movements in order to develop properly, they also need to learn how to play the less active, quiet games that will enable them to use skillfully the smaller muscles of the body. Like adults, children need to know how to have fun with things in their everyday environment—how to entertain themselves rather than be entertained.

Specific objectives to be realized through classroom activities might well include the desire to:

1. Share with the child interesting "fun to do" activities for classroom and after-school play.
2. Add variety and completeness to the total physical education program.
3. Develop a sense of fair play and the ability to play with others.
4. Develop good leadership and fellowship techniques.
5. Aid in developing good all-round social, physical, and emotional development.

In order to reach these worthy objectives, the teacher needs to utilize all available indoor space to the greatest advantage in carrying out a carefully planned program. If she is fortunate enough to have moveable chairs in the room, circle tag and "It," or other such active games are desirable. If, however, desks and chairs are fastened to the floor, quiet games are

327

more suitable. Knowledge of a wide range of activities and how to modify them to fit into one's own particular situation is imperative.

Rules of conduct should be set up by the children aided by the teacher. Activities chosen by the group should not infringe upon the rights of others in nearby classrooms.

CRITERIA FOR CHOOSING ACTIVITIES

In selecting games for indoor play the teacher should strive for participation of the whole class. Good questions to keep in mind when selecting activities are:

1. How many children can be active safely at one time?
2. How quickly can new players replace those who have been active?
3. How much activity will each child actually engage in during the period?
4. Do the chosen games reach our pupil-teacher objectives?

SAFETY PRECAUTIONS

Learning to take chances wisely should be stressed throughout the period. Over-protected children often are denied rich learning experiences. This does not imply that they should be encouraged to cut their fingers in order to learn that a knife is sharp, but does connote that many dangers can be avoided best when one learns from a painful experience. Pupil-teacher safety rules are most adhered to; group-discovered hazards are most avoided.

Suggested safety precautions are:

1. Avoid running around in small circles or changing directions suddenly.
2. Establish goal lines away from wall.
3. Use beanbags or balloons rather than regulation balls; reduce the amount of equipment used.
4. Limit the number of players to fit into a given space, but be certain that each child gets a turn and takes part in meaningful activities.
5. Keep noise at a minimum.

Additions to this list should be made after the teacher gains from the experience of playing with the children in her own room; she should make a collection of activities most favored by the children and be constantly on the search for new materials.

EQUIPMENT

A magic box, which is used only on stormy, dark days, can help turn a dull day into one of great adventure. Checkers, cards, table games, beanballs, ring toss, jacks, and miniature bowling pins are among the treasures. Small-group or couple play should be encouraged, or a group of six might choose games they want to play. Each group might be allowed to play their favorite game for the entire period or change with any other willing group at half-period time.

A construction box is often found in the rooms of creative, experienced teachers. In it are found games made by the pupils on previous rainy days, along with some half-completed ones. Some children made checkerboards, others toss boards for fruit-jar rubbers. Still others have made miniature table shuffleboard sets on which checkers can be finger snapped up, down, and into given areas. Two boys made a jumping standard by driving nails into two boards and using an old fishing pole to move up and down on the nails to show how high one must jump in order to clear the pole. Two girls and four boys made a balance beam using blocks to steady a railroad tie size board.

These and numerous other pieces of equipment and games can be made in the classroom. Home- or class-made equipment often is more meaningful to pupils than expensive items furnished by the school. The creative teacher, when and if she has a "will," will find the "way" to get equipment for her group. She can even stimulate the class into making many of the things with which they can play.

Suggested minimum equipment includes:

1. Four ring toss games
2. Four rubber balls
3. One treasure box
4. Card and table games

5. Jump ropes
6. One long rope
7. Phonograph or piano
8. Empty milk cartons and tin cans of varying sizes

GAME LEADERSHIP

Successful game or play leadership requires skill. The leader must know games best suited for the group, how to get play started, when to stop one activity and go on to the next, as well as a wide range of things to play. Mastery of these skills comes from experience, providing one has learned from past mistakes. The novice may gain additional experience with church or neighborhood groups in order to become more expert.

Mastery of a best method to gain attention is important. A sudden clapping of hands, playing a piano cord, and blowing a whistle are recommended techniques. Although the teacher may ordinarily have control over her group, it may be lessened or even lost during this classroom recreation. She may find it necessary to stop activities entirely or momentarily in order to regain control. However, the pupils should not be bargained with when they are "bad" or have been particularly "good." The plea, "Please let us play five minutes longer and we will be quieter" or the promise, "Now children, if all of you get your arithmetic lesson we will play ten minutes longer this afternoon" are often significant signs of this type of leadership technique. In the former, the children have found that they can bargain with the teacher. In the latter, the teacher is slipping carrots into the daily diet by promising dessert. Next to compulsion, bargaining is the lowest form of leadership.

An atmosphere of fun should permeate the classroom. If the first game has been wonderful, obtaining class cooperation will be easier when the second one to be played is introduced. If, however, a game that looked like fun when described in the book should fall flat, it is best to change to another rather than insisting "now children this game really *is* fun" when obviously it is not.

Rules and the setting of necessary boundaries should be briefly explained. A description of how to play, coupled with actual demonstrations, is ideal. If, when saying, "Everyone get into a circle," the teacher will join hands with a youngster on either side, the pupils will quickly get into this formation. The use of imitation is a standard teaching method, for children are copycats. A major portion of their learning comes through what they see and try to do. Educators call this trial-and-error learning through imitation.

Changing activities at their fun peaks adds to their enjoyment. Children often say then, "Oh, let's keep on playing, please!" Grownups realize that stopping the activity at the climax will cause the children to have greater desire to play the game again because it was such fun. This need for completeness, as psychologists call it, drives us to take up willingly or return joyfully to interrupted tasks or pleasures. Recognition of fun peaks can be developed.

Going from the known to the unknown is an educational principle applicable to game as well as subject matter material, for basically the same principles of teaching underline all learning materials. Each new game period should begin with the most favored game from the previous period. Because we all like to do those things which we can do well, the wise teacher aids children to learn many skills with above-average ability. It is wise to learn at least two new activities during the game period as well as review others. It is unwise to insist upon skill perfection at the sacrifice of an unpleasant experience or unfavorable attitude.

ACTIVE CIRCLE GAMES

KICK THE PIN

Grades: 4, 5, 6   Players: 10 for each circle

Equipment. A volley or rubber play ball; an Indian club or milk bottle for each group.
Directions. Each circled group with approximately 6 feet between each player tries to kick the ball so as to knock down the centered pin. All kicking is done from this circle. Each team tries to knock over the pin first. The succeeding team scores one point. Ten points constitute a game.

RING THE BOTTLE NECK

Grades: 1, 2, 3   Players: 4 to 6 on each team

Equipment.   Catsup or pop bottle and brass or wooden ring suspended from the end of a two-foot stick with 20 inches of string; both for each group.

Directions.   Player holds the stick at end opposite from where the string is fastened, and tries to get the ring over the neck of the bottle. Each player on each team gets one try while the leader counts slowly from 1 to 10. Score one point for each successful attempt. The team scoring 10 points first wins.

BALL BOUNCE

Grades: 1, 2, 3   Players: 4 to 6 on each team

Equipment.   A soccer, rubber playground or tennis ball, a chair, and one wastebasket for each player.

Directions.   From a distance of 8 feet each player tries to bounce the ball over the chair and into the upturned wastebasket. Each player gets one turn. The team scoring 10 points first wins.

BULL IN THE RING

Grades: 2, 3   Players: entire class

Equipment.   None.

Directions.   Players form a circle around the chosen "bull," who tries to break through. If he gets through, all chase him. His catcher becomes the "bull."

STRIDE BALL

Grades: 4, 5   Players: 10 players in each circle

Equipment.   One volley, soccer, or basketball.

Directions.   "It" stands in a circle. Outside players stand with feet in straddle position touching those of players on their right and left. "It" tries to roll the ball outside the circle between the legs of some players. The players try to stop the ball with their hands. If they can, they roll the ball back to center player. When "It" rolls the ball between the legs of a player, the two exchange places.

POISON CIRCLE

Grades: 4, 5, 6   Players: 8 to 10 in a circle

Equipment.   Chalk.

Directions.   Draw circle 4 feet in diameter. Place players around the ring. The object of the game is to keep out of the poisoned circle by trying to pull others into it. When a player steps in or on the poisoned circle he is out.

CIRCLE CATCH BALL

Grades: 4, 5, 6   Players: 8 to 10 in a circle

Equipment.   Volley, soccer or basketball for each group.

Directions.   "It" stands inside the circle of players standing 3 feet apart. Players throw the ball around or across the circle to each other while "It" tries to catch the ball. If he succeeds, he trades places with the person who last threw the ball.

CLUB GUARD

Grades: 2, 3   Players: 8 to 10 in a group

Equipment. Indian club, volley or playground ball.

Directions. Players form circle around one guarding club in the middle. The object is to knock the club down with the ball. The guard protects it with his legs or body or bats it with his hands. The new guard is the one who gets the club down. Divide a large group into several smaller circles for the greatest game success and fun. Avoid having more than eight in each group, if possible.

SCHOOLROOM TAG

Grades: 1, 2, 3   Players: entire class

Equipment. Chalk.

Directions. A circle is drawn about 4 feet across in the front of the room. "It" stands near the circle. The leader names any 3 children to try to get into the circle without being tagged. The one tagged first becomes "It." If no one is tagged, the first player becomes "It."

RING MASTER

Grades: 1, 2, 3   Players: entire class

Equipment. None.

Directions. All players form a circle without holding hands. A ring master stands inside and pretends to flourish a whip. As he turns, he calls out the name of some animal and all move around the circle imitating that animal. When the ring master says, "Now all join the circus parade" each imitates any animal he wants to. The teacher or class chooses the one who has done the best imitations.

EXCHANGE TAG

Grades: 1, 2, 3   Players: entire class

Equipment. None.

Directions. "It" faces the group and calls out the names of any two players who must exchange seats. "It" tries to tag one of them before he reaches a seat. The tagged player becomes the new "It."

INDIAN RUNNING

Grades: 1, 2, 3   Players: entire class

Equipment. None.

Directions. Six are chosen to leave the room. They arrange themselves in any order, return to the room and run around it, then go out again. When they return, the children try to name their running line-up. The child who is successful may choose five others to leave with him and the game continues.

PALM BALL

Grades: 4, 5, 6   Players: entire class divided into small circles

Equipment. A rubber ball for each side.

Directions. Circled players cup hands behind their backs. "It" places the ball in someone's hands, who must turn and run in the opposite direction. Each tries to get back to the vacant spot first. The loser becomes "It."

NUMBERED CHAIRS

Grades: 4, 5, 6   Players: entire class

Equipment. A chair for each player, plus one extra.
Directions. Seat players and place extra chair in a line. Players number off. The space retains the number throughout, though players change. Number one calls "four." Immediately "four" responds with another number. When a player whose number is called does not respond immediately he must go to the end of the line. Thus "nine" becomes "eight," etc. Numbers are called rapidly. The object of the game is to send top players to the end of the line.
Variations. Have players clap hands on knees, then together. Then snap fingers on left hand. Then on right hand in rhythm to 1, 2, 3, 4 count. All players must keep this rhythm up while calling out or responding to a number. Failure to keep the rhythm going will send a player to the end of the line. This game may also be played in a circle.

BIRDS HAVE FEATHERS

Grades: 1, 2, 3   Players: entire class

Equipment. None.
Directions. One player is the leader. He and all others flap their arms like birds. He calls out names of something with feathers. If a player flaps his wings on calling out something that does not have feathers, he is out. The leader flaps his wings on almost all things to confuse the group and calls as rapidly as possible, "Birds have feathers, bats have feathers, babies have feathers," etc.
Variations. Thumbs up and thumbs down. Cats have fur, trees have leaves.

I AM VERY TALL

Grades: 1, 2, 3   Players: entire class

Equipment. A blindfold.
Directions. One player is blindfolded. Then another says, "I am very, very tall, I'm very, very small, sometimes I'm tall, sometimes I'm small. Guess which I am now." He stands or squats. "It" guesses whether the player is standing or stooping. If "It" chooses correctly he chooses someone to take his place.
Variations. The whole group stands or squats. Chosen player holds hands up for "tall" and low for "small."

FIND THE LEADER

Grades: 1 to 6   Players: entire class

Equipment. None.
Directions. Players stand or sit in a circle. A leader is chosen. One player goes out. The group starts clapping and continues until the returned player stands in the center of the circle. The leader changes from clapping to waving his hands, swinging his feet, etc. All other imitate the changed actions by watching someone opposite. The player has three chances to find the leader. If he finds him, he chooses a player to take his place. If he does not find him, he again is "It." A new leader is chosen.

CENTER PITCH

Grades: 2, 3   Players: 3 to 5 on a team

Equipment. 1 beanbag, eraser, or ball for each team.
Directions. Players on each team take single turns throwing the beanbag into a metal wastebasket 8 feet away. Add players' scores. The winner is the team scoring 21 points.
Variations. (1) The players begin and stop pitching the bags at the leader's whistle. The winner is the team scoring the most points in five minutes.
(2) Draw chalk circles at one end of the room. Players throw the bags into the circles.
(3) Draw three circles on a board or cardboard. Each player gets three tosses. Team scoring largest number of points in a given time wins. First circle counts 25, second 15, third 5.

QUIET CIRCLE GAMES

ELECTRIC SHOCK

Grades: 1 to 3   Players: 10 to 15 in each circle

Equipment.   None.
Directions.   Players sit or stand in a circle. "It" stands inside and tries to guess where the shock is. All players hold hands; one player begins the shock by squeezing a player's hand on his right or left. The shock may move any direction and at any time a player may send it back the other way. "It" tries to find the position of the shock. The caught player becomes "It."

AIR BALLOON

Grades: 1, 2, 3   Players: circles of 8 to 10 players

Equipment.   One balloon for each group.
Directions.   Divide the group into equally numbered circles. On count of "3" each group competes with the other to see which one can keep the balloon in the air longest by tapping it. Each player may tap the balloon only once, but may tap it after another player has done so.
Variations.   Music may be played. Each player may tap in rhythm to the music or on one separate rhythmic beat.

POISON BALL

Grades: 1, 2, 3   Players: circles of 8 to 10 players

Equipment.   Two rubber balls for each circle.
Directions.   Players form into circles, each circle has two balls. When music stops or the whistle blows, players in possession of either ball are poisoned and must leave the group. When the group gets down to four only one ball is used. The last player to stay in the circle is the winner.
Variation.   Musical chairs.

WHO HAS GONE?

Grades: 1, 2   Players: entire class

Equipment.   None.
Directions.   "It" closes his eyes. One player leaves the room. "It" tries to guess who has gone. If he guesses correctly, he and the player who went out change places. If not, the game begins again.

ELECTRIC TAG

Grades: 1, 2, 3   Players: entire class

Equipment.   None.
Directions.   Players sit in rows with their hands in their laps and eyes closed. At a signal, the last pupil in each row touches the shoulder of the person in front of him, he touches the next person, etc. The row that has its first pupil stand, wins.

STILL WATER

Grades: 1, 2, 3   Players: entire class

Equipment. None.
Directions. "It" faces the rest and picks out the quietest one when he says "still water." On the words, "running water" the pupils can move around and talk. The winner chooses the quietest and she becomes "It."

ANGELS DO IT

Grades: 1 to 5   Players: entire class

Equipment. None.
Directions. Pupils place hands behind their necks to look like angel wings. The leader gives the direction, "Touch your nose, angels do it." All players must quickly touch their nose and get back to angel position. The first angel team scores 1 point. Suggested "do its"—touch right foot, left foot, clap twice behind you, stand up, touch wood, whistle a tune.

STAGE COACH

Grades: 4, 5, 6   Players: entire class

Equipment. None.
Directions. Players are each given a name of a stagecoach part. One starts telling a story of the stagecoach, mentioning all parts assigned. As the child's part is named he gets up and runs around his chair. When the leader says, "Stagecoach" all must change chairs with anyone except the player on his left and right. The leader tries to get a seat. The person left seatless becomes the new story teller.

I PASS THESE SCISSORS TO YOU

Grades: 4, 5, 6   Players: entire class

Equipment. A pair of scissors.
Directions. Players are seated in circle formation. The leader passes a pair of scissors. The next player passes them on saying, "I have received them crossed and I pass these scissors to you uncrossed." The crossed and uncrossed refers to the passer's legs or feet, and not to the open or closed scissors being passed as the players think. If the receiver's feet were crossed when the scissors are passed, and crossed as he passes them, he says, "I received them crossed and I pass these scissors to you crossed." The game continues until everyone catches on.

THE GUESSING BLINDMAN

Grades: 1, 2, 3   Players: entire class

Equipment. One blindfold and a stick or ruler.
Directions. Players are seated in circle formation. One is blindfolded and turned around three times while all others change seats. The blindman walks forward and touches someone with the stick saying, "Can you guess." The touched player, trying to disguise his voice, repeats this question three times. If the blindman guesses who is speaking, he and the discovered player exchange places. Otherwise, he is "It" again.

BUG

Grades: 3 to 6   Players: individual or 4 to 10 on each team

Equipment. Make two or more hexagon-shaped tops with the letters B, H, T, E, L, F on six sides; paper; pencils.

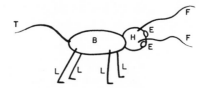

Directions. Each player spins the top. If "B" comes up he draws the body of the bug and spins again. If he gets an "E" he loses his turn, for there is no head into which to fit the eyes. The second best throw, therefore, is an "H" for the head. "T" means tail, "L" means leg, "F" for feeler. Each bug must have two eyes, two feelers, and six legs along with its body, tail, and head before it is a complete bug. When a player tosses something he already has, he loses his turn. A player cannot start drawing his bug until he gets a "B" for body. The team or individual drawing a complete bug first wins.

MUFFIN PAN BOWLING

Grades: 1, 2, 3   Players: 4 to 6 on each team

Equipment.   One muffin pan; one small rubber ball for each group.
Directions.   Set the pan upright against a wall or on a table. Place a board against one edge of the pan to form an incline. Roll the ball up the incline into the compartments. Score one point for each successful attempt. Each player is given 3 trials. The team scoring 10 points first wins.

RING ON A STRING

Grades: 1, 2, 3   Players: divide class into circles of 10 players

Equipment.   Ring on a string.
Directions.   One stands in the circle. A string with a ring on it is held loosely in both hands by all players in the seated circle. The object of the game is to slip the ring along the string from one player to the next while "It" tries to locate the ring or who has it. If he is successful, he exchanges places with the one under whose hand it was. If unsuccessful he continues as "It."

CATCH THE CANE

Grades: 3, 4   Players: entire class

Equipment.   Cane or yardstick.
Directions.   "It" stands inside the circle. All players, including "It" are given a number. "It" holds the cane upright with one end on the floor. As he calls out a number he lets go of the cane. The player whose number has been called attempts to catch it before it touches the floor. If he fails he becomes "It." If he catches the can, the first player remains "It."

THE TOY SHOP

Grades: 1, 2   Players: entire class

Equipment.   None.
Directions.   One child is chosen shopkeeper; one the customer, who leaves the room while the others choose which toy they want to be. When the customer returns he asks to buy some toys. If he asks for a ball the player representing a ball bounces up and down, or for an airplane, the player flies around the room, etc. The shopkeeper guides his buying by suggesting and showing certain toys. The customer selects the three best toys.

How Many Can You Remember?
(Kim's Game)

Grades: 4, 5, 6   Players: entire class

Equipment.   A wide variety of objects.
Directions.   Place 20 to 30 objects on table. Everyone looks at them 2 to 3 minutes. Then a cover is placed on them. The winner is the person writing down the greatest number of the objects.

TABLE AND CARD GAMES

MAKING SQUARES

Grades: 4, 5, 6   Players: 2

Equipment.   Five or more vertical rows of dots on a piece of paper.
Directions.   Players take turns connecting any two dots with a straight line. No diagonal line may be drawn. Each places his initial in each square his line completes. When all dots have been connected the player having the largest number of initialed squares wins.

THROW THE CARDS

Place a wastebasket, box or hat two or more feet before lines of three or four players. Award one point to each for cards thrown successfully into the container.

PIG

Players seated around a table are dealt eight cards: fours, fives, sixes, sevens, eights, nines, etc., making the deck up according to the number playing. On the signal, "go," each passes one card face down to the player on his left. When anyone can make a book of four cards having the same number, he puts his cards down and places one finger to his nose while the rest continue playing. The last one to copy him or who has failed to notice that the others have their fingers touching their nose, is a P. If the same player is last to do so again, he is a PI: on the next failure he becomes a PIG. Anyone he can get to answer any question with yes or no, also becomes a PIG. Play continues until all are out of the game.

STUNTS AND GAMES OF SKILL

HAND TOUCH

Grades: 3, 4   Players: individual

Equipment.   None.
Directions.   Put one hand where the other cannot touch it. After the players try unsuccessfully, have him put the right hand to the left elbow, for this is the secret of the trick.

JUMP THE SHOT

Grades: 4, 5, 6   Players: 6 to 8 in each group

Equipment.   A long rope with a shoe tied on it for each group.
Directions.   Pupils form a circle around the center player who swings the rope in a circle. He gradually increases the swinging part of the rope until it reaches the knees of the group, and at the same time increases the speed of the swing. All try to jump over the weighted rope as it reaches them. A circle player touched by the rope is eliminated.

CIRCLE SQUAT

Grades: 4, 5, 6   Players: entire class

Equipment.   None.

Directions.   Players run, skip, hop, and march as directed by the leader. All must squat when the leader's whistle blows. Play continues until all but one have been eliminated.

CLOTHES PIN DROP

Grades: 4, 5, 6   Players: groups of 4 to 6

Equipment.   Milk bottles and 5 clothes pins for each group.

Directions.   Each player in each line drops 5 clothes pins one at a time in the milk bottle from an upright position. The scores for each player are added together. The winner scores 20 points.

PING-PONG BOUNCE

Grades: 4, 5, 6   Players: groups of 4 to 6

Equipment.   3 ping-pong balls and a box for each group.

Directions.   Each player in each line bounces all of the ping-pong balls into the box from a 10-foot line. Team scores are added together. Then winner scores 25 points first.

PICK UP

Grades: 2 to 6   Players: individual

Equipment.   A coin.

Directions.   Stand with back against a wall, heels touching. Try to pick up the coin without moving the heels away from the wall.

CIRCLE TWO

Grades: 2 to 6   Players: individual

Equipment.   None.

Directions.   Move the arms in large circles of opposite directions—the right hand away from the body; the left toward the body.

Variations.   (1) Swing right foot in a circle moving left; then left in a circle moving right. (2) Pat the head with one hand and rub the stomach with the other simultaneously.

STAND UP

Grades: 2 to 6   Players: individual

Equipment.   None.

Directions.   Lie flat on the back; arms to the side; hands flat against the hips. Arise without using the hands. First come to a sitting position; then stand up.

Variations.   Lie flat on the back; cross arms on chest. Stand up without uncrossing the arms or using the elbows.

BALANCE WRITING

Grades: 4, 5, 6   Players: individual

Equipment.   A milk bottle, pad of paper, pencil.

Direction.   Sit down on an upright milk bottle. Cross legs with only the heel of one foot touching the floor. Write your full name on the pad while trying to maintain your balance.

Variations.   (1) Light a match.
                (2) Thread a needle.

JUMP THE BROOK

Grades: 1, 2, 3   Players: divide the class into two groups

Equipment. Chalk or two ropes.
Directions. Players line up in two single lines. Each runs and jumps across the brook (chalk marks or ropes placed about 8 inches apart). If a player misses, he must drop out to get his feet dry. After each round the brook is made wider until one is proclaimed champion.

BEANBAG TOSS

Grades: 4, 5, 6   Players: groups of four

Equipment. Plywood with three holes and a beanbag for each group.
Directions. The board has three holes with 5-, 10-, and 15-point values. Players toss the beanbag through the holes and play for total individual or group points.
Variations. Paint a clown's face on the plywood. Score 5 points for hitting the mouth hole, 10 for each eye.

CARD TOSS

Grades: 4, 5, 6   Players: 4 to 6 on a team

Equipment. 10 cards for each group.
Directions. Each pupil tosses 10 cards singly into a propped-up hat or wastebasket 10 feet away. Score one point for each successful toss.

HE CAN DO LITTLE

Grades: 4, 5, 6   Players: entire class

Equipment. A cane or stick.
Directions. Players sit in a circle. The leader starts the game by saying, "He can do little who can't do this." He passes the cane to the player to the left who must repeat the action as nearly as possible and then pass the cane on to the player on his left. The leader tells the player whether or not he has done the stunt correctly. The secret is that the tapping is done with the cane in the right hand, and the cane is then taken in the left and passed on to the next person. The leader may beat out a special rhythm and go through extra flourishes to distract attention.

ACTIVE RELAYS

CHINESE HOP

Grades: 4, 5, 6   Players: two teams

Equipment. Ten sticks, candles or tenpins.
Directions. Place sticks in a straight line 1 foot apart. Each player hops on one foot over the sticks without touching any of them. He is disqualified if he touches a stick. After jumping over the last stick, the player, still on one foot, picks up that stick and hops back over the other nine. Next he hops over the nine sticks, the eight, etc., each time hopping back down the line of remaining sticks. He continues until all sticks have been picked up. A player is disqualified if he fails to tag the next player to start hopping up his line, if he touches both feet to the ground at any time, or if he touches a stick with his foot. The second player puts down the ten sticks. The third picks them up, etc., until all players have hopped up and down the line.

HORSE AND RIDER

Grades: 5, 6   Players: 8 to 10 boys

Equipment. None.
Directions. Divide the group into equal teams. One player mounts the back of another; legs around his waist and arms around his shoulders. They race to and around line where they exchange positions and race back to the starting line to tag off the next couple.
Variations. The "horse" goes down on all fours. The "rider" straddles his back. They race to the finish line and exchange positions.

HURDLE RACE

Grades: 5, 6   Players: 10 boys for each team

Equipment. A rope or broomstick.
Directions. Players 1 and 2 on each team hold a broomstick or rope between them 6 or more inches from the floor. They run down the line with their teammates between them jumping the hurdle as it moves to the end of the line. As soon as they reach the end, number 2 returns to the head of the line and starts down with number 3 in the same manner. Number 3 then runs with number 4 and so on until number 1 is back at the head of the line.

BLACKBOARD RELAY

Grades: 4, 5, 6   Players: entire class

Equipment. Blackboard, chalk.
Directions. Played as any relay except instead of touching the goal, player writes a number on the board in a line. The last player must add all numbers correctly. The team with the first correct answer wins.

TAG THE WALL RELAY

Grades: 4, 5, 6   Players: entire class

Equipment. None.
Directions. Seat players in even-numbered rows. On a signal, the last player in each row runs forward and tags the wall. As soon as this player is past the first seat in the row, everyone moves back one seat, leaving the first seat vacant for the runner. As soon as the runner is seated, he raises his hand and the last person seated begins. The line whose players all finish running first wins.

NEWSPAPER RACE

Grades: 2 to 6   Players: two equally divided teams

Equipment. Two newspapers.
Directions. Each contestant is given a newspaper, on which each step of the race must be made. He puts down a sheet and steps on it, puts down another sheet and steps on it, reaches back to get the first sheet and move it forward, and so on until he reaches the goal line, from which he returns in the same fashion and tags off the second player.

SPIDER RACE

Grades: 1, 2, 3   Players: equally divided teams

Equipment. None.
Directions. Player number 1 in each line faces the goal. Player number 2 stands with his back turned and they link elbows and race to the goal. Player number 2 runs back facing the end line while player number 1 runs forward. Players 3 and 4 and on down the line repeat the actions.

Rapid Fire Artist

Grades: 2 to 6   Players: 2 to 10 on each team

Equipment.   Pencil or crayon, paper.
Directions.   Divide the group into equal teams. Each group sends an "artist" to the leader, who tells him an animal, person, tree, etc., to draw. The "artist" rushes back to his group and begins to draw the likeness of the person, place, or thing given him. As soon as the group recognizes what is drawn, the members yell it all together. The group guessing first scores 1 point. 10 points constitute a game. The "artist" cannot talk or give any hints other than drawing as to what he is creating.

Nature Guess

Grades: 2 to 6   Players: 2 to 10 on each team

Equipment.   None.
Directions.   Divide the group into four teams. Each group sends a different member up each time to the leader who tells him an animal, or person to act out. The first group to guess who or what the person represents scores 1 point. 10 points constitutes a game.

QUIET GUESSING GAMES

Grocery Store

Grades: 1, 2, 3   Players: entire class or divide into teams of 4 to 10 in a group

Equipment.   None.
Directions.   Divide group into equally numbered lines. One player from each line steps forward. The leader calls out any letter. The player who first calls out the name of any grocery article beginning with that letter scores a point for his team. 10 points constitutes a game.
Variations.   Players call out the name of any animal, a person's name, state, etc.

Nursery Rhymes

Grades: 1, 2, 3   Players: entire class

Equipment.   None.
Directions.   Give each pupil or a group of three a nursery rhyme to act out.
Variations.   A poem; a song.

Hand Puppets

Grades: 1 to 4   Players: entire class

Equipment.   Paper sacks and crayons.
Directions.   Each pupil or group of four makes hand puppets out of paper sacks and each group puts on a brief show.

Magic Music

Grades: 2, 3, 4   Players: entire class

Equipment.   None.
Directions.   One leaves the room while others hide a small object. The player returns and tries to find the hidden treasure by getting his clue from the singing of the group. As he draws nearer the object, the singing grows louder, or softer when he moves away. Piano music may be substituted.

WHAT AM I?

Grades: 4, 5, 6   Players: entire class

Equipment.   Any picture from a magazine and one straight pin for each player.
Directions.   Pin a picture on the back of each pupil. Players mingle around trying to find out what the picture is that he is wearing. He may only ask questions calling for a no or yes answer. When he discovers what he represents, he reports to the leader who pins the picture on his lapel. Pictures of animals, cars, famous people, flowers, etc., may be used.

I SAW

Grades: 1, 2, 3   Players: two circles

Equipment.   None.
Directions.   "It" stands in each circle and each "It" says "On my way to school today I saw—" and imitates what he saw. The others guess what he saw. The one guessing correctly becomes "It." If no one guesses, "It" tells what he was imitating. If his imitation was poor as decided by the group, he must choose a new "It." If the imitation was good, "It" is praised and remains "It."

ALPHABETICAL GEOGRAPHY

Grades: 4, 5, 6   Players: entire class

Equipment.   None.
Directions.   One pupil calls out the name of a state, or city. The next player must call out a state or city with the last letter in the name called.
Example.   New York, Kansas City, Yucatan, New Hampshire, etc.

GAMES FROM OTHER LANDS

STONE, PAPER, SCISSORS
Japan

Grades: 4, 5, 6   Players: entire class

Equipment.   None.
Directions.   Divide players into two equal lines. Each player faces his partner with hands behind him. The leader counts "1, 2, 3"; on "3" each player brings his hands forward with hands in any of the three positions, depending upon his choice. The stone is represented by clenched fists; the paper by open hands, palms down; scissors by extending the first two fingers. Because the stone dulls the scissors it beats them. The scissors beat the paper because it can cut. The paper beats the stone because it wraps the stone. Points are scored, the team scoring the most wins.
Variations.   (1) All players advance. At "4" one, two, three or four fingers are held out to represent 1—stone; 2—scissors; 3—paper; 4—stone.
(2) Man, gun, rabbit, bear.
(3) Man, gun, tiger.

CHICKEN MARKET
Italy

Grades: 4, 5, 6   Players: entire class

Equipment.   None.
Directions.   All players are chickens except the two strongest class members. One becomes the buyer; the other the seller. All players squat down and clasp their hands around

their knees and are told not to smile or laugh. The buyer comes to test each chicken by pinching, chin chucking, or tickling. At last he says, "This one is just right." He and the seller take hold of the chicken's arms and swing it counting "1, 2, 3"; as they do so, if the chicken laughs he is eliminated. If he does not laugh he is not sold but remains safe.

HEN AND WILD CAT
Africa

Grades: 1, 2, 3   Players: entire class

Equipment.   None.
Directions.   The "Hen" leads her flock of other players around a chosen "Cat." She warns them of danger and the "Cat" tries to catch any foolish chickens who come too near.

THE TIED MONKEY
Africa

Grades: 1, 2, 3   Players: entire class

Equipment.   Rope, handkerchief with one end tied into a knot for each player.
Directions.   One boy is chosen to be the "monkey." He is tied to a chair. The others try to hit him with their handkerchiefs while he tries to catch them. If successful he changes places with his victim.

CALABASH
Africa

Grades: 4, 5, 6   Players: 3 in each group

Equipment.   None.
Directions.   Two players lock arms to pen in a third one who stands between them. The middle player is locked in or is "caloshed." He tries to wiggle out while his jailers move their locked arms up and down to keep him in.

SAND BAG BALL
Alaska

Grades: 4, 5, 6   Players: 10 in each circle

Equipment.   One playground volleyball or balloon for each group.
Directions.   Players kneel in a circle. The ball is batted in the air and players try to keep it aloft by striking it with one hand. A player is out if he uses both hands, or if he fails to strike the ball and misses. The winner is the last remaining player.

GUESSING GAME (Tlingit Tribe)
Alaska

Grades: 3, 4   Players: entire class

Equipment.   20 or more small sticks.
Directions.   "It" arranges the sticks in small bundles while others hide their eyes. Each guesses quickly how many sticks are in each bunch. The new "It" is the first to call out the correct number.

FROG DANCE
Burma

Grades: 4, 5, 6   Players: entire class

Equipment.   None.
Directions.   Pupils squat in a circle. They hop forward around the ring by throwing out

one foot, and then the other. As each hops, he claps his hands (1) in front of his knees, (2) in back, and tries to make others fall over. A player who falls is out. The winner is the one who frog dances longest without falling.

CALL THE CHICKENS HOME
China

Grades: 1, 2   Players: entire class

Equipment. A blindfold.
Directions. A blindfolded player stands apart from the "chickens" who run by and touch him after he says, "Tsoo, Tsoo—come and find your mother." Any chicken caught exchanges places with the blind man.

CATCHING FISHES IN THE DARK
China

Grades: 1, 2, 3   Players: entire class

Equipment. A blindfold.
Directions. A blindfolded player tries to catch the "fish" who runs past. If one is caught the blindman tries to guess what kind of a "fish" the player has chosen to be. If he succeeds, the "fish" and he exchange places, otherwise one "fish" has won freedom.

CATCHING THE FISH'S TAIL
China

Grades: 1, 2, 3   Players: 10 in each line

Equipment. None.
Directions. The players grasp arms around the waist of the person ahead so that the line becomes compact. The first player is the "head," the last the "tail." The "head" tries to catch hold of the "tail." Any player who breaks hold is eliminated.

SKIN THE SNAKE
China

Grades: 4, 5, 6   Players: 10 in each line

Equipment. None.
Directions. Players stand in a single line, each putting his right hand between his legs and holding the left hand of the boy behind him. All walk backward. The last one lies down. The others pass over him and also lie down. The last one gets up first and walks forward outside the line and helps pull the other one up until all are standing again. All players must keep holding hands.

MENAGERIE
England

Grades: 1, 2, 3   Players: entire class

Equipment. Chalk, blackboard.
Directions. Each chooses an animal sound he wishes to imitate. The leader writes down all names given on the blackboard and tells a story, weaving in each animal. When a pupil hears the name of his animal, he imitates the sound. When the leader calls out, "Menagerie" all give their sounds at once.

PEBBLE GAME
Greece

Grades: 4, 5, 6   Players: entire class

Equipment.   10 or more pebbles or jacks for each player.
Directions.   Place pebbles on back of the hand. When a signal is given, turn the hand over and try to catch as many pebbles as possible with the same hand.

PHUGADI
India

Grades: 1, 2, 3   Players: couples

Equipment.   None.
Directions.   Two players face each other with toes touching. They grasp each other by the waist, lean back as far as possible and turn together.

PAINTING COLORED SAND PICTURES
Italy

Grades: 4, 5, 6   Players: groups of four

Equipment.   Bags of colored sand for each group, white notebook paper.
Directions.   Give each group bags of yellow, red, black, blue, and white sand. The white sand is scattered over the paper to form a frame. Next the outline of a bird, person, animal, or object is formed by letting the black sand slowly ooze between the fingers. The remaining colors are used to complete the design. Groups can compete to "paint" the most attractive picture.

SATSUMA KEN
Japan

Grades: 2, 3, 4   Players: entire class

Equipment.   Blindfold.
Directions.   The pupils stretch out the fingers of one or both hands simultaneously. "It," who is blindfolded, tries to guess the total number of extended fingers of all players.

BEAD GUESSING
American Indian

Grades: 1, 2, 3   Players: entire class

Equipment.   Bead.
Directions.   One player holds a bead in one hand behind him. He stops before one player who tries to guess in which hand the bead is held. At each guess the one holding the bead must bring his hands forward and open them. If the guesser guesses correctly three times, the one holding the bead runs to his seat. If the "guesser" catches him he gets to hold the bead. Each player may guess three times, but unless he guesses correctly all three times the one holding the bead moves on.

CHINESE HOLD UP
China

Grades: 3, 4, 5   Players: entire class

Equipment. None.

Directions. Seat players in a circle. One starts the game by holding his hands to both ears. Immediately the players to the right and left of him must hold their ears. The last one to do so is out and starts the game again by pointing to any player. This player grasps his own ears and players on his right and left grasp theirs. The eliminated player starts the game again. The game continues until only two are left.

YEMARI
Japan

Grades: 4, 5, 6   Players: 6 in each circle

Equipment. One tennis or rubber ball for each group.

Directions. Players stand in a circle. One bounces the ball up and back to himself with his open hand. He continues as long as the ball is in reach, but cannot move from the circle. When the ball moves near another player, that person keeps it bouncing. The game continues until some one fails to hit the ball and is eliminated. The last remaining player wins.

SUGGESTED READINGS

American Association for Health, Physical Education, and Recreation: *Classroom Activities.* Washington, D.C., 1957.

Boy Scouts of America: *Scout Field Book.* New York.

Culin, Stewart: *Games of the Orient (Korea, China, Japan).* Rutland, Vt., Charles Tuttle Company, 1960.

Eisenberg, Helen and Larry: *Omnibus of Fun.* New York, Association Press, 1957.

Girl Scouts of America: *Games for Girl Scouts.* New York, 1948.

Harbin, E. O.: *Games of Many Nations.* New York, Abington Press, 1964.

Hunt, Sarah and Cain: *Games The World Around.* New York, A. S. Barnes & Co., 1950.

Macfarlan, Allan: *Book of American Indian Games.* New York, Association Press, 1958.

Macfarlan, Allan and Paulette: *Fun with Brand-New Games.* New York, Association Press, 1961.

Ripley, G. Sherman: *The Book of Games.* New York, Association Press, 1960.

Van Hagen, Winifred; Dexter, Genevieve; and Williams, Jesse Feiring: *Physical Education for Elementary Schools.* Sacramento, California, State Department of Education, 1951.

Vannier, Maryhelen: *Methods and Materials in Recreation Leadership,* Rev. Ed. Belmont, Calif., The Wadsworth Press, 1967.

Chapter 19

Camping and
Outing Activities

Now I see the secret of the making of the best persons,
It is to grow in the open air and eat and sleep with the earth.

WALT WHITMAN

Increasingly, camping and outing activities become an integral part of the total school program. Ideally, these activities can best be stressed from grades 4 through 12, although some may be begun at any time in the first three grades. Crowded classrooms and gymnasiums often create a problem, yet every school in America, whether it be located in a village or teeming city, has access to wide-open spaces, city parks, or even school grounds where a camping program might be initiated. Many cities now operate public school camps on a year-round basis. Still more provide some kind of overnight, day, or weekend camping experiences for their students.

Such camps have been launched primarily as a means of supplementing and integrating indoor learnings centered around verbalized theory with outdoor experiences focused around learning to live in the out-of-doors. At these school camps where there are no truant officers, no school buildings, no bells, no traditional school subjects taught by ordinary school teachers, no detention rooms, and no failures, youths are gaining experiences that peak all others in their educational lives.

Here children are discovering the real meaning of the words nature, trees, hills, ferns, cooperate, share, and contribute. Boys and girls are living the thrill of seeing, touching, and smelling the earth and all its magic, and experiencing the joy of hearing the indescribable music of wind in the pine trees and of rushing water. For many of these children, camping and outing activities are opening up a world about which they have been told, seen in movies or on television, about which they dreamed and are eager to learn. And here, too, children from rural areas are having the thrilling discovery of learning to play in the out-of-doors with others. City children are learning new skills in a new world of adventure.

What these far-sighted American school systems have done in establishing school camps and outdoor education programs can and should be duplicated. The local community, the state, and the federal government all have vital roles to play in this new educational movement.[1]

TYPES OF EXPERIENCES

Camping and outing activities possible for elementary schools include learning to:

1. Live independently of one's family.
2. Adjust and contribute to group life.
3. Care for and select one's own clothing according to the kind needed for changing weather conditions.
4. Make one's own bed and care for it.
5. Set and clear tables; act as host and hostess.
6. Plan group meals confined to a definite budget according to nutritional standards.
7. Make a number of different kinds of fires and cook over them.
8. Use a compass; tell directions from trees, sun, and grass.
9. Lay trails.
10. Pace and measure distance.
11. Read maps; construct maps of local areas.
12. Hike long or short distances with the maximum of pleasure and the minimum of fatigue.
13. Know the sky above, the meaning of stars, and their use to man.
14. Understand and know as much as possible for one's age about birds, animals, trees, rocks, insects, and flowers.
15. Recognize harmful plants, trees, insects, animals.
16. Care for and use camp tools including axes, saws, ropes.
17. Enjoy out-of-door sports and games. The school does not provide such sports as ice skating, tree climbing, snow shoeing, wood chopping contests, fishing, canoeing, trapping.
18. Make useful articles from native materials—pans from clay, spoons from wood, pan racks from tree branches, hats from reeds.
19. Take an active part in some community project, such as protection from camp soil erosion, building an outdoor theater, making a new road.
20. Build a number of different kinds of shelters.
21. Use the camp environment to its fullest extent.
22. Practice good health and safety habits.
23. Lashing.
24. Blanket rolling.

Classes in camping should be held out-of-doors for a double period or be the last scheduled in the day. The physical education class is the logical place for the inclusion of camping in the school program. Weekend or afternoon camping trips can easily be incorporated in the program, especially if teachers, as well as the students, are camping-minded. Interested parents, local Girl or Boy Scout leaders are usually available as chaperones or assistant leaders.

The key person in the program is the teacher. If she is interested in learning as well as teaching others how to do camping and outing skills, and if she is enthusiastic, she will find ways to include and develop this as

---

[1] Macmillan, Dorothy: *School Camping and Outdoor Education.* Dubuque, Iowa, William C. Brown Company, Publishers, 1956.

an integral part of the total school program. Camping experts in the community can and will offer valuable help, for camping-minded leaders are usually eager to sell outdoor education. Increasingly, colleges and universities are requiring camp leadership training courses for major's and minor's in physical education.

THE OUTDOOR LEARNING LABORATORY

One of the most vital outdoor education programs in the country is thrilling many youngsters at the Ladera Elementary School in Thousand Oaks, California, where a large, outdoor wooded area has been set aside for new kinds of educational experiences. Part of this large area has been left in its natural state so that conservation, plant, and wild animal projects abound. An adjacent plot of level land is used for mapmaking, digging, landscaping and sheer fun in the out-of-doors.

The children have built a model weather station. There is a pen enclosing domestic pets and a small lake for fishing, aquatics, and other recreational purposes. The youngsters have also built a model of an early California mission from their own handmade adobe bricks.

In another nearby school, the pupils have used their outdoor education area to dramatize the small size of the "wee" plane Charles Lindbergh

Figure 55. Camping activities for children should revolve around food, shelter, and recreation in the out-of-doors. (Courtesy of AAHPER.)

first flew across the Atlantic Ocean. Elsewhere children have devised a framework model of the *Goodspeed,* one of the first ships to arrive at Jamestown in 1607. Such experiences give children a rich educational tool with which to explore their world and that of our ancestors. These and many other outdoor learning experiences, such as that in a New England pine forest where the children sweep the ground clean early every morning in order to learn how to read the tracks made by nocturnal animals, as well as about the animals themselves, all help to make learning the great adventure it can be and to make the world, in which each living thing is a vital part, an exciting place in which to live.

Camping and outdoor education have also been used successfully to help prevent juvenile delinquency as well as to rehabilitate youthful law breakers and emotionally disturbed youth.[2]

THE PROGRAM

The program of outdoor education and school camping should be built around: (1) learning to live with others in the out-of-doors, (2) healthful personal and community living, (3) basic campcraft skills, (4) work experiences, and (5) conservation projects. Subject areas which have been found to be best taught, in part, in the out-of-doors through first-hand experiences are physical education, health education, science and nature, dramatics, music, arts and crafts, mathematics, local history, geography, English, as well as government or civics.

Program activities at the Tyler Texas Public School Camp include:

Intra-group evening programs	Outdoor cooking
Felling, chopping, splitting wood	Planting trees, grass, gardens
Conservation hikes	Farm chores
Learning how to use an axe, saw, wedge	Camp maintenance projects
Map and compass hikes	Trail blazing
Trapping animals	Logging
Cabin clean-up duties	Visit to the school farm
Construction—carpentry	Swimming
Weather study	Visits to community places of interest
Making check dams	Scavenger hunts
Making posted signs	Lard making
Pottery	Milking
Fishing	Soap making
	Sketching

Camping and outdoor living skills which should be included in the school program of outdoor education can best be taught in wooded areas.

---

[2] Read the book *Wilderness Road* by Campbell Loughmiller (University of Texas Press, 1965) for a report of one of the most unusual and successful rehabilitation camp programs for school dropouts and emotionally disturbed boys. It is an amazing success story, showing what leadership and nature can do to help heal the emotionally disturbed.

However, the following may also be taught on the play field or on a vacant lot:

Camping and Outdoor Living Skills

A. CAMPCRAFT

1. Knife—selection, use, care, whittling, safety measures
2. Use of axe, hatchet, cross-saw; selection, use, care; splitting, chopping, cutting down trees; safety measures
3. Use of saws, shovels, picks, hammers; safety measures

B. FIRE BUILDING

1. Fixing a fireplace
2. Selection of wood and common kinds of fires for outdoor cooking
3. Fire safety hints

C. OUTDOOR COOKING

1. Menu planning—selection according to daily nutritional standards
2, Packing for hikes and overnights
3. Care of food—refrigeration, protection, waste disposal
4. Types of outdoor cooking devices
5. Preparation and serving of food

D. HIKES AND OUTINGS

1. Kinds of hikes
2. Where to go, what to do, what to take, and what to do when you arrive
3. Hiking games, pacing
4. Camp site selection
5. Camp making and breaking; tent pitching, ditching and striking
6. Bed rolls and sleeping bags
7. Packing a knapsack, personal needs[3]
8. Light camping equipment

E. KNOTCRAFT AND LASHING

1. Rope whipping
2. Square knots, sheet bend, bowline, clove hitch
3. Ways to use knots
4. Square, diagonal, sheer, continuous lashing
5. Things to lash

F. NATURE AND WOOD-LORE CONSERVATION

1. Common plants, edible and poisonous
2. Common animals—harmful and friendly

---

[3] Boy Scouts of America: *The Boy Scout Handbook.* 2 Park Ave., New York.

3. Common insects and snakes—harmless and harmful
4. Common birds
5. Knowledge of astronomy
6. Knowledge of common myths and legends concerning the heavens
7. Common fossils, minerals
8. Fishing, hunting, and trapping skills
9. Forestry conservation
10. Trail blazing, map reading, use of compass
11. Weather casting
12. Improvised shelter, equipment, and rustic construction
13. Soil conservation

G. INFORMAL GROUP ACTIVITIES

1. Group singing
2. Simple dramatics, including stunts, skits, hand puppets
3. Story telling
4. Games—active, quiet, folk, nature
5. Crafts—nature, junk, rise of native materials, sketching and painting, and others suitable for camp

H. CONSTRUCTION PROJECTS[4]

Suggested projects include making:

Rustic entrance for cabin, unit, or camp	Rustic furniture
Totem poles	Dam up a creek
Outdoor kitchen	Rustic bulletin boards
Outdoor theater	Nature aquarium
Campfire trail	Outdoor chapel
Log cabin	Camping equipment and eating utensils
Nature exhibit, nature trail	Repair of boats and other equipment and facilities
Rock garden	Clearing paths
Campcraft exhibit	Lean-to-shelters
Outpost camp	Bows and arrows
Weathervane	Sundial
Tree house	Bridge across a creek
Council ring	Soil erosion control
Pottery kiln	Shelves, tables, and benches
Nature trails	Cleaning up the campsite
Fernery	

I. CAMPCRAFT SKILL CONTESTS

Groups will enjoy the following:

Water boiling	Fire building—with and without matches
Wood chopping	Wood saving
Lashing camp tables, bridges, etc.	Whittling
Making functional crafts from native materials	Pie, cookie, and cake making contests
Fishing for the most fish, the largest fish, or a specific kind of fish	Casting at white tire targets placed at different distances
Knotcraft relays	Knot tying for speed
Trail blazing	Tent ditching and pitching for speed

---

[4] Mitchell, Viola, and Crawford, Ida B.: *Camp Counseling,* 3rd Ed. Philadelphia, W. B. Saunders Company, 1961, pp. 109–110.

Skills taught in campcraft should well terminate in a day, weekend, or summer camping. Activities included in the program must be geared to the interests, needs, and capabilities of the children. Fourth graders may not be as keen about knotcraft as sixth graders; they may, however, be thrilled with going on a vagabond hike or learning how to fry eggs on a heated rock.

Hiking

A hike is a walk with a purpose. It is one of the best of all outdoor activities, for it builds physical fitness through vigorous use of the big muscles of the body. There are many kinds of hikes ranging from early morning bird walks to mountain climbing.

Teacher and pupils should plan together where they want to hike, what each will take and how it will be packed or carried, what kind of clothes, and especially shoes and socks, would be the best to wear, what to do on the way, how to walk on the highway, or through the forest, and what to do when the group reaches its destination.

Places to hike might include going to some local park, a nearby lake or forest, someone's farm, some place of local interest, the local zoo, or some camp nearby. Group singing or round-robin story telling will add to the fun along the way.

Hiking distances should be increased gradually as the pupils become more expert in covering more ground with a minimum of fatigue and more adept in seeing interesting treasures along the way. Cookouts can add to the joy of the hike's end. Simple meals such as fried bacon and egg sandwiches, carrot sticks, cocoa, and fruit are easily prepared and great fun to do.

Types of suitable hikes, some for class time, others for longer periods:

1. *Nature Hike*—to collect, study, or see as many kinds of wild flowers, birds, insects, or animals as possible.
2. *Treasure Hunt Hike*—each squad is given a sealed envelope containing a list of clues leading to the hidden treasure. The first squad to find the treasure wins.
3. *Scavenger Hunt Hike*—each squad is given a sealed envelope containing a list of articles to be brought back to a certain spot in a given time limit. The group which has found the most articles wins.
4. *The Lost Baby or Object Hike*—each squad searches for a doll hidden by the teacher or a squad.
5. *Exploration Hike*—a walk along back roads, through forests, or other places unknown to the children.
6. *Coin Flip Hike*—a coin is tossed in the air at every road crossing to see which direction the group will go.
7. *Star, Sun or Cloud Hike*—a trip to a hill to catch and hear legends about the stars, sun or clouds.
8. *Moonlight Hike*—a night's stroll to see and hear the beauties of night.
9. *Stream Hike*—the class follows a creek, river or stream as far as possible in a given time to see how it winds, turns, and changes.
10. *Trail Blazing Hike*—the class finds and clears a new trail or path.

11. *Compass Hike*—each squad selects a direction and hikes that way. The groups exchange news of their adventures upon returning.

12. *Walk Out—Ride Back Hike*—one group walks while the second one rides and vice-versa for the return trip.

13. *Overnight Hike*—the group hikes to and from the established camp where they will stay overnight.

What one wears upon a hike depends upon where he is going, when, and the kind of weather expected. However, a good general rule to remember is that old comfortable clothes are best. Blue jeans or slacks may be preferred by the group to shorts. Shoes worn must be appropriate with room enough in them for the hiker to wear one or two pairs of heavy socks. Both shoes and socks must be free from rips or holes. Sweaters, jackets, or flannel shirts can be tied around the waist. Sandwiches wrapped in bandanas and tied to a stick carried over the shoulder will leave hands and arms free for easy rhythmic swinging a-tuned to easy rhythmic walking.

Hiking is one of the few cost-free physical activities left in our land. Children, who learn early the joy of strolling, seeing, and absorbing the beauty and wonder of life which ever surrounds them, can well be started on a life-long pleasurable hobby.

Fire Building

Fire has many uses: to cook, heat, burn rubbish, and give off warmth. The appeal of fire is omnipresent among all peoples of the earth, for everyone, regardless of age, is drawn to it. Children can be taught how to use fire—the desire for this knowledge can be constructively channeled.

Types of wood best for cooking are:

1. For fast flames needed for boiling purposes use pine, spruce, balsam fir, red maple, basswood, or elder.

2. For even flames and coals needed for frying or broiling use the hickories, oaks, birches, sugar maple, white ash, eucalyptus, locust, beech.

Points to remember about fire building are:

1. Clear the ground around the area.
2. Use small match-sized twigs, shavings, or bark for the foundation.
3. Add finger-size dry sticks laid crisscross or tepee-shaped over the foundation.
4. Have all wood ready before starting the fire.
5. Light the fire with the wind at your back, remembering that fire needs air.
6. Build the fire by adding wood of graduating size.
7. Be sure the fire is out before you leave it; water is best to use.

TEPEE FIRE

TYPES OF FIRES

TEPEE OR WIGWAM

Used for boiling purposes. Place the wood in a tepee formation.

CRISSCROSS

A slow burning fire best for frying, baking, or heat. Start with a foundation of tinder. Make a crisscross of sticks placing larger ones at the bottom.

CRISSCROSS

REFLECTOR

A slow burning fire used for baking. Bank the wood against larger pieces of green wood so that the heat is thrown forward. Have the baker in place before the fire is lighted.

REFLECTOR FIRE

INDIAN STAR OR LAZY MAN'S FIRE

A slow burning fire which can be used for heat, comfort, and slow roasting. Start with a tepee fire. Use long poles, which are pushed into the fire as their ends burn.

INDIAN FIRE

HUNTER-TRAPPER FIRE

Use for slow boiling, stewing. Two heavy logs of slow-burning wood are laid parallel with the narrowest end placed facing the wind. Sticks of green wood are laid across the two to be used for supporting pans. Start from a tepee fire which will catch other tinder laid between the two big logs.

HUNTER-TRAPPER FIRE

BEAN HOLE FIRE

Used for cooking a one pot meal. Fire is laid in a hole 1 foot wide and 8 to 10 inches deep. Green sticks are laid across the top of the hole for supporting pans.

BEAN HOLE FIRE

BACKLOG FIRE

Used for frying and boiling. Fire is built in front of a back-log for boiling purposes. Coals are raked forward between the two logs for frying purposes.

BACKLOG FIRE

Suggested Easy-to-Prepare Outdoor Meals

Menu planning will aid children to learn the esentials of good nutrition. Outdoor cooking is great fun! Roasting wieners, and burning marshmallows is easy, but real outdoor cooking takes skill. Simple one-pot meals are best for young children to cook.

Each meal should include:

Meat, fish, cheese, beans, or eggs.
Milk for cooking or drinking.
Some kind of fruit.
One vegetable, preferably two—one cooked, one raw.
Enriched bread.

If the children are to be at camp all day the three meals eaten there should include:

At least 1 pint of milk per person.
Fruit of some kind for two meals.
Cereals or enriched bread.
Two vegetables—one raw, of the green leafy variety; one cooked.
One potato, in addition to the other vegetables.
Meat, fish, cheese, beans or eggs.
Butter or fortified margarine.
Various types of outdoor cooking will be fun to try.

TENNIS RACKET BROILER

TENNIS RACKET BROILER

Toasting bread on sticks is an easy beginner. Broiling meat on green sticks shaped like snowshoes is more advanced and more fun to do.

TIN CAN STOVE

TIN CAN STOVE

Pan broiling, frying, and stewing can be done individually over tin can stoves made from large-sized, number 10 coffee cans with a wedge cut out of the end from which the lid has been removed.

FLAT ROCK COOKING

FLAT ROCK COOKING

On-a-rock cooking is sheer delight to all who can do it. A flat rock is laid across several smaller ones and is used as a frying pan.

BAKING BREAD DOUGH

BAKING BREAD STICKS

Green stick cooking is an art, but also one not difficult to master. Prepared biscuit dough to which water or milk has been added is twisted around the end of a green stick and slowly toasted.

GREEN STICK COOKING

GREEN STICK COOKING

Barbecues are more advanced but sixth graders could cook small pieces of meat this way. Two V-shaped sticks driven into the ground support a green stick on which the meat is speared through. A special sauce is used for basting the slowly-turned meat. Pans and skillets are used, too, but are not as novel for the novice as the ingenious methods suggested.

PLANKING

PLANKING

Planking, a method of cooking meat on a board by reflected heat, is great sport especially for all Roy Rogers' fans.

PARAFFIN BUDDY BURNER

PARAFFIN BUDDY BURNERS

Buddy burners made of tuna fish cans, paraffin, and cardboard are fun to make and use. One end is taken from the can, paraffin made from old candle stubs is dripped around a piece of cardboard wound in a loose spiral with one end pulled out as a wick. The burner can be used inside a tin can stove. It is ideal for egg frying or cooking pancakes.

Suggested things to cook by any of the mentioned methods are:

Green Stick or Green Stick Broiler
Steak, bacon, ham, liver
Bread twists
Kebobs

REFLECTOR OVEN

Fry Pans
Any meat that can be fried
Eggs—scrambled, fried
Toasted sandwiches
Pancakes
Fried potatoes

One Pot Meals
Chili
Corn chowder
Hunter's stew
Baked beans
Chop suey
Ring tum diddy

Reflector Ovens or Backlog Reflector
Biscuits
Cookies
Cakes
Corn bread
Muffins

Bean Hole Cooking
Stews
Beans
Cooked cereals

Barbecue
Pork
Beef
Chicken

Coal Baking
Potatoes
Roast corn
Apples

Plank Cooking
Fish
Steak
Chops
Liver
Ham

Foil Cooking

Aluminum foil cooking is ideal for beginners. Almost any kind of food which can be baked or steamed can be cooked in it. The secret of success is in folding the food in a double wrapper into a neatly pressed package, and placing it on or covering it with coals. Children tend, like the novice adult, to put the food directly into flames and should, consequently, be instructed that this will only ruin it.

Types of food which can be prepared best by beginners include:

1. Chicken parts, frozen fish, or other kinds of meat or fowl, thoroughly cleaned; place these and thinly sliced potatoes, carrots and onions in the package.
2. Hamburger meat or canned Spam, using the vegetables mentioned above.
3. Canned prepared biscuits; wrap singly and spread with either brown sugar and cinnamon or butter and jelly, or both.
4. Bacon and eggs; lay flat two or three slices of bacon and break an egg over them; season, and fold into a package.
5. Corn roasting; spread butter, salt and pepper over the corn, sprinkle water or insert ice cubes for steaming purposes.
6. Apples, squash, potatoes or other fruits and vegetables baked over the coals.
7. Franks in a blanket.
8. Cakes and cookies.
9. Shish-kebobs made of beef, veal, or franks alternated on skewers, or green stick with slices of onions, tomatoes, potatoes, and mushrooms. Wrap each skewerful with barbecue sauce and lay it on the coals for 15–20 minutes.
10. Frozen vegetables cooked in a pan with a lid made from the foil.

Foil skillets and pans can also be shaped and used in frying or baking almost every type of meat, fish or vegetable. Corn popped in foil is especially recommended for beginners.

Recipes for types of dishes that are unique to camping follow.

CHILI CON CARNE

Serves 8   One pot
4 tablespoons of grease
4 chopped onions
1½–2 lbs. of hamburger
2 cans tomatoes
2 cans kidney or red beans
Salt
Pepper

Fry onions and meat until brown. Season. Add tomatoes and beans. Add chili powder or 2 tablespoons of Worcestershire sauce.

CAMPFIRE STEW

Serves 8   One pot

1½–2 lbs. of hamburger
3 teaspoons of grease or cooking oil
4 onions
2 cans of concentrated vegetable soup
Salt
Pepper

Make and fry little balls of hamburger. Fry onions in bottom of the pan until they and the meat balls are brown. Pour off excess grease. Add the soup. Cover and slowly cook until the meat is thoroughly cooked.

SAVORY BEANS

Serves 8   One pot

6 wieners or 2 slices of ham
1 can of whole corn
2 cans of baked beans
1 can tomatoes
2 onions
Salt
Pepper

Fry onions and meat together. Add tomatoes, corn and beans. Cook slowly.

FISH IN A BAG

Individual   No utensils

¼–⅓ lb. of fillet fish per person
Salt
Pepper
Small piece of butter
Heavy wax paper
Newspaper

Wrap the seasoned, buttered fish in wax paper so it is all covered. Wrap again in wet newspaper. Leave in coals 20–30 minutes, turning it once. Keep paper wet enough to cook the fish by steaming. Season with lemon, if desired. Tin foil may be used instead of wax and wet paper.

CORN ROAST

Individual   No utensils

2–3 ears per person
Salt
Pepper
Butter

Soak ears of corn in their husks in water 2–3 hours. Cook in good bed of coals. (Or, each water-soaked ear may be wrapped in aluminum foil, after removing the husks, and cooked in the coals.) Cook 20–35 minutes. Eat with lots of butter.

PIONEER DRUMSTICKS

8 persons   On-a-stick

2 lbs. of chopped beef
1 cup corn flakes crumbled fine
2 eggs
Pepper
Salt
2–3 onions
16 rolls or pieces of bread
8 green sticks thumb size

Mix chopped beef with onions, two eggs, one cup of crumbled corn flakes, and seasoning. Wrap this around the end of a green stick, squeezing it evenly in place. Cook over coals, turning frequently. Slightly twist to remove it from stick. Serve on bread.

KEBOBS

Individual   On-a-stick

¼ lb. round steak cut in squares about 1 inch square
    and ¼ inch thick
Small onion peeled and sliced
Partially boiled potato, sliced ¼ inch thick
2 strips of bacon cut in squares
1 fresh tomato cut in thick slices
2 rolls or sandwiches

Alternate cubes of beef (raw or partially cooked), onion, bacon, potato, and tomato on green stick or pointed wire, leaving little space between pieces. Repeat in same order. Sear quickly all over. Then cook slowly over coals, turning frequently. For variation try alternate pieces of lamb and onion, or bacon and liver, or oysters and bacon.

LOTS-MORES

Individual   On-a-stick

3 marshmallows
3 squares of chocolate
green stick thumb size

Split marshmallows and insert chocolate. Toast slowly.

MARGUERITES

Individual   On-a-stick

2 marshmallows
2 soda crackers
2 walnuts, pecans, or peanuts

Split marshmallows and place nuts on top. Insert between crackers and toast.

POTATOES BAKED IN TIN CAN

Serves 8   Baking

8 potatoes
No. 2 tin cans, with wire handles
Heavy wax paper

Scrub potatoes well and rub with butter or wrap in wax paper. Put in a large coffee can that has five holes punched in the top. Place in coals and pile them around the sides. Cook about one hour.

Other recipes for types of dishes that are unique to camping are:

Bread Twists: Add water, according to directions, to prepared biscuit dough or Bisquick. Mix in a paper bag until a stiff dough is formed. Wind this around a green stick or a broom handle covered with foil, browning it slowly. Stuff holes with butter, bacon, or jam.

MIX DOUGH IN A PAPER BAG   USE ROCKS AND STICKS

Pancakes: Add water to prepared mix. Have pan hot and well greased. Pour a spoonful on the pan. Cook until bubbles appear, turn. For variety, add to the batter cinnamon, cooked rice, blueberries, or a cup of whole-kernel canned corn.

Somemores: Make a sandwich of two white or graham crackers, add a piece of chocolate and one marshmallow. Toast slowly, and sample. Judge for yourself whether you would like "Somemore."

Baked Fish: Wrap a piece of frozen fillet in aluminum foil with a piece of raw carrot, potato, onion, and celery. Cook over coals.

Baked Chicken: As above, wrap your favorite piece of chicken in the foil and cook with the vegetables.

Eggs in Mud: Cover eggs or potatoes with wet clay or mud. Cook eggs twenty minutes in hot coals, potatoes one hour.

Camper's Stew: Have each person wrap the lower part of a large coffee can with foil. Put in alternate layers of chopped onions, carrots, celery, corn, and beef. Sprinkle tomato juice, canned tomatoes or catsup over the top. Put on lid. Wrap the entire can with foil. Cook in hot coals for fifteen to twenty minutes.

Chili Con Carne: Brown diced onions and hamburger. Add meat and cook until done. Season with chili powder. Add one can of Mexican chili beans, one can of tomatoes, two tablespoons of catsup, and cook slowly.

Camp Cocoa: Use one teaspoon of cocoa to every two of sugar. Add one cup of milk for every person, or four tablespoons of powdered milk to every cup of water, or ½ cup of evaporated milk to every ½ cup of water. Mix cocoa and sugar with water in kettle and cook to a smooth paste. Add milk, a pinch of salt, and stir all together. Heat almost to a boil. Serve with a marshmallow for each cup.

Nature

Too many children are oblivious of their world around them. The role of the adult in helping youth discover the magic and beauty of nature is to help them really see and appreciate living things in their everyday life. Emphases should be placed on nature *exploration* rather than on nature study, for the former spells adventure, the latter, school and patterned drudgery. Teachers untrained in botany and biology often are more successful in helping children find things to smell, touch, watch, and love than teachers who answer eager questions of "What is this?" or "Why do the birds do that?" in a flat, all-knowing tone which quickly quenches a flickering flame of curiosity. Too often adults have succeeded in robbing children of the thrill of finding things for themselves.

Numerous free and inexpensive sources of help in this area are available from local and federal government sources.[5] Other sources of aid include farmers, rangers, scout officials, hobbyists, and science teachers. Reference books, beautifully illustrated in color, should be readily available so that those eager to learn more about nature can do so.

Program possibilities in nature education include:

Trail-making in scenic wooded areas.
Forestry projects (tree planting, making seed beds, transplanting, trail blazing by marking trees).
Nature guessing games.
Rock, fern, flower, vegetable garden making and care.
Building tree houses for the discovery of bird and animal habits.
Crafts from native clay, shells, woods.
Vegetable dyeing.
Sketching, painting.
Cloud, tree, flower, animal photography.
Making a lily pond.
Building fish shelters in streams.
Constructing bird refuges.
Fishing, fly and bait casting, fly tying.
Berry and other fruit picking.
Hobby collections of Indian relics, spore prints, rocks, minerals, butterflies.
Making a sundial or Indian clock.
Driftwood collecting.
Making mats, bed frames, and other useful articles from reeds and willows.
Tanning skin for purses or belts.
Collecting feathers for ornaments.
Constructing canoe paddles, arrows, bows from native woods.
Rope-making.
Bone- and sandstone-carving.
Making a weather forecasting station.
Constructing weather flags.
Collecting weather signs and sayings.
Taking trips to local fire patrol stations, tree nurseries, wild game preserves, or fish hatcheries.
Telling star and other nature legends of Indians.
Making a camp nature museum of local wild life.
Boat and canoe rides to see the wonders of night on the water.
Rainy-day hikes to discover how nature adapts itself to inclement weather.
Making and observing rules for conservation of the local natural resources.
Composing creative writing, music, dance and dramatic activities around nature themes.
Making musical instruments from gourds, hollow reeds or corn stalks.

---

[5] Vannier, Maryhelen: *Methods and Materials in Recreation Leadership.* Belmont, California, Wadsworth Press, 1966, pp. 204–205.

NATURE GAMES

Wise is the leader who has a large supply of carefully selected nature games to add zest and sparkle to his or her program, or variety and surprise during adverse weather conditions. Even adults enjoy testing their wits or newly acquired nature knowledge in a game similar to "Twenty Questions." Each selected game should add to the effectiveness of the total program and not be a tacked-on unnecessary fringe to an already attractive garment. The leader might well make a large collection of such games, writing each on a separate card based upon the pattern used below to describe each of the following active and passive games:

ONE FOOT SQUARE
Outdoor—Quiet

1. Divide the group into teams.
2. Place a book or other object over a piece of ground approximately one foot square.
3. Give each group 5 minutes or less to collect as many living things as possible in that square.
4. Reward the winning group with the privilege of choosing the next activity.

RETRIEVING
Outdoor—Active

1. Divide the group into teams.
2. The leader holds up one specimen (rock, maple leaf, etc.) and says "Go!"
3. Award one point to the group that returns first with a similar object.
4. Play for ten or fewer points.

I SAW
Outdoor or Indoor— Active

1. Arrange players in a circle.
2. One acts out what animal, fish, or bird he saw recently.
3. He remains inside the circle if anyone or all fail to guess what he saw.
4. The winner remains in the circle longest.

TRAILING
Outdoor—Active

1. Leader goes cross country into the woods, marking his trail by bending twigs, footprints, or similar signs.
2. The group tries to find him 10 to 15 minutes later.
3. The first to find him is winner.

TRUE OR FALSE
Outdoor or Indoor— Active

1. Divide the group into two teams, naming one side True, the other False.
2. The leader reads a statement that is either true or false such, as "Dogs fly."
3. Each side runs behind own safety line depending upon the statement. If true, the True group runs while the False chases.
4. Winning team ends up with the most players.

TOUCH
Indoor—Quiet

1. Place bird nests, leaves, fruit, etc., into a paper sack.
2. All players close their eyes and each handles all articles inside the bag.
3. When all have removed blindfolds, the winner is the one who records the largest correct number of articles.

KIM'S GAME
Indoor—Quiet

1. Place a nut, vegetable, leaf, etc., into an uncovered box.
2. Have all players look into the box for 2 minutes.
3. Winner has recorded the largest correct number of articles.

SOUNDS
Outdoor—Quiet

1. Give each player pencil and paper.
2. All remain silent for 5 minutes, noting down all natural sounds heard during that period.
3. The winner is the one who has recorded the greatest number.

SHARP EYES
Indoor—Quiet

1. Show all a bird or animal picture for 2 minutes.
2. Have all record the answers to specific questions such as "What color was the bird's left wing?", etc.
3. Winner has recorded the greatest number correctly.

DRAW
Indoor—Quiet

1. Divide into teams.
2. Call one from each team to see the name of a bird or beast you have written down.
3. Each goes back to his own group and without talking must draw a picture of the bird or animal.
4. Winning team guesses correctly first and is given one point.
5. Play to five points.

BLIND AS A BAT
Outdoor—Active

1. Leader blindfolds and ties rope to wrist of one representative from each team.
2. Leader holds rope ends and allows each 5 feet of rope.
3. All walk around and call out the identity of as many objects as possible in 5 minutes.
4. Winner has named most objects correctly.

FLASH NATURE GAME
Outdoor or Indoor— Quiet

1. Give each player a number and divide into two teams.
2. Leader has 10 or more specimens from wide variety of nature objects in a bag.
3. Holds each one above his head, turning it around slowly, allowing all to see.
4. Calls a number and player with that number guesses what object is.
5. Award one point to team member who correctly idenfies object.
6. Play for ten points.

CHANGING COVER
Outdoor—Active

1. While leader counts ten, all players hide themselves 30 feet away.
2. Leader eliminates anyone he can see.
3. Leader closes his eyes and counts to nine while players move closer.
4. Continue counting one less each time and eliminate all those seen as they all move closer each time.
5. Winner gets closest to the leader at the most reduced count.

NUMBER ONE MAN
Outdoor—Active

1. Leader arranges hikers in single file behind him.
2. He sees an object of nature and asks person behind him (the Number One Man) to identify it.
3. Failure to do so means that player goes to the end of the line and second person has chance to move up if he can answer. If he fails, he goes to the end of the line, too.
4. Winner remains in first place longest.

HARE AND HOUNDS
Outdoor—Active

1. Divide group into Hare and Hound teams.
2. Hares hide in groups of three and must remain in this group.
3. Hounds search until all groups are found.
4. Hares become Hounds and game continues.
5. Team finding others in shortest time wins.

CURIO COLLECTION
Outdoor—Active

1. Leader names an oddity of nature such as a tree with red leaves, a tree bent by a strong wind, etc.
2. Players search until the curio is found.
3. Winner finds the greatest number.

FETCH IT
Outdoor—Active

1. Divide the group into two lines, each player numbered so that opposite players have same number.
2. Leader asks any two with same number to "fetch" (bring him) a certain object, such as a milkweed, etc.
3. Line scoring ten points first wins.

WHO AM I?
*Outdoor or Indoor—
Active*

1. One player pretends to be some character in nature.
2. He tells brief facts about himself but conceals his identity, such as "I live along the seashore and am an animal."
3. The one guessing correctly becomes the new leader.

FIND ME
Outdoor—Active

1. Divide the group into teams.
2. Give each team a list of various nature objects to find with points given according to difficulty for each article.
3. First group to make 15 points wins.

I SPY
Outdoor—Active

1. Hike with a group.
2. Leader says "I spy a robin" (or any other nature object).
3. All who also see the object sit down.
4. Others remain standing until they see it.
5. Award points to each of the first three in the group who see the object named.
6. Play until one wins 10 points.

MATCH IT OR KNOW IT
Outdoor—Active

1. Divide group into two teams.
2. Allow each team 15 minutes to collect objects of nature (leaves, twigs, seeds, nuts, etc.) and to take them back to their side.
3. One representative from each goes to opposite side with an article.
4. If opposing team can name it, award one point; if they can match it from their collection, award two points.
5. Play for 15 points.

NATURE SCAVENGER HIKE
Outdoor—Active

1. Divide group into teams of 6 to 10 on each.
2. Give each a list of nature objects to find within a given time.
3. Winning team finds the greatest number within the allotted time.

NATURE SCOUTING
Outdoor—Active

1. Divide group into teams and send each on a 15- to 30-minute hike going East, West, North, or South.
2. Representative from each team tells most interesting things seen by the group.
3. All vote which team saw the most interesting things.

TREE TAG
Outdoor—Active

1. "It" tries to tag players.
2. Designate one kind of tree which players are safe when touching.
3. Tagged players assist "It" until all are caught.

SCRAMBLE
Indoor—Active

1. Arrange 20 or more nature objects in a pile.
2. Divide players into teams, giving each corresponding numbers.
3. Call out all number two's to find the bird nest (etc.) and to bring the object to their teams first.
4. Winning team has secured the most objects.

NATURE BASEBALL
Indoor—Quiet

1. Arrange nature questions on cards.
2. Divide players into two teams.
3. Draw baseball diamond on floor with chalk.
4. Leader asks batter a question. If he answers correctly he goes to first base; if he fails he is out.
5. Play according to regular baseball rules.
6. Play four innings or for 10 to 15 minutes.

PROVE IT
Outdoor—Quiet

1. Arrange players in a circle.
2. One says, "From where I sit I see a tree with moss on it." (Or any other natural object in sight.)
3. If anyone challenges his seeing the tree, he must prove it by touching the tree.
4. If challenged and unable to prove what he saw, he must drop out; if he can prove it, his challenger must leave the game.

STRING-BURNING CONTEST
Outdoor—Active

1. Stretch two strings between stakes, one 12 inches above the ground, the other 18 inches above it.
2. Contestants must collect tinder kindling and build a fire to burn the upper string.
3. No wood may be piled higher than the 12-inch string.
4. Each one tries to burn the upper string apart first.

Knotcraft

Although there are hundreds of knots with a specific use for each, the elementary school child should learn to tie a few basic ones well and know the unique value of each, rather than trying to master the art of knowing how to tie many. The pupil should learn that a good knot is one that is easily tied and untied and one that will serve its purpose. Knots are used for: (1) joining rope, cord or string, (2) stopping the end of the rope, string or cord from slipping, (3) looping, (4) securing, (5) shortening other ropes, and (6) holding articles.

The teacher should have each pupil bring a piece of clothesline or small rope, demonstrate how the knot is tied, or show a picture if she herself cannot tie the knot and have the pupils copy the instructions step by step. The pupils should tie the knot on a chair, box or tree, and practice until the skill is mastered.

Learning how to tie the following knots and their use might well be included in the program.

SQUARE KNOT

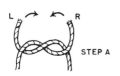

STEP A

STEP B

Used for joining two ends of rope or to tie a bundle, bandage, or shoestring, as well as to make a longer rope from several short ones.

a. Take each end of the rope in each hand. Cross the end in the right over the end in the left, twisting it back down and up in front so that a single knot is made. The end you started with should now be in the left hand.

b. Take the end in the right hand and bend it over the left making a loop that lies along the knot already made.

c. Take the end in your left hand into the loop you have made.

d. Take hold of the knot on both sides, tighten by pulling the ends in opposite directions. To loosen, take hold in the same way and push toward the center.

SHEET BEND

SHEET BEND

Used to join two ropes of different sizes. Two ropes, one smaller, are needed.

Make a square knot with two ends. Take the end of the smaller rope (*A*), cross it under the other piece of the rope at (*B*), and then up and over the loop of the bigger rope at *C*. This makes one end of the smaller rope on top and one underneath the loop of the larger rope. As you pull the knot tight, the extra turn will secure the small end in place. The knot is completed after making the extra twist with the smaller rope.

BOWLINE

BOWLINE KNOT

Used to make a loop in the end of a rope to slip over a hook or secure something to a post.

a. Take one end of the rope only but tie the other one to a tree or round object. Make a loop and judge the place where the knot will be. Let the rope lie in the palm of your left hand.

b. With the right hand, make a loop up and back of the fingers of the left hand, coming down in front, and catching the rope with the thumb as it crosses.

c. Slip your fingers out of the loop, take the end of the rope in the right hand with left thumb and finger. Pass the rope up from underneath to make a small loop.

d. Pull this end to make the main loop the size you want it, then pass the end in back of the standing part of the rope and back to the front and down into the small loop again so that it is beside itself.

e. Take these two pieces of rope in one hand and the main part of the rope in the other, pull the knot by pulling in opposite directions.

f. To make the loop around a tree or round object, pull around it before you pull through the small loop; pull tightly and proceed as before.

g. Try to tie the knot with one hand as sailors do, but remember with even both hands you always should use just one end of the rope.

CLOVE HITCH

Used to tie something securely.

a. Take an end of the rope around a tree or rung and cross it over its own part.

b. Take end around the tree or rung again and under the bend just made.

SLIP KNOT

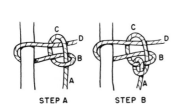

STEP A   STEP B

Used to tether a horse, or attaching a rope to a bucket handle, or for neckties.

a. Draw end *A* (as shown in step A) around a tree or rung and make a small loop in it.

b. Bring *A* up behind and across the standing part of the opposite rope end (*D*), then down through bight *B*, and then up around and down through bight *B* again (as shown in step B).

Knifemanship and Toolcraft

Use of the knife can be taught to girls as well as boys. A Boy or Girl Scout knife is recommended. The pupils should be taught the parts of the knife, safety measures to use when opening and closing it, how to sharpen it, and how to care for it.

The group can be taught how to whittle useful articles from native materials including buttons, name tags, candle holders, letter openers, paper weights, lapel pins, napkin rings, knives, forks, and spoons. How to make and use fuzz sticks and kindling wood might well be included.

THE USE OF THE HATCHET AND AXE

THE AXE

A hand axe is a good tool for general use. To use the axe properly, grasp the end firmly with the thumb around the first finger. Bring the axe down carried by its head and strike sharp direct blows on the wood. To cut a heavy log, strike diagonal blows, never cut square across. To fell a small tree, first clear the brush around it. Cut diagonally down the trunk and alternate this with blows up the trunk. To split a log, drive the axe into the wood, raise both together, striking on the edge of a block. Or lean the log against another log or block and strike in the center where it touches the block. Practice splitting larger logs into small pieces of kindling.

STEP 1

STEP 2

STEP 3

AXEMANSHIP

Teach your pupils to use first a light single-headed axe. Have them first try to chop a log that is on the ground. To hold the axe, grasp it easily, right hand with the palm under the handle of the axe and with left palm over the end. These positions are reversed for left-handed pupils. Balance weight easily and practice letting the axe fall from above your head on to the log. Then (1) raise the axe head with the right hand over your head while the left hand moves up slightly to the front. Keep elbows bent; (2) let the right hand slip down the handle to other hand as the axe falls, but guide the handle and keep your eyes on the spot to hit; and (3) let the axe head do the swinging and the work. Keep practicing until a rhythmic easy swing develops. Practice by cutting heavy logs before you begin chopping down small trees.

Sleeping Equipment and Tents

THE BED ROLL

Sleeping bags are ideal camping equipment. However, blanket rolls are simple to make and prove almost as good.

First lay a poncho or raincoat on the ground. Place the first blanket on the poncho near the middle so that half of it extends out on the side. Place a second blanket on its end at the center of the first blanket so that it lies directly above the poncho. Lap each additional blanket over the underneath one. Fold a sheet and place it on last. Fold all blankets over in reverse order, 1, 2, 3, etc. Pin through all sides and the bottom with horse-blanket pins. Snap the poncho over and tightly roll all the blankets into a bed roll. Carry the roll over the shoulder or on your back.

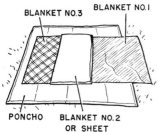

BLANKET NO.3   BLANKET NO.1

PONCHO   BLANKET NO.2
OR SHEET

TENTS

The simplest type of shelter is a poncho tent made by throwing a poncho over a rope stretched between two trees, and pegging it down.

A wall tent is also recommended. These can be bought at nominal cost at Army and Navy stores. The campers can be taught how to pitch and ditch these tents with skill as well as how to make wooden tables and chairs, brooms, waste baskets, and other housekeeping articles from native materials. Caches used for storing food and keeping it cool are also fun to make.

PONCHO SHELTER

Lashing

This skill aids campers to use native materials for needed articles, for lashing is a way to bind sticks or poles together without nails. Its use serves to protect trees which would be damaged by nails, and adds to the over-all rustic setting of camp. Because it requires only cord and sticks or poles, it is easily set up or taken down.

SQUARE LASHING

SQUARE LASHING

This type joins two sticks together at right angles.
Tie a clove hitch to the vertical stick at one end of the stick. Bring the standing part across the horizontal stick, then around behind the vertical stick. Repeat until both sticks are secure.

DIAGONAL LASHING

DIAGONAL LASHING

This type joins two sticks at a diagonally formed X.
Tie a clove hitch around both. Make as many as six turns joining in one direction, then as many the other way. Finish off with a square knot.

ROUND LASHING

ROUND LASHING

This type is used to join two short sticks to make one long one.
Tie a clove hitch around one, then wrap the cord around both. Finish off with a square knot or half hitches.

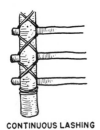

CONTINUOUS LASHING

CONTINUOUS LASHING

This type is used to make ladders or bridges.
Use small short sticks and long narrow ones. Notch the long sticks where the smaller ones will be lashed. Use a cord four times longer than the long sticks and start with a clove hitch at the end of the long stick at the middle of the cord, thus having equal lengths on either side of the long stick. If the hitch has been properly placed, the ends of cord will pull the knot tight as they came up from the under side of the long stick. Next bring the cords around this knot over the first small stick, following the lines of the long stick. Pull down and under, crossing the cord on the under side of the long stick. Pull cords over the second small stick, following the lines of the long stick by going under and crossing underneath the long stick, and coming up for the next one. The rope should always run parallel to the long stick on the top and should cross on the under side. End with two half inches and tuck ends of the rope under the last stick.

Lashing is fun to do. It is a useful camp skill, for the campers can learn to lash pieces of wood together to make coat hangers, mirrors, picture frames, tables, shoe racks, suitcase racks, a tripod for pots and pans, bridges, chairs as well as the other articles previously mentioned.

Other Camp Skills

FINDING YOUR WAY

Knowing how to find one's way in the woods even when lost is a valuable skill. Teach pupils how to find their way by the sun, a watch, stars, tree moss, and a compass. At the same time introduce trail blazing by using trees, rocks, or grass. Map making and reading of places in the local community will be interesting to the students. Signaling by means of the Morse Code, or flags and smoke should also be included. Care should be taken, however, not to duplicate skill areas already covered by the pupils in their Girl and Boy Scout work. Use of a skill inventory sheet before classes begin will prevent any duplication.

SOIL CONSERVATION

The pupils can learn much in this area about our land and how to conserve our national resources. Learning about how to build dams and understanding their use, soil erosion and correction, forest conservation, how to plant trees, shrubs, fruits, and vegetables will increase in each student a deeper appreciation of the soil and land on which he lives. That we all live on the land is often forgotten in our modern world. Learning how to live simply in the out-of-doors, utilizing what is in one's environment, can add much to a child's wise use of present and future leisure time.

Fishing

Every child should learn how to fish, for this is one sport that can bring lifetime enjoyment. Cane poles can be used, or the children can cut and fashion their own from tree branches. Fly and bait casting is more fun, but requires special equipment, which is relatively inexpensive.

Bait casting is done with live, artificial, or fresh bait. Worms, spoons, or pork rind are often used. The rod is made from wood, steel, glass, or bamboo.

Hold the rod easily in one hand with the thumb on the spool where it feels best as you apply pressure to control the speed of the lure. Do the overhead cast on three counts:

Count One—Hold the rod almost horizontal.

Count Two—Bring it back to an imaginary twelve o'clock; then eleven o'clock.

Count Three—Snap your wrist, bringing the rod back down slightly above your original horizontal position.

Practice to develop a smooth, relaxed, accurate cast. Use the rod tip for aiming and whip the line straight ahead each time. Avoid back casting too far or tensing up. Stand squarely, or with the opposite leg forward in a stride position (right leg forward for a left-handed person and vice versa for a right-handed one).

Fly casting is done with artificial or live bait. Artificial flies are multicolored and have colorful names such as the royal coachman, grizzly bear, and so forth. Live bait includes salmon eggs, worms, grasshoppers, and minnows. The rod is made from tubular steel, split bamboo, or glass.

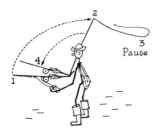

Hold the rod easily in one hand with the thumb on top or at one side (whichever is more comfortable). Learn to cast on these four counts:

Count One—Hold the rod horizontal. Take up the line slack with an outward pull of the oposite hand.

Count Two—Snap the line back over your head to one o'clock.

Count Three—Make a momentary pause until the lure completes its backward movement.

Count Four—Snap the rod back down almost to its original horizontal position.

Our American Heritage

The early history of America is a brilliantly colored tapestry recording as its dominant pattern man's struggle to carve a unique life and culture out of a wilderness. Pictured there are Indians, explorers, trappers, prospectors, Pilgrims, lumberjacks, and ranchers—campers all, to whom life itself was camping—rugged human beings dependent upon the land, respectful of it, and seeing in it a good life. These dynamic pioneers, pushing beyond boundaries, blazing new trails into regions marked "unknown," left behind them rich sagas of daring courage. Today's youth needs to learn and appreciate this treasure.

Campfire programs should be built around folk themes. Songs and stories from all regions of the country will increase appreciation of other groups. Folk and square dancing, and party games will add much sheer fun. Games of low organization, including nature guessing games and contests in campcraft skills, will add much to build group unity and a spirit of good fellowship. Camping has no equal in bringing out and developing the best in youth and helping them find real adventure.

SUGGESTED READINGS

Donaldson, G. W.: *School Camping.* New York, Association Press, 1952.

Empleton, Bernard et al.: *The New Science of Skin and Scuba Diving.* New York, Association Press, 1962.

Goodrich, Warren, and Hutchins, Corleen: *Science Through Recreation.* New York, Holt, Rinehart and Winston, 1964.

Harty, William: *Science for Camp and Counselor.* New York, Association Press, 1964.

Hunt, W. Ben: *Crafts and Lore.* New York, Golden Press, 1965.

Ickis, Marguerite: *Nature in Recreation.* New York, A. S. Barnes & Co., 1965.

Lynn, Gordon: *The Golden Book of Camping and Camp Crafts.* New York, The Golden Press, 1959.

Mitchell, Viola, and Crawford, Viola: *Camp Counseling.* Philadelphia, W. B. Crawford, 1961.

Peterson, Gunnar, and Edgren, Harry: *The Book of Outdoor Winter Activities.* New York, Association Press, 1962.

Saunders, John: *The Golden Book of Nature Crafts.* New York, The Golden Press, 1958.

Smith, Julian; Carlson, Reynold; Donaldson, George; and Masters, Hugh: *Outdoor Education.* Englewood Cliffs, N.J., Prentice-Hall, Inc., 1963.

Chapter 20

Adapted Programs for Atypical Children

No child should be excused from physical education classes because of a physical, emotional, or social handicap. Until recently, it has been the practice to allow the exceptional boy or girl to stay in the study hall or go to the library while his classmates had their physical education periods. Or, if the child were not too badly handicapped, he might have been allowed to be official score keeper during class athletic contests. Handicapped children need not and must not be mere spectators instead of participants, regardless of their disability. For some, lying down resting is physical education, for still others playing cards or throwing darts is an activity which, when learned, may be the magic ticket that will admit them into peer groups. The unskilled child, if he is further handicapped by being physically crippled, is, indeed, in for a lonely, isolated, miserable future. Children need to learn how to live successfully in our highly competitive society, how to mix with people, and how to use their leisure time wisely. Through individual help in corrective physical education, handicapped children increasingly are being educated to face and recognize their limitations, and to learn how to work around them. They should be encouraged and required to learn how to play. Although no one group of children needs physical education more than any other, all groups must be included in the program.

NUMBER OF HANDICAPPED CHILDREN

It is estimated that between 5 and 10 per cent of all school children should be in some program in special education. The following table shows the handicaps of which these children are classified:[1]

Low physical fitness	20 to 25%

---

[1] Fait, Hollis: *Special Education.* Philadelphia, W. B. Saunders Company, 1966.

Poor body mechanics	50 to 60%
Nutritional disturbances	1 to 2%
Visual handicaps	1 to 2%
Auditory handicaps	1 to 2%
Cerebral palsy	Less than 1%
Cardiac conditions	1%
Arrested tuberculosis	Less than 1%
Diabetes	Less than 1%
Anemia	Less than 1%
Asthma and hayfever	2 to 4%
Hernia	Less than 1%
Epilepsy	Less than 1%
Mental retardation	1%
Other	1%

Mental retardation affects nearly 6 million Americans. In the foregoing chart, although this is only 1 per cent of all school age children, the vastness of this and other equally startling number of handicaps requires that these children be given more educational attention than ever before.

In addition to these figures the National Society for Crippled Children has estimated that between 25 to 50 per cent of all school children could be helped by better programs in corrective physical education.

CLASSIFICATIONS

All atypical children fall into two classifications: (1) the physically handicapped, and (2) the socially handicapped. Within each of these groups each child differs widely, for no two of these children are alike any more than are any two normal children.

Types of physical handicaps among children are:

1. Postural	5. Speech
2. Crippling	6. Respiratory
3. Visual	7. Cardiac
4. Hearing	8. Nutritional

Types of social handicaps among children are:

1. Feeble-mindedness or mental retardation
2. Delinquents or those with remedial emotional maladjustments.

NEEDS OF EXCEPTIONAL CHILDREN

The needs of exceptional children can be met if the following items are recognized:

1. Their needs are practically the same as those of normal children.
2. They can profit usually more from being with normal groups than from being segregated; they need to be encouraged to mix with those who are normal.

Figure 56. No children should be excused from physical education because of a physical, emotional, or social handicap. Rather, an adaptive program should be established for them. (Courtesy of Public Schools of Lincoln, Nebraska.)

3. Normal children can often help them to recognize their limitations and to work around them. Although children are often cruel, they accept any handicapped child who proves he has licked his problem and can do many other things better than they can.

4. Few children can be helped to any great extent who have been too sheltered by parents who have allowed them to remain helpless over a long period of time.

5. All children need to solve their own problems, to take and assume responsibilities, and to have good friends to help them become adjusted to their own limitations, environment, and society.

6. Work and play programs must be geared to their limitations, environment, and ability, yet be challenging enough so that the children can and will progress.

THE ADAPTED PROGRAM

All exceptional children should be encouraged and required to take part in the physical education program, just as are all normal children. Points to be remembered by the teacher in charge of the adapted program are:

1. The program must be built upon the individual needs of each child.

2. The program must be conducted under the supervision and direction of a recognized medical authority.

3. The teacher should have specialized professional preparation to enable her to do this work successfully.

4. The parents' cooperation must be sought and secured.

5. The children follow the same procedures and rules in as many things as possible in normal groups, including class participation, costumes, and grading.

6. Classes for severely handicapped children should be kept small. The kind of defect will determine grouping possibilities. Malnourished children, for example, may have classes with those suffering from cardiac and respiratory defects.

7. Pupils should be assigned to special classes according to the amount of physical work permitted.

8. Complete records should be kept for each child, including results of the physical examination, health history, observation and data from his family, reports sent to other staff members, a record of his behavior, and his personality rating.

9. The program should be set up in the gymnasium or chair-free room large enough for adequate equipment. The following minimum items are recommended:

Stall bars	Cots
Mats or mattresses with washable covers	Full-length mirrors
Scales	Punching bags
Individual benches without backs	Iron boots
Flying rings	Horizontal ladders
Bulletin boards	Knee, ankle, and leg exercisors
Individual exercise cards	Muscle-testing instruments
Filing cabinet for records	Recreational games
Screens	

PROGRAM OBJECTIVES

The aim of the adapted program should be to enable each pupil to obtain his optimum physical, social, mental, and emotional potential in a well planned, progressive program which has been built around his special needs, interests, and limitations. The objectives of such a program might well be to assist each pupil to:

1. develop total fitness.

2. develop and improve physical skills and movement efficiency.

3. develop a wide variety of leisure-time recreational skills.

4. gain an understanding of the nature of his handicap and its limitations, along with insight of potentials which might be developed.

5. develop a happy attitude and wholesome philosophy of life.

6. gain recognition from his peers for positive actions and widen his circle of friends.

7. learn how to adjust to, and compensate for, his limitations.

8. develop physical strength, body flexibility, explosive power, balance, reaction time, and movement efficiency.

TEACHER QUALIFICATIONS

In addition to knowledge and skill in teaching a wide variety of physical education activities, the teacher working with atypical children should have a working understanding of the human body, first aid, and the causes, nature, and effects of handicapping disabilities. Above all, she must have the patience to work with these pupils (for their progress in learning skills is often painfully slow), as well as a feeling of acceptance of the pupil (for many of them are repulsive looking and often grotesque). The more the teacher knows about each pupil and his particular handicap, the more successfully she can teach him. Parent conferences will prove helpful, but should be well planned so that both parties concerned develop a feeling of rapport, support, and willingness to work together in order to help the individual child involved. Such a conference may also afford the teacher the opportunity to establish the controls necessary for protecting the condition from aggravation.[2]

SAMPLE LETTER SENT TO THE FAMILY PHYSICIAN

Cooperation with the family physician should be sought. The school doctor may wish to write to him and include a copy of the following blank to be filled out and returned, or this may be sent by the teacher.

DOCTOR'S BLANK

Physical Education Recommendations

Name of pupil _____ Sex _____

Address _____ School _____

Age _____ Grade _____

All pupils are required by the Education Law in this State to attend courses in instruction in physical education. Those pupils who are unable to participate in the regular program because of defects are required to take a corrective class built around their individual needs.

Special activities are provided for children who require special attention. Check below the defect this pupil has according to your findings:

_____ Postoperative   _____ Defective posture

_____ Convalescent   _____ Flabby musculature

_____ Cardiac   _____ Foot defects

_____ Malnutrition   _____ Others

_____ Chronic fatigue

Check below the activities you recommend that this pupil take part in:

_____ Apparatus   _____ Recreational sports (ping-pong, shuffleboard, deck tennis)

_____ Athletics

_____ Stunts   _____ Quiet table games

_____ Rhythms (folk, square,   _____ Corrective exercises
social)
                                          _____ Walking

_____ Swimming   _____ Complete rest

---

[2]Fait, Hollis: *Adapted Physical Education.* Philadelphia, W. B. Saunders Company, 1960, p. 49.

This is to certify that I have examined _____ and recom-

mended that he(she) participate only in these checked activities for a period of _____ weeks,

_____ the whole semester.

Dr. _____ Phone _____

Date _____ Address _____

Additional comments or recommendations: _____

_____

_____

_____

PARENT COOPERATION

The teacher should gain the cooperation of the parents by helping them understand the importance of the corrective program. This may be done by a letter or by a personal conference. The teacher should explain the nature of the child's defect and what is being done to help him. A list of specific exercises recommended by the doctor to be done at home may be included in the letter to the parents, or given to them at the conference.

CLASS WORK

Adapted physical education classes should be as individual as possible. The program needs to be varied, stimulating, and challenging. Each pupil should be taught how to relax, how to do his own prescribed individual exercises, games and sports suitable for his handicap, and group activities. Additional work in the swimming pool is highly recommended for most cases. Whenever possible, activities may be co-educational, for the social values of mixed group play are important.

A 40-minute class period might include:

1. Relaxation	5 minutes
2. Light group exercises done to music	5 minutes
3. Individual exercises done to music	10 minutes
4. Group games	15 minutes
5. Relaxation	5 minutes

Exercises might well be incorporated into games whenever possible, or games made out of the exercises. Progress charts should be kept with the aid of the pupil. The teacher should also have individual talks with each child to help him gain insight into his own condition, and to encourage him to grow in skills. Together they might work out specific objectives toward which the pupil will work. This might be built around the following form:

STUDENT OBJECTIVE SHEET IN ADAPTED PHYSICAL EDUCATION

Name of student _____ Age _____

Defect _____ Grade _____

Things I want to accomplish this semester in Corrective Physical Education:

A. *Physical*

_____ 1. How to play one or more team games

_____ 2. How to play one or more individual games

_____ 3. How to do one or more social, folk, or square dances

_____ 4. How to increase my score on physical fitness tests

_____ 5. How to do one or more campcraft skills

_____ 6. How to swim

_____ 7. How to play longer without fatigue

_____ 8. How to gain or maintain the weight proper for my build

_____ 9. I can and will play after school

B. *Social*

_____ 1. Accept responsibilities

_____ 2. Cooperate more with others

_____ 3. Be more considerate of others

_____ 4. Be more tolerant of others

_____ 5. Be more able to see the humorous side of things

_____ 6. Get more people to like me

_____ 7. Get to know more about myself

Activities suitable for class work *upon the recommendation of a physician* are:

1. Games (without equipment) of the low organization type—(Simon Says, Still Water, I Spy, etc.)
2. Games of high organization or isolated sport skills (soccer, soccer dribble relay, basketball, basketball goal shooting, football, football throw for distance)
3. Dancing (folk, modern, square, social)
4. Marching and moving to rhythm
5. Gymnasium apparatus work (stall bars, balance beam, the horse, etc.)
6. Golf, clock golf, putting, miniature golf, driving
7. Handball, hand tennis
8. Tennis, paddle tennis, deck tennis
9. Ping-pong

10. Volleyball, sitting volleyball, newcomb
11. Archery
12. Darts
13. Standard gymnastic stunts (cartwheels, somersaults, head stands, etc.)
14. Swimming, water basketball, diving
15. Hiking and camping
16. Shuffleboard
17. Box hockey
18. Quiet card games
19. Table games (checkers, pick up sticks, jacks, etc.)
20. Self-testing activities—basketball and baseball throws for distance and accuracy, etc.
21. Fly casting and fishing
22. Skating
23. Horseshoes
24. Wrestling
25. Weight lifting
26. Rope spinning
27. Tenniquoit
28. Tether ball
29. Conditioning exercises

TEACHING METHODS

Teaching-learning situations that are natural and desirable will be the most productive. Pupil self-direction should be a goal to be reached. Gradually more and more responsibility should be given him concerning his own use of class time. Each child should assist in building the program and have a strong voice in selecting activities. A relaxed atmosphere of adventure and friendliness should permeate the room. All children should be trained to practice habits of safety in order that they may feel secure in what they are doing without the fear of being hurt.

ADMINISTRATIVE DETAILS

When exceptional children can safely be included in physical activity programs with normal children, they should be so scheduled. Those with mild cardiac conditions, for example, can play shuffleboard, those wearing leg braces can learn archery, and those in wheelchairs can learn to swim in classes with well children.

The teacher should work closely with school and family doctors in order to select the best recommended developmental activities for each child.

Since some students have special health and safety problems, these should be carefully taken into account when planning the program. These include the poorly coordinated child who tires easily or the diabetic who sometimes pushes himself beyond his fatigue level.

The following special equipment is suggested:

Full length mirrors	Weighted shoes
Weights of varying sizes	Stationary bicycle
Punching bags	Rowing machine
Wall pulleys	Scales
Stall bars	Shoulder wheels
Knee and ankle exerciser	Slantboards

Since many handicapped children are obese and poorly skilled and lack strength, every effort should be made to provide them with modified activities that will eliminate this problem. Gaining parental cooperation is vital and every effort should be made to encourage family recreational activities in which the handicapped child can be included, such as roller skating or swimming for the blind.

SPECIFIC CASES

Posture

Posture is a result of habit of the mind as well as of the body. There are many postures each person assumes rather than the static ram-rod one our grandparents considered ideal, for postures vary according to what one does. In general, good posture means proper body alignment in standing, sitting, and lying positions—all done with the minimum of fatigue, with ease, grace, and efficiency. In short, good posture is the maximum result produced by minimum of effort of the body when moving or held stationary. The body is properly balanced, the step is buoyant, the movements zip rather than drag, the head is erect rather than drooped, the hips are tucked under rather than thrust out, and the shoulders straight, not hollow. There are many postures the body assumes rather than one static posture, as each person moves about.

Causes of poor posture are:

1. *Poorly balanced diet*—muscles of the body are affected to such a degree that they do not have the power to hold the person up. An overweight child may have foot defects because the bones in his feet are not strong enough to support his body correctly.

2. *Environmental conditions*—poor lighting affects the posture habits of the child trying to do homework, as does a sagging bed mattress or the use of a large pillow.

3. *Rapid growth*—because different parts of the body may sometimes develop at faster rates, the child may slump. This is often true of adolescent girls who develop large breasts at an early age.

4. *Fatigue*—weary children droop because tired muscles are unable to hold the body in the best position. This fatigue may be the result of insufficient sleep, rest, food, and exercise.

5. *Mental and emotional tensions*—worry, strain, lack of security, fear, feelings of inadequacy, all tell on the bodies of their victims.

6. *Vision and hearing*—these defects sometimes cause one to assume incorrect body movements in order to see and/or hear what is going on in the world. Fixed habits of holding the head to one side or craning the neck forward may result.

7. *Structural and orthopedic defects*—some children are born with non-remedial defects, such as a hunchback or short leg, others may acquire defects from accidents.

TYPES OF POSTURE DEFECTS

Three types of posture defects are the most common: (1) scoliosis (curvature of the spine), (2) lordosis (hollow lower back), and (3) kyphosis (round shoulders). Commonly observed defects include forward head, round shoulders, protruding shoulder blades, round upper back, sway back, flat back, flat feet, ankle pronation or supination, and shoulder imbalance. Many deviations of a functional nature can be corrected, whereas defects due to a structural cause are difficult to correct by means other than surgery.

POSTURE EXAMINATIONS

Posture examinations for elementary school children should be conducted wherever possible by an orthopedic specialist or a medical doctor. Serious defects in young children can be corrected more succesfully than those found among secondary school students. The following suggested form may be used by the examining physician:

ORTHOPEDIC SCREENING EXAMINATION

_____ School

Name _____   Address _____

Age _____   Phone _____

Grade _____   Sex _____

Weight _____   Race _____

Height _____

Body Type

1. Short and stocky   (   )
2. Long and angular   (   )
3. Athletic, broad shoulders and
   narrow hips   (   )

Gait

Normal   (   )
Abnormal   (   )

Remarks: _____

_____

Legs

Normal   (   )
Bowed   (   )
Knock-kneed   (   )
Hyperextended   (   )
Knee-caps normal   (   )

Feet

Longitudinal arch
Normal   (   )
Very low   (   )
Very high   (   )
Fallen   (   )
Callouses   (   )

Remarks: _____   Remarks: _____

_____   _____

Feet

    Transverse arch
    Normal   ( )
    Very low ( )
    Very high ( )
    Fallen   ( )
    Callouses ( )

    Remarks: _____

Toes

    Normal   ( )
    Hammer   ( )
    Overriding   ( )
    Athlete's foot ( )
    Corns   ( )
    Callouses   ( )

    Remarks: _____

Arms and Hands

    Normal   ( )
    Deformity ( )
    Bitten nails ( )
    Tremors   ( )

    Remarks: _____

Ankles

    Normal   ( )
    Pronated ( )
    Supinated ( )

    Remarks: _____

Posture

    Good   ( )
    Superior ( )
    Fair   ( )
    Poor   ( )

    Remarks: _____

Spine

    Normal   ( )
    Kyphosis ( )
    Lordosis ( )
    Scoliosis ( )

    Remarks: _____

Chest

    Normal   ( )
    Hollow   ( )
    Deformity ( )

    Remarks: _____

Shoulders

    Normal   ( )
    High (both) ( )
    Low (both) ( )
    High (one) ( )
    Low (one)   ( )
    Winged   ( )

    Remarks: _____

Recommendations   *Describe*

    1. Corrective exercises _____

    2. No correction needed _____

    3. Condition not correctable _____

    4. Rest _____

    5. Improved nutrition _____

                  Name of Physician _____

                            Address _____

                               Date _____

Records such as the above are only functional when used. The teacher in charge of the adaptive program needs to have a conference with the examining physician, the parents, and the pupil as soon after the examination as possible. A remedial program based upon the findings and recommendations made by the medical authority should be started as soon as possible.

Activities selected for the student who has poor body mechanics due to functional reasons may be learned from any course of study used for the other children.

Those selected for students who have difficulties stemming from structural defects (lordosis, kyphosis, or scoliosis) may include the following:

1. Lead-up games to basketball, football, softball, and volleyball
2. Speedball
3. Soccer
4. Tennis (regular, deck, paddle, hand)
5. Hand and Indian wrestling
6. All types of dancing except acrobatic tap
7. Individual stunts
    a. Cartwheel
    b. Head and hand stands
    c. Push ups
    d. Chinning and bar work
    e. Rope climbing
    f. Animal walks (crab, centipede, duck, and elephant)
    g. Human croquet
    h. Leapfrog
8. Hiking, camping, fishing, and bait casting
9. Archery
10. Golf (tenpin, clock, regular)
11. Relays
    a. Throwing
    b. Passing
    c. Receiving
12. Recreational swimming

The Feet and Ankles

Defects of the feet and ankles include:

1. Flat feet
2. Weak feet
3. Ankle pronation (turned-in foot)
4. Ankle supination (turned-out foot)

Many parents and teachers have the mistaken idea that the child will outgrow a foot deformity or walking habit. This is rarely true. Children who complain of aching feet and legs and who quickly turn their shoes over to the sides should receive corrective devices to alleviate difficulties. Specially built shoes, arch supports, and ankle supports may be advisable.

Corrective exercises, along with instruction concerning proper shoe fitting, foot care, proper methods of weight bearing, and means of relaxing and refreshing tired foot muscles, can be most beneficial.

Figure 57. Weak foot muscles can be corrected by this type of activity. (Courtesy of *The Instructor*. Photograph by Edith Brockway.)

The restricted program should be a broad one containing almost the same type of activities found in the regular program. Relays that involve picking up marbles with the toes, or moving objects with the feet, as well as track and field events, are especially recommended. However, those which call for heavy landing, or sudden twists and turns can be dangerous and should not be included. Aquatics are highly beneficial.

More serious foot defects, such as a shortened Achilles tendon or heel cord, rigid flatfoot, as well as others due to structural causes, often limit participation in active games. If bearing the weight is painful, table and quiet games are more suitable.

Suggested activities for those having more serious defects include:

1. Foot marble games
2. Croquet
3. Bowling (lawn, duck pin, regular)
4. Shuffleboard
5. Tether ball
6. Simple rhythmic activities
7. Stunts and self-testing activities on mats and apparatus
8. Archery
9. Swimming, boating
10. Bicycling
11. Camping, fishing, fly casting

Heart Disease

Organic and functional heart disturbances are relatively common among young children. Rheumatic fever is more serious among school youngsters than has been formerly believed, for it often damages the heart of its victim. Even in lighter cases it is often referred to as the disease that is seldom cured, and as the disease that licks the joints and bites the hearts of children. Repeated attacks often follow lowered resistance and extreme fatigue. Over 70 per cent of all children suffer some degree of heart damage.

Signs and symptoms of the disease are: swelling, temperature, increased breathing rate, pallor, listlessness, irritability, frequent nose-bleeds, and often tenderness and swelling in the joints of the body. Some cases are so slight that parents, thinking their child is just hot, tired, and cross, fail to call the doctor or even to put the child to bed. Leakage of the heart or heart murmur due to the toxins of the disease and fever are the result of both mild and severe attacks, although the chances of serious heart damage are greater in the more serious cases. Rheumatic fever is caused by a streptococcus and no child can be immunized or protected against the malady: all children are potential victims of the disease.

Restricting these children entirely from any kind of physical activity can cause negative emotional reactions. Children want and need to play with others, repeated warnings and threats from parents can produce harmful fears. Rather, the child should be taught activities in which he can safely participate, made aware of fatigue signs, and urged to drop out of activity when he wishes. The family physician needs to recommend not only the kind of activity to be played, but also the amount advisable.

Suggested activities from which the physician could make recommendations include.

Archery	Mild roller skating
Circle games	Rope spinning
Bag punching	Social dance
Croquet	Swimming and light water games
Camping	Shuffleboard
Fishing, hiking, hunting	Ping-pong
Juggling	Paddle tennis
Horseshoes	Ring toss
	Volleyball

Deaf and Hard of Hearing

It is claimed that one out of every ten persons in our society has hearing difficulties or is completely deaf. Special schools are provided for advanced cases, but the majority of those affected are enrolled in public schools, or mingle with normally-hearing members of our society. Lip-reading instruction, voice training, hearing aids, and proper emotional channeling have aided afflicted persons.

Because children suffering from hearing impairment often isolate themselves from others and thus develop needless feelings of fear, frustration and insecurity, normal urges for activity must be re-emphasized and directed. These individuals might well take part in practically all the activities in the regular program. Individual stunts, such as push and pull ups, gymnastics, the usual athletic games offered to other pupils, and individual sports, such as tennis, archery, badminton, and deck tennis, are recommended. Because the sense of balance may be damaged, rhythmic activities may offer too much of a challenge to any child who has not had many opportunities to play or develop good coordination. Social dancing may gradually be included in the program.

The following is a student teacher's description of a movement exploration experience using car tires with a group of deaf children:[3]

I would put the spontaneous reactions of the deaf children at Pilot School for the Deaf toward the tires into separate classifications. There were six tires in the gymnasium, and gradually twenty children entered the room!

At first the children descended on the tires so that each one had his own. One lifted it in the air waist high with himself in the middle and his arms holding it up and ran laughing around the room. Another stood on the edge and started jumping . . . slowly at first and then faster and faster. A third simply curled up inside and clutched the edges peering out at the rest of the group coming in; another simply sat for a few minutes thoughtfully and then started making a noise like a jet engine taking off. He was grinning from ear to ear, and I wondered to what special place he was traveling! Still another curled up inside with his eyes closed. Imagine the privacy of your very own tire just to think in?

The next step came in getting the children to understand that they must share these possessions with two others. At first they each were furious but all of a sudden they realized that two or three in a tire was that much more fun. They bounced on them by holding hands and jumping; they balanced by holding hands and walking carefully around the edges; or they sat in them like three men in a boat. It was even more fun to squeeze two or three inside and jump, run, or just wiggle around. Everything they did was their own invention and they were wild about the newness and fun of it all.

After about fifteen minutes we got the tires into circle and had them follow the leader: jumping into a flat tire . . . wiggling through an upright tire; hopping into one . . . skipping . . . going backwards, and so on. Then we got them into teams for a tire relay. Two children held two tires upright while the rest went through and touched the wall. The "holders" loved just clutching onto the hard rubber! They themselves got the idea of a backward relay. Their activity period was up too quickly and they were quite upset at having to leave the gym.

We used the tires and beanbags later for a "basket-ball" game and relay. They still wanted just to sit, jump, crawl into, roll over, or run with them. The tires seemed indestructible and usable in many ways. Besides serving as a piece of equipment for hard usage, the children seemed to delight in using them for shelter. When I watched them just sitting in them and grinning I wondered exactly what thoughts were going through their minds and if they realized how lucky they were to be able to have so much adventure and privacy all their own. It seems to me you could conduct an entire gym program with the tires and beanbags we took to these small deaf children that day.

Blind and Partially Sighted

Special schools are provided for those totally or partially blind. Although the number of children attending public schools who have serious eye difficulties is small, there are some known cases. The physical educa-

---

[3] Reported by Rita Newman, a student in the class "Teaching Health and Physical Education in Elementary Schools," at Southern Methodist University, Spring Semester, 1967. Each student in this class is required to work two hours weekly teaching physical activities to exceptional or normal children.

tion program for these children should stress good body mechanics, the development of courage, and happiness. Individual activities, such as body-building stunts, self-testing activities, and camping activities, are recommended for the upper elementary group. Social, folk, and square dances can add much joy to the lives of these children, as can games of low organization, simple stunts and self-testing activities.

It is truly amazing what physical activities blind children, with patient teaching, can learn to do! Many play golf, bowl, roller and ice skate, swim, and dance. Track and field, wrestling, and all kinds of modified games are ideal for these children.[4]

The Mentally Retarded

There are about 5.5 million known mentally retarded people in America and this number is increasing. Although many are moderately retarded, thousands are profoundly so. If a child has lived up to the age of six, his chances for living an average life span are good. Our many state schools and institutions for these people of all ages are vastly overcrowded. Many children are not discovered as being severely retarded until they are in the third grade in school, when reading and mathematics skills are being stressed.

Retardation has many causes, including rubella or German measles during the first three months of the mother's pregnancy, the Rh factor, chromosomal abnormalities, inborn errors of metabolism, lack of prenatal care, physical malformation of the brain, brain injury and damage before, during, or after birth, and other unknown factors. Most retarded individuals have psychomotor, perceptual, and sensory difficulties and those most severely damaged have extremely poor motor coordination.

Retardates can learn an amazing number of physical activities from a teacher with great patience who shows them much tender, loving care and understanding. In planning programs for this group it is suggested that one:

1. stress big motor movement activities such as running and hopping.
2. use color as much and in as many ways as possible.
3. "show" more, explain less.
4. keep rules simple.[5]
5. use large equipment, remembering that the smaller the child, the larger the ball should be.
6. provide for many kinds of rhythmical activities.
7. stress the "fun" element in play.
8. learn from the pupils—modify and improvise with them as they play and learn.
9. emphasize big muscle mimetic play (elephant trunk swing, bunny hop, etc.).

---

[4] For helpful information see the splendid book by Dr. Charles Buell listed in the Suggested Readings.

[5] Franklin, C. C.: *Diversified Games and Activities of Low Organization for Mentally Retarded Children.* Carbondale, Illinois, Southern Illinois University, 1966.

10. perform many kinds of simple calisthenics to music.
11. include many camping and outing activities in the program.
12. stress all kinds of dancing and, if possible, have the group perform in public.
13. include many kinds of stunts and tumbling activities.
14. teach in small areas or rooms with small groups and, when needed, on a one home basis.
15. keep each child active.
16. demonstrate and take part in the activities so that the children can "see" and "copy."
17. correlate good health habits with physical education.
18. give all students recognition for what they do as much as possible and in as many different ways as possible.
19. enlist the aid of volunteer "normal" peers and adults to help these children learn a variety of movement skills.
20. stress the development of social and physical skills.

Poliomyelitis (Infantile Paralysis)

This disease, now known to be caused by a filterable virus that attacks the spinal cord in its nerve centers, is often a crippler of young and old alike. Medical authorities now have found that although many persons who have contracted the disease are paralyzed as a result, still more recover from it without any or few bad effects. In fact, it has now been discovered that many persons have had the disease in a mild form and have, consequently, built up an immunity due to repeated exposure to small virus doses. Some few people may even have a natural immunity.

Children crippled from the malady and who are able to be in school should be assigned to classes in physical education. Those who have mild defects may well have classes with normal children. Those wearing braces, using crutches, or who are in wheel chairs may be assigned to the special corrective class.

Although programs in muscle re-education for these children must be built almost entirely upon specific exercise prescribed by medical authorities, the child can often receive great benefits from functional activities found in sports and games. Recreational activities high in social and carryover values need to be stressed.

The victims of this disease above all need to learn to do things for themselves. They should never be waited upon or pampered. They should mingle with normal children as quickly and as much as possible.

Suggested activities for those in wheel chairs include:

Table games	Card games
Darts	Archery
Bait and fly casting	Swimming

Activities suitable for those wearing leg braces, or using crutches include:

Archery	Horseshoes
Shuffleboard	Individual stunts and self-testing
Camping and outing	activities
Swimming	Tether ball
	Bait and fly casting

Activities suggested for those having paralysis of one arm are:

Social dancing	Swimming
Running and other relays using the legs	Individual stunts and self-testing activities
Camping	Roller skating
Rope jumping	Hiking

Cerebral Palsy

Brain-injured children, the victims of cerebral palsy, often have keen intelligence. Authorities claim that approximately 60,000 of the half million children affected are highly educable. Formerly, many persons believed that many of the children were feeble-minded because they looked that way. We now believe that if the child is mentally capable of learning, is emotionally stable, and can get around well enough without a special attendant, he will be better off in a public school than in a special one. Often when cerebral palsied and other exceptional children are too carefully shielded by their parents they become spoiled and maladjusted. For these children especially the value of attending a public school is great.

Types of cerebral palsy most common include: (1) the *spastic,* which makes up the largest number, (2) the *athetoid* which is characterized by involuntary, uncontrollable, jerky movements and which makes up between 25 to 30 per cent of all cases, and (3) the *ataxic* which is characterized by disturbance in balance and posture, inability to control direction, and proneness to perform a multiplicity of eye movements, and which makes up 5 to 10 per cent of all cases. Muscle rigidity and tremor often are found in all three types. Speech disorders and seizures are also common. Deafness is found in some cases of the athetoids.

Children who have cerebral palsy often possess intensified fears of falling, repeated failure, and resulting frustration. Timidity, self-consciousness, and resentfuless may be marked. Many are courageous, happy, and well adjusted, especially if they have had friendly, determined, patient parents. Most of those able to be in school have contributed greatly to the school in the way of spirit and talent.

The teacher needs to explain to all physically normal children and adults the nature of the child's defect, enlist their cooperation to accept him, and help him to help himself. Consideration should be the right of this pupil, just as it is for all others.

The child, if his condition is not too serious, may well be placed with a class of normal children. Because games are the normal outlet of all children, it is important for the exceptional child to receive special aid in learning to do a number, or even a few, with average or above skill. Play activities should be adapted to meet the pupil's own limitation. Highly competitive games and relays should be avoided, for under stress the child may be hurt more than helped.

Those children suffering from more serious injuries should be segregated from the group of normal children and placed in special corrective classes. However, they may well be assigned to classes in which are found those with heart, posture, or other defects previously mentioned. Games stressing balance, timing, and relaxation should be included in the program.

The teacher at all times needs to work not only with the doctor but also the parents. Special exercises recommended by the physician must be carried on at home. Parent training, in the case of the cerebral palsied child, is often almost as important as pupil training.

Suggested activities other than corrective exercises and techniques in relaxation include:

Simple folk dances	Simple singing games
Social dance	Camping and outing
Rhythmic activities	Games of low organization
Simon Says	Horseshoes
Yo-yo or Hi-Li	Shuffleboard
Going to Jerusalem	Target throwing
Swimming	Rope skipping

Epilepsy

A pupil suffering from epilepsy has the same desires, interests, and drives for play as any other child. But, unlike others, he is faced with the great problem of living in a society or group where his affliction is met with great prejudice, ignorance, superstition, and fear. Even the word epilepsy carries great stigma. Fear of rejection from the child's peers and adult associates is constant and may be greatly magnified.

Epilepsy is caused by irritative injuries to the brain. The specific symptoms depend upon which part of the brain has been irritated. The symptoms vary from seizures lasting only a few seconds (Petit Mal or "Little Sickness") to twitching and convulsions in which the person becomes unconscious (Grand Mal or "Big Sickness").

Accurate statistics on the number of cases are not available, due primarily to concealment and stigma. It is, however, a major health problem, and from the standpoint of numbers, it is far more prevalent than most people realize.[6] Some medical authorities now state that one out of every 100 persons in the United States has some form of epilepsy.

Children whose seizures are mild may and do attend public schools. Those with more serious difficulties are in special classes in public schools,

---

[6] International Council on Exceptional Children, Special Committee on Epilepsy: *Education for All American Children, Do We Really Mean It?* 130 North Wells Street, Chicago, Illinois, 1964.

or in private schools. Afflicted persons are educable, many are extremely intelligent, but a few are feeble-minded and non-educable in the usual sense.

Increasingly, medical authorities are turning their attention to epilepsy. The new drugs Dilantin, Tridione, Paradione, Mesantoin, and Phenurone have been found to be most effective; proper use of these medications has reduced the number of seizures in about one-half of the cases. Diagnostic techniques are being improved constantly. The electroencephalograph, an instrument for measuring electrical impulses of the brain, has proved to be of great diagnostic value.

If the epileptic child is in school, he can be helped by understanding teachers who can help the other teachers and pupils to realize that, with the exception of a possible seizure, the child is normal in other ways. Should a seizure occur, the teacher can help the child by not showing fear, horror, or repulsion at the sight. By setting this pattern that the pupils will copy, the teacher can then explain to the others that Johnny or Mary is having an attack which does not hurt him, that he is temporarily asleep or unconscious and when he wakes up he will not even know what happened but will be very tired. The child, after the attack, should be taken to the first-aid room and be allowed to sleep or rest until he wants to get up. When he regains consciousness following a seizure, the first sight that he beholds should not be a circle of classmates and the teacher standing over him terror-stricken. During the seizure the teacher should place a tightly-rolled handkerchief between the child's back teeth, and place him on the floor where he cannot injure himself from convulsive reactions.

Epileptic children placed in school with normal children must be under the care of a physician, who should work closely with the physical education instructor in selecting activities suitable for them. Because they rarely have seizures while engaging in play activities, group participation with the normal should be encouraged. Activities that call for concentration might well be stressed. The controlled epileptic may benefit greatly from competitive sports and team relays which require physical conditioning and much concentration. Swimming, rope climbing, and other activities in which the child would be in danger if an attack might occur must be avoided at all times.

Suggested activities include as many as possible which other children do, and increased rhythmic activities calling for concentration, such as learning intricate tap, social, or folk dance steps.

Lowered Vitality

Children who are underweight, overweight, anemic, or who have had operations, rickets, tuberculosis or other chest ailments fall into this group. All should be given modified school programs, little if any homework, and few responsibilities in both the home and school. Regular physical checkups, an increased balanced diet, sleep and rest, and proper amounts as well as kinds of exercise should be recommended to the pupil and parents by the teacher and the physician. Allowing the pupil to rest or sleep during his physical education class may be for this person the type of physical education he most needs. However, the child should also learn quiet games and take part in modified sports as a part of this program.

Suggested activities include:

Archery	Jacks
Bait and fly casting	Table games, such as checkers,
Building games	pick up sticks, etc.
Hiking	Table card games
Camping and outing	Ping-pong
Games of low organization	Self-testing activities
Marbles	Social, folk and square dance
Singing games	Swimming

Other Deviations

Other deviations of school children include:

Diabetes	Emotional disturbances
Birth injuries	Convalescence
Congenital deformities	Mental deviations
Speech defects	Inefficient body mechanics
Hernia	Nutritional disturbances

Each child requires individual attention. Recommendations made by the physician concerning the type and amount of physical activity best suited for each pupil must be followed to the letter by the teacher. Whenever possible the child should be placed in classes with normal children.

Physical education has much to contribute to the enrichment of the lives of all children. No child with defects need be restricted or denied the opportunity to learn how to play skillfully, or the joy of playing with his classmates and friends. In as much as possible, afflicted children should play the same games as their peers, but the teacher should have the approval of a physician of the suggested individual program for each such child in her group.

SUGGESTED READINGS

American Association for Health, Physical Education, and Recreation: *Bibliography on Research in Psychomotor Function* (Physical Education and Recreation for the Mentally Ill). Washington, D.C., 1966.

Baker, Harry: *Introduction to Exceptional Children,* 3rd Ed., New York, The Macmillan Company, 1961.

Buell, Charles: *Physical Education for Blind Children.* Springfield, Illinois, Charles C Thomas, Publisher, 1966.

Carlson, Bernice, and Ginglend, David: *Play Activities for the Retarded Child.* Nashville, Abingdon Press, 1961.

Clarke, H. Harrison, and Clarke, David: *Developmental and Adapted Physical Education.* Englewood Cliffs, N.J., Prentice-Hall, Inc., 1963.

Fait, Hollis: *Special Education, Adapted, Corrective, Developmental,* 2nd Ed. Philadelphia, W. B. Saunders Company, 1966.

Franklin, C. L.: *Diversified Games and Activities of Low Organization for Mentally Retarded Children.* Carbondale, Ill., Southern Illinois University, 1966.

Hunt, Valerie: *Recreation for the Handicapped.* Englewood Cliffs, N.J., Prentice-Hall, Inc., 1964.

Mathews, D.; Kruse, R.; and Shaw, W.: *The Science of Physical Education for Handicapped Children.* New York, Harper & Row, 1962.

Monkhouse, Ruth: *Proposed P. E. Programs for Educable Mentally Retarded Children.* Master's thesis, University of Texas, 1963.

National Association for Retarded Children: *Day Camping for the Mentally Retarded.* New York, 1966. (25¢)

Pomeroy, Janet: *Recreation for the Handicapped.* New York, The Macmillan Company, 1964.

Rathbone, Josephine: *Corrective Physical Education,* 7th Ed. Philadelphia, W. B. Saunders Company, 1966.

ORGANIZATIONS FROM WHICH HELPFUL INFORMATION CAN BE OBTAINED

American Academy for Cerebral Palsy, Inc., 4743 N. Drake Avenue, Chicago 25, Illinois
American Diabetic Association, 1 E. 45th St., New York 17, N.Y.
American Hearing Society, 817 14th St., N.W., Washington, D.C.
American Medical Association, 535 N. Dearborn St., Chicago 10, Illinois.
American Neurological Association, 710 W. 168th St., New York 32, N.Y.
American Psychiatric Association, Inc., 1270 Avenue of the Americas, New York 20, N.Y.
American Public Health Association, 1790 Broadway, New York 19, N.Y.
Council for Exceptional Children, 1201 16th St. N.W., Washington 6, D.C.
National Association for Retarded Children, 420 Lexington Ave., New York, N.Y.
National Epilepsy League, Inc., 130 N. Wells St., Chicago 6, Illinois.
National Multiple Sclerosis Society, 270 Park Avenue, New York 17, N.Y.
National Society for Crippled Children and Adults, 11 S. LaSalle St., Chicago 3, Illinois.
National Society for Medical Research, 208 N. Wells St., Chicago, Illinois.
Shut-In Society, 221 Lexington Avenue, New York 16, N.Y.
United Cerebral Palsy, Inc., 50 W. 57th St., New York 19, N.Y.

Chapter 21

Recess and
Noon-Hour Activities

Playground activities include recess, before- and after-school play, and noon-hour recreation. Such times are for spontaneous free play in which each child engages in games or does things of his own choosing. These are rich educational times, far more so than most teachers realize. The child of today has now, and will have as tomorrow's adult, more free time than his grandparents or own parents ever dreamed possible. As future adult citizens who are prepared for life, our children must learn how to use their ever increasing free time wisely, how to create their own fun without being constantly or passively entertained, and how to gain refreshment and release from tension.

A small boy once defined recreation as "doing what you do when you don't have to." The college professor explains that it is those activities voluntarily done during leisure which bring satisfaction and joy and are socially approved. Both are right, for recreation does mean re-creation, renewal, refreshment, relaxation, fun, spontaneity, joyfulness, and fullness of life. Aristotle, born 384 B.C., claimed that the whole end and object of education is the right use of leisure. Present-day educators are increasingly seeing the great wisdom of his statement.

Recess and noon-hour play helps the child maintain and develop good health through increased exercise, provides opportunity for him to practice and improve in physical and social skills, and gives him a chance to let off steam in legitimate ways. Above all, these are valued free-choice and experimental learning times in which the youth prepares for his own unsupervised adulthood when he must be ably skilled at making his own choices regarding life and living his daily 24 hours on and off the job. Education for positive use of leisure time is a *must* in our contemporary society.

Figure 58.   Recess and noon-hour play help the child maintain and develop good health through increased exercise, provide opportunity for him to practice and improve in physical and social skills, and give him a chance to let off steam in legitimate ways. (Courtesy of Elizabeth Glidden, Specialist in Elementary Physical Education, Los Angeles City Schools, Los Angeles, California.)

ADMINISTRATIVE DETAILS

It is imperative that the school provide adequate and safe facilities as well as teacher leadership and supervision during these periods of play. Schedules for recess time should be staggered so that not too many children are on the grounds at one time. The allotted period should be long enough to allow each child to use some of the apparatus, run and play with others, as well as have enough time to go to the bathroom, wash his hands, and get a drink of water. For safety reasons primary classes should be assigned a permanent play space next to the main building that has enough shade and sunlight to produce and safeguard health. Older children should be given their own play area far enough away from the younger ones so that both groups can play safely.

All free-play periods should be well supervised. No teacher should be assigned more than 50 to 75 children. Male teachers might well be asked to supervise both sexes on the upper elementary level. A first-aid box

Figure 59.   Education for positive use of leisure time is a *must* for all children in our society, for they and all other Americans must learn how to use their ever-increasing free time wisely. Youth must learn how to create their own fun without being passively entertained or constantly supervised by adults. (Courtesy of Youth Services Section, Los Angeles City Schools.)

should be located on the grounds or just inside the door of the main building. Records and careful study should be made of all accidents which occur. Both students and teachers will profit from making a careful study of these reports and together devising ways to make the play area safer for all classes and individuals.

Noon-hour recreation should follow a supervised and unhurried lunch period. If one hour is allowed for this activity, only half of it should be given over to free-choice play. No child should be permitted to gulp down his lunch in order to join his friends in rugged play, because such action would not be educationally sound. Together, youth and adults should set up rules regarding how long students should be expected to stay in the lunchroom and how much time may be given over to play. Quiet games, social dancing, and such dual games as box hockey or deck tennis are recommended. It is unwise to schedule highly competitive intramural games during this period because the development of good eating habits in a relaxed atmosphere is as important in the life of growing boys and girls as outdoor exercise.

SAFETY PRECAUTIONS

Although there should be few rules regarding the playground, these might well be devised by the children themselves with teacher guidance. All hazardous equipment should be discovered and marked by each class group when taken on a tour of the area by its teacher. Bright yellow paint or white markings striped with red for protruding rocks, swing apparatus, posts, etc., is recommended. Children should be taught how to use correctly each piece of apparatus and equipment, as well as how to care for perishable articles such as rackets and balls. All apparatus should be inspected by a reliable adult at least once monthly.[1]

ACTIVITIES

Most of the games mentioned in this book can be played outdoors. However, the following ones are especially suitable for recess and noon-hour play.

MARBLES

This game is best for two or not more than six players. Ten or more marbles are encircled in a drawn ring. All players stand behind a line 4 to 6 feet away. Each "lags" or rolls his shooting marble, the largest one called his "taw," toward the ring trying to knock out as many of the enclosed marbles as possible. Players then take turns, each shooting his taw, by flipping it with his tumb out of his curved hand and from his bent index finger.

FOX AND GEESE

Two players sit 4 to 6 feet away facing each other with legs spread apart. Each arranges his 20 to 30 marbles in lines or in a flying geese V formation before a line drawn in front of his feet. Players take turns rolling 4 to 6 big taws (foxes) toward the others' marbles (geese) trying to hit and knock them behind the line. Play continues until one has destroyed all the others' geese.

---

[1] See Chapter 4, *The Gymnasium, Playground, Pool, and Classroom,* for suggested outdoor play areas, apparatus, and equipment.

HOPSCOTCH

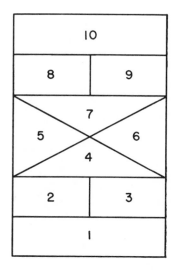

Playground, tennis courts and sidewalks
Grades: Girls 1 to 4; boys 1 and 2
Players: 4 to 6 to court

This game is enjoyed by all children but is particularly suitable in remedial cases where limited activity is recommended.

1. Second through fourth grades.

   Player throws pebble into square 1, hops in on one foot, picks up pebble and hops out.

   The pebble then is thrown into square 2, the player hops on one foot into 1, straddles 2 and 3, picks up the pebble, puts weight on left foot and hops into 1 and out. The player may continue until the pebble fails to land in the proper square or he steps on a line or puts a foot down when he should not. He hops on one foot into 1, 4, 7, and 10 and straddles the lines to retrieve the pebble in 2, 3, 5, 6, 8, and 9.

2. First graders like more activity so they follow the above instructions but hop to the end and back each time.

Variations: Play the game as above, hopping from one number to the next without missing.

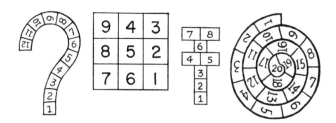

JUMP ROPE

Class instruction should be given in progression as follows:

Rope is swung back and forth in pendulum fashion. Child jumps from one side to the other.

Child stands by rope and jumps as it describes a large full circle.

Front door—Child learns to run in as rope comes toward jumper.

Back door—Child learns to run in as rope goes away.

Hot pepper—Fast jump.

Jump rope ditties—The most popular ditties chanted by today's children as they skip rope are included below. These ditties are made up by the children and apparently understood by the young fry though the connotation in some may seem vague to adults. Sometimes the words dictate certain movements while others simply give each jumper a fair turn at the rope.

Figure 60. Jumping rope provides practice in developing coordination and rhythm as well as being good exercise. (Courtesy of Elizabeth Glidden, Specialist in Elementary Physical Education, Los Angeles City Schools, Los Angeles, California.)

DITTIES

1. Had a little radio
   Put it in free
   Only station I could get
   Was W-B-Z. (*Hot pepper until jumper misses*)

2. Bubble gum, bubble gum,
   Chew and blow,
   Bubble gum, bubble gum,
   Scrape your toe.
   Bubble gum, bubble gum,
   Tastes so sweet
   Get that bubble gum off your feet. (*Runs out*)

3. Momma, momma, I am sick
   Call the doctor quick, quick, quick
   How many pills must I take? (*Count 1, 2, 3 until misses*)

4. Ice cream soda
   Delaware punch
   Tell me the name
   Of your honey bunch.
   Alphabet a, b, c, etc.,
     (*When jumper misses she names a boy to take her place
     whose name begins with the letter on which she missed*)

5. Blue bells, cockle shells
   Evie, Ivy, Over. (*Count 1, 2, 3, etc., until misses*)

6. Cinderella dressed in yellow
   Went upstairs to kiss her fellow
   How many kisses did she get? (*Count 1, 2, 3, until misses*)
   Cinderella dressed in green
   Went upstairs to eat ice cream
   How many spoonfuls did she eat? (*Count jumps 1, 2, 3*)
   Cinderella dressed in black
   Went upstairs and sat on a tack
   How many stitches did it take? (*Count jumps 1, 2, 3*)

7. One, two, buckle my shoe
   Three, four, shut the door
   Five, six, pick up sticks
   Seven, eight, lay them straight
   Nine, ten, big fat hen
   Eleven, twelve, bake her well. (*Count 1, 2, 3*)

8. Down in the meadow
   Where the green grass grows
   There sat Mary (*name of jumper*)
   As sweet as a rose.
   She sang and she sang
   And she sang so sweet
   Along came Joe (*boy friend*)
   And kissed her on the cheek.
   How many kisses did she get? (*Count*)

9. Teddie Bear, Teddie Bear
   Turn around
   Teddie Bear, Teddie Bear
   Touch the ground
   Teddie Bear, Teddie Bear
   Go upstairs (*jumps toward head of rope*)
   Teddie Bear, Teddie Bear
   Say your prayers
   Teddie Bear, Teddie Bear
   Turn out the light
   Teddie Bear, Teddie Bear
   Say good night.

10. Mable, Mable
    Set the table
    And don't forget
    The Red Hot Pepper.

11. *Twenty-four robbers.*
    Not last night but the night before
    Twenty-four robbers came knocking at my door.
    I ran out and they ran in
    And this is the song they sang to me.
    Spanish dancer, do a split
    Spanish dancer, do a high kick
    Spanish dancer, turn around
    Spanish dancer, touch the ground
    Spanish dancer, do the kangaroo (*squat and jump*)
    Spanish dancer, skit, skat, skidoo!

12. Shirley Temple (or Charlie McCarthy) went to France
    To teach the children how to dance
    A heel and a toe and around you go,
    A heel and a toe and around I go,
    Salute to the Captain,
    Bow to the King,
    Turn your back on the Ugly Ole Queen.
        (*Run out back door*)

13. *Nonsense.*

    Buster Brown went to town
    With his britches up-side down.
    Out rolled a nickel
    He bought a pickle
    The pickle was sour
    He bought some flour
    The flour was yellow
    He bought him a fellow
    The fellow was mean
    He bought a bean
    The bean was hard
    He bought a card
    And on the card
    It said, Red Hot Pepper.

PADDLE TENNIS

This game is played like regular tennis except that the ball is served underhand and hit with a wooden paddle. The server stands behind the serving line in the right court and serves the ball diagonally across the net in one or two tries into his opponent's receiving court. After the ball bounces once, it is hit back across the net and the game continues until one hits the ball into the net, out of bounds, or misses it. The game is scored like tennis: 15, 30, 40, Game, except when both have a tie score of 40–40 or "deuce," after which two consecutive points must be made. The game may be played by two of four players.

Variations: *Hand Tennis:* played by batting a ball back and forth with one or another hand. *Kick Tennis:* played by kicking a soccer or playground ball back and forth across the net using the same rules.

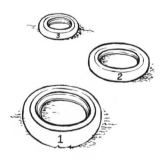

PLAYGROUND GOLF

Tennis balls or beanbags can be thrown into numbered tin cans or rubber tires scattered over the area. Players take turns trying to throw the ball into these in as few tosses as possible.

Variation: Sink numbered poles in partially buried tin cans in a widely scattered area. Hit a golf, ping-pong or jack ball into the can with a broomstick.

Figure 61. Paddle tennis is similar to regular tennis except that the ball is served underhand and is hit with a wooden paddle. (Courtesy of Elizabeth Glidden, Specialist in Elementary Physical Education, Los Angeles City Schools, Los Angeles, California.)

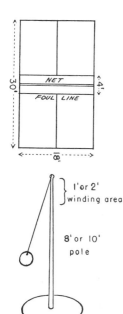

DECK TENNIS

This game is played with a round rubber deck-tennis ring or rope ring by two or four players. The rules are similar to volleyball in that one continues serving as long as he wins a point; when he loses it, "side out" is called and his opponent now serves. The server begins the game by throwing the ring underhand, across, or to one side of his body into the diagonally opposite half court. Loss of serve occurs from catching the ring with both hands, changing it from one hand to the other, stepping on or over the serving line, throwing the ring into the net or out of bounds.

The game consists of 15 points. If the score becomes tied at 14-all, two consecutive points must be made. As many as 20 players can play, but the game is best for smaller groups.

TETHER BALL

The game object is to hit the ball so that it will wind around the pole, one person choosing to hit it always in one direction and his opponent hits in the other. Score one point for winding the ball around the pole. Play for 5 or 10 points. Players must take turns hitting the ball.

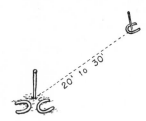

Shuffleboard

(Children's Game)

Equipment: 4 cues shaped to curve around the disc, 8 discs, each set of 4 being of separate colors (red, green, etc.)

The object is to score the most points. Players alternate turns. To count, the disc must be inside but not touching any line. A player may move his own disc by hitting it into a better position. Scoring is done after each has shot all of his discs. In doubles, two opponents play side by side at one end, alternating turns until all have been hit. Then their partners play in the same manner, starting from the oposite court end. Their scores are tallied with those previously made by their partner.

Horseshoes

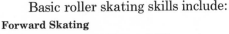

Equipment: Two stakes placed 20 to 30 feet apart, 4 regular or hard rubber horseshoes.

In singles, two players start from the same stake by taking turns before throwing from the opposite stake. In doubles, each team member takes turns at each court end. The closest shoe scores 1, a ringer 3. The game consists of 21 points.

Roller Skating

Upper elementary children greatly enjoy roller skating. Many schools include instruction in this activity in their physical education programs. Although pupils can best be taught to roller skate individually, after the basic movements have been mastered, the children can be grouped according to achievement levels for recess and noon-hour activity, as well as for needed practice.[2] The children should learn how to skate forward, stop, make turns, skate with a partner, do the crossover or corner turn, and skate with a partner and three or more pupils in a single line. More advanced pupils will enjoy skating to music during the noon hour, as well as learning how to waltz, fox-trot, and perform many other kinds of dance steps on skates. Square dancing on skates is especially exciting to those older pupils who have already learned how to do successfully the many movement skills this type of dancing offers.

Basic roller skating skills include:

Forward Skating

1. Pretend you are running and sliding on ice.
2. Push forward on one skate, glide on the other. Repeat.
3. Take bigger movements, trying to cover more distance on each foot.

---

[2] Price, Herbert, and Koch, Claire: Teach roller skating skills. *The Journal of Health, Physical Education, Recreation,* March, 1960.

Figure 62. Roller skating is a splendid noon-hour activity, for it can lead to better use of leisure time during after-school hours. (Courtesy of AAHPER.)

Stopping

1. Put weight on the inside skate.
2. Point the toe of the outside skate outward; bring heels closely together.
3. Press weight down on the outside skate and drag it behind the forward skate.

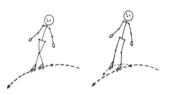

The Cross-over Turn

1. For the two-foot learning turn, place the inside skate in front of the outside skate and lean to the inside.
2. For the one-foot leaning turn, glide on the inside skate and bring the outside skate forward in front of the body as the turn is made.

Skating Backward

1. Point toes in and push one skate backward and glide on the other.
2. At corners, cross the inside skate behind the outside skate.

The Waltz

1. Boy skates forward; girl backward.
2. Skate in rhythm, accenting the first beat.

Trio Skating

1. Two boys, girl in the middle.
2. Hook elbows and all move forward on the right foot, or back on the left in unison.

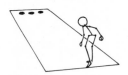

PIT BOWLING

Play with up to four individual players or in teams of three.

Each player rolls croquet balls or softballs toward three pits dug in the ground 20 feet away.

Score three points for each ball that lands in the hole. Play for individual or team points.

TIN CAN GOLF

Sink tin cans in the ground for holes. Players use improvised sticks and old tennis balls, croquet mallets and balls, or hockey sticks and balls.

Arrange the cans like a clock face with each hole across the circle from the preceding one, i.e., 1, 3, 5; 7, 9, 11; 6, 8, 10.

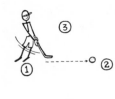

Use posts that extend about a foot above the ground instead of sunken cans, if desired. Each hole is made when the ball hits the proper post. A ball may be kicked instead of hit with the hands.

The winner completes the course in the least number of strokes.

CROQUET

Played with a wooden ball and mallet, the object of this game is to be the first to hit the ball through all the arches up and down the court. Simplified rules include:

1. Each player alternates turns hitting the ball, starting a mallet's distance in front of the starting stake and attempting to drive the ball through the first two wickets.
2. Each players is given another hit for going through an arch or hitting another's ball or the turning stake at the opposite end of the court. Two more hits are earned if the ball goes through both first arches, but if through any other two arches, the player has the right of a mallet's length ahead in any direction, plus one stroke.
3. One loses a hit for playing out of turn.
4. Each ball must go through each numbered arch in proper progression.
5. A ball driven out of bounds may be put back on the boundary line where it went off.
6. One missing the ball entirely with the mallet may have a second turn.
7. If one's ball hits another, the owner may put it next to the one struck, step on it while she hits her own ball hard enough to send the other's far down the court or out of position, or she may measure a mallet's distance in any direction and hit her ball from there.

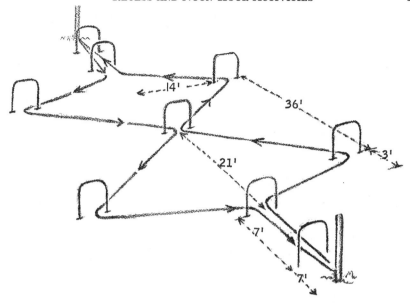

SHUFFLEBOARD

Played by two or four, the game object is to propel discs, using a cue, onto scoring diagrams at the opposite end of the court in order to score, or prevent one's opponent from scoring. Simplified rules are:

1. The red disc is shot first and then the two players alternate shooting black and red discs until all are shot from one end of the court and then the other.
2. In doubles, after all discs are played at the head of the court, play starts at the foot with red leading. Red player and a black one stand at each end of the court, alternating turns, each shooting 2 discs.
3. A game consists of 50, 75, or 100 points.
4. After players have shot all four discs, score all within the court area but do not count those on any line.

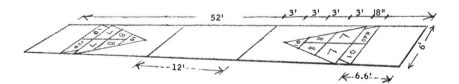

ROPE QUOITS

Played by two or four or any number, with either purchased or improvised equipment.

Rules

1. Each player shoots 4 quoits per frame, when it is his time to shoot.

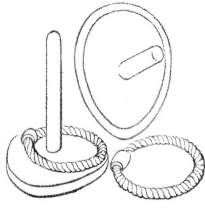

2. Opponents then shoot 4 quoits in the same manner.
3. "Ringers" count 5 points each. All other quoits remaining on the base count one point each. Quoits that go off the board are lost, and do not score any points.
4. A game consists of 10 frames for each player in the game.
5. The player having the highest score wins.
6. Players' feet must be behind the foul line or designated shooting point when the quoit is thrown; otherwise the shot is a foul and does not score.
7. The distance from foul line or shooting line to the rope-quoit base should be as near 15 feet as possible.
8. Any number of partners may play in a game as in shuffleboard or bowling. Partners having the highest score win.

JACKS

Equipment: 6 jacks, small rubber ball
Players: 4–6 in a circle
Play area: Sidewalk, hallway, classroom, cafeteria

1. All jacks are tossed on the ground.
2. Player tosses ball into air, picks up a jack, and catches the ball before it hits the ground.
3. Each continues until misses or all single jacks are picked up; players take turns and go as far as possible.
4. After picking all jacks up by 1's, proceeds in the same manner by 2's (picks up two jacks when ball is tossed): then by 3's, 4's, 5's, and 6's.
5. All jacks tossed on ground, tosses ball into the air, brushes jacks singly into cupped other hand (Pigs in a Pen), does 2's, 3's, etc.
6. All jacks tossed on ground, ball into air, picks up jack with other hand and catches it on the back of the hand before catching the ball; does 1's, 2's, 3's, etc.
7. Add as many variations as possible.

Variations: *Eggs in the Basket:* jacks are picked up and transferred to the other hand before catching the ball. *Pigs in the Pen:* jacks are swept into opposite hand between spread fingers. *Lambs Over the Wall:* jacks are lifted over the opposite hand held in wall position. *Lazy Susan:* the ball is bounced twice before the jacks are picked up. *Rapid Fire:* the ball is never allowed to bounce or hit the playing surface.

SUGGESTED READINGS

Armbruster, David, and Irwin, Leslie: *Basic Skills in Sports,* 2nd Ed. St. Louis, C. V. Mosby Company, 1967.

Blake, O. William, and Volp, Anne: *Lead-up Games to Team Sports.* Englewood Cliffs, N.J., Prentice-Hall, 1964.

Carter, Joel: *How to Make Athletic Equipment.* Englewood Cliffs, N.J. Prentice-Hall, Inc., 1960.

Donnelly, Richard, et al.: *Active Games and Contests.* New York, Ronald Press, 1958.

Kraus, Richard: *Recreation Today, Program Planning and Leadership.* New York, Appleton-Century-Crofts, 1966.

Mulac, Margaret: *Games and Sports for Schools, Camps and Playgrounds.* New York, Harper & Row, 1964.

Van der Smissen, Betty, and Knierim, Helen: *Recreational Sports and Games.* Minneapolis, Burgess Press, 1964.

Vannier, Maryhelen, and Poindexter, Hally Beth: *Individual and Team Sports for Girls and Women,* 2nd Ed. Philadelphia, W. B. Saunders Company, 1968.

Chapter 22

Intramural and After-School Activities

CLASS COMPETITION AND TOURNAMENTS

Competitive class tournaments are suggested for grades, squads, teams, and individuals. Basically and in itself, competition for children is good if conducted under the proper conditions of good leadership and if too much stress is not placed upon winning. Children like to compete, to match and test their skill with others. However, games and athletic activities best suited for their own age groups must be selected for competitive purposes. Types of competition possible are: (1) Single Elimination Tournaments, (2) Winning-Loser Tournaments, (3) Ladder Tournaments, and (4) Round Robin Tournaments.

SINGLE ELIMINATION TOURNAMENTS

If the original number of contestants is a perfect power of two, no modification of this diagram is necessary. When the number of contestants is not a perfect power of two, byes are added until this is reached. The number of byes should equal the difference between the number of competitors and the next higher power of two. When fifteen are entered there will be one bye (16 − 15 = 1) etc.

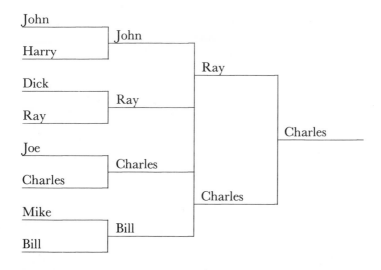

The number of byes should be divided so that one-half of them appear at the top of the drawing and the remaining half at the bottom.

WINNER-LOSER TOURNAMENT

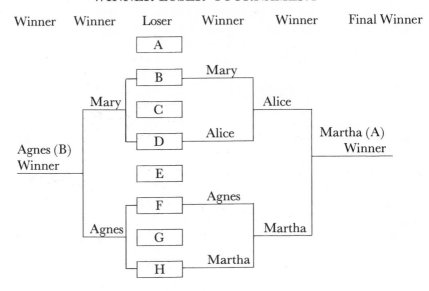

The principle for adding byes in this type of tournament is the same as in the elimination tournament. Winners move out to the right of the chart; losers move out to the left in the second round, and winners continue to move out to the left or right in all continuing rounds.

LADDER TOURNAMENT

Individuals or teams are arranged in ladder formation. Any player may challenge another player directly above. If the challenger is successful in defeating the opponent, his name takes the place of the defeated team, and vice versa. The final winner remains in the first position at the completion of the tournament.

| Team 1 |
| Team 2 |
| Team 3 |
| Team 3 |
| Team 4 |
| Team 5 |
| etc. |

ROUND ROBIN TOURNAMENTS

In this type of competition the revolving column is the simplest for pairing opponents. Numbers are given to teams or individuals. Bye is used in the place of teams or individuals if there is an uneven number of competitors. Pairing of competitors is done by placing them in two columns. Once teams or individuals are given a number and once the numbers appear on the tournament chart, that order must be maintained. Competitors are arranged in the following manner:

1 Jack	bye Ray
2 Agnes	7 Peggy
3 Martha	8 Bill
4 Alice	9 Catherine
5 Harry	10 Greg
6 Charles	11 Betty

Players are moved either clockwise or counterclockwise to meet their opponents. If there is a bye it remains stationary, each number jumping over it to the next place:

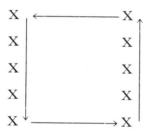

One fewer round is played than the number of teams or individuals entered. The pairings and series for a round robin tournament for eight teams are given below:

	First Round		*Second Round*		*Third Round*
1	8	1	7	1	6
2	7	8	6	7	5
3	6	2	5	8	4
4	5	3	4	2	3

	Fourth Round		*Fifth Round*		*Sixth Round*		*Seventh Round*
1	5	1	4	1	3	1	2
6	4	5	3	4	2	3	8
7	3	6	2	5	8	4	7
8	2	7	8	6	7	5	6

The pairings will be different in each round. The team winning the most games is declared the winner. The above procedure may be followed for any number of teams if a bye is used for an uneven number. When all players have played each other in each round, the tournament is completed.

TYPES OF COMPETITION SUITABLE FOR CHILDREN

Suggested games and sports for tournament competition for young children include:

Athletic games—(Soccer dodgeball, kick ball, newcomb, base football, touch football for grade 6, circle goal shooting, softball, etc.)
Hopscotch
Jump rope
Kicking soccer balls for distance
Kite making and flying
Marbles
Relays of all kinds
Running races
Stunts and self-testing activities (individual)
Target throws

SUGGESTED COMPETITIVE ACTIVITIES FOR UPPER ELEMENTARY CHILDREN

Suggested competitive activities for upper elementary children include:

Team Games

Touch Football
Modified touch football games
Football keep-away
Centering relays
Passing relays
Pass or punt back game
Place kick, punt, and/or pass for accuracy and/or distance

Soccer
7 or 9 player soccer, speedball, and/or speed-away
Circle and/or line soccer
Soccer goal kick
Passing and dribbling relays
Goal kicking for accuracy

Volleyball
Modified volleyball
Ball keep-up
Newcomb
Serving, passing, and/or volleying for accuracy

Softball

> Throws for accuracy and distance
> Timed base running
> Lead-up games (Beat the Ball, Throw It and Run, etc.)
> Modified softball

Basketball

> Basket shooting contests
> Dribbling, passing for accuracy and speed
> Lead-up games (Twenty One, Drop In, Drop Out, etc.)
> Sideline basketball
> 6 or 9 court basketball

Other

> Circle team dodgeball
> Modified field hockey
> Modified lacrosse

Individual Sports

Swimming

> Speed and distance team and individual contests using a variety of strokes
> Swimming for form

Track and Field

> 20–40–60 yard dashes
> 220–440 yard distance events
> Hurdles
> High jumps
> Running and standing broad jumps
> Lighter shot put
> Standing hop-step-jump
> Throws for distances using balls of various weight and size
> Shuttle relays

Other

> Deck, table, and paddle tennis
> Badminton
> Tennis
> Shuffleboard
> Horseshoes
> Rope jumping
> Yo-Yo tops
> Hula hoop contests
> Camping and outing activities
> Lawn and alley bowling
> Handball
> Bicycle races and obstacle courses
> Roller and ice skating
> Marbles

ORGANIZATION OF PROGRAMS

An intramural director should be in overall charge of the program, assisted by the individual leader and student leaders from each competing unit. The latter are best peer-elected rather than teacher-selected and they should assist as team captains, equipment helpers, officials, scorers and timers, record keepers, and news reporters. An intramural council made up of the director and student leaders is suggested, thus providing opportunities for student leadership development and an overall governing body.

The program should be for *all* children, including the handicapped and those of various skill abilities; grouping may be by classroom or grades, age, sex, skills, height and weight, and interest. All school and community facilities should be used for the program.

Activities can be scheduled before and after school, during extended lunch periods, as a scheduled part of the school day, on Saturdays and holidays, and during school vacations.

Written policies should be drawn up regarding awards, transportation, finance and budget, records, eligibility and parental approval, medical care, safety and first aid, and accident and liability insurance. The program should be evaluated frequently to determine its effectiveness in relationship to the stated aims, goals, and objectives. No program can be measured realistically by the number of participants, for it is the increased growth of each child who takes part in it that matters most.

CLASSIFICATION OF PLAYERS

Intramural activities are those physical activities conducted between groups of students within one school. A successful program depends upon equality between competing teams or individuals. It is advisable to classify students according to a plan which includes the factors of age, height, weight, and sex. For safety reasons, boys and girls should be separated for most competitive sports after ten years of age, for boys at this age tend to surpass girls in strength, flexibility, endurance, and speed. However, because of social values inherent in team play, opportunities should be provided for boys and girls to be members of the same team as many times as possible during each semester.

Younger children of primary age should be classified in different groups according to their capacity to enter into different levels of graded activities. Physical examinations and skill tests are the best way to determine this capacity.

Individual players may be classified for all competitive events according to age, height, and weight or a combination of these factors.

The teacher, aided by squad leaders, might well select team mem-

Figure 63. Competition for children is good if conducted under good leadership and if too much stress is not placed upon winning. (Courtesy of AAHPER.)

bers, who in turn will elect their captains. This provides for a more reliable equalization of team skill, for children tend to choose their best friends rather than skillful players. Often the class ugly duckling or motor moron is either left out or is usually the last one chosen. Children, like adults, want to be first; it is ego-damaging to be last always.

Another suggested way for selecting teams is for the group to select the needed number of captains. These chosen leaders stand facing the class, who will count off according to the number of captains. As each one calls out his number, he goes and stands behind the captain having the corresponding number. This method is often superior to having circled groups number off in teams, for some pupils will be wise enough to count ahead and change places with one or two others in order to be on the desired team. Another method is selecting captains by pupil vote, having each player draw a number out of a hat, and stand behind the numbered captain drawn.

If the major emphasis is placed upon fun rather than winning, the children will gradually select the method which to them seems fairest for classifying and forming teams. They should be encouraged to experiment with as many methods as possible. We learn to know what we want by finding out from experience what we do not want. Experience is not only the best teacher, it can also be an ideal way for learning how to make good judgments.

CLUB ORGANIZATION

Pupils may be organized into clubs for competitive purposes. Class, grade or team and homeroom teams are suggested. Group or physical education class groups may compete with members from other classes in after-school play. Interest groups may be organized into teams or individuals to compete against each other. Whatever sub-division or organizational play is followed, the teacher should stress 100 per cent group participation and work toward that end.

An after-school leader's club might well be developed. Members may be either teacher-selected or pupil-elected. These pupils can be trained to organize competitive groups, assist in officiating, scoring, and record-keeping as well as planning and evaluating the complete program for a season, term, or year. The club might also be responsible for issuing, caring for, and checking-in equipment. Bulletin board publicity, loud speaker announcements, and newspaper reports offer splendid means for integrating the total program with English as well as other subjects.

THE SEASONAL PROGRAM

The total after-school program should be organized around seasonal sports and games. Kite flying contests, marble, jack, or jump rope tournaments are best in the spring. Lead-up games to football are best in the fall season, whereas basketball-type games are most ideal for the winter.

The following seasonal program might serve as a guide around which the leader could make additions:

Fall Season

Line soccer	grade 4
Shuttle-pass soccer relay	grades 5, 6
Simplified soccer	grades 5, 6
Pin soccer	grade 4
Relays	grades 1, 2, 3, 4, 5, 6

Winter Season

Dodgeball	grades 4, 5, 6

Basketball shuttle relay	grades 4, 5, 6
Newcomb	grades 2, 3
Keep away	grades 2, 3
Captain ball	grades 4, 5, 6
Relays	grades 1, 2, 3, 4, 5, 6

Spring Season

Base kickball	grades 3, 4
Kickball	grades 3, 4, 5, 6
Jacks	grades 1, 2, 3
Hopscotch	grades 1, 2, 3
Jump rope	grades 1, 2, 3
Kite flying	grades 4, 5, 6
Relays	grades 1, 2, 3, 4, 5, 6
Camping skill contests	grades 4, 5, 6

A seasonal program provides a logical progression from lesson to lesson and season to season. Simple games that use the basic skills of running, throwing, catching, jumping, hopping, creeping, and hanging should be stressed through grade 4. More advanced games into which these fundamental movements are integrated should be stressed beginning at the fifth grade level.

SPECIAL EVENTS

Play Days

Play days or community get-together days are excellent ways to get parents to come see what their children have learned. The primary purpose of the play day is to provide mass participation in all the games, stunts, rhythmic activities, hunting games, campcraft skills, and individual events. Every student should take an active part, not just the best from each school or class.

Play days may be organized for all the children (1) within one school, (2) in two or three neighboring schools combined, (3) from all schools in the district, or (4) for the whole county. Small play days organized at the close of the fall, winter, and spring programs offer incentive for teachers and children to plan and carry out a systematized progressive program.

Suggestions for conducting a successful play day include:

1. Have a definite theme such as a rodeo day, national airplane, car or horse race, the olympic games, a popular holiday, etc.
2. Separate pupils from each school or class so that each team will be made up of members from different schools or classes.

3. Divide the players into teams built around the chosen theme:
   a. Rodeo—bronchos, mustangs, cowboys, etc.
   b. Airplane race—T.W.A., Braniff, American, United, etc.
   c. Olympic games—U.S., Germany, England, Italy, etc.
   d. Popular holiday (Christmas)—trees, toys, reindeer, etc.
4. Have each team wear a favor or symbol representive of the theme.
5. Play games known to all, but change their names to fit the theme.
   a. Rodeo—a running race becomes a wild horse race across the plains, etc.
   b. Airplane—a running race becomes a non-stop flight from Los Angeles to New York, etc.
   c. Olympic games—a running race becomes a foot race of contestants bringing a lighted torch from Mt. Olympus to Helsinki, etc.
   d. Popular holiday—a running race becomes a race for reindeers for an honored place on Santa's Christmas team, etc.
6. Have each group make up a team yell, motto, or song.
7. Have each group compete in other areas too, such as singing, charades, dancing, guessing games.
8. If refreshments are served, change the name of the food to fit the theme.
9. Award simple prizes to winning team members, such as magazine pictures, ribbons, tin cups. etc.
10. Have a definite beginning and ending to the entire program and to each event.

Other Special Events

Assembly programs, demonstrations, field days, special exhibits, motion-picture films and colored slides, special programs prepared for community groups, festivals, along with other such events are rich opportunities for selling physical education to the public. People support the things in which they believe. They can see values in a football game. They rarely have an opportunity to see a good physical education program. Special events call for hard work, but values gained from extra hours of labor pay great dividends in increased student-parent interest and support to the teacher and what she teaches.

DEMONSTRATIONS

An annual public demonstration should be the outgrowth of the regular physical education program. It should be the best of the year's program but never its goal. All children should participate rather than the few selected best. Demonstrations may show (1) a typical class period, (2) a survey of all activities covered during the year, (3) pupil-parent activities in which the pupil demonstrates first, then the parent, or (4) a program centered around a general theme.

Rehearsals of the demonstration should be held largely during class period and little after-school time should be taken up with practice. Mass rehearsals held one or two days before the performance aid in smoothing out rough spots. These practices should include the procession and recession order, the finale and large numbers, each separate number on the program taken up in order, plus a check of the general effect of costumes, music, etc.

Rhythms, 5th Grade

Demonstration

Figure 64.   Children should be provided with opportunities to demonstrate to adults the many skills they have learned in their physical education classes. (Hastings Public School, Hastings, Nebraska.)

Scenery and costumes should be of secondary importance but should be made, in as far as is practicable, largely by the pupils. A scarf tied around the regulation uniform can do much to change its appearance.

The sample program which follows may serve as a suggested guide for a demonstration program showing the work done in six elementary classes.

A. Entrance March   all pupils

B. Singing Games   grades 1, 2

    Hickory, Dickory, Dock
    Little Jack Horner
    The Muffin Man
    Did You Ever See A Lassie?

C. Stunts and Tumbling   grades 3, 4
    Inchworm Walk
    Elephant Walk
    Forward and Backward Somersaults
    The Merry-Go-Round
    Pyramids

D. Relays   grades 4, 5
    Wheelbarrow Relay
    Ropejump Relay
    Tenpin Relay
    Forty Ways to Get There Relay

E. Grade Games   4th grade boys
    Line Dodgeball
    Line Soccer
    Hit Pin Baseball

F. Grade Games   4th grade girls
    Newcomb
    Shuffleboard
    Kickball

G. Square Dancing   grades 5, 6
    Old Dan Tucker   boys and girls
    Virginia Reel
    Starlight Schottische
    Butterfly Polka

H. Gymnastic Drill   grades 4, 5, 6
    Five minutes of exercises done to command.

I. Departure March   all pupils

SCHOOL ASSEMBLY PROGRAMS

Special programs given in assembly can be a rich educational experience. It can be an excellent means of educating the principal and other teachers, and can lead to better understanding and appreciation on the part of the pupils.

The presentation may be (1) a general orientation, (2) a recognition assembly, or (3) a special subject assembly.

The general orientation assembly is best held at the beginning of the new year. It is a grand means of acquainting newcomers with the objectives and activities included in the physical education program. Pupils can demonstrate games, dances, and other activities. Films might be shown which stress good sportsmanship, or playground safety. The program can also be used to stimulate interest in coming events. Outside speakers may give illustrated talks or demonstrations.

The recognition assembly is the time leaders are given public acclaim for skill, leadership ability, or some contribution made to the school. Pupils can give short speeches stressing values of good health, fair play, or team loyalty. Songs or short poems may be interspersed with the talks. Awards given to outstanding pupils may be in the form of verbal recognition or actual presentation of a tangible inexpensive object.

The special subject assembly is often used to introduce new activities to the pupils or re-acquaint them with familiar ones. Posture, safety, Indian dancing, and games from other lands might be used.

EXHIBITS

Although exhibits are often associated with a large occasion, such as National Education Week or National Safety Week, the school exhibit can be a separate type of demonstration. A corridor, bulletin board, or room may be used for the display. Pupils should make, gather, and assemble all materials to be shown, working under the guidance of the teacher. Emphasis may be placed around such themes as the total physical education program, safety, good health habits, leisure-time, play, posture, or illustrated materials showing the work done in the department or class. Snapshots taken of pupils on the playground might be arranged attractively on a bulletin board. Mimeographed material may also be laid out for free distribution. Samples of toothpaste, cereal, soap, etc., may be obtained from companies interested primarily in using this type of advertising. Hobby samples often make an interesting exhibit and sometimes start new enthusiasts on a pleasurable pursuit of developing a new skill or interest.

PROGRAMS FOR COMMUNITY GROUPS

The physical education department or classroom teacher is frequently asked to prepare programs for civic groups. As far as possible, these programs should be drawn from the actual program in the school and be a fair representation of it. Spectacular performances given by a few should be kept at a minimum. Preferably as many pupils as possible should take part. Such programs often make a valuable contribution toward developing better understanding and appreciation between the school and community, the teacher and parent.

In conducting all special events, the teacher should assume the responsibility for organizing, conducting, and evaluating them. Student chairmen and their various committees should assist with all aspects of the event. Questions to be answered honestly both by the teacher and pupils when evaluating the outcome of each program are:

1. What changes were made in pupil growth in developing desirable attitudes, new skills, and new knowledge?

2. To what degree did the program acquaint others with the real purpose and content of our physical education classwork and program?

3. What increased opportunities should be given to students next time in planning, conducting, and evaluating the program?

4. How many school people commented favorably on it? How many parents? What did other pupils say about it?

FOOTBALL, BASEBALL, AND BASKETBALL COMPETITION

One major problem facing the elementary teacher is when to allow boys and girls to compete on a sponsored school team against other schools. When the question is raised as to whether elementary school children should compete against others or not, teachers take sides on this issue, almost all immediately thinking of competition in basketball and football. Increasingly, competition in these two sports and its place in American schools is being questioned on all levels, but especially in high schools and colleges. Some believe too much emphasis is placed on these major sports and on too few players instead of the majority of students. Actually, competition in itself is not undesirable; it is only what one does when competing that may be negative, in how one feels when winning or losing. In reality, children compete for family status the day they are born. A group of boys playing marbles are competing against each other, as are a group of girls playing jacks for fun. Certainly we, as educated adults must avoid stereotype thinking, realizing that we all must guard against thinking all policemen are "dumb," all detectives "smart," all teachers "old maids," all professors "absent-minded," or all competition "bad." But at the same time, as educated adults, we must be cognizant that increasingly outside groups are putting greater pressure on teachers to allow sixth, fifth, and in some schools even fourth grade children to play competitive athletic sports. There are many pro and con arguments to this highly debatable question.

ARGUMENTS FOR

Some sporting goods salesmen, sports writers, parents, physical educators, coaches, and teachers present the following arguments in favor of competitive sports:

1. Because children will play these games anyway in sand lots and streets, why not teach them how to play so fewer will get hurt.

2. Because these are our national games, children should learn how to play them well early in life.

3. We will develop better high school and college players if we can teach players earlier in life and, thus, the game will be more thrilling to play and to watch.

4. The individual player who is beyond his age in growth and skill should not be held back by being forced to play baby or sissy games.

5. It is better to be skilled in one or two sports than just an average player in several.

6. We live in a highly competitive society and the sooner a child learns how to compete, the more successful he is apt to be as an adult.

7. The program gives children a chance to represent their school and to develop school spirit, as well as good sportsmanship.

8. Such a program will help eradicate juvenile delinquency.

9. Our children are maturing earlier, are taller and heavier than their predecessors, and thus need more challenging activities.

10. Competition is good at any grade level, and highly organized athletic contests can stimulate some children as does an advanced academic class challenges the mentally superior child.

ARGUMENTS AGAINST

On the other hand, some physicians, leading physical educators, coaches, teachers, and parents argue that:

1. Children may receive permanent bone and ligament deformities from playing these adult games while they are in a period of rapid growth and body change.

2. There is little carry-over value in these games, for the modern world offers little opportunity to play these games throughout life. Few will play them when they are 28, 48, 68, 88.

3. The games are superimposed upon children by adults, often for their own selfish gains.

4. The games tend to reward professionalism by demanding ever increasing specialization and thrills.

5. Children should learn to do things set aside for children, to have something toward which to look forward when they become adults.

6. Such a program for a few already "good" diverts attention from all children, thus causing the already "poor" to become poorer.

7. Children should be exposed to many generalized activities, whereas specialized activities should be reserved for older children who are more emotionally mature.

8. Although children naturally protect themselves from fatigue or stress, in such sports they are too often pressured by their coach, team, or others to push themselves beyond their physical and health limits.

9. Too often too much emphasis is placed upon winning, advertising, gate receipts, and concessions rather than upon children.

10. Experts claim juvenile delinquency is caused by at least five major factors of which having opportunities to compete successfully is not one of them.

11. We should devote our energies to broaden and strengthen all existing programs rather than entering into such controversial ones.

Because a challenging varied program in a wide range of physical activities should be provided for every child of grade school age, the above pro and con arguments should be viewed in this light. The American Association for Health, Physical Education and Recreation, the American Medical Association, and the American Society for State Directors of Health, Physical Education and Recreation have all taken definite stands *against* regularly scheduled inter-scholastic competition below the senior high school level.[1] Any school, therefore, and any grade or

---

[1] Scott, Harry: *Competitive Sports in Schools and Colleges.* New York, Harper & Brothers, 1951, pp. 480–481.

junior high school teacher who bases physical education on after-school programs in football, basketball or any other competitive athletics, limits participation to those of certain physical size, strength, ability and/or all three, and does so without the aproval of the physical education profession, experts in this field, or those in medicine.

These leading experts endorse the following recommendations drawn up at the National Conference on Program Planning in Games and Sports for desirable athletic competitions for children of elementary school age:

1. Programs of games and sports should be based on the developmental level of children. Boxing, tackle football, ice hockey and other body contact sports should not be included in any competitive program for children twelve and under.

2. These programs should provide a variety of activities for all children throughout the year.

3. Competition is inherent in the growth and development of the child and, depending upon a variety of factors, will be harmful or beneficial to the individual.

4. Adequate competitive programs organized on neighborhood and community levels will meet the needs of these children. State, regional and national tournaments, bowling, charity and exhibition games are not recommended for these age groups.

5. Education and recreation authorities and other community youth-serving agencies have a definite responsibility for the development of adequate neighborhood and community programs of games and sports and to provide competent leadership for them.

6. The competent, professionally prepared physical educators and recreation leaders are the persons to whom communities should look for basic leadership.

Although today's children will enter tomorrow our highly complex and adult society, their elementary school teachers are morally and professionally obligated to reserve, as well as provide, for them those simple, unspoiled, carefree and abundant joys of childhood for which they are physically, mentally, and emotionaly best suited.

SUGGESTED READINGS

American Association for Health, Physical Education, and Recreation: *A Platform Statement Prepared by the Division of Men's Athletics,* Washington, D.C., 1963.

Brosman, Alan: Little Leaguers have big problems—Their parents. *Atlantic,* March, 1963.

Athletic Institute, *Intramurals for Elementary School Children.* Chicago, Illinois, 1964; *Desirable Athletic Competition for Children,* 1967.

Harp, William: Only when competition is properly guided is it beneficial to children. *Journal of Health, Physical Education, Recreation,* January, 1967.

Means, Lois: *Intramurals: Their Organization and Administration.* Englewood Cliffs, N.J., Prentice-Hall, Inc., 1963.

Neil, Donald: Little Leaguers aren't big leaguers. *Reader's Digest,* June, 1961.

Neilson, N. P.: *Problems in Physical Education.* Englewood Cliffs, N.J., Prentice-Hall, Inc., 1965.

Neilson, N. P.; Van Hagen, Winifred; and Comer, James: *Physical Education for Elementary Schools,* 3rd Ed. Englewood Cliffs, N.J., Prentice-Hall, Inc., 1966.

Oberteuffer, Delbert, and Ulrich, Celeste: *Physical Education.* New York, Harper & Row, 1962.

Salt, Benton; Fox, Grace; and Stevens, B. K.: *Teaching Physical Education in the Elementary School,* 2nd Ed. New York, The Ronald Press, 1960.

Sanborn, Marion, and Hartman, Betty: *Issues in Physical Education.* Philadelphia, Lea & Febiger, 1964.

Soloman, Ben: The Little League, *Youth Leaders,* April, (Entire Issue) 1953.

Voltmer, Elmer, and Esslinger, Arthur: *The Organization and Administration of Physical Education.* New York, Appleton-Century-Crofts, 1967.

Chapter 23

Evaluating the Results

Evaluation is a method of appraising, measuring, and checking progress. It is finding out where you are in relationship to where you want to go. When correctly used, it can help the teacher discover: (1) pupil progress, health status, behavior, and reaction to the program and fellow classmates, (2) her own ability to teach and reach successfully individuals as well as a class group, (3) strengths and weaknesses of the program, and (4) better ways to explain to parents, profesional colleagues, school administrators, and the general public what physical education is all about. To be most effective, evaluation should be continuous, be done by all who participate in and/or are affected by the program, and be concerned both with end products and the means with which to reach these ends.

Methods of evaluating pupil progress and the physical education program include:

Skill tests	Questionnaires
Written tests of knowledge, attitudes, and habits	Posture tests
	Attitude tests
Observation	Social development tests
Check lists	Physical examinations
Rating scales	Health records
Interviews	Personality inventories
Case studies	Progress reports by school health
Diaries	personnel
Parental conferences	School surveys of the use of school
Self-appraisal	facilities for after-school recrea-
Group discussions	tion, the school lunchroom, etc.

The results gleaned from such measuring techniques may be used for motivation, self-evaluation, grading, grouping, guidance, as well as other purposes.

The teacher most frequently uses observation, a type of subjective evaluation. To be of value, such appraisal must be precise and skilled. Both appearance and behavior can be observed and accurate deductions made by those with educated eyes and ears who are adept in noting "telling things" children say and do. Every effort should be made to discover what each child thinks, feels, knows, and does. A teacher must be more than a sounding board, yet each should realize that to an educated, child-sensitized adult, everything a youngster does is revealing; the more freely the child can and does communicate to the adult, the more he will divulge about himself. Children will and do "speak" in *every* way to the *real* teacher. The more the teacher talks, the less she will learn from and about each child in the class.

Success in objective evaluation, which is often more accurate than subjective measuring, requires careful, detailed, planned step-by-step procedures, because the effective administration of such tests includes:[1]

Advanced preparation
> Selecting the test.
> Gaining complete knowledge and understanding of test to be used and how it is to be administered.
> Obtaining needed equipment and facilities.
> Preparing score cards for individuals by class roll or squads.

Administrating the test
> By paired groups with one-half scoring, the other taking the test, in reverse order.
> By squads, by the squad leader or other trained class assistants.
> Using the station-to-station method, rotating groups to certain testing areas.
> Using any combination mentioned above.

Devising scoring methods, recording results by the teachers, assistants, squad leaders, or paired partners

Duties during the test
> Providing a warm-up period.
> Demonstrating each item.
> Motivating each pupil to do his best.
> Taking many safety precautions.

Duties following the test
> Collecting score pads.
> Converting raw scores to percentage on a scoring table.
> Comparing results with norms and constructing profiles.
> Informing pupils of the results.
> Using the results for classification, guidance, research grading, and motivation.

THE PURPOSE OF EVALUATION

Good testing can produce more orderliness in teaching and effectiveness in gaining desired results. Clarke points out the following specific purposes which can be achieved through physical education testing:

1. To determine the status of boys and girls in relation to fundamental human values amenable to improvement through physical education activities and methods.

---

[1]See the splendid article by Harold Barrow, "The ABC's of testing," pp. 35–37 in the May-June, 1962, issue of *The Journal of Health, Physical Education, Recreation* for detailed instructions for administering objective tests effectively.

2. To determine the status of boys and girls in relation to basic body traits which affect physical performances.

3. To classify pupils according to their abilities in physical activities.

4. To measure the results of instruction in physical and motor skill activities.[2]

EVALUATION OF HEALTH STATUS AND PHYSICAL GROWTH

Although some school authorities believe in annual physical examinations, other recommended four periodic examinations from grades 1 to 12, to be given when the child enters first grade, during the middle elementary experience, at the beginning of adolescence (during the junior high school years), and before leaving the senior high school. However, throughout a child's school experience he may be referred to the school physician or a specialist because of a teacher's observation or the result of a screen test. The physical examination should include:

Nutritional status	Muscle tone
Eyes and eyelids	Posture
Ears and eardrums	Bones and joints
Skin and hair	Abdomen
Heart	Nose, throat, and tonsils
Lungs	Thyroid glands
Nervous system	Lymph nodes
Pulse rate when resting and after exercise	Teeth and gums

A record should be kept of all findings, and there should be a follow-up corrective or remedial program, if necessary, for this appraisal is not an end to itself, but rather a means of helping each pupil gain better health. Although ideally as much time as possible should be spent with each child, because of the number of children to be examined by the available physicians, this sometimes is impossible. In such cases, a minimum of ten minutes should be given per pupil to be examined at school by one or more doctors.

All children should be weighed and measured each month in the elementary school and an accurate record should be kept for each pupil. Although weight norms are available from insurance companies, each teacher should use these only to compare the records of *each* pupil in relationship to those of many children of the same age and grade in school, for each child may have inherited a small, large or medium skeletal frame, may have had a recent or lingering illness, or a deep-seated emotional involvement—all of which affect growth.

---

[2]Clarke, Harrison, and Haar, Franklin: *Health and Physical Education for the Elementary School Classroom Teacher.* Englewood Cliffs, N.J., Prentice-Hall, Inc., 1964. p. 69.

The Wetzel Grid is often used in elementary schools for recording a child's growth pattern over several years.[3] Such a record is valuable in noting growth patterns and deviations.

It is important that those conducting screen tests for vision, hearing, and posture, capitalize upon teachable moments as they arise, as well as know how to answer the questions children ask, for it is then that they *want* to learn and often can best have fears eliminated. Educators call this "having a need for learning" and have discovered that "wanting to know" is basic to "getting to know." Recommended screen tests are:[4]

> *For Vision*
> The Massachusetts Vision Test
> The Holmgren Wool Test for color blindness
>
> *For Hearing*
> Discrete Frequency Audiometer Test
> The Watch Tick
> The Massachusetts Group Pure Tone Test
> The Coin Click Test
>
> *For Posture and Body Mechanics*
> The New York State Posture Test
> The Kraus-Weber Refined Posture Test
> The Kelly Foot Pain Test
> The Footprint Angle

---

[3] Vannier, Maryhelen: *Teaching Health in Elementary Schools.* New York, Harper & Brothers, 1963.

[4] Complete directions for giving all of these screen tests can be found in Willgoose, Carl: *Evaluation in Health Education and Physical Education.* New York, McGraw-Hill Book Co., Inc., 1961.

EVALUATION OF SOCIAL GROWTH AND PUPIL BEHAVIOR

The following suggested chart can be used for recording and studying pupil behavior:

PUPIL BEHAVIOR SHEET

Name _____ School Year _____ Age _____

Physical Education Class _____

Does the child:

	Frequently	Seldom	Never
Take an active part in planning group activities?			
Take an active part in playing?			
Express himself confidently?			
Accept criticisms and suggestions from his peers?			
Accept criticisms and suggestions from adults?			
Take turns with others?			
Show above average leadership ability?			
Have many consistent friends?			
Change friends often?			
Play fairly?			
Seem interested in improving skills or learning new ones?			
Assume responsibility without being reminded or threatened?			
Seem happy and well adjusted?			

Comments

1. _____
2. _____
3. _____
4. _____
5. _____

Areas in which the child needs help:

1. _____
2. _____
3. _____
4. _____
5. _____

What I will do to help him help himself:

1. _____
2. _____
3. _____
4. _____
5. _____

Signed _____

Date _____

These records can be of invaluable help to the teacher in gaining insight of all of her pupils. Changes in behavior that indicate growth and improvement should be noticed and commented upon to the pupil by the teacher.

The use of a sociogram is also recommended. Here the children are asked to help the teacher group them into activity, and write the names of class members they would like on a team. By this device, the teacher can identify group isolates, rejects, and leaders.

Children are not miniature adults. We, who are older, must increasingly help them to develop their own unique personality. Above all, we need to help them develop necessary work and recreational skills, good health and character, and all else needed for them to find true happiness in life.

EVALUATION OF MOTOR SKILLS AND PHYSICAL FITNESS

Numerous tests have been developed to measure motor ability, motor intelligence, and physical fitness. Almost all measure strength and endurance, innate coordination, speed, reaction time, balance, kinesthesis, flexibility, agility, and body explosive power. Suggested tests for doing so on the elementary level are:[5]

Brace Motor Ability Test
Vertical Jump Test
Burpee Test
Carpenter Motor Ability Test
Iowa Brace Test
Kraus-Weber Floor-Touch Test for Flexibility
AAHPER Youth Fitness Test
New York State Physical Fitness Test
Oregon Motor Fitness Test
Amateur Athletic Union Junior Physical Fitness Test[6]
President's Council on Physical Fitness Test[7]
Washington Motor Fitness Test[8]
California Physical Performance Test[9]
The Carpenter General Motor Capacity Tests[10]
Latchaw Motor Achievement Test[11]

---

[5] See Clarke's or McCloy's book listed in the bibliography for complete directions for giving each test.

[6] Available from The Amateur Athletic Union, 233 Broadway, New York, N.Y.

[7] Available from U. S. Government Printing Office, Washington, D.C., 1961.

[8] Available from Dr. Glenn Kirchner, Eastern Washington State College, Cheney, Washington.

[9] Available from The Bureau of Health Education, Physical Education and Recreation, California State Department of Education, Sacramento, California.

[10] Carpenter, Arleen: Measuring general motor capacity and general motor achievement in the first three grades. Research Quarterly, *13*:444, December, 1942.

[11] Latchaw, Marjorie: Motor achievement. Research Quarterly, *25*:429, December, 1954.

EVALUATION OF PUPIL KNOWLEDGE AND ATTITUDES

Written tests include objective questions which require short answers, longer essay answers to general questions, rating scales, and problem situation questions which require short but well-thought-through answers.

Written tests are of the greatest value when the teacher fully understands what it is she wants to test, knows what to do with the results, and has found the best measuring instruments for these purposes.

TRUE AND FALSE TESTS

Educators contend that these are the poorest and weakest kind of objective test questions to use. Pupils tend to read meaning into each statement; few can tell the difference between a correct or incorrect statement or can resist mentally tinkering with it; few things are really completely true or entirely false.

All true and false statements should be short and simple. Avoid using the words "never" or "always." Have the pupils use the symbols (+) or (0) instead of (T) or (F), because those unsure of the answer often deliberately make the marks hard to tell apart. Other ways to score the test include encircling T if the statement is entirely true, or F if it is only partly true, or blocking out X in the first column if the sentence is correct and encircling it if the second one is wrong. In the first grade, have the children draw a face (☹) with the mouth turned down if the statement is false, or draw it with mouth turned up if it is true. (☺)

Example: Write + if the statement is true, 0 if it is false.

Hit pin baseball for sixth grade pupils.

- 0   1. Five Indian clubs are used in this game.
- 0   2. Each run scores two points.
- +   3. The ball, when kicked fair, must be sent to first, second, third, home base, in this order.
- 0   4. The pitcher may throw the ball to the kicker.
- +   5. The kicker is out on the third strike.

MULTIPLE CHOICE TESTS

These questions should be short, clearly written, and not copied word for word from a textbook. Care must be taken not to make all possible answers so wrong that it is obvious which one is correct, or set a pattern through which the correct answer can usually be found.

Example: Place the letter of the most correct answer in the provided blank.

Tennis

<u> c </u> 1. A lob is a stroke used in (a) serving, (b) smashing, (c) sending the ball high into the air, (d) driving it directly to the net player.

<u> d </u> 2. The term deuce is used in (a) serving, (b) volleying, (c) rallying, (d) scoring.

<u> a </u> 3. A fast hard drive which "kills the ball" or "puts it away for keeps" is a (a) smash, (b) lob, (c) volley, (d) line drive.

<u> d </u> 4. A point made by the server after a deuce score is called: (a) add out, (b) 40–15, (c) 30–40, (d) add in.

<u> b </u> 5. A set is won by a player who first wins (a) four, (b) six, (c) eight, (d) three games, providing he has won two games more than his opponent.

MATCHING TESTS

These questions are best for measuring the mastery of "where," "when" and "who" types of information. They do not develop the ability to interpret or express one's self. The responses to the matched items should be placed alphabetically or numerically in the right-hand column. Blank spaces should be provided in the left column before each item to be matched. There should be at least two more answers in the right column than in the left.

Example: Match the items in the left column with those in the right. Some answers in the latter may be used twice:

Folk Dance

<u> c </u> 1. Crested Hen	a. England
<u> b </u> 2. Jig	b. Ireland
<u> a </u> 3. Sellinger's Round	c. Denmark
<u> c </u> 4. Little Man in a Fix	d. France
<u> a </u> 5. Green Sleeves	e. Spain
<u> h </u> 6. Broom Dance	f. America
	g. Scotland
	h. Germany
	i. Italy

FILL-IN BLANKS

The chief drawback to this type of examination is that pupils have difficulty filling in blanks in the exact words the teacher expects; thus, they are often given the benefit of the doubt or cause the teacher to become irritated and more exacting as she continues to grade the paper. Also, it is time-consuming to grade such questions. One advantage to using this type of test is that the pupil is not guided to the answer.

Example: Write the correct answer in the blank provided for it below.

Square Dance

1. The head couple is usually standing with its back to the caller.
2. The lady usually is on the gentleman's right side.
3. Honor your partner means to bow to your partner .
4. The last line of the call "all jump up and never come down" is swing your honey round and round .
5. Three running steps followed by a hop is done in a schottische .

ESSAY QUESTIONS

These questions provide pupils with opportunities to write and read aloud complete sentences and whole paragraphs using good grammar, and to think through problems carefully. Their drawback is that they are time-consuming to read and difficult to grade. However, such answered questions help teachers to gain additional insights concerning their pupils and their unique personal problems. Suggested questions are:

1. What are the values of being physically educated?
2. How have your own recreational patterns been improved as a result of taking this class?
3. What is your definition of good sportsmanship?

RATING SCALES

Pupils enjoy rating and evaluating their work or habits in school. The best scales for doing so are those devised by the class. Teachers can help children gain benefit from this type of experience by a personal follow-up conference with each child.

Example: Pupil's Personal Evaluation of Daily Health Habits.

	Always	Frequently	Seldom	Never
1. I brush my teeth after eating.	_____	_____	_____	_____
2. I eat fruits and vegetables every day.	_____	_____	_____	_____
3. I drink a quart of milk daily.	_____	_____	_____	_____
4. I usually go to bed before 9:00 p.m.	_____	_____	_____	_____
5. I worry about my school work.	_____	_____	_____	_____

EVALUATION BY THE PUPILS

Children should be given many opportunities to evaluate what progress they have made in relationship to the goals set individually and by the class. Teachers should appraise their progress with them, as well as be ever observant of their reactions to what they are doing, their attitude toward her, the class, themselves, and life in general. Time should be taken frequently to discuss these reactions, problems which have arisen concerning individual or group behavior, good sportsmanship, as well as formulate future goals and plans.

Deeper insight and a clearer understanding of the group as a whole, as well as the feelings of the class toward the teacher, can be gained by having each pupil write on an unsigned paper answers to the following questions at the end of a semester or a major class project.

1. Did you enjoy this experience? Why?
2. List the new things you have learned in order of importance to you.
3. What activities did you do away from school that you learned here?

Figure 65. Children, too, should be given many opportunities to evaluate what progress they have made. (Courtesy of Elizabeth Glidden, Specialist in Elementary Physical Education, Los Angeles City Schools, Los Angeles, California.)

4. What person do you most admire in our class? Why?
5. How could you be like this person, if you wanted to?
6. What did you hope to do or learn that you did not?
7. What pupil do you think improved the most? In what ways?
8. Are the pupils here learning to be good citizens? In what ways?

Much information can also be gained concerning each pupil by having him complete statements which show his inner feelings, fears, or inner thoughts. Suggested questions include the following:

1. My greatest fear when I am in this class is that I _____

_____ .

2. I think my ability in sports and games is _____

_____ .

3. I dislike _____ because _____ .

4. I would like to be just like _____ when I grow up because _____

_____ .

5. I _____ this class, because here I _____

_____ .

There is great educational value found in having pupils submit sample objective test questions with their correct answers, and in grading each other's paper in class as the teacher reads the correct answer. Every real educator will find ways to utilize any time spent in evaluating progress to its utmost, and will make good use of test findings in order to improve as an effective youth leader.

The pupils may feel freer to speak truthfully if they are asked to write suggestions for class improvement and turn them in unsigned. Another method is to have each pupil fill in the following suggested check list:

PUPIL EVALUATION SHEET

	Always	Frequently	Seldom	Never
Do you enjoy classes in physical education?	_____	_____	_____	_____
Do you feel as though you are getting enough individual attention in learning to do new things?	_____	_____	_____	_____
Do you play the activities learned in class after school and during your leisure time?	_____	_____	_____	_____
Do you like to take showers after class?	_____	_____	_____	_____
Do you feel as though your class gives you enough opportunities to get to know a number of activities and people?	_____	_____	_____	_____
Do you feel as though you have gained in skills?	_____	_____	_____	_____

List the things you like most about physical education.

1. _____

2. _____

3. _____

List the things you like the least about physical education.

1. _____

2. _____

How do you think our class could be made better?

1. _____

2. _____

TEACHER EVALUATION

Every teacher should take a frequent realistic look at herself and her work. A suggested evaluation sheet for doing so follows:

	Always	Frequently	Seldom	Never
1. I like teaching.	___	___	___	___
2. I enjoy my students and try to understand them.	___	___	___	___
3. I am democratic.	___	___	___	___
4. I feel inadequately prepared to do my job well.	___	___	___	___
5. I make the best use of student leadership.	___	___	___	___
6. I make the best use of facilities and equipment.	___	___	___	___
7. I have my own teaching objectives clearly in mind for each class.	___	___	___	___
8. I have my objectives clearly in mind for the development of each unique individual student.	___	___	___	___
9. I plan my work ahead.	___	___	___	___
10. I teach something new every class period.	___	___	___	___
11. I am cognizant of carry-over values in what I am teaching.	___	___	___	___
12. I give skill and written tests periodically and use them to evaluate my work.	___	___	___	___
13. I feel that the students admire me.	___	___	___	___
14. I have discipline trouble.	___	___	___	___
15. I try to cooperate with my administrators.	___	___	___	___
16. I feel the other teachers respect me.	___	___	___	___
17. I join professional organizations, attend their meetings, and read their periodical literature.	___	___	___	___
18. I feel that I am making a real contribution to my professional field.	___	___	___	___

Things I should do to improve myself as a teacher are:

a. _____ e. _____

b. _____ f. _____

c. _____ g. _____

d. _____ h. _____

Date _____

My progress on this so far has been:

a. _____ c. _____

b. _____ d. _____

Date _____

EVALUATION BY THE PHYSICAL EDUCATION SUPERVISOR

Although the classroom teacher in most primary grades teaches physical education and other subjects, many of them, as well as those specialized physical educators on the upper elementary level, have supervisors to assist them in their work. The use of a supervisor's evaluation sheet seen below should be followed by personal conferences, so that improvement, if needed, can be made:

Name of teacher _____   Name of school _____

Date of rating _____   Rated by _____

Instructions: Using a scale of 1 to 3, rate each teacher in each item below. Rate 3 for above average, 2 for average, 1 for below average.

	1	2	3
1. Shows an understanding of people.	____	____	____
2. Uses democratic methods.	____	____	____
3. Has an understanding of the community, the school, and is aware of their relationships to each other.	____	____	____
4. Shows ability to organize and plan his work carefully.	____	____	____
5. Shows ability to measure pupil progress.	____	____	____
6. Recognizes individual differences.	____	____	____
7. Understands group behavior.	____	____	____
8. Helps groups plan, conduct, and evaluate their own program under his direction.	____	____	____
9. Develops student leadership.	____	____	____
10. Has ability to build group unity.	____	____	____
11. Can solve discipline problems.	____	____	____
12. Is respected and liked by students and fellow teachers.	____	____	____
13. Can demonstrate well.	____	____	____
14. Can speak well, using correct grammar.	____	____	____
15. Safeguards the health and safety of all.	____	____	____
16. Provides a well-balanced graded program.	____	____	____
17. Provides definite progression in a graded program.	____	____	____
18. Uses well a wide variety of teaching methods.	____	____	____
19. Is attractive, neat, and looks like a leader.	____	____	____
20. Is creative.	____	____	____
21. Shows knowledge of the entire school curriculum and realizes the contribution of his own area.	____	____	____
22. Uses the bulletin board, realizing that it is a silent teacher.	____	____	____
23. Keeps adequate records and realizes their importance.	____	____	____
24. Shows ability to maintain proper teacher-pupil relationships.	____	____	____
25. Shows professional promise.	____	____	____

EVALUATION WITH THE PRINCIPAL

The school administrator should be aware of the work accomplished by all teachers during the school year. He should visit each teacher regularly and offer suggestions for improvement. As the chief administrator of the school system, he often must be the go-between for teachers and the general public. By observing classes in physical education and reading reports submitted by the teacher, he may gain insight into the program.

The task of teaching also includes that of educational diagnosis. The teacher's analysis of each class should include consideration of what the children accomplished during their class period, learning problems that were evident with the entire group as well as with individuals, and possible solutions for learning stumbling blocks.

Tests are useful tools for evaluating learning in skills, rules, and attitudes. Each unit of work should include a written and skill test. These should be easily administered and not be too time-consuming to grade or record. Not more than two class periods should be taken for these tests.

EVALUATION OF THE SCHOOL PROGRAM

Three major areas of the elementary school physical education program should be evaluated periodically: the effectiveness of the teacher conducting the program, the facilities, and the program content. Such an evaluation could be made by a visiting team of physical education experts, the teachers involved in the program, and the school administrator. Periodic meetings should be held to review the results of such an evaluation made by any two of these groups, and specific plans should be drawn up to eliminate existing weaknesses. Consultants should be brought in to work with the teaching staff to improve offerings, if need be.

The following evaluative form might well be used by those reviewing the program in its entirety:

PROGRAM EVALUATIVE FORM

A. *The Instructional Staff*

                                                                  Yes   No

1. Is the teacher a college graduate with a major in elementary education? ___ ___

2. Has the teacher had at least one three-hour course in elementary physical education within the past five years? ___ ___

3. Has the teacher attended any clinics or workshops in elementary physical education within the past three years? ___ ___

4. Is the classroom teacher assisted by an elementary school physical education specialist in planning and conducting the program? ___ ___

5. Can the teacher demonstrate a wide variety of movement skills or sport skills correctly? ___ ___

Yes No.

6. Can she diagnose faulty movement patterns and correct movement imperfections?

7. Does the teacher follow a graded course of study in elementary physical education?

B. *The Facilities*

Outdoor

1. Is the outdoor play space a safe place for children to play?

2. Is the area fenced?

3. Are all playing areas well marked, drained, and free of debris?

4. Are the youngest children assigned a place to play that is (a) furthest away from the oldest children's area; (b) near the school building?

5. Is there sand, tanbark, or sawdust under all apparatus to protect pupils from injury?

6. Are all pieces of equipment thoroughly checked periodically for safety purposes?

7. Are all pupils taught the safest way to use all outdoor equipment?

8. Are the pupils well supervised during recess, before and after school when playing, and during noon hour?

Indoor

1. Is there a well-lighted, well-ventilated gymnasium used for both instructional and free play purposes?

2. Is the gymnasium a safe place for pupils at active play?

3. Are all court and boundary lines well marked?

4. Is there adequate storage space for all equipment and supplies?

5. Can all needed equipment be easily and quickly moved to all teaching areas?

C. *The Program*

1. Do teachers help plan and revise periodically a printed graded course of study?

2. Are the teachers and pupils aware of the objectives of the program in its entirety and of each daily lesson therein?

3. Does the program contain a variety of activities under the broad headings of aquatics, rhythmical activities, movement exploration, stunts and tumbling, elementary gymnastics, simple games, lead-up games to team sports, and camping and outdoor education?

4. Does the instructional program really produce skill learning in a variety of activities or is it merely a supervised play period?

5. Are there adequate established ways in which the program can be evaluated by the teacher, the pupils, and the school administrator?

6. Is the program correlated with the school health and safety programs?

7. Does the program meet the amount of time designated for daily class instruction in physical education set by state law?

8. Is there a modified program provided for those children who are handicapped or atypical?

According to the above findings, the weaknesses of our total physical education program seem to be:

a. _____

b. _____

c. _____

d. _____

Things we should do to improve our program are:

a. _____

b. _____

c. _____

d. _____

GRADING AND REPORTING TO PARENTS

It is usually not customary to record separate physical education grades other than Pass or Fail for primary children. However, most report cards for this age group contain blanks for the teacher to rate each child's ability to play well with others, show good sportsmanship, and development in play skills. In grades 4, 5, and 6, many schools report a separate grade in physical education for each pupil. Such a grade may be of the number or letter type, and is based largely upon achievement, attitude, and attendance. All grades should be given on an educational basis and those who have done the best work in accordance to the stated objectives of social, physical, and emotional development, receive the best grades.

The far-reaching influences of a good physical education program should reach into the home and local community. Individual conferences with parents, home visits if possible, and telephone conversations can help teachers gain needed information regarding the effectiveness of their teaching. When parents and teachers become working partners, their joint efforts can and will produce many fruitful results!

SUGGESTED READINGS

American Association of School Administrators, Council of Chief State School Officers, and National Association of Secondary-School Principals: *Testing, Testing, Testing.* Washington, D.C., National Education Association, 1962, 32 pp.

Clarke, H. Harrison: *Application of Measurement to Health and Physical Education,* 4th Ed. Englewood Cliffs, N.J., Prentice-Hall, Inc. 1967.

Latchaw, Marjorie, and Brown, Camille: *The Evaluation Process in Health Education, Physical Education and Recreation.* Englewood Cliffs, N.J., Prentice-Hall, Inc., 1962.

Lewis, Gertrude: *The Evaluation of Teaching.* Washington, D.C., National Education Association, 1966.

Meyers, Carlton R., and Blesh, T. Erwin: *Measurement in Physical Education.* New York, The Ronald Press Company, 1962, 473 pp.

Rothney, John W. M.: *Evaluating and Reporting Pupil Progress: What Research Says to the Teacher,* No. 7. Washington, D.C., National Education Association, 1960, 33 pp.

Scott, M. Gladys, and French, Esther: *Measurement and Evaluation in Physical Education.* St. Louis, The C. V. Mosby Co., 1960.

Scott, M. Gladys: *Research Methods in Health, Physical Education, Recreation, for the Research Council.* (See especially the chapter on "Construction of Tests.") Washington, D.C., American Assn. for Health, Physical Education, and Recreation, 1959, 536 pp.

Smithells, Philip, and Cameron, Peter: *Principles of Evaluation in Physical Education.* New York, Harper & Brothers, 1962.

Willgoose, Carl E.: *Evaluation of Health Education and Physical Education.* New York, McGraw-Hill Book Co., Inc., 1962, 478 pp.

Appendices

RECOMMENDED FILMS ON ELEMENTARY PHYSICAL EDUCATION

After School Activities for Boys and Girls (filmstrip), American Council on Education, Washington, D.C.

Archery for Girls, 10 min., Coronet Films.

Ball Handling in Basketball, 10 min., Encyclopaedia Britannica Films, Inc.

Ball Handling in Football, 11 min., Encyclopaedia Britannica Films, Inc.

Basketball for Girls—Fundamental Techniques, 10 min., Coronet Films.

Beginning Camping, 30 min., Athletic Institute.

Beginning Swimming, 30 min., Athletic Institute.

Beginning Tumbling, 11 min., Coronet Films.

Beginning Volleyball (filmstrip of 208 frames—four units, 10 min. each), Athletic Institute.

Careers in Physical Education, 30 min.; *Careers in Recreation,* 30 min., Athletic Institute.

Children Growing Up With Others, 45 min., National Film Board of Canada.

Evaluating Physical Abilities, 15 min., Athletic Institute.

Exercise and Health, 8 min., Coronet Films.

Focus on Fitness, 18 min., American Assn. for Health, Physical Education, and Recreation.

Fundamentals in Track and Field, 26 min., Encyclopedia Films.

Intermediate Tumbling, 11 min., Coronet Films.

Mat Mann's Swimming Techniques for Boys, 18 min., Coronet Films.

Mat Mann's Swimming Techniques for Girls, 11 min., Coronet Films.

Methods of Teaching Physical Education, 40 min., All American Productions, Box 801, Riverside, California.

New Designs in Elementary Physical Education, 30 min., American Assn. for Health, Physical Education, and Recreation.

Play Ball, Son! 20 min., Young America Films, Inc.

Play in the Snow, 10 min., Encyclopaedia Britannica Films, Inc.

Play Softball, 86 frames with script, Association Films.

Playground Safety, 10 min., Coronet Films.

Playtown U.S.A., 35 min., Athletic Institute.

Primary Safety: In the School Building, Coronet Films.

Primary Safety: On the School Playground, Coronet Films.

Readiness—The Fourth R, Athletic Institute.

Share the Ball, 32 frames with text, Simmel-Meservey, Inc.

Simple Stunts, 11 min., Coronet Films.

Skip to My Lou, 5 min., Indiana University.

Soccer for Girls, 11 min., Coronet Films.

Social Dancing, 11 min., Coronet Films.

Softball for Boys, 10 min., Coronet Films.

Softball for Girls, 11 min. (B&W and color), Coronet Films.

Sports Teaching Aids (3x5 card file bibliography of films, filmstrips, and slides), Division of Girls' and Women's Sports, American Assn. for Health, Physical Education, and Recreation.

Squirrel in Trees, 5 min., Indiana University.
Swimming for Beginners, color, Visual Educational Films.
Teaching Aids for Health, Physical Education, and Recreation (a list of free and inexpensive teaching aids), Thomas Flanigan, Box 2, Mokena, Illinois.
They Grow Up So Fast, 27 min., color, American Assn. for Health, Physical Education, and Recreation.
Three Deep, 6 min., Indiana University.
Trampolining, 28 min., Athletic Institute.
Volleyball for Boys, 11 min., Coronet Films.
Volleyball Techniques for Girls, 9 min., McGraw-Hill Book Co., Inc., Text-Film Department.

RECOMMENDED FILM STRIPS

The following film strips are available both for rental and purchase from The Athletic Institute, 805 Merchandise Mart, Chicago, Illinois:

Apparatus Activities for Boys and Men
Archery
Badminton
Campcraft Shelters
Campcraft Series
Fishing
Gymnastics for Girls and Women
Lifesaving
Skiing
Soccer
Swimming
Table Tennis
Track and Field for Elementary School Children
Tumbling
Volleyball

FILM SOURCES

The following are the full addresses of the sources (sale, rental, or loan) of the films listed:

AAHPER Film Sales: 1201 16th Street, N.W., Washington 6, D.C.
A.F.R.: American Film Registry, 24 East Eighth Street, Chicago 5.
A.M.N.H.: American Museum of Natural History, Department of Education, Central Park West at 79th Street, New York 24.
Association: Association Films, Inc., Broad at Elm, Ridgefield, New Jersey.
Bailey: Bailey Films, Inc., 6509 DeLongpre Avenue, Hollywood 28, California.
Castle: Castle Films—Distributor, United World Films, Inc., 1445 Park Avenue, New York 29; 542 S. Dearborn St., Chicago 6; 6610 Melrose Avenue, Los Angeles 38.
Commerce: New York State Department of Commerce, Film Library, 40 Howard Street, Albany 7, New York.
E.B.: Encyclopaedia Britannica Films, 1150 Willamette Avenue, Willamette, Illinois; 202 E. 44th Street, New York 17; 5625 Hollywood Blvd., Hollywood, California.
I.C.S.: Institutional Cinema Service, Inc., 1560 Broadway, New York 19.
Ideal: Ideal Pictures, 1558 Main Street, Buffalo 8; 233–239 West 42nd Street, New York 36; 58 E. South Water Street, Chicago 15.
I.F.F.: International Film Foundation, Inc., 1600 Broadway, New York 19.
Indiana: Indiana University, Audio-Visual Center, Bloomington, Indiana.
N.E.M.P.: New England Movie Production, 83–85 Winter Street, Exeter, New Hampshire.
N.F.B.: National Film Board of Canada, R.K.O. Building, Suite 2307, 1270 Avenue of the Americas, New York 20.
Simmel: Simmel Meservey, Inc., 321 S. Beverly Drive, Beverly Hills, Calif.

Syracuse: Educational Film Library, Syracuse University, Collendale at Lancaster Avenue, Syracuse 10, New York.

U.W.F.: United World Films, Inc., 1445 Park Avenue, New York 29.

FILM GUIDES

A Directory of 2600 Films, 16 mm. Film Libraries, 1953. Available from Supt. of Documents, Government Printing Office, Washington 25, D.C.

Educational Film Guide. The H. W. Wilson Company, 950 University Ave., New York 52, New York. (Contains information on 13,762 films.)

Educators' Guide to Free Films. Educators' Progress Service, Randolph, Wisconsin.

Free and Inexpensive Learning Materials. Division of Surveys and Field Services, George Peabody College for Teachers, Nashville, Tennessee.

1961–62 Guide to Sports, Physical Education, and Recreation. The National Audio-Visual Journal.

Sport Film Guide. The Athletic Institute, 2095 State Street, Chicago 4, Illinois.

Sports Teaching Aids: Audio-Visual. AAHPER, 1201 16th Street, N.W., Washington 6, D.C.

INDEX

Accidents. See also *Safety*.
  prevention of, 72, 73
  reporting of, 73
    form for, 74
  safeguards against, 71–73
Accompaniment, for rhythms and dance, 200
Ace of Diamonds (international dance), 218
Activities, competitive, suitable for children, 412, 413
  for after school, 409–424
  for atypical children, 378–380, 384–393
  for classroom, 327–346
  for grades 1–3, 44, 111, 112, 113
  for grades 4–6, 46, 113, 114, 115, 116
  for playground, 67
  for recess and noon hour, 395–408
  graded, list of, 111–116
  group, for outdoors, 352
  intramural and after-school, 409–424
  locomotor, movement exploration and, 238, 239
  self-testing, list of, 261
Adolescent, characteristics of, 49
Adult(s), recreation and, 15
After-school activities, 409–424
Age, groupings according to, 33
  maturation and, 32
Air Balloons (classroom game), 334
All Up Relay, 162
Alphabet Game, 156
Alphabetical Geography (guessing game), 342
Aluminum foil cooking, 358
Angel Balance (pyramid stunt), 282
Angels Do It (classroom game), 335
Apparatus. See *Equipment*.
Aquatics, accident prevention in, 72
  class organization for, 313–316
  control of class in, 315
  deep water activities in, 323
  fun time in, 322

Aquatics (*Continued*)
  games in, 323
  races in, 323
  relays in, 323
  safety in, 72
  shallow water activities in, 322
  skills in, 316–321. See also name of skill.
  teaching aids in, 322
  testing procedures in, 324–325
Arch Goal Ball Relay (basketball relay), 168
Arms Length Tag, 146
Assembly programs, 420
Athletics. See name of specific sport or activity.
Attendance laws, 36
Attitudes, and learning, 12
  evaluation of, 431–433
Atypical children, adapted programs for, 373–393
  administrative details and, 380
  class work for, 378
  classifications of, 374
  methods for teaching, 380
  needs of, 374–375
  objective sheet for, 379
  parent cooperation and, 378
  physician's recommendations for program for, 377
  recognition of, 51, 52
Automobiles or Airplanes (simple game), 138
Axe, use of, 368, 369

Back crawl (aquatic skill), 320
Back drop (trampoline skill), 289
Back glide (aquatic skill), 318
Back to Back (simple game), 139
Back-to-back roll (stunt), 277
Backlog fire, 355
Backstroke (aquatic skill), 319

Backward jump (stunt), 262
Backward kick (stunt), 263
Backward roll, progressions in, 277
Bait casting, 371
Balance beam, 296
Balance Relay, 163
Balance stand (stunt), 263
Balance Writing (classroom game), 338
Ball(s), bouncing, rhythm and, 195
    games using, 174–193. See also name
        of game.
    in movement exploration, 246
Ball Bounce (classroom game), 331
Ball Puss (lead-up game), 174
Ball receiving (volleyball skill), 187
Ball Toss (lead-up game), 175
Balloon Relay, 170
Bamboo Hop (rhythm game), 196
Bar(s), horizontal, 297
    stall, 299
Base Football (soccer skill game), 181
Base running (baseball skill), 183
Baseball, competition in, arguments
        against, 423
    arguments for, 422
    skills in, 182, 183
        games for developing, 183–186
Baseball Overtake Contest (baseball
    skill game), 184
Baseball Relay, 169
Basket shooting (basketball skill), 190
Basketball, competition in, arguments
        against, 423
    arguments for, 422
    skills in, 188–191
        games for developing, 191–193
Basketball Pass Relay, 168
Basketball relays, 168
Basketball Shooting Relay, 168
Bat Ball (baseball skill game), 183
    Progressive (baseball skill game), 185
Batting (baseball skill), 182
Bead Guessing (American Indian
    game), 345
Bean hole fire, 355
Beanbag Toss (classroom game), 339
Beans, savory (recipe), 359
Bear Dance (stunt), 263
Bear Walk (stunt), 263
Beat the Ball (baseball skill game), 183
Beater Goes Round (simple game), 139
Bed roll, 369
Behavoir, of pupils, evaluation of, 428–
    430
    records of, 52
    problems of, signs of, 51
Bells (stunt), 263
Belonging, as social need, 38
Bent knee hop (stunt), 263
Bird, Beast, Fish (simple game), 139

Birds Have Feathers (classroom game),
    333
Blackboard Relay, 340
Blanket roll, 369
Blast Off! (simple game), 148
Bleking (international dance), 223
Blind as a Bat (nature game), 364
Blindness, 387
Bluebird (singing game), 204
Board games, 149, 155. See also name of
    game.
Bobbing (aquatic skill), 317
Body mechanics, tests for, 428
Body position, in social dancing, 226
Bombs Away! (target game), 153
Bounce pass (basketball skill), 189
Bouncing (trampoline skill), 288
Bouncing Ball (stunt), 273
Boundary Ball (lead-up game), 175
Bowline (knot), 367
Bowling (relay), 163
Bowling (lead-up game), 175
Bowling Game, 157
Box, in movement exploration, 245
Box Ball (baseball skill game), 184
Box Hockey, 156
Box Relay, 171
Box waltz, basic steps in, 228
Bread, green stick baking of, 357
Bread twists (recipe), 361
Breast stroke (aquatic skill), 320
Breath-holding (aquatic skill), 316
Broad jump, 310
Broiler, for outdoor cooking, 356
Bronco Relay, 171
Broom Dance (international dance),
    220
Broomsticks, in movement exploration,
    239, 245
Buddy burners, paraffin, 357
Bug (classroom game), 335
Bull in the Ring (classroom game), 331
Bulldog Pull (stunt), 275
Bulletin board, games for, 149

Cage Ball (volleyball skill game), 188
Calabash (African game), 343
Call Ball (lead-up game), 176
Call the Chickens Home (Chinese
    game), 344
Campcraft. See Camping.
Camper's Stew (recipe), 361
Campfire Stew (recipe), 359
Campfires, 354–355
Camping, activities in, 347–372
    experiences in, 348
    skills in, 351–372
        contests using, 352
        sleeping equipment for, 369

Cap Transfer (relay), 163
Captain Jinks (singing game), 202
Card games, 337
Card Toss (classroom game), 339
Cartwheel, progressions in, 277
Casting (fishing skill), 371
Catch the Bat (simple game), 139
Catch the Cane (classroom game), 336
Catch, Throw, and Sit (basketball skill game), 191
Catching (baseball skill), 182
Catching (basketball skill), 190
Catching Fishes in the Dark (Chinese game), 344
Catching the Fish's Tail (Chinese game), 344
Center Pass Relay (football relay), 167
Center Pitch (classroom game), 333
Cerebral palsy, activities for children with, 390
Certification, of physical education teacher, 22
Changing Cover (nature game), 364
Charlie Brown (simple game), 147
Cherkessia (international dance), 220
Chest pass (basketball skill), 189
Chicken, baked (recipe), 361
Chicken Market (Italian game), 342
Children, atypical, 373–393
    characteristics of, 43–51. See also *Growth* and specific age or grade level.
    competitive activities for, 412, 413
    conflicts in, 40
    exceptional, 51. See also *Atypical children*.
    games created by, 246–247
    handicapped, 373–374. See also *Atypical children*.
    lower elementary, competitive activities for, 412
    needs of, 37–40
    population changes affecting, 34
    retarded, 388. See also *Atypical children*.
    socio-cultural effects on, 35, 36
    upper elementary, competitive activities for, 412–413
    value of play to, 14
Chili Con Carne (recipe), 358, 361
Chimes of Dunkirk (international dance), 218
Chinese Get-up (stunt), 275
Chinese Hold Up (Chinese game), 346
Chinese Hop (relay), 340
Chinning, in rope climbing, 295
    on horizontal bar, 297
    on still rings, 298
Churn the Butter (stunt), 273
Circle Catch Ball (classroom game), 331

Circle Club Bowls (lead-up game), 176
Circle formation, for class instruction, 101
    for relays, 160
Circle games, active, 330–333. See also name of game.
    quiet, 334–337. See also name of game.
Circle Kick Ball (lead-up game), 176
Circle Kick Soccer (soccer skill game), 180
Circle Relay, 163
Circle Squat (classroom game), 338
Circle Two (classroom game), 338
Circle Volley Relay (volleyball relay), 167
Class, control of, 104
    in aquatics, 315
    excuses from, reasons for, 95
    formations for, 100–102
    management of, 94
    organization of, 99–105
        for aquatics, 313–316
        for stunts and tumbling, 259
        for team sports, 178–179
Class competitions, 409
Classification, of players for competition, 414–416
Classroom, games for, 327–346
    physical education activities in, 60
    safety in, 328
Classroom games, 327–346. See also name of game.
    criteria for choosing, 328
    equipment for, 328–329
    leadership in, 329–330
    objectives of, 327
    safety precautions in, 328
Classroom relays, 339–341
Climbing ladder, in movement exploration, 239
Clothes Pin Drop (classroom game), 338
Clove hitch (knot), 368
Club Guard (classroom game), 332
Club Snatch (simple game), 140
Clubs, competitive, organization of, 416
Cock Fight (stunt), 275
Cocoa (recipe), 361
Coffee Grinder, 263
Coin Flip Hike, 353
Color Me (simple game), 148
Color Tag, 146
Come Along (simple game), 144
Come Let Us Be Joyful (singing game), 201
Community groups, recreation programs for, 421
Compass Hike, 354

Competition, classification of players
for, 414–416
for children, 412, 413
in sports, arguments against, 423
arguments for, 422
organization of clubs for, 416
organization of programs for, 414
Conditioning theory of learning, 81
Conferences, parent-teacher, 52
Conflicts, in children, 40
Connectionism, theory of, 82
Conservation, 351, 371
Constructed games, 148–149. See also
name of game.
outdoor. See *Outdoor cooking.*
Copycat (simple game), 147
Corkscrew (stunt), 264
Corn Roast (recipe), 359
Corner formation, for class instruction,
101
Corner Spry (lead-up game), 177
Costumes. See *Uniforms.*
Cotton-eyed Joe (couple dance), 212
Couple dances, 212–213. See also name
of dance.
Couple formations, for class instruc-
tion, 102
Couple stunts, 261, 262, 273–276
Cowboy Loop (square dance), 210
Crab Walk (stunt), 264
Crane Dive (stunt), 264
Crawl (aquatic skill), 320
Creative games, 138–157. See also name
of game.
Creative movement, progressive pre-
sentation of, 247
Creative play, 240–246
movement in, 245
Crested Hen (international dance), 221
Crisscross fire, 355
Croquet (recess activity), 406
Cross Over Relay (softball relay), 169
Csebogar (international dance), 217
Culture, effects of on children, 35, 36
Curio Collection (nature game), 365
Curriculum, aims of, 5, 7
Curriculum study, 28
Cut the Wand (stunt), 264

Dance walk (dance step), 227, 228
Dances, international, 214–225. See
also name of dance.
Dancing, accompaniment for, 200
recordings for, 232, 233
for couples, 212–213
for mixing, 213–214
social, 225–229
basic steps of, 227
patterns in, 228

Dancing (*Continued*)
square, 206–214
terminology of, 229–231
Danish Dance of Greeting, 217
Dash (track and field activity), 309
Deafness, adapted programs in, 386
Deck tennis (recess activity), 403
Deformities, activities for children
with, 384, 385, 389
Demonstration(s), importance of, 10
of motor skills, 93
public, 418
program for, 420
Development, of children. See *Growth*
and specific age or grade level.
Diamond Ball (baseball skill game),
184
Dip (stunt), 264
Discipline, techniques of, 42–43
Distance kicking (soccer skill), 181
Ditties, for jumping rope, 399–402
Dive Over One (stunt), 278
Diving (aquatic skill), 321
Dizzy-izzy (relay), 164
Dodgeball (lead-up game), 177
Dog Catcher (simple game), 140
Dog Run (stunt), 264
Double Circle (simple game), 140
Double line formation, for class in-
struction, 102
for relays, 160
Double ropes, use of, 296
Double walk (stunt), 273
Draw (nature game), 364
Dribbling (basketball skill), 190
Dribbling (soccer skill), 179
Driving the Pig to Market (relay), 163
Duck Walk (stunt), 264
Ducking (aquatic skill), 316

Education, advanced, for teachers, 30
goals of, 16
in elementary school, 7
in-service, for teachers, 27
physical. See *Physical education.*
principles of, 25
Egg Roll (stunt), 265
Egg Sit (stunt), 265
Eggs in mud (recipe), 361
Eight year old, characteristics of, 48
Electric Shock (classroom game), 334
Electric Tag (classroom game), 334
Elementary backstroke (aquatic skill),
319
Elementary grades, primary. See
Grades 1–3.
upper. See *Grades 4–6.*
Elementary school, objectives of, 7
Elephant Walk (stunt), 275

Epilepsy, activities for children with, 391

Equipment, accounting for, 97
  commercial sources of, 75
  defective, legal liability for, 62
  first aid, 73
  for gymnastics, improvised, 294
  for locomotor activities, 239–240
  for movement exploration, 239–240
  for outdoor cooking, 356, 357
  for physical education program, 69
  for relays, 162
  for track and field activities, 309
  for tumbling activities, 258
  increased use of, 61
  playground, 65, 66, 67
    for young children, 66
  sleeping, for camping, 369
Eskimo roll (stunt), 278
Essay tests, 433
Evaluation, of lessons, by pupils, 433–435
  of physical education program, 438–440
    principal and, 438
  of pupil progress, methods for, 425
  purpose of, 426
Exceptional children, 51. See also *Atypical children*
Exchange Tag (classroom game), 332
Excuses, from class, reasons for, 95
Exercise(s), for posture, 133–135
  law of, 83
  warm-up, description of, 292–294
    objective of, 291
Exhaling (aquatic skill), 317
Exhibits, public, 421
Exploration, movement. See *Movement exploration.*
Exploration Hike, 353
Eyes, opening of, in water (aquatic skill), 317

Fan formation, for class instruction, 100
Fasten Seat Belts (simple game), 148
Feather Relay, 170
Fetch and Carry (relay), 164
Fetch It (nature game), 365
Field theory of learning, 85
Fielding (baseball skill), 183
Fill-in blank tests, 432
Find Me (nature game), 365
Find the Leader (classroom game), 333
Finger Polka (international dance), 222
Finger Shuffleboard, 154
Fingerling test (aquatic test), 324
Finning (aquatic skill), 318
Fire building, principles of, 354
  skills in, 351

Fires, for outdoor cooking, types of, 354–355
First aid equipment, 73
Fish, baked (recipe), 361
Fish Hawk Dive (stunt), 265
Fish in a Bag (recipe), 359
Fish test (aquatic test), 325
Fishing, 371
Fist Fungo (volleyball skill game), 187
Fitness, physical, 128. See also *Physical fitness.*
  postural, 132–133
Flash Nature Game, 364
Flat rock cooking, 356
Floating (aquatic skill), 317, 318
Fly casting, 371
Foil cooking, 358
Folded Leg Walk (stunt), 265
Foot, deformity of, activities for children with, 385
Football, competition in, arguments against, 423
  arguments for, 422
Football relays, 166, 167
Forearm headstand, 278
Formations, for aquatic demonstrations, 314
  for aquatic practice, 315
  for class instruction, 100–102
  for relays, 160
  for square dancing, 211
Forward roll, progressions in, 278
Foul shooting (basketball skill), 190
Fox and Geese (recess activity), 398
Fox trot, 227
Free standing (stunt), 265
Free-play periods, supervision of, 396
Freeze Out (basketball skill game), 192
Frog Dance (Burmese dance), 343
Frog Dance (stunt), 265
Frog Hop (stunt), 265
Front crawl (aquatic skill), 320
Front drop (trampoline skill), 289
Full squat (stunt), 266

Games. See also name of game.
  aquatic, 323
  board, 149, 155
  card, 337
  circle, active, 330–333
    quiet, 334–337
  classroom, 327–346
  constructed, 148–149
  created by children, 246–247
  creative, 138–157
  for bulletin board, 149
  fundamental play and, 138–148
  guessing, 341–342
  international, 342–346

Games (*Continued*)
  lead-up, 174–178
  map, 150
  nature, 363–366
  of skill, 337–339
  pitching, 149, 156
  playground areas for, 67
  quiet. See *Classroom games.*
  related to sports, 150
  relay, 339–341
  rhythm, 195–196. See also *Games, singing.*
  simple, 138–157
  singing, 201–205. See also *Games, rhythm.*
  table, 337
  target, 153–156
  using balls, 174–193
  using target skills, 153–156
Gestalt psychology, learning and, 85
Gie Gordon's (international dance), 222
Give Me a Light (simple game), 141
Gliding (aquatic skill), 318
Goat Butting (relay), 164
Grades, reporting of, to parents, 440
Grades 1–3, activities for, 111–113
  characteristics of children in, 43–45
  couple stunts for, 273–275
Grades 4–6, activities for, 113–116
  characteristics of children in, 45–46
  couple stunts for, 275–276
Grasp the Toe (stunt), 266
Green Sleeves (international dance), 219
Green stick cooking, 357
Grocery Store (guessing game), 341
Growth, mental, in grades 1–3, 44
  in grades 4–6, 46
  physical, evaluation of, 427–428
  groupings based on, 33
  in grades 1–3, 43
  in grades 4–6, 45
  professional, of teachers, 26
  social, evaluation of, 428–430
  social-emotional, in grades 1–3, 43
  in grades 4–6, 45
  types of, 32
Guessing Blindman (classroom game), 335
Guessing Game (Alaskan), 343
Guessing games, 341–342. See also name of game.
Gustaf's Skoal (international dance), 217
Gymnasium, determining size of, 57
  locker requirements for, 58, 59
  use of, 58
Gymnastics, apparatus for, 294
  elementary, 291–306
  safety in, 294

Hand Baseball (baseball skill game), 184
Hand Puppets (guessing game), 341
Hand Touch (classroom game), 337
Hand wrestle (stunt), 273
Handicapped children, 373–374. See also *Atypical children.*
Hands and knee drop (trampoline skill), 289
Handspring, progressions in, 278
Handstand, 278
  stall bars and, 300
  supported at hips (pyramid stunt), 282
Handstand archway (pyramid stunt), 282
Hang Tag, 146
Hare and Hounds (nature game), 365
Hatchet, use of, 368
Have You Seen My Sheep? (simple game), 141
He Can Do Little (classroom game), 339
Heading (soccer skill), 180
Headspring, progressions in, 279
Headstand, 279
  forearm, 278
  stall bars and, 300
Health, physical fitness and, 135–136
  status of, evaluation of, 427–428
Hearing, defects in, activities for children with, 386
  tests for, 428
Heart disease, activities for children with, 385
Hen and Wild Cat (African game), 343
Here We Go Over the Mountain Two by Two (singing game), 203
High jump, 310
High Windows (simple game), 141
Hikes, types of, 353
Hiking, equipment for, 354
  principles of, 353
  skills in, 351
Hindu Tag, 146
Hitting (baseball skill), 182
Hobbies, teacher education and, 29
Hog Tying (stunt), 275
Hokey Pokey (singing game), 203
Home study courses, in-service education and, 29
Hook On (simple game), 142
Hook-On Tag, 146
Hoop Obstacle Course (simple game), 157
Hoop Rolling (relay), 164
Hopping, movement exploration and, 238
Hopscotch (recess activity), 398

Horizontal bar, use of, 297
Horizontal float (aquatic skill), 318
Horizontal stand (pyramid stunt), 282
Horse, side, vaults using, 301
Horse and Rider (relay), 340
Horseshoes (recess activity), 404
  for indoors, 154
Hot Ball (lead-up game), 177
How Many Can You Remember?
  (classroom game), 337
Human Ball (stunt), 266
Human Hurdle (relay), 169
Human Obstacle (relay), 170
Human Rocker (stunt), 266
Hunter-trapper fire, 355
Hurdle Race (relay), 340

I Am Very Tall (classroom game), 333
I Pass These Scissors to You (classroom
  game), 335
I Saw (guessing game), 342
I Saw (nature game), 363
I Spy (nature game), 365
Inch Worm (stunt), 267
Indian leg wrestle (stunt), 276
Indian Running (classroom game), 332
Indian star fire, 355
Infantile paralysis, activities for chil-
  dren with, 389
In-service education, for teachers, 27
Instruments, musical, for dance accom-
  paniment, 200
International dances, 214–225. See also
  name of dance.
International games, 342–346. See also
  name of game.
Intramural activities, 409–424
Inverted hang (rope climbing skill), 296
Inverted hang (still rings skill), 299

Jacks (recess activity), 408
Jamaica Holiday (international dance),
  223
Jesse Polka (couple dance), 212
Jingle Bells (singing game), 204
Jump(s), broad, 310
  high, 310
Jump and reach (stunt), 267
Jump and slap heels (stunt), 267
Jump foot (stunt), 267
Jump Over the Stick (stunt), 267
Jump rope (recess activity), 398
  ditties for, 399–402
  rhythm and, 195
Jump the Brook (classroom game), 339
Jump the Creek or Brook (simple
  game), 142
Jump the Shot (classroom game), 337

Jump the Shot (simple game), 142
Jumping, movement exploration and,
  238
Jumping Jack (stunt), 267
Jungle Jim (game), 246

Kalvelis (international dance), 215
Kangaroo Hop (stunt), 268
Kebobs (recipe), 360
Keep Away (basketball skill game), 191
Keep It Up (volleyball skill game), 187
Keeper test (aquatic test), 325
Keyhole Basketball (basketball skill
  game), 192
Kick Ball (soccer skill game), 181
Kick the Pin (classroom game), 330
Kicking (soccer skill), 180, 181
Kickover Ball (soccer skill game), 181
Kim's Game (classroom game), 337
Kim's Game (nature game), 364
Knee dip (stunt), 268
Knee drop (trampoline skill), 288
Knee lift (stunt), 268
Knee mark (stunt), 268
Knee-shoulder stand (pyramid stunt),
  283
Knee walk (stunt), 268
Knuckle down (stunt), 268
Knives, use of, 368
Knotcraft, 366–368
  skills in, 351
Knots, types of, 367, 368
  uses of, 366

Ladder, in movement exploration, 239
Ladder tournament, 410
Lame Puppy Walk (stunt), 268
Lashing, skills in, 351, 370
Law(s), liability, 62
  of learning, 83
  requiring physical education, 5
  school attendance, 36
Lazy man's fire, 355
Leaders, choice of, 179
Leadership, by pupils, use of, 103
  classroom games and, 329–330
  of squads, duties in, 103
Leading, in social dancing, 226
Lead-up games, 174–178. See also name
  of game.
Leapfrog (stunt), 276
Leapfrog Relay, 170
Learning, evaluation of, 431–433
  Gestalt psychology and, 85
  kinds of, 86
  laws of, 83
  outdoor, 348, 349
    program for, 350

Learning (*Continued*)
  principles of, 80, 86
  theories of, 81–86
Leisure time, physical education and use of, 12, 13
Lemme Sticks (rhythm game), 196
Lesson plan, daily, 121–124
  for stunts and tumbling, 260
  weekly, 116, 117, 118
Liability, of schools and teachers, 62, 64
Limbo (rhythm game), 195
Line Bowling (baseball skill game), 184
Line Dodgeball (lead-up game), 177
Line formation, for class instruction, 100
Line Relay, 162
Line Relay (soccer relay), 165
Line Soccer (soccer skill game), 182
Locker room, accident prevention in, 72
  regulations for, 94
  specifications for, 58
Locomotor activities, movement exploration and, 238, 239
Locomotor movements, rhythm and, 199–201
Locomotor skills, relays using, 162
Log roll (stunt), 269
Long Base (baseball skill game), 185
Long stretch (stunt), 269
Loose Caboose (simple game), 142
Lost Baby Hike, 353
Lots-Mores (recipe), 360
Love, as social need, 39
Lower elementary grades. See *Grades 1–3.*
Lummi Sticks (rhythm game), 196

Magic Music (guessing game), 341
Maine Mixer (dance), 213
Making Squares (classroom game), 337
Maladjustment, signs and symptoms of, 51
Map games, 150
Marbles (recess activity), 398
Marching, principles of, 197–199
Marguerites (recipe), 360
Match It or Know It (nature game), 365
Matching tests, 432
Mats, for stunts and tumbling, 258
  rolled, use of, 304
Maturation, levels of, 32. See also *Growth.*
  skill development and, 9
Mayim (international dance), 221
Meals, outdoor preparation of, 356, 357, 358. See also *Outdoor cooking.*
Meetings, of professional staff, 27
Menagerie (English game), 344

Mental retardation, 388
Mercury (pyramid stunt), 283
Merry-go-round (relay), 164
Merry-go-round (stunt), 276
Mexican Mixer (international dance), 214
Midnight (simple game), 143
Mimetics, progressive presentation of, 247
Mixers (dances), 213–214. See also *Dancing* and name of dance.
Monkey run (stunt), 269
Moonlight Hike, 353
Motor skills, evaluation of, 430
  techniques of teaching, 92–94
Movement(s), creative, progressive presentation of, 247
  locomotor, rhythm and, 199–201
Movement exploration, balls in, 246
  locomotor activities for, 238, 239
  equipment in, 239–240
  teacher's role in, 234
  techniques of teaching, 236–237
  tires in, 240, 246
Muffin Pan Bowling (classroom game), 336
Mule kick (stunt), 269
Multiple choice tests, 431
Music, for dancing, 200
  recordings of, 232, 233
  for marching, 197
Musical instruments, for dance accompaniment, 200

Nature Baseball (nature game), 365
Nature games, 363–366. See also name of game.
Nature Guess (classroom game), 341
Nature Hike, 353
Nature Scavenger Hike (nature game), 365
Nature Scouting (nature game), 365
Nature skills, list of, 351
Nature study, activities for, 361, 362
Needs, of atypical children, 374–375
  of children, 37–40
  unfilled, conflicts arising from, 40
Newcomb (volleyball skill game), 188
Newspaper Race, 340
Nine Court Basketball, 193
Nine year old, characteristics of, 49
Noon-hour activities, 395–408
  supervision of, 396
Nose-and-Toe Tag, 146
Nose Dive (stunt), 264
Novelty relays, 170–172
Number One Man (nature game), 365
Numbered Chairs (classroom game), 333

Numbers Change (simple game), 143
Nursery Rhymes (guessing game), 341

Object Hike, 353
Objectives, for atypical children, 379
Observations, of children playing, 52
Obstacle relays, 169–170
One Foot Square (nature game), 363
Organization, of class, for aquatics, 313–316
   for stunts and tumbling, 259
   for team sports, 178–179
  of clubs, for competition, 416
Organizations, for teachers, 29
Orthopedic screening examination, form for, 382
Ostrich Tag, 146
Outdoor activities, 347–372. See also *Camping* and name of activity.
Outdoor construction projects, 352
Outdoor cooking, equipment for, 356, 357
   fires for, 354–355
   in aluminum foil, 358
   skills in, 351
Outdoor learning, experiences in, 348, 349
   program for, 350
Oven, reflector, 357
Over and Under (relay), 164
Overhead pass (basketball skill), 189
Overnight Hike, 354

Paddle tennis (recess activity), 402
Painting Colored Sand Pictures (Italian game), 345
Palm Ball (classroom game), 332
Palm the Ball (lead-up game), 177
Pancakes (recipe), 361
Paper Bag Relay, 171
Paraffin buddy burners, 357
Passing (basketball skill), 188, 189, 190
Passing (soccer skill), 180
Passing (volleyball skill), 187
Paul Revere Relay, 172
Pebble Game (Greece), 345
Peg board, 154
Phugadi (Indian game), 345
Physical development, youth fitness and, 126–136
Physical education, aims of, 5, 6
   attitudes toward, 3
   for atypical children. See *Atypical children.*
   goals of, 7–13, 16, 17
   in history, 3

Physical education (*Continued*)
   in total curriculum, 26
   program for. See *Physical education program.*
   teacher of. See *Teacher physical education.*
   techniques for teaching, 90
Physical education program, 107–124
   areas of, 119
   evaluation of, 438–440
   graded activities in, 111–116
   period divisions of, 109
   planning of, 108–109
   progression in, 121
   time percentages for, 107, 108
   weekly plan for, 116, 117, 118
Physical education teacher. See *Teacher, physical education.*
Physical fitness, definition of, 128
   development and, 126–136
   evaluation of, 430
   goals of education and, 8
   health and, 135–136
   program for, 128–130
   safety and, 135–136
   screening tests for, 130–132
Physical growth. See *Growth, physical.*
Physiological needs, of children, 37
Pick Up (classroom game), 338
Pig (classroom game), 337
Pilot Relay, 171
Ping-pong Bounce (classroom game), 338
Pioneer Drumsticks (recipe), 360
Pioneers and Indians (simple game), 141
Pit bowling (recess activity), 406
Pitching games, 149, 156
Plan(s), daily lesson, 121–124
   for stunts and tumbling, 260
   weekly lesson, 116, 117, 118
Planking (outdoor cooking skill), 357
Planning, with pupils, 98
Play, creative, 240–246
   movement tasks in, 245
   fundamental, simple games and, 138–148
   types of, 13
   value of, 13–16
Play days, 417
Playgrounds, equipment for, 65, 66, 67
   game areas of, 67
   recommendations for, 64–68
   safety precautions for, 398
Playground golf (recess activity), 402
Plug (simple game), 143
Poison (simple game), 143
Poison Ball (classroom game), 334
Poison Circle (classroom game), 331
Poliomyelitis, activities for children with, 389

Population, changes in, effect of on children, 34
Post Ball (basketball relay), 168
Post Relay (softball relay), 169
Posture, defects of, activities for children with, 384
   types of, 382
  examination of, 382
  exercises for, 133–135
  fitness of, 132–133
  poor, causes of, 381
  tests of, 428
Potatoes, recipe for, 360
Primary grades. See *Grades 1–3.*
Professional growth, of teachers, 26
Professional organizations, membership in, 29
Program(s), assembly, 420
  competitive, organization of, 414
  for atypical children, 375–376. See also *Atypical children.*
  for community groups, 421
  physical education. See *Physical education program.*
  seasonal, 416
Program Evaluative Form, 438
Progressive Bat Ball (baseball skill game), 185
Prone float (aquatic skill), 317
Prone glide (aquatic skill), 318
Prove It (nature game), 365
Psychology, Gestalt, and learning, 85
Pull across (stunt), 273
Pupils, as leaders, use of, 103
  behavior of, evaluation of, 428–430
  planning by, 98
Pupil Behavior Sheet, 428
Pupil Evaluation Sheet, 435
Push Ball (relay), 165
Push-ups, 269
Put a Spook in a Haunted House (simple game), 156
Pyramid(s), poses for, 285, 286
  requirements for, 280, 281
  stunts for, 281–284

Quiet games. See also *Classroom games* and name of game.
  circle, 334–337
Quoits, rope (recess activity), 407

Raatikko (international dance), 222
Rabbit jump (stunt), 269
Race Around the Bases (baseball skill game), 186
Races, aquatic, 323
Radar Screen (game), 247
Rapid Fire Artist (classroom game), 341

Rating scales, for pupil's self-evaluation, 433
Rebound tumbling. See *Trampolining.*
Recess, activities for, 395–408
  supervision of, 396
Recipes, for outdoor cooking, 358–361
Recognition, as social need, 39, 41
Records, behavior, 52
  keeping of, 97
Recordings, musical, list of, 232–233
Recreation, value of, 13–16
Red Light (simple game), 144
Red River Valley (square dance), 208
Red Rover (simple game), 144
Reflector fire, 355
Reflector oven, 357
Relaxing (aquatic skill), 317
Relay games, 339–341. See also name of game.
Relays. See also name of relay.
  aquatic, 323
  basketball, 168
  classroom, 339–341
  equipment for, 162
  football, 166, 167
  formations for, 160
  games using, 339–341
  novelty, 170
  obstacle, 169–170
  organization of teams for, 159
  self-testing activities and, 161
  soccer, 165, 166
  softball, 169
  240-yard, 311
  types of, 159, 160
  using locomotor skills, 162
  volleyball, 167
Report cards, grading and, 440
Rescue Relay, 162
Research, in-service education and, 28
Retardation, mental, 388
Retarded children, 388. See also *Atypical children.*
Retrieving (nature game), 363
Rhythm, 195–196
  jump rope and, 195
  locomotor movements and, 199–201
  marching and, 197–199
  methods of introducing, 194–199
  time and, 194
Rhythm games, 195, 196. See also *Singing games* and name of game.
Rhythmic Limbo (rhythm game), 195
Rig-A-Jig (singing game), 204
Ring Master (classroom game), 332
Ring on a String (classroom game), 336
Ring the Bottle Neck (classroom game), 331
Rings, use of, 298

Road to the Isles (international dance), 222
Rocker (stunt), 274
Roll call, methods for, 95
time allotted to, 96
Roll pass (basketball skill), 190
Roller skating (recess activity), 404
Rooster Fight (stunt), 274
Rope climbing, 295, 296
Rope quoits (recess activity), 407
Rotation (volleyball skill), 187
Round robin tournament, 411
Round the Bases (softball relay), 169
Row Boat (stunt), 274
Run and Punt Relay (football relay), 166
Run and Roll Relay (soccer relay), 166
Running, movement exploration and, 238
Running broad jump, 310
Running Relay, 162

Sack Relay, 171
Safety, in aquatics, 72
in gymnastics, 294
in stunts and tumbling, 258–259
physical fitness and, 135–136
precautions for, in recess activities, 398
singing games and, 205
Sand Bag Ball (Alaskan game), 343
Sand pictures (classroom activity), 345
Sardines (simple game), 145
Satsuma Ken (Japanese game), 345
Scatter formation, for class instruction, 101
Scavanger Hunt Hike, 353
Schnozzle (simple game), 155
School, elementary, objectives of, 7
Schoolroom Tag (classroom game), 332
Scissors jump, 310
Scramble (nature game), 365
Sculling (aquatic skill), 318
Seal Crawl (stunt), 270
Seat drop (trampoline skill), 289
Security, as social need, 38
Self-testing activities, graded, 261
Serpentine (relay), 170
Service (volleyball skill), 186
Seven year old, characteristics of, 48
Sharp Eyes (nature game), 364
Sheet bend (knot), 367
Shooting baskets (basketball skill), 190
Shooting fouls (basketball skill), 190
Shoulder rest (pyramid stunt), 283
Shoulder stand (pyramid stunt), 283
Shower Ball (volleyball skill game), 188
Shower rooms, specifications for, 58

Shuffleboard, 407
for children, 404
Shuttle formation, for class instruction, 101
for relays, 160
Side horse, vaults using, 301
Side Line Basketball (basketball skill game), 192
Side stroke (aquatic skill), 319
Side-arm pass (basketball skill), 189
Sight, defects of, activities for children with, 387
tests for, 428
Singing games, 201–205. See also Rhythm games and name of game.
safety and, 205
Single elimination tournaments, 409
Single file formation, for relays, 160
Single squat (stunt), 270
Sitting balance (pyramid stunt), 283
Sitting mount (pyramid stunt), 283
Sit-ups, 270
Six year old, characteristics of, 47
Skill games, 337–339. See also name of game.
Skills. See also name of skill.
aquatic, 316–321
baseball, 182, 183
games for developing, 183–186
basketball, 188–191
games for developing, 191–193
bowling, 175
camping and outdoor living, 351–353
development of, maturation and, 9
in ball handling, games requiring, 174
in outdoor cooking, 351
locomotor, relays using, 162
motor. See Motor skills and name of specific skill.
nature, list of, 351
soccer, 179, 180
games for developing, 180–182
target, games employing, 153–156
teaching of, role of teacher in, 10
team sport, methods of teaching, 179
trampoline, 286–289
volleyball, 186, 187
games for developing, 187–188
Skin the Cat, on horizontal bar, 297
on still rings, 298
Skin the Snake (Chinese game), 344
Skin the Snake (stunt), 276
Skip Rope Relay, 165
Skip Tag, 145
Skipping, movement exploration and, 238
Sleeping bag, 369
Sliding, movement exploration and, 238
Slip knot, 368

Soccer, skills in, 179, 180
    games for developing, 180–182
Soccer relays, 165, 166
Social dancing, 225–229
  basic steps in, 227
  patterns of, 228
Social growth, evaluation of, 428–430
Social needs, of children, 38
Softball relays, 169
Softball throw (track and field skill), 311
Soil conservation, 371
Somemores (recipe), 361
Somersault, 270
Sounds (nature game), 364
Spanker (stunt), 270
Spider Race, 340
Spoke Relay, 169
Spoon and Ping-pong Ball Relay, 171
Sports. See also name of sport.
  competitive, arguments against, 423
    arguments for, 422
  games related to, 150
  skills and rules related to, 150–153
  team. See Team sports.
Spotters, in stunts and tumbling, 259, 260
Springboard, 302
Squad leader, duties of, 103
Squads, use of, 102
  leadership of, 103
Square Ball (lead-up game), 178
Square dancing, 206–214
  teaching progressions for, 207
Square formation, for class instruction, 101
Square knot, 367
Squat Tag, 146
Squirrels in Trees (tag game), 146
S-R-Bond theory of learning, 82
Stage Coach (classroom game), 335
Stairs, in gymnastics, 306
  in movement exploration, 239
Stall bars, 299
Stance, in basketball, 188
Stand on partner (pyramid stunt), 284
Stand on partner's knee (pyramid stunt), 284
Stand Up (classroom game), 338
Standing broad jump, 310
Standing mount (pyramid stunt), 284
Star, Sun, or Cloud Hike, 353
Step Over the Wand (stunt), 270
Stick cooking, 357
Stiff knee pick-up (stunt), 271
Stiff leg bend (stunt), 271
Still rings, 298
Still Water (classroom game), 335
Stilts, 157

Stone, Paper, Scissors (Japanese game), 342
Stool Hurdle (relay), 170
Stoop and throw (stunt), 271
Stoop Tag, 146
Stove, tin can, 356
Stream Hike, 353
Stride Ball (classroom game), 331
Stride Ball (lead-up game), 178
Stride Ball (relay), 165
String-burning Contest (nature game), 365
Strokes, swimming, 319–321. See also name of stroke.
Students. See Pupils.
Stump walk (stunt), 268
Stunts, class organization for, 259
  couple, 261, 262
    for primary grades, 273–275
    for upper elementary grades, 275–276
  description of, 262–276. See also name of stunt.
  equipment for, 258
  for pyramid building, 281
    description of, 282–284
  graded, 260
    uniforms for, 257
  group, 262
  individual, 261
  lesson plan for, 260
  pyramid, 281–284
  safety in performing, 258–259
  tumbling, description of, 277–280
    grade level of, 277
  use of spotters in, 259, 260
Supervisor, role of, 22, 23
Survey(s), as in-service education, 28
Swedish box and buck, vaults using, 300
Sweep Up Relay, 172
Swimming. See also Aquatics.
  strokes in, 319–321. See also name of stroke.
  teaching aids in, 322
Swimming pool, recommendations for, 59, 60

Table games, 337
Tag, 146. See also specific names.
Tag the Wall Relay, 340
Take a Little Peek (square dance), 209
Tantoli (international dance), 215, 216
Target (baseball skill game), 185
Target Ball (lead-up game), 174
Target games, 153–156. See also name of game.
Target skills, games employing, 153–156

Target Throw (target game), 153
Teacher(s), advanced degrees for, 30
  evaluation of, by supervisor, 436–437
  evaluation sheet for, 436
  in-service education for, 27–30
  physical education, certification of, 22
    in primary grades, 21
    philosophy of, 24
    preparation of, 22
    qualities of, 24
    responsibilities of, 4
  qualifications of, atypical children and, 376
  self-evaluation by, 435–436
Teaching, by television, 105
  methods for. See *Teaching methods.*
  of skills, role of teacher in, 10
  pitfalls in, 91
  principles basic to, 25, 26
  team method of, 105
Teaching methods, discipline problems and, 42
  for grades 1–3, 44
  for grades 4–6, 46
  for team sports, 179
Team sports. See also name of sport.
  lead-up games to, 174–178
  methods of teaching, 179
  relays related to, 165–169
  skills in, 174–193
    methods of teaching, 179
Team teaching, 105
Teams, division of class into, 178
  selection of, for competition, 414–416
Television, teaching by use of, 105
Tents, 369
Tepee fire, 354
Test(s), administration of, 426
  of aquatic skills, 324
  of physical fitness, 130–132
  types of, 431–433
Tether Ball (recess activity), 403
Theories, of learning, 81–86
Thigh mount (pyramid stunt), 284
Thorndike's laws of learning, 83
Thread the Needle (stunt), 271
Three Deep (tag game), 147
Three-legged Relay, 172
Through the Stick (stunt), 271
Throw and Catch (volleyball relay), 167
Throw It and Run (baseball skill game), 186
Throw the Cards (classroom game), 337
Throwing (baseball skill), 182
Tied Monkey (African game), 343
Tight rope walking (stunt), 271
Time, period division of, 96
  rhythm and, 194

Tin can golf (recess activity), 406
Tin can stove, 356
Tin can walkers, 157
Tinikling (rhythm game), 196
Tires, in movement exploration, 240, 246
Toe wrestle (stunt), 276
Tools, use of, 368
Toothpick and Ring Relay, 172
Touch (nature game), 363
Tournaments, types of, 409–412
Toy Shop (classroom game), 336
Track and field activities. See also name of activity.
  equipment for, 309
  indoor, 308
  outdoor, 309
Trail Blazing Hike, 353
Trailing (nature game), 363
Trampoline, class organization for, 259
  routines in, 287–289
  safety in, 258
  skills in, 286–289
Trapping (soccer skill), 180
Travel, teacher education and, 29
Treading water (aquatic skill), 318
Treasure Hunt Hike, 353
Tree Tag (nature game), 365
Triangle (pyramid stunt), 284
Tripod (stunt), 279
Troika (international dance), 218
Tropanka (international dance), 219
True and false tests, 431
True or False (nature game), 363
Tuck float (aquatic skill), 317
Tumbling, class organization for, 259
  equipment for, 258
  lesson plan for, 260
  rebound. See *Trampolining.*
  safety in, 258–259
  spotters in, 259, 260
  uniforms for, 257
Tumbling stunts, description of, 277–280
  grade level of, 277
Turk Stand (stunt), 272
Turning bar, in movement exploration, 239
Twenty-one (basketball skill game), 191
Two step (dance), 227, 228

Under the Bridge (stunt), 272
Uniforms, for stunts and tumbling, 257
  recommendations for, 94
  specifications for, 71
Unit, teaching, organization of, 121
Upper elementary grades. See *Grades 4–6.*

Up-spring (stunt), 272
Up-swing (stunt), 272

Vaults, on side horse, 301
    on Swedish box and buck, 300
Veleta (couple dance), 213
Virginia Reel (square dance), 211
Vision, defects in, activities for children
    with, 387
    tests of, 428
Volleyball, skills in, 186, 187
    games for developing, 187–188
Volleyball relays, 167

Walk Out-Ride Back Hike, 354
Walking, movement exploration and,
    238
Walking Chair (stunt), 276
Wall boards, 155
Waltz, teaching suggestions for, 229
    types of, 228
Wands, in movement exploration, 239,
    245
Warm-up exercises, description of, 292–
    294
    objective of, 291

Wash Day (game), 247
Way Down in the Paw Paw Patch
    (singing game), 202
Weather Cock (simple game), 147
Weather Vane (stunt), 272
Weave In (simple game), 140
Weekly lesson plan, 116, 117, 118
Western roll (track and field skill), 311
What Am I? (guessing game), 342
Wheelbarrow (stunt), 274
Who Am I? (nature game), 365
Who Has Gone? (classroom game), 334
Wicket Walk (stunt), 272
Wigwam fire, 354
Winner-loser tournaments, 410
Wood-lore, skills in, 351
Workshops, as in-service education, 28
Wring the Dishrag (stunt), 275

Yemari (Japanese game), 346
Youth, value of play to, 15

Zigzag formation, for class instruction,
    101
Zigzag Relay (soccer relay), 166
Zigzag Volley (volleyball relay), 167